BAYREUTH

BAYREUTH

A History of the Wagner Festival

Frederic Spotts

Yale University Press
New Haven and London
1994

Set in Bembo by Best-set Typesetter Ltd., Hong Kong
Printed and bound in Great Britain by The Bath Press, Avon

Library of Congress Cataloging-in-Publication Data

Spotts, Frederic.
    Bayreuth: a history of the Wagner festival/Frederic Spotts.
        p.   cm.
    Includes bibliographical references and index.
    ISBN 0–300–05777–6
    1. Bayreuther Festspiele.   2. Wagner, Richard, 1813–1883.
    3. Music—Germany—Bayreuth—History and criticism.   I. Title.
ML410.W2S6   1994
782.1'079'43315—dc20   93–36805
                                                                                    CIP

A catalogue record for this book is available from the British Library.

Contents

Preface

Richard Wagner is the most controversial artistic figure of all time. And the operatic Festival which he founded at Bayreuth in 1876 is not only the world's oldest and best-known but likewise the most controversial. The composer conceived of this novel venture early in his career in the conviction that his highly unorthodox operas required highly unorthodox arrangements for their presentation. The unique atmosphere of the Festival and its immense prestige have made Bayreuth a model for opera houses everywhere, a place of pilgrimage for music-lovers and an artistic goal for singers and conductors.

A history of Bayreuth is first of all the story of an institution—its origins, productions and performances. At the same time it is also a chronicle of the Wagner family, a clan which Karl Marx found as bizarre as the Nibelungs and equally deserving of an epochal four-part opera. The eccentric, feuding, scandalous descendants—'the royal family of Bayreuth', as the dynasty came to be known—merit a book, if not an opera, but are relevant here only in so far as the institution was their property, on which they imposed their very idiosyncratic wills. Some aspects of this story can probably never be known, victims of death, silence and bonfire.

A third strand of the history concerns Bayreuth's place in the life of the German nation. In a country where music has been supremely important and every artistic act ultimately a political act, any great cultural venture was bound to be entangled in the national destiny. In this case, however, the involvement was entirely unparalleled—in part because Wagner was a political figure in his own right, in part because the Festival became caught up in the hubristic nationalism which followed German unification in 1871, but above all because of the nature of the operas themselves. Although these sagas aroused in the non-German a purely aesthetic reaction, in the German they struck a tremendously resonant chord deep inside the communal psyche. Their myths and romanticism, their gods and heroes, their social outcasts and self-immolating heroines coincided with the vague but powerful yearning, the sense of struggle and the longing for redemption that was embedded in the national character. 'Wagner's art is the most sensational self-portrayal and self-criticism of German character that is conceivable,' observed that astute Wagnerian Thomas Mann.

Even so, Wagner without Bayreuth would have been like a country without a capital, a religion without a Church. Had the Festspielhaus not been erected, the link between the operas and the German psyche would have remained platonic, harmlessly confined to such endeavours as Wagner societies, lectures and newsletters. But once consummated in a physical centre and site of a recurring celebratory Festival, the enterprise was inevitably drawn into the ideological vicissitudes of the young country. The fateful development occurred when the composer's most fanatical and conservative followers transformed the Festival into the temple of a pseudo-religion—a cult complete with messianic saviour, holy scripture, revelation and oral tradition; with a Holy See claiming infallibility and a sacred pilgrimage site; with apostles, loyal disciples and schismatics; with orthodoxy and heresy, submission and excommunication—and converted Bayreuth into a mighty fortress in defence of 'true German values', in other words a stronghold of reaction, nationalism and anti-Semitism.

As a result, operas meant to have universal meaning and a Festival intended to be at most a national but certainly not a nationalistic institution were hopelessly compromised. Thus evolved the fatal equation: Wagner = Bayreuth = fascism, a concatenation that was not broken until recently. As such, Bayreuth has always been a paradigm of German national development. 'Bayreuth is Germany', Wagner's biographer Carl Friedrich Glasenapp overheard an English member of the audience exclaim in amazement in 1876. And so it has ever been—sometimes its pride, sometimes its shame, but always its fascination. As the Wagner expert Hans Mayer has grandly written, 'To try to compile a history of Wagner, a history of the Festival, is to write at the same time German history and world history.'

Acknowledgements

For research material and publications relating to the Festival, it is my pleasure to thank the Richard-Wagner-Gedenkstätte in Bayreuth, in the persons of Dr Manfred Eger, Günter Fischer, Susanne Kutschera and Monika Seeser. I am deeply grateful for their unfailing kindness and efficiency. Equally am I indebted to the Harvard University music library, whose superb Wagner collection was indispensable. Nor could I have done without the support of the Center for European Studies at Harvard and specifically that of Professor Stanley Hoffmann and Abby Collins. Of the many others who helped in one way or another, I must invidiously single out Peer Baedeker, Brigitte Barkley, John Bovey, Claus Frankel, Agnes Habereder, John Lichtblau, Bernd Mayer, Erich Rappl, Anthea Morton-Saner, Philip Wolfson, William Youngren and Jürgen Zinkler for particular thanks.

For the illustrations, I express my gratitude above all to the Richard-Wagner-Gedenkstätte for those prior to 1945 and to the Bayreuther Festspiele for those since 1951. Appreciation is due as well to the Landesbildarchiv Oberfranken, Bayreuth, for the aerial view of the Festspielhaus; the Bildarchiv preussischer Kulturbesitz, Berlin, for the photographs of Hitler at Wahnfried and the soldiers marching to the Festspielhaus; Leo Schneiderhahl for the photograph of the expellees at the Festspielhaus and Roger Wood for that of the 1983 stage model. The longitudinal section perspective and the Festspielhaus floor plan have been published by permission of the George C. Izenour Archive, New Haven, Connecticut.

For permission to use copyright material, I wish to thank Valerie Eliot and Faber & Faber for T.S. Eliot's *The Hollow Men*; Stephen Fay and Roger Wood and Secker & Warburg for *The Ring*; Houghton Mifflin for Erich Leinsdorf's *Cadenza*; the *New Yorker* for Joseph Wechsberg's 'Letter from Bayreuth'; the *Observer* for articles by Peter Heyworth; *Opera* for various reviews; Random House and Cassell & Company for

Acknowledgements

Ernest Newman's *The Life of Richard Wagner*; Geoffrey Skelton and Victor Gollancz Ltd for *Wieland Wagner: The Positive Sceptic*; The Society of Authors on behalf of the Bernard Shaw Estate for *The Perfect Wagnerite* and *Shaw's Music*; the *Sunday Times* for articles by Ernest Newman and *The Times* for unsigned critical reviews.

Introduction

From a distance it looks as though it might be an antiquated brick warehouse. Irreverent locals deride it as having the charm of an Oktoberfest beer tent and the elegance of a railway station. It put Cosima Wagner in mind of an 'Assyrian edifice'. Friedrich Nietzsche described it as 'a colossal four-towered Nibelung structure'. Igor Stravinsky found it 'lugubrious' and said it looked like 'a crematorium, and a very old-fashioned one at that'. To Romain Rolland it resembled an 'industrial structure more than a cultural establishment'. Richard Wagner's Festspielhaus at Bayreuth has been described in many ways— utilitarian, sober, naïve, meagre, ugly, majestic even—but never as beautiful. Nor did the composer wish it to be. 'I agree to a structure entirely of wood,' he wrote in 1872 before construction began, 'however much this will vex my dear Bayreuth fellow citizens, who would very much like to see a building of stately exterior.'[1] Yet generations of Wagnerians who have made their musical *hadj* would have it no other way, in fact love it for its very homeliness.

Were Wagner to return to his opera house today, he would find it almost as it was when he last saw it in 1882. As he walked up the tree-lined avenue so familiar to his devotees, the exterior would look just the same. Only at close range would changes be apparent. Invisible to almost any eye but his own would be the renewed front façade, the result of reconstruction work in the late 1950s, when the original half-timbered brick exterior was replaced by concrete beams and brick infill. Proceeding further, he would observe that the rear of the building had been expanded. The backstage areas were slightly enlarged in 1924–5 to accommodate the solid stage sets which replaced the old canvas backdrops, a modest west wing was added in 1931 for offices and the east side was expanded a bit in 1963 to provide space for rehearsals and workshops. What he would be unable to see is the pre-stressed concrete and steel interior frame installed between 1958 and 1968 to replace the old

Modern aerial view of the Festspielhaus.

wooden beams. The alterations were overdue; the wood was rotting and the building was a fire-trap. Had it been anything but Wagner's theatre, state inspectors would have closed it long before. By remarkable technical legerdemain, the old structure, which the composer had not expected to last more than a few decades, was made permanent without any compromise of the original appearance.

The complex of buildings—workshops, rehearsal areas and storage facilities—constructed behind the theatre since his time would immediately catch his attention. Every detail of opera production absorbed him, and he would be fascinated by the excellent facilities and modern equipment. Today there are three large rehearsal stages. The principal one was constructed to simulate the stage of the theatre itself in size and floor inclination, so that it could be used in developing and testing stage sets for new productions. Since the *Ring*, *Parsifal* and three or four other operas are performed every season, rehearsal time for each is limited. These new stages in addition to the opera stage itself make it possible to rehearse four works simultaneously. In addition there is a practice hall for the ballet groups in *Parsifal* and *Tannhäuser*, a carpentry shop, a metal

2

shop, a painting studio and the like. Returning to the front, the composer would observe that the two rickety refreshment halls have vanished. The one on the right and its descendants down the years have been used for orchestra rehearsals. The latest structure, a glass and wooden barrack constructed in the centenary year of 1976, was the first to be designed with acoustics in mind. Next to it, but almost impossible to see in the thick shrubbery, is a strange-looking round building—known as the snail because of its shape—which was constructed in 1987 as a site for chorus rehearsals.

Stepping inside the opera house, Wagner would find the amphitheatrical auditorium exactly as he knew it. The same thirty descending rows of seats are there, though not the original cane and wooden ones. These were sold off to Bayreuth enthusiasts in 1968 and replaced with bentwood seats, still without arm rests and, some think, even more unobliging to the human shape, despite an exiguous covering of upholstery. The wooden floors remain uncovered, since carpeting would absorb sound and disturb the delicate acoustical balance. Turning to the rear of the auditorium, he would immediately notice that between the old princes' gallery and the artists' gallery above them, a balcony had ingeniously been inserted. It was constructed in 1930, for the purpose at the time of accommodating the press. With these various alterations over the years, the number of seats increased from 1,645 in 1876 to the present 1,925. Otherwise, the interior remains unchanged, with the original solemn rows of wooden Corinthian columns along the sides, the same 124 gasolier lights and the sail-cloth ceiling cover painted to simulate a velarium.

A nineteenth-century photograph of the interior of the auditorium as Wagner himself would have seen it. On stage are the original *Parsifal* sets of the temple of the grail, designed by Paul von Joukowsky in 1882 and used until 1934.

Nothing would have pleased the composer more than to see that his architectural invention, the sunken orchestra pit, has been preserved. This was the structure's central feature, and Wagner essentially built his theatre around it. By constructing the pit below the level of the auditorium and partially covering it with a hood, he made the orchestra invisible and was able to plunge the theatre into complete darkness. Wagner and his architects also designed an enormous stage and then made it seem larger still by devising another original feature, a double proscenium. By framing the stage with these arches, they found they had achieved an amazing illusion of depth. Ernest Newman, Wagner's famous biographer, once described the effect:

> It may seem incredible that a few extra feet of height or depth in a mountain rock or pass can have any particular psychological import, but here it is so; the generous scale of the setting of itself gives you the feeling that the characters are in every way more than life-size, that they are not merely physically but mentally free of the limitations of ordinary humanity, that they are creatures not only of the earth but of the sky and the regions below the earth.[2]

Though he left technical questions to others, Wagner would have been intrigued by the stage machinery. It is especially important at Bayreuth since some of the operas require set changes as near to instantaneous as possible. The composer's successors have insisted on having the most modern equipment available; with the current facilities it is possible to change a scene in complete silence in a matter of seconds. Even more would Wagner have been impressed by the stage lighting system. He had been dependent on gas lamps, with a few electric devices for spotlights. In 1888 the Festspielhaus was completely electrified and, in the years that followed, stage lighting gradually developed into a cardinal feature of Bayreuth's production technique. The most up-to-date equipment has accordingly always been maintained, even when funds have been available for little else.

After completing an inspection of his opera house, Wagner would no doubt be equally amazed, pleased and disappointed—amazed to see that what he intended as a temporary construction was still there; pleased to know that the auditorium had been left untouched but disappointed to learn that a later generation, more appreciative of his genius, had failed to replace it with an imposing structure. The disappointment, however, would no doubt have turned to ironic satisfaction when he came to realize that though later generations have constructed grandiose opera houses around the world, his alone continues to be recognized as the perfect, functional structure for opera and any notion of replacing it is unthinkable.

In realizing a long-held dream of having his own opera house for annual performances of his works, Wagner invented the modern music festival. Not until Max Reinhardt, Hugo von Hofmannsthal and Richard Strauss established a festival at Salzburg in 1920 was there anything like it, and only when John Christie established Glyndebourne in 1934 was there a similar family enterprise. Though there is now a multitude of music festivals, Bayreuth remains the most famous and, if the proportion of ticket requests to tickets available is a measure, the most esteemed. It also remains the most serious—serious to a fault, in the view of conductors and singers who are intimidated by the knowledge that a Bayreuth audience can be counted on to know the scores so well that the slightest error is bound to be detected. Bayreuth demands seriousness. Who would go to the inconvenience of travelling to an out-of-the-way place to endure the discomfort of sitting on a hard seat for hour after hour in an auditorium without air-conditioning at the height of summer except out of deep devotion to Wagner's works? The composer deliberately planned it that way, and that is the way it has always been.

Since its beginning in 1876 the Festival has followed an invariable routine. The season begins at the end of July and lasts for a month. The operas are performed in cycles which, with rare exception, include both the *Ring* and *Parsifal* and one or more of the other works which Wagner considered representative of his developed style and worthy of Bayreuth: *Der fliegende Holländer, Tannhäuser, Lohengrin, Tristan und Isolde* and *Die Meistersinger von Nürnberg*. Before the Second World War, the Festival was much slower paced. Then, only three works were normally performed and there was a 'rest year', usually every two years, to prepare a new production. Consequently, works other than the *Ring* and *Parsifal* were in the repertory only for two or three seasons in the course of a quarter century. *Tannhäuser*, for instance, was performed in 1891, 1892, 1894, 1904, 1930 and 1931; *Lohengrin* in 1894, 1908, 1909, 1936 and 1937. And though *Meistersinger* made it to the stage in nine seasons and *Tristan* in eleven, *Holländer* was performed only in 1901, 1902, 1914 and 1939. Expanding the canon to include *Rienzi* has been considered but rejected on the ground that the work is too problematical for the Bayreuth stage.

The *Ring* and *Parsifal* are Bayreuth's particular specialities. The Festspielhaus was built for the *Ring*, while *Parsifal* was scored with its acoustics in mind. And nowhere else are the two works given in such ideal conditions. The *Ring* is by far the greatest challenge to any producer. Among the four individual parts—*Rheingold, Walküre, Siegfried* and *Götterdämmerung*—there are thirty-four roles to direct and thirty-six scenes to stage, many of them the most difficult in all opera. The orchestra and conductor must perform for a total of fifteen hours. The principal roles—Brünnhilde, Siegfried and Wotan—are horrendously demanding, more so than any others in the operatic repertory. The work is invariably done in its entirety, with days off between

Walküre and *Siegfried* and between the latter and *Götterdämmerung* to allow the principals to recover from the strain, the brass players to rest their lips and the audience to regain its emotional composure. Until 1953 there was only a single rest day—between the final two operas. But with the modern-day Bayreuth orchestra playing a half-tone higher and singers apparently no longer possessing the sheer physical stature and stamina of the old-time Wagnerians, a two-day pause was considered necessary for the sheer survival of the principals.

Such was Wagner's festival concept: the same seven works and only those works, performed over and over in a provincial town. It should have been an infallible recipe for artistic and financial disaster—and it very nearly was. But in the end, as usual, Wagner succeeded against all the odds. And, as always, he triumphed through a combination of his own dogged determination and the fanatical devotion of his admirers.

Wagner's music inspired a passion that was, if not downright irrational, at least difficult to explain. Or perhaps it was simply as Thomas Mann maintained, that his works are a uniquely explosive mixture of myth and psychology, rousing the most sensitive emotions, the deepest primordial passions. In nature and degree, this Wagnermania was unprecedented, quite unlike the devotion inspired by any other composer, or indeed by any other artistic creator in any field. It was almost religious in its fanaticism and self-sacrificing dedication. Those who participated in the *Ring* première in 1876, as their memoirs testify, gave themselves to it as though to a sacred rite. Thus was born the *Bayreuther Geist*, the Bayreuth spirit, that has permeated the Festival ever since. It is a sense that to participate in the Festival is the greatest privilege one can have, whether one is a singer, conductor, musician, lighting technician, stage engineer, carpenter, seamstress or ticket-taker. Countless autobiographies and interviews over the years have remarked upon it. 'I still remember the exact moment when I first saw the Festspielhaus situated up on the hill', begins a typical comment, in this case by Birgit Nilsson a century after the original première.[3] 'I thought my heart must burst. I simply could not believe that I might be allowed to sing in this temple, in this hall, where Wagner lived and worked. It just seemed a dream. With a pounding heart, I entered the Festspielhaus and had the feeling that Wagner's spirit hovered over everything.' This is the sort of humility and dedication, remarkable in a profession not unknown for self-promotion and vanity, that Bayreuth has invariably evoked. 'In no other house do you have the sense of artists leaving their egos in the dressing room in order to give their all in the cause and tradition of Wagner', a critic could write even in the 1980s.[4]

In the earliest days, some singers and conductors refused any remuneration—as did Karl Muck, Arturo Toscanini and Hans Knappertsbusch later on. Even today singers and conductors accept fees that are considerably less than in other major houses. Bayreuth has always refused to be drawn into the 'star system' and now maintains a set fee for the role rather than for the person who sings it. Performing at Bayreuth naturally offers unpaid compensation, since it is a ticket to success—and high fees—elsewhere. None the less, the attitude remains very much one expressed by Astrid Varnay, Bayreuth's Brünnhilde of the fifties and sixties: 'One goes to Bayreuth to work; to earn money, one goes elsewhere.'[5]

Bayreuth is special in another way. One of Wagner's shrewdest decisions was insisting that the Festival should be held in relative isolation. 'Island' is a word recurring again and again when artists try to explain Bayreuth's singular atmosphere. The seclusion has a remarkable psychological effect, not only encouraging total concentration on work but creating a remarkable familial spirit. As a notoriously difficult singer told an interviewer, 'In Vienna, I'm fed up with a rehearsal before it starts. Here I enjoy it right down to the end. The place is inspiring. Even the air is inspiring.'[6] Comparing his experience in the 1970s and 1980s producing operas at Bayreuth with that in London, Berlin and other places in Europe, Götz Friedrich commented that he doubted whether many singers were any longer attracted to Bayreuth out of devotion to Wagner alone, since his operas were at times done as well or better elsewhere. 'No, the esprit de corps has more to do with the fact that one is part of a team that temporarily lives together, almost as if on an island.'[7] Wistfully he added, 'I only wish that those who have sung at Bayreuth had the same feeling toward their work—and toward Wagner—when they sing Wagner in other places.' August Everding, another Bayreuth producer of the 1970s and long-time general manager of the Munich Opera, was also convinced that the comparative solitude makes all the difference. 'For work, the cloister cell is best.'[8]

The extent to which Bayreuth has been able to preserve its original character is extraordinary. For the most part it is due to the continuity of control by the composer's heirs. From the time of Wagner's death in 1883 until 1906, the Festival was managed by his widow, Cosima. She was succeeded by her son, Siegfried, and he in turn was followed in 1930 by his widow, Winifred. After the Second World War, she retired in favour of her sons, Wieland and Wolfgang. These successive generations of Wagners have tenaciously refused to make any significant change in the way the Festival is put on—by stretching out the season, changing the repertory, holding other events during the season or performing the works of other composers. To be sure, some singers and musicians now commute during the season to other engagements, a practice that would have been unthinkable not many years ago. Even so, Bayreuth remains largely immune from the drastic changes wrought by jet-setting, publicity-conscious singers and conductors and the pressures that have transformed many other festivals into social and commercial events. Wheat fields still border one side of the opera house and a park, laid out in the composer's time, continues to grace the others, while the distant view beyond the town is of the same meadows and forests that Wagner himself might have set his eyes on.

But important as the isolation, continuity and unique atmosphere may be, what has made Bayreuth special is above all the building itself, this strange 'old barn', as Wagner once called it.

> Then there was silence—and out of the silence and the darkness came a sustained E flat, so low I could not distinguish exactly when the silence ended and the sound began. Nor could I be sure where the sound came from. It might have come from the sides of the auditorium, or the rear, or the ceiling. Slowly the invisible orchestra began to play melodic passages, barely audible at first and gradually increasing until the auditorium was filled with music, the music of the waters of the Rhine. I will never forget that moment.[9]

Of all the impressions evoked by a Bayreuth performance, it is the magic of the sound that is most immediate and striking. The description by Joseph Wechsberg, the writer and opera critic, of his first experience of it—at a rehearsal of *Rheingold* in 1956—echoes what countless others have said or written since the Festival began. The darkness, the silence and then the incomparable sound that seems to come from nowhere and everywhere, that envelops singers and audience alike, that flows with immaculate purity and smoothness, this above all is what makes the Festspielhaus supreme.

The Bayreuth sound results from an optimal mix of the basic ingredients of good acoustics. Chief of these is reverberation time—roughly speaking, the period it takes for sound to die. In the Festspielhaus it is 1.55 seconds. This is ideal for 'heavy' sound, such as Wagner's, which requires a longer reverberation time than lighter and more transparent music, such as that of Mozart and Stravinsky. Furthermore, the theatre's reverberation time is greatest at low frequencies, which is also exemplary for the rich colour of Wagner's scores. Hence a secret of Bayreuth's acoustical preeminence is that the house needs to accommodate only a single type of music and is ideal for that type. Since very little was known about acoustics at the time of construction, the excellence must essentially be credited to Wagner's usual luck and intuition.

Another factor is the effective diffusion and projection of sound. Fundamental is the theatre's wooden fabric. The house is a carpenter's building, in fact is the largest free-standing timber structure ever erected. The types of wood used—local pine, fir and maple—have a splendidly resonant quality. Speaking of how he found singing there, the tenor Manfred Jung said, 'Wood breathes, takes in and then gives back.'[10] Similarly, when asked if it made a difference where she sang, Leonie Rysanek replied: 'Yes. It is incomparably more beautiful to sing in Bayreuth. I hear myself and that is ideal. I say this not in vanity but because I can control my voice. There are many houses, for example, the Met, where the voice is simply lost. In Bayreuth it comes back.'[11]

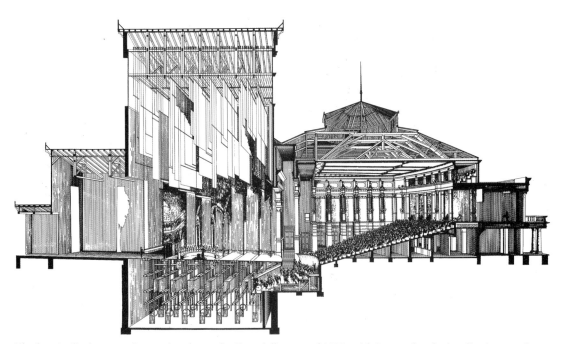

The longitudinal perspective section shows the Festspielhaus as of 1882, with its steeply raked auditorium, sunken orchestra pit, stage, fly tower and rear stage. A performance of *Parsifal* is under way; on stage are the settings for the temple of the grail.

The sound is enhanced by other features of the design and construction. The empty space under the auditorium acts as a resonator. The wooden roof and sail-cloth ceiling-cover function as a reflector. The irregular surface created by the pillared buttresses along the walls, with their hollow wooden columns, diffuses acoustical energy which is finally grounded in the shallow galleries at the rear. The auditorium is therefore an exceptional receptor of sound, which it blends, distributes and softens while enhancing its clarity. The resulting sound quality and the balance between voice and orchestra are unmatched. The Festspielhaus is a more subtle house than any other. The slightest nuance makes itself felt throughout the auditorium. The clarity of words and the refinements of vocal colour are revealed here as nowhere else.

The Bayreuth auditorium is above all kind to voices. As a venerable Karl Muck told a fledgling Karl Böhm, 'Should you ever get to Bayreuth, you will never make the orchestra too loud for the stage; you can turn it up full volume, but you will not obscure even a singer with a weak voice; that is the miracle of Bayreuth.'[12] Soloists and chorus can sing piano when in another opera house they would have to sing mezzoforte or even forte. Vocalists immediately become aware on their initial appearance that they need less power and that in fact they must restrain their voices. In pianissimo passages a soloist can almost sing sotto voce, while a voice that has volume as well as delicacy finds its resonance greatly augmented without any loss of beauty. Comparing Friedrich

A view from behind the stage with the curtain closed. Given the extreme importance of lighting at Bayreuth, the best and latest equipment has always been maintained. In this 1953 photograph of the cat-walk, the control console can be seen on the upper left.

Schorr's performance at Covent Garden in the summer of 1930 with that which he also attended a few weeks later at Bayreuth, Ernest Newman commented:

> Here in Bayreuth not only does his great voice sound greater than it does in London, but the increased volume brings with it not the usual coarseness of 'amplification' but an extraordinary fineness of texture. In most theatres a big orchestra drowns the singers. Here it is quite a common thing for the singer's resonance to overpower the orchestra.[13]

Maintaining a balance between singers and orchestra while achieving a fusion of orchestral sound were in fact two of Wagner's aims in designing his opera house. His orchestration from *Lohengrin* onward often had an almost organ-like quality in which the specific sound of individual instrument groups was submerged in the whole. As his compositional style evolved into its maturest phase, with richer and heavier orchestral textures, the sound threatened to overwhelm the singers. At Bayreuth he wanted to dampen the volume somewhat and at the same time blend the instruments more effectively and in that way also exploit the chromatic idiom that he had initiated with *Tristan* and followed in the later parts of the *Ring*. Even before the Festspielhaus had been constructed, he had apparently tried to imagine how the *Ring* would sound in the auditive conditions he hoped to create. In the view of Peter Schneider, who conducted the *Ring* in the 1980s, Wagner began scoring the work, from the third act of *Siegfried* onward, for his dreamed-of opera house. 'From this point on the dynamic indications, the enrichment and strengthening of the instrumental texture correspond with the house acoustics.'[14]

To achieve the sound he wanted, Wagner introduced a number of innovations, which he tried out with the *Ring* première in 1876 and slightly altered for the *Parsifal* première in 1882, since which time they have been considered sacrosanct. One of these is the peculiar deployment of the musicians. They are seated not in the usual semicircle, but in nine rows, on six ever deeper levels of the sunken pit. In the front are two rows of violins, ranged together; contrary to orthodoxy, the first violins are on the right, the second on the left. In the third and fourth rows are violas, then a row of cellos, with double basses on either side. Next are the woodwinds, flanked by harps, and finally at the deepest level—under the stage—sit the brass and percussion. Although this arrangement is credited with enhancing the balance and homogeneity of the orchestral sound, as Wagner wished, some believe that it is ideal only for *Parsifal* and that other operas would benefit from different seating.

Another novelty is the covered pit, with a hood in front and a sound damper at the rear. The forward cowling was originally intended to shield the auditorium from reflected light from the pit while the rear overhang was added in 1882 for acoustical purposes. The effect of the two together is to modulate the volume, especially of the woodwind and brass, and to force the sound forward to the front of the pit where it mixes with that of the strings, to create a sound that is fully blended and balanced. Because low frequencies escape from the pit more readily than high ones, the orchestral sound is exceptionally dark and silky.

After hearing the *Ring* performed in 1876, Wagner was able to score *Parsifal* with the house acoustics in mind. These enabled him to create the type of sound and the constant, subtle shifting of instrumental colour and the balance between voice and orchestra that he desired. So it is not surprising that having been scored specifically for the Festspielhaus, *Parsifal* is the opera heard to best effect there—and by general consent better than anywhere else. Whether he would have rescored his other operas for Bayreuth, had he lived, has been debated ever since.

Wagner's arrangements create enormous problems for everyone in the pit. Most obvious is the sheer difficulty for the conductor and musicians to see each other. The conductor can scarcely catch a glimpse of the players on the lower levels, while the cellists must constantly turn

Hans Knappertsbusch conducting the Festival orchestra in the covered pit; the view is from the double basses, with violas in the foreground and second violins above them.

their heads to see him. Coordination is another problem, especially for the basses and harps, divided at separate ends of the pit. And with so much sound trapped inside the pit, the unfortunate musicians are at times nearly overpowered by the volume. Able to hear only the players next to them, they have no sense of the overall orchestral sound, much less the voices on stage, and therefore cannot be certain whether they are playing too loud or too soft, too fast or too slow. As a result they are exceptionally dependent on the conductor. 'We are machines, not musicians', the players have sometimes complained, if not in quite those words. Keeping the players together, maintaining proper volume and tempo and all the other essentials of good conducting and playing are therefore vastly more difficult than anywhere else. During a rehearsal of the 1983 *Ring*, Georg Solti commented: 'If anybody had told me when I was at music school that I would one day be in a pit where I couldn't hear anything or see all the players, I would have become a doctor.'[15]

A more serious drawback results from the architecture of the pit itself. Eduard Hanslick, the Viennese critic and Wagner's great nemesis, was the first to observe—at the time of the *Ring* première—that the pit had the effect of compromising 'if not the precision, at least the brilliance of the orchestra'.[16] And Camille Saint-Saëns, who knew Wagner's scores well, complained: 'There is a great deal of musical wastage at

12

Bayreuth. Many interesting details evaporate in the great orchestra pit.'[17] Loss of intensity and detail—such has been the main criticism over the years. The moderation and blending of sound at times results in blandness. For all the beauty of tone, there is consequently a loss of the sheer physical thrill of the orchestral sonorities, especially in the climaxes. After conducting for several seasons in the 1930s, Wilhelm Furtwängler said he found not only that delicate passages at times lost some of their 'intricacy, illumination and plasticity'[18] but also that 'the sensual sound and splendour of the orchestra, which were the composer's objective, are not fully realized'.[19] On attending his first Bayreuth performance in 1982—the year before he himself conducted there—Georg Solti echoed this view. 'It was an entirely different Wagner sound than I had ever heard before. I missed the masses of sound and the colours that I love so much in Wagner.' Most critical of all was Richard Strauss. On the basis of his three seasons conducting there, he maintained that the covered pit was effective only in *Parsifal*, *Tristan* and the *Ring*. Otherwise, 'many of the inexhaustible riches of the score are lost at Bayreuth—I need only mention *Meistersinger*'.[20] In short, though the composer succeeded in redimensioning the orchestral sound to the

Wolfgang Wagner and James Levine. 'For a conductor Bayreuth has the advantage of being able to conduct unseen. And the audience is able to give itself entirely over to the music, and this creates a different mood. Wagner's works need this intensive concentration' (James Levine).

advantage of the voices, he paid a substantial price. It is in fact difficult to dissent from Strauss's own conclusion: Wagner the composer was willing to sacrifice his music for the sake of Wagner the dramatist.

Meistersinger is, as Strauss said, the main musical casualty. In stark contrast to *Parsifal*, its polyphonic style and the almost chamber music quality of some passages call for highly articulated rather than suffused sound, sharp contrasts rather than smooth transitions, and differentiated orchestral sonorities rather than constant blending. It is indicative that a year before the work was first performed at Bayreuth in 1888, Hermann Levi, the original *Parsifal* conductor, warned Cosima Wagner that there were bound to be problems. Sure enough, the rehearsals went badly. 'Despite the most assiduous efforts,' one of the musical assistants at the time recorded, 'it proved impossible to produce clear sound; the intricacies of the score, the sonorous "gothic" of this music was lost in the confusion of sounds; ambiguity and turgidness were all that remained of fruitless efforts.'[21] Since the Second World War conductors have occasionally been permitted to remove some of the sound blender, which itself has been reconstructed, to overcome some of these problems.

Meistersinger also poses a practical difficulty. More than in any other of Wagner's operas, the voices are accompanied by woodwinds. Yet since the woodwind players can scarcely hear the singers, they have no choice but mechanically to follow the conductor, and it depends on him alone to make certain they stay in time with the singers.

Keeping time with the singers. That is still another difficulty caused by the covered pit. The orchestral sound does not flow, as in other opera houses, directly into the auditorium but instead is projected onto the stage where it is further refracted in a largely inexplicable interaction with the sets, the cyclorama and proscenium walls before rebounding into the auditorium. Only then and there do voices and orchestra meet. Holding what are in effect two waves of sound in synchrony is consequently a great challenge to conductors, soloists and chorus alike. In other houses, singers follow the conductor's baton. Were they to do so at Bayreuth, their voices would reach the auditorium before the instrumental sound. They must therefore lag behind the beat, how much behind depending on the stage sets. In sets that conventionally lack depth—Sachs's workshop, Senta's spinning room or Hunding's hut, where there is a sound wall directly behind the singers—soloists and chorus can almost sing along with the orchestra. The deeper the sets, the longer they must delay. In Götz Friedrich's 1979 *Lohengrin* production, in which even the rear stage was open and the chorus ranged along the entire depth, the sound of the chorus varied by as much as half a beat, depending on where the singers stood.

Soloists are apparently able to make the adjustment in timing fairly easily. The chorus must be meticulously guided by its director and his three assistants. They watch the conductor on television monitors while at the same time listening to the chorus with one ear and to the orchestra

through a headphone with the other. Moving around, as their director
Norbert Balatsch once said, like acrobats—from one end of the stage to
the other, up a ladder, down a ladder—they signal with red-tipped
pencil lights whether to speed up or to slow down. But it is the
conductor who needs the coolest nerves. He must ignore the delay in
hearing the voices from the stage and resist an impulse to adjust his
tempo. Attempts to compensate can mean that the voices and the
orchestra never come together. In practice one tends to wait on the
other, with the result that the tempo drags. Said Solti of his experience:
'I have never been so confused in my life.'[22]

Yet timing is almost the least of a Bayreuth conductor's headaches.
Down in the pit—'like being 150 feet under water without a diver's
helmet', in Daniel Barenboim's words[23]—a conductor can see and hear
remarkably little either in the pit or on the stage, just as singers and
chorus members are able to catch scarcely a glimpse of him. 'The
conductor is the one who hears worst,' Wieland Wagner once said.[24]
Rudolf Kempe, well known as a virtuoso conductor, was so terrified by
it all that he later confessed to having been tempted to pack up and leave
after his first rehearsal in 1960. How do conductors cope? In Cosima
Wagner's day it helped somewhat that singers were required to follow
stringently stylized gestures and that tempi were slow. Of more recent
conductors, Hans Knappertsbusch learned to read the singers' lip movements, and others have done the same.

Worse still, a conductor has little or no idea how the music sounds to
the audience. He is usually tempted to dampen the violins, which
surround him, but if he does so, they are too subdued. The brass sounds
unbearably loud in the narrow confines of the pit but is much softer
when heard in the auditorium. Only by sending an assistant into the
auditorium and occasionally going there himself during rehearsals can a
conductor gradually form an impression of the sound he is creating. Solti
said that his rule of thumb was: 'When I can't hear anything on stage, I
know I am too loud, and when I can hear easily I know I am too soft.
When I can hear a little of the singers' voices above the orchestra, I think
it must be right.'[25]

Not surprisingly, some conductors fail and leave after a year. But even
the staunchest find they need several seasons to catch on. Joseph
Keilberth summed up his own experience from 1952 to 1956 in a way
that doubtless reflects that of others:

> Richard Wagner created a wonderful sounding board when he designed this
> house, but he didn't make it easy for the conductor. I've worked here for
> several summers now, but every time it takes me a good while to catch on.
> I can hardly hear the singers. And they can't see me very well. So I work in
> shirt sleeves. Some of the conductors wear shirts that reflect light. The
> musicians don't hear the singers at all; in some sections of the pit they don't
> even hear themselves. Right here, though, the music literally beats around

your ears. Under the circumstances, the conductor has a hard time keeping singers and orchestra together. He has to rely on instinct, float along with the singers, and keep the orchestra moving. I've worked in a lot of places, but, I assure you, Bayreuth is the toughest.[26]

Soothing conductors, encouraging singers and generally keeping the Bayreuth family happily engaged during the season is a vital but only a minor part of the management's work. Wolfgang Wagner, the composer's grandson and since 1966 sole head of the Festival, has described his job as ninety per cent administration and only ten per cent art. Helping him is a permanent staff of around seventy employees which grows to nearly 800 once everyone—singers, musicians, chorus and conductors, carpenters, electricians, mechanics, painters and seamstresses—has arrived by the third week of June.

In common with all opera managers, Wolfgang Wagner's main administrative worry is finance. With its divas, choruses, large casts, elaborate settings and costumes, enormous backstage crews, large orchestras and expensive conductors, opera is by far the most costly of art forms. In only two places, Bayreuth and Glyndebourne, has it been successful as a family concern.

The Festival has from the start been nagged by financial difficulties. It went bankrupt once and verged on insolvency on four other occasions. Today it is in healthy if not opulent financial condition, its position based on a combination of private and public support on the one hand and its own income and careful spending on the other. The budget has risen exponentially, from 1.5 million marks in 1951 to 6.5 million marks in 1971 and just short of 19 million (£6.8 million; $12 million) in 1992. Roughly forty-two per cent of this latest sum was covered by government grants—from Federal, Bavarian and local authorities—which amounts to only half what other major German opera houses receive. The other major donor is the Society of the Friends of Bayreuth, whose 3,700 members—almost a quarter of them non-Germans—together regularly give around two million marks a year. Close to half the total is therefore earned by the Festival itself, from ticket sales, radio broadcasting fees, royalties from recordings and video films and the sale of publications and photographs. To reinforce his position as manager and minimize the risk of interference, Wolfgang Wagner has always sought to keep his dependence on outside support at less than half the total income.

With the drastic increase in staff wages and artists' fees, the Festival has had to devote a steadily increasing proportion of its income to personnel expenditure. By the early 1990s this stood at around 80 per cent, up from 46 per cent when the Festival was revived in 1951. The other major—and highly variable—expenditure is for new productions.

For a producer Bayreuth is ideal. Wolfgang Wagner does his best to make available whatever funds are necessary. The Festival offers a highly skilled staff along with the most up-to-date mechanical and lighting

Early in a new production, a stage model is produced and studied for its feasibility. Here William Dudley and Peter Hall explain their proposed stage platform for the 1983 *Ring* to Gudrun and Wolfgang Wagner.

equipment. The time allotted to develop, test and rehearse a production is exceptionally generous—for the *Ring* around three years, for other works about eighteen months. And after it has gone on stage, a new production is treated as a work-in-progress, to be revised in succeeding years as the producer wishes, with additional money available for changes.

Given the ever longer commitments of an ever smaller number of Wagnerian singers and conductors, planning for a new production must begin years in advance. Once the artists are sounded out and a producer enlisted, preparations can begin. At the outset the producer describes his general concepts to his set designer, who prepares sketches or models of the proposed staging. House experts study these proposals for their technical feasibility and suggest changes they consider necessary. A rough budget is then calculated. In the following months the sets are constructed and the costumes and masks are made. Tests of the staging follow in the main rehearsal stage behind the Festspielhaus. These are concerned not only with the feasibility of the sets themselves but with their effect, for example, on choral sound.

'I can only say I have never been able to work under such conditions anywhere else,' Götz Friedrich commented of his own experiences as a Bayreuth producer.[27] What he had in mind, he explained, was the amount of time and resources available—technical rehearsals nine months in advance and then as much as a week for them, lighting rehearsals on the stage with a lighting team not long after that and further tests of the sets on one of the special rehearsal stages. And everything done in an unhurried way. Only the stage itself was less available than in other houses, since no single production has priority

At an acting rehearsal of the 1962 *Tannhäuser*, Wieland Wagner demonstrates a gesture to Wolfgang Windgassen, who sang the title role.

and each producer has equal access. All in all, he concluded, 'One can accomplish much more at Bayreuth in three or four weeks than in other places in two or three months.'[28]

It is one of the historic Bayreuth conventions that the dramatic presentation is paramount and the music subordinate. Even such famous Bayreuth conductors as Hans Richter, Hermann Levi, Arturo Toscanini and Wilhelm Furtwängler presided over an orchestra and cast they did not select and productions they did not influence. When Fritz Busch had the temerity in 1924 to raise questions about some of the singing and orchestral playing, Siegfried Wagner politely told him to mind his own business. Conductors have always been expected to feel honoured at being invited and expected to serve without murmur. Not until 1930—and then as a concession to Toscanini—was the name of the conductor even mentioned in the programme.

Considering the gigantic egos of most conductors, it is not surprising that the tradition has not always been accepted. The first to challenge it was Furtwängler. Inevitably he failed and left. After the Festival was revived in 1951, several conductors also quit, either because they regarded the production as intolerable or would not agree to the casting. Beginning in the 1970s, certain conductors—Boulez and Solti, for example—were enticed to Bayreuth by being promised a greater role.

18

They were signed on first and permitted to choose the producer and outline the overall conceptual approach. And it is generally accepted that Götz Friedrich's production of *Parsifal* was retired because the conductor, James Levine, refused to go on conducting anything so avant-garde, and for a variety of reasons he was less dispensable than Friedrich. All that said, however, the producer retains independence and Bayreuth remains a producer-director's opera company.

The orchestra which a Bayreuth conductor leads is exceptionally large. In part this is simply due to the unprecedented role Wagner gave the orchestra in his operas. Far from merely accompanying voices, it narrates what is visually and psychologically taking place on stage; it describes what cannot be conveyed by singers and settings and it even creates its own images—a toad, a dragon, a bird as well as fire, forest, darkness and dawn, wind and waves, lightning and thunder. So successful are these musical pictures that some listeners have always been more absorbed in the sound than in the dramatic events on stage. George Bernard Shaw said his favourite way of enjoying the *Ring* was to sit at the back of the house, close his eyes and 'listen without looking'.[29] Others would frankly have preferred Wagner as a symphonist. Richard Strauss himself once rhetorically asked whether a 'cultivated audience' liked Wagner's operas for the singing or for the orchestra. 'I think the latter,' was his rhetorical answer.[30]

To create his 'speaking orchestra', Wagner needed music of unprecedented richness, colour and detail, even new sounds. He not only augmented the normal orchestra but also equipped it with novel, modified and seldom-used instruments—such as 'Wagner tubas' in the *Ring*, a cattle horn in the second act of *Walküre*, a wooden trumpet in the third act of *Tristan* as well as a 'Beckmesser harp' and Night Watchman's horn in *Meistersinger*, not to mention 'bells' for *Parsifal* and 'anvils' for *Rheingold*. Some instruments were given a role almost equivalent to that of a vocalist—as the English horn in the final act of *Tristan*. To express everything he had in mind in *Götterdämmerung*, the composer said he would have needed two orchestras. And so emerged the Wagner orchestra and, eventually, the Bayreuth orchestra.

The Festival orchestra is also larger for reasons unique to Bayreuth. Here Wagner wanted not only the instrumentalists prescribed in the scores, but also an augmented string section—16 first violins, 16 second violins, 12 violas, 12 cellos, 8 double basses and from 2 to 6 harps—up to 27 more instruments than in the conventional Wagner orchestra. This string section is invariable; the number of woodwinds, brass and percussion, however, varies from opera to opera. Hence the total number of musicians for *Lohengrin*, for example, is 89; the total for the *Ring*, 124. The Bayreuth orchestra is also supplemented by ten 'stage musicians'— trumpeters and trombonists who play fanfares outside the opera house to announce the beginning of each act as well as music from the stage, as in the first and last acts of *Lohengrin*.

The complement of players has steadily grown over the years. Today there are 183 musicians, a figure dictated both by the increased number of performances in a season and by modern working conditions. No one is any longer willing to play extremely long scores day after day for a month. A musician these days normally plays in four of the seven or so operas in any season. In addition, horn players are often changed between the second and third acts of *Götterdämmerung*.

For most of its history, it has been a specially recruited orchestra. This follows a tradition established by the composer himself, who for his *Ring* première in 1876 selected the best players available from orchestras throughout Germany rather than relying on a single, existing band with certain weak sections. For financial reasons, however, it was necessary to accept the hospitality of the Munich Court Opera for the première of *Parsifal* in 1882 and for several years thereafter. But by 1886 Felix Mottl, then principal conductor, reconstituted a special orchestra. It took him years of effort before he succeeded in putting together a solid group and, even so, he had to bring much of it with him every summer from the Karlsruhe Court Opera where he was chief conductor. He was succeeded in 1903 by Karl Muck, an extremely fastidious musician and no doubt for that reason rarely content with his musicians. After the First World War Fritz Busch recommended inviting Toscanini to rebuild the orchestra — as he had done with the La Scala orchestra after 1918 — but his suggestion was rejected. The quality of the musicians was especially high in the 1930s when most players came from Berlin. After the Second World War, the difficulties of forming a new orchestra seemed insurmountable, and serious thought was given — as it had been from time to time in the past — to engaging an existing one. Talks were held with the Dresden Staatskapelle and the Bavarian Radio Symphony Orchestra. In the end it was decided that the old system was the best way to maintain quality and retain control.

Bayreuth musicians are not so much recruited as coopted. In the past they were primarily recommended by conductors; now they are normally proposed by other musicians. No one is offered more than a year's contract and anyone considered below standard is not invited back. An assessment is made at the end of the season by the concert master and representatives of the various instrument groups in consultation with the orchestra director and Wolfgang Wagner. Conductors are asked for their views but apparently have little or no influence on who comes, who stays or who goes. A few players last only a year, most at least a decade and some for as long as thirty years. Hence it is essentially the same orchestra year after year, a self-reproducing organism, with usually no more than a dozen or so changes.

The Festival orchestra has always been a German orchestra. Occasionally a few foreigners have been invited; there was even a New Yorker — Orleana Boker, a harpist — in the 1876 orchestra. But since rehearsal time is short, instrumentalists must know their Wagner well.

German musicians, playing Wagnerian works—in particular the highly demanding *Ring* operas—more often than do others, are considered better prepared. Even so, the majority of players currently come from relatively few orchestras—two in Hamburg, two in Cologne, two in Berlin and, since 1990, ensembles in Dresden, Leipzig and the Berlin State Opera.

A sense of being part of a great tradition has always been strong among Bayreuth musicians. The honorarium, which is the same for each player, does little more than compensate for expenses. There is no Bayreuth musicians' union; consequently, union rules which would normally limit rehearsal time, for instance, do not apply in Bayreuth. Players willingly accept a punishing schedule. 'It could only happen here' is a comment that occurs over and over in one phrasing or another. 'It's what they call the miracle of Bayreuth,' said one. 'Of course it could not go on forever. The good thing about Bayreuth is that it lasts for only two months. We could not keep up this pace for any longer than that.' While the sense of single-minded devotion has diminished somewhat in recent years as musicians also play in other summer events on free days, by and large the Bayreuth spirit still flourishes.

While relations between the orchestra and its conductors are veiled behind mutual discretion, respect is not surprisingly identified as the key to the relationship. Toscanini lost some of the orchestra's confidence in 1931 by walking out of a rehearsal and refusing to conduct at a memorial concert for Cosima and Siegfried Wagner. Far worse is inadequate professional skill, and in Bayreuth the standards are of the highest. 'A Bayreuth musician can tolerate just about anything in a conductor,' said one of them, 'but what he cannot accept is his not understanding the score, and that is occasionally the case.' The worst row in Bayreuth's history broke out over this issue when Pierre Boulez conducted a new production of the *Ring* in 1976. In the opinion of most of the musicians, Boulez had neither mastered the score nor had any feeling for it. His interpretation, which among other things was deemed to have suppressed the leitmotifs, incited an open revolt by nearly three-quarters of the orchestra. The players even disavowed him publicly by refusing to appear with him on stage at the conclusion of the première performance. Boulez offered to resign; Wolfgang Wagner stood by him. The following year at least a third of the musicians did not return, some by their own choice and some by that of Boulez.

The chorus has always been Bayreuth's particular glory. 'It makes tears come to the eyes by the sheer nobility of the sound' is typical of the sort of critical comment repeated through the decades. Since the very beginning in 1876 it has been the best opera chorus in the world. Year in and year out, whatever critics and audiences might say of the production, staging, soloists, conductors or orchestra, the chorus has invariably been judged a flawless wonder, moving critics and audiences alike by its sheer perfection. In other opera houses a chorus is an ensemble of singers; at Bayreuth it is a single, seamless, uniform voice with an intonation of crystalline clarity. At times it is the inspiration, the one impeccable achievement of a performance.

The quality of the chorus is primarily due to the straightforward excellence of the individual singers. A fair number of them are soloists or proto-soloists, and the Bayreuth chorus is the only one in which many would sing. Also important is the Bayreuth tradition of rigorous drilling in the weeks before the season and a final run-through before each performance. Training and rehearsing go on throughout the day, day after day. Newcomers are coached in the morning; a rehearsal of the full chorus often follows in the afternoon or evening. The initial fort-night is critical. It is then that the individual voices are forged into one single voice, one sound. Usually the most outstanding singers, with their own technique and vocal colour, must make the greatest effort to submerge their voices in the mass. Given the Bayreuth acoustics, mem-bers must also learn to keep their voices softer than normal. That is a principal aim of the initial rehearsals; thereafter the volume is gradually increased, though always kept at a level lower than it would be in another opera house. When the director is satisfied with the singers' sound and articulation, the chorus practises its stage movements, first in a rehearsal stage and then, with the full orchestra, in the theatre itself.

Until the 1960s, members of the chorus were exclusively German and Austrian. Nowadays they come from as many as two dozen countries, and annual trials are held in London, Manchester, Frankfurt, Hamburg, Vienna and Bayreuth. There are 134 members—76 men and 58 women—with a turnover of 20 or so a year. For certain operas their number must be augmented—as many as 120 boys are brought in from local schools to be Nibelungs in *Rheingold* and a hundred or more are recruited from local choral groups for the finale of *Meistersinger*. Finding and rehearsing the singers has been the responsibility of the Festival's chorus masters over the years: Julius Kniese, Hugo Rüdel, Friedrich Jung, Wilhelm Pitz and, since 1972, Norbert Balatsch. Each seemed at the time irreplaceable, yet each was somehow equalled or even surpassed by his successor.

For soloists the route to Bayreuth has been more or less the same since the earliest years. A singer may be recommended by a conductor, or may be heard in a performance at another house or may request an audition during the Festival. During much of its history Bayreuth has been as interested in discovering and cultivating new talent as in having the most outstanding soloists of the day. The notion of putting a few world-famous stars on stage and letting the rest of the performance take care of itself is a vice to which Bayreuth has never succumbed.

Today the great problem for Bayreuth, as for opera houses every-where, is the small number of Wagnerian singers and the very small number of those who are outstanding. 'The Wagnerian mode of singing has today already begun to die out; it is extremely difficult to find any singer equal to its demands,' the musicologist Theodor Adorno wrote in 1963.[31] Two years later Wieland Wagner himself frankly complained in the Festival's annual publication that the shortage of singers was so acute he found it almost impossible to assemble 'even a moderately good cast' for any of Wagner's operas. On another occasion he jested that were anything to happen to Wolfgang Windgassen, then Bayreuth's leading male singer, he would have to post a sign: 'Festspielhaus closed—no tenor.'

There is no fixed schedule for singers; they may arrive early or, if the opera has been in the repertory for some time, late. Rehearsing is initially done in one of the rehearsal rooms alternately with the director, discussing the role and practising the stage movements, and with the conductor, working on the music. By late June, rehearsals with the director move to the opera house and those with the conductor and orchestra to the restaurant. These are followed by one or more full stage rehearsals with the orchestra. Since these cannot easily be interrupted, a subsequent run-through for the singers with piano accompaniment is held. The penultimate phase is the main rehearsal, when for the first time soloists, orchestra and chorus, along with sets and lighting, are rehearsed together. Then, in the final fortnight are held the dress rehearsals, a great Bayreuth tradition when friends of the Wagners and relations of the performers are invited to attend.

By the end of July all is in readiness. The Festival begins with a new production, if any is presented that year. On the opening day there is a brief choral concert at the composer's grave. Wreaths are laid there and at the tombs of his descendants. Respects paid, the audience ascends to the Festspielhaus, ready for the old magician to do his tricks.

The usual way of attending a Wagnerian opera in Paris, Milan, London or New York—on those relatively rare occasions when one is performed—is to race across town through evening rush-hour traffic, queue at the box office, sink exhausted into a seat, damn latecomers, try to forget the day's problems and concentrate on the music, have a drink in the first intermission to prevent physical collapse and a snack in the second to stave off famine, doze off for a minute or two during the last act and, finally, after hand-to-hand combat for a taxi, arrive home around midnight. Even in the more civilized days of the nineteenth century, a night at the opera was just as frantic. To Wagner, it was intolerable. He was determined to make his devotees give over the better part of the day to a performance in a location where there would be no distractions. The place he chose was Bayreuth.

Bayreuth is a pleasant city, situated in Franconia, one of the loveliest corners of Germany—an area of charming towns, architectural gems and forested hills known as Franconian Switzerland. An English visitor in the 1930s described it as 'a lovable old town, with unexpectedly picturesque little winding by-streets, a stately palace, an exquisite rococo opera, churches and shady parks'. The lovable old town was largely blasted to bits by the American air force in April 1945, but it has been rebuilt and is today prosperous and attractive. The Old Schloss has been reconstructed, the New Schloss refurbished and the rococo opera house beautifully maintained; a few picturesque back streets are still to be found and the parks remain as shady as ever. It is still possible to have a rendezvous where Brünnhilde Straße meets Gunter Straße or where Lohengrin Straße crosses Elsa Straße or, ominously perhaps, where Siegmund Straße runs into Hunding Straße. One can also still buy an aspirin at the Parsifal, Meistersinger, Ring, Siegfried or Tannhäuser pharmacy, bread at the Richard Wagner bakery, a drink at the Holländer bar and china at the Walküre porcelain factory.

Yet Bayreuth has always been disparaged. Foreign visitors in particular have complained that it is ugly and boring, the people unpleasant and money-grubbing, its restaurants bad and its accommodation difficult to find and inadequate. Apart from the Festival itself, there is little to see and less to do. That, at least, is exactly as Wagner wanted it. One was to come to Bayreuth for the opera and nothing but the opera.

These days visitors complain less about food or rooms or boredom than about the scarcity and price of tickets. During the early Festivals it was impossible to fill the house. At the end of the 1880s attendance suddenly picked up; by 1891 tickets were selling for more than their face value and by 1904 a stationery shop was openly advertising seats at 'increased prices', a euphemism for black market tickets. Sales continued to be good through the 1920s and even for two years into the great depression. In 1931, when both Toscanini and Furtwängler conducted, tickets on the black market fetched more than five times their normal price. After the Second World War ticket sales revived rapidly; from 1955 on the Festival was always sold out and by the 1990s nearly half a million people were applying for the 58,000 available tickets. There is still a black market—discreetly at the west side of the Festspielhaus and less discreetly in the columns of a local paper.

Today ticket requests must be made in writing in the autumn. They are entered into a computer and sorted by nationality, fame and demonstrated interest in the Festival. Members of the Society of Friends of Bayreuth and other patrons enjoy priority along with, in recent decades, French and Americans. Applicants must usually wait at least five years, but the process is a lottery which some applicants never seem to win.

For the lucky ones, the ritual on the day of a performance has remained essentially unchanged since 1876. For those who wish to attend one of the private lectures on the opera of the day, it begins at 10:30 in the morning. Then at least an hour before curtain time—that is, by three o'clock, or by five o'clock in the case of *Rheingold* and *Fliegender Holländer*—the audience begins to assemble. Some still make their way up the hill on foot; in the old days there were few carriages and today there are just as few taxis.

The time before the performance is traditionally spent strolling outside the theatre or taking refreshments. There are no foyers inside the opera house where spectators can sit or walk; indeed the doors are locked until shortly before the beginning of each act. Fortunately, as Nietzsche remarked of the first Festival, 'In Bayreuth even the spectator is a spectacle worth seeing.'[32] So most members of the audience spend the time gazing at one another. The more intellectually intrepid, however, peruse the Festival programme. This booklet is not light reading. Unlike the usual opera programme, it runs nowadays to 75 pages of learned articles, sometimes related to the day's opera but more often about other aspects of Wagner's works and Bayreuth history—'Richard Wagner and Russian Musical Life', 'Adolphe Appia's Meaning for the Development of Modern Staging', 'The Psychological Meaning of Keys in Wagner's Works' and the like. What is not to be found is a synopsis of the day's opera since it would be infra dig to imply that a member of the audience did not know the opera more or less by heart.

Dress has always been mixed. Wagner had tried to impose a dress code—morning coats and grandes toilettes—but it was ignored even in his day. Before 1914 there was a good deal of dressing up, but also much dressing down—evident in often-published photographs of G.B. Shaw and others in wrinkled lounge suits. Between the wars and in the 1950s and 1960s dress was informal. During the 1970s, the years of ostentatious prosperity were celebrated by an escalation in stylishness. But by the 1990s anything was acceptable—from the startling to the staid, from T-shirts to tails.

Of late the audience has included increasing numbers of young people, even teenagers, something that would have been unimaginable in earlier years. Roughly a third of the audience are now foreigners, and they are more widely international than ever. In the beginning Wagner had overestimated the interest of his own countrymen, and in some early years almost half the audience were non-German. In the two decades before 1914 several hundred French normally showed up, but their number was greatly exceeded by the British, the most numerous, and by Americans. Americans often aroused derision, sometimes relatively good-natured, more often slightly malicious. These 'Wagnerized Yankees', in one critic's phrase, were derided as rich, philistine poseurs. In fact 'American' as an adjective was widely used in Bayreuth circles as a synonym for whatever was materialistic, commercialistic or vulgar. Even the sober critic of the staid *Frankfurter Zeitung* considered it necessary in his report on the 1931 season to inform his readers: 'Behind me someone from the U.S.A. slept through at least three-quarters of *Parsifal*. When at the end she woke up, no doubt because everyone else rose to leave, I heard her say to her neighbour, "Was it not wonderful?" Perhaps she had had a pleasant dream.'[33] Would the incident have been considered worth recording had the woman been German or of another nationality?

Fifteen minutes before the performance, a single fanfare sounds from the balcony over the front entrance—a theme from the act about to be performed. At ten minutes it sounds twice and at five, three times. This is the final signal for the audience to take their seats. Tickets are checked by young women known because of their long blue skirts as 'girls in blue'. There are thirty-two of them, Wagner enthusiasts for whom the job is a means of seeing the opera free and of catching a glimpse of what goes on behind stage.

What first strikes a newcomer on entering the Festspielhaus is the excellence of the sight lines even from the sides and the way the eye is ineluctably drawn to the stage and, in the absence of any architectural or decorative distraction, to the stage alone. From that moment on, one is caught in the web of Wagner's elaborate musical-theatrical-psychological design. Opera in this place is a total experience from the moment of arriving to the moment of leaving.

A minute or so before the lights go down, the audience, as if by collective telepathy, falls quiet. Once the auditorium darkens, it subsides into the famous 'Bayreuth hush'. The mood of solemnity is unspoiled by applause for the conductor, who is already invisibly ensconced in the pit, or by latecomers, who are never allowed entry. That nearly 2,000 people can then remain seated in motionless silence for hours on end has always been one of the marvels of Bayreuth. Rarely is there a cough, sniff, sigh, wiggle, twitch, squirm or quiver. The audience might have turned to stone. Or, as Mark Twain discovered in 1891, 'You seem to sit with the dead in the gloom of a tomb.'[34] In the old days, however, the seats could be perilous since some of them squeaked with the slightest movement. Stravinsky had a bitter recollection of his attendance at *Parsifal* in 1912: 'Crack! Now I had done it! My chair had made a noise which drew down on me the furious stares of a hundred pairs of eyes.'[35]

The intervals between acts are generous, a full hour. One dines or, again, walks outside the theatre or in the nicely landscaped park in front. 'During the intermissions,' Romain Rolland wrote in 1891, 'the French flirt, the Germans drink beer and the English read the libretto.' Five years later he took a grimmer view, recording in his journal: 'A miserable public—phonies, Jews, snobs, hypocrites, Yankees, slow-witted English and repulsive Germans, stinking as high as the Alps.'[36] Alban Berg was equally choleric on attending *Parsifal* in 1909. Profoundly moved by the music, he was disgusted by the levity of the audience, which to his jaundiced eye appeared to be mostly Americans and Bavarians, who looked as though they had stepped out of a caricature in a satirical magazine. In his account, the Bavarians drank beer, the Americans champagne, and both sat around chattering and laughing. He described the experience as an 'empty delusion' and swore he would never return—an oath he kept—and had no doubt that Wagner himself would, if it were possible, rise from his grave and also flee.[37]

The Festspielhaus during intermission, with the brass ensemble about to summon members of the audience to take their places.

In one respect the Bayreuth ritual has changed drastically. Before the Second World War the audience applauded at the end of an opera and even on occasion called for the conductor—who refused to appear. After the performance one gathered in the Festival restaurant where, as the noted French Wagnerian Albert Lavignac recorded in 1897, it was 'not rare to see everybody spontaneously rise to give a warm and noisy ovation' when the artists joined them.[38] This hallowed tradition was broken in 1951 when the Siegfried and Brünnhilde of that season were permitted to take a curtain call at the end of *Siegfried*. In the following years the practice was steadily broadened to include curtain calls after every act. Then in the late 1960s audiences in German opera houses were ever more frenzied in their cheering and even more in their booing. The phenomenon attained its height—or depth—at Bayreuth, as Festival productions became increasingly controversial. Audiences divided into one group that hollered its approval and another that screamed its opposition, or the entire audience might boo one year and cheer the next.

Eight hours after having left for a performance, one returns down the hill. There was something oddly religious about the day—a shared experience of deep meaning, like-minded participants, everyone familiar with the ritual and equally moved. How to explain the continuing spell of Bayreuth? Why is one's musical life incomplete without attending the Festival? The music and staging, a long and famous tradition, the theatre itself, the civilized way of doing things, the 'island' atmosphere—do these add up to the mystique that surrounds the Festival and that for over a century has drawn millions on what even today retains the character of a pilgrimage? And how did it all come about?

1

'Strong and fair, see it stand'
(*Rheingold*)

It has been raining hard since early morning. On a hill above Bayreuth mud is everywhere and ankle deep. Long banners—twenty-one of them—with the national and Bavarian colours, hang wet and limp in the incessant downpour. No less soggy is a waiting crowd, people from all around Germany. A military band stands in place, but the dripping platform for dignitaries and singers is empty. Just after eleven o'clock a carriage draws up, and out steps a small man with one of the most famous and frequently caricatured profiles in Europe. He is Richard Wagner, and it is Wednesday, 22 May 1872, his fifty-ninth birthday. It is also one of the most important days in his life. 'Everything that had happened up to now', Nietzsche later wrote, 'was a preparation for this moment.'[1]

The moment was the occasion when the foundation-stone of Wagner's own opera house was to be laid. Once the composer and his friends had arrived, the band struck up his *March of Homage* to King Ludwig II of Bavaria. The stone was then lowered into place and with it a capsule containing a telegram of congratulation from the King, several Bavarian and German coins and a holograph scrip with the composer's own quatrain: 'Here I enclose a secret, And if it remains many hundred years, As long as the stone preserves it, It will reveal itself to the world.'[2] Wagner took a hammer and tapped the block three times, saying with the first stroke, 'Be blessed, my stone, endure for long and be steadfast.' Deathly pale, he was near to tears.

Because of the foul weather the remainder of the ceremony was transferred to the Margrave's Opera House in the centre of town. Nietzsche was among those who accompanied Wagner down the hill, recording:

He was silent and for a long time looked in upon himself with a gaze which cannot be described in words. But what Wagner saw inside himself on that day—what he was, what he is and what he will become—that is something

29

we who are closest to him can to some extent see as well, and only in that Wagnerian gaze can we for the first time understand his great accomplishment—and with that understanding be certain of its fruition.[3]

The Opera House was already overcrowded when Wagner entered. On rising to speak, he turned to his patrons and friends and said he had that day been honoured as no other artist in history. The theatre he envisaged was to be a modest structure, made of the simplest materials and without any adornment. In fact it might best be likened to the sort of temporary construct at a fair which was afterwards pulled down. That the building would not be a permanent and stately one was due to the German parliament's lack of interest in his work and beyond that to the deplorable state of German art.

With the oration having ended on a note similar to Hans Sachs's lamentation which concluded *Die Meistersinger*, a choral group fittingly broke into the *Wacht auf!* chorus from that opera, with its message of hope triumphing over adversity. The ceremony continued with Wagner himself conducting Beethoven's Ninth Symphony. For the occasion he had insisted on having not an existing orchestra and chorus but rather artists he had individually recruited from the best houses in Germany. Nothing was ever casual with Wagner, and this was in fact a trial run for an arrangement that was later very important to him. The memorable symphonic performance was followed by a huge banquet which finally brought the celebrations to a close. By the end of the day, Wagner was, as Ernest Newman wrote, exhausted but proud and contented as never before in all his life.

What memories had run through the composer's mind that day? Did he recall all the places from Riga to Rio de Janeiro that had directly or remotely played some role in shaping the building now to be erected? Wagner the creator of music dramas is famous; Wagner the architect, the man who picked up ideas with a voracious eclecticism and put them together with astounding success, is almost unknown. The story of how his utopian fantasies took concrete form is not only a significant aspect of Wagner's artistic career but offers a remarkable example of how determination and serendipity combined to produce a singular achievement.

The original impetus is clear. In revolutionizing opera, Wagner realized he would have to revolutionize opera production. What he confronted was a situation where opera was primarily a social rather than a musical event. This was even obvious from the physical arrangements in opera houses. Spectators were seated in hierarchical tiers of boxes in a horseshoe-shaped auditorium where seeing the stage was not as important as seeing, and being seen by, other spectators. The stage itself was small and ornate, and the theatre remained lit throughout a performance. Members of the audience, chattering among themselves, were almost as much a part of the show as the singers on stage. The operas themselves were apt to be mangled at the whim of a stage-manager; the music might be cut or altered and the settings for one work were often used for another, irrespective of the dramatic content of either. Soloists usually lacked acting—and at times singing—ability and in any case tended to be more interested in playing to the gallery than in playing a role on stage.

To someone who saw music as a means of redeeming society, such antics were an unspeakable outrage. In Wagner's view the core of the problem was money. That, not art, was what animated impresarios. To them opera was a business and the objective was profit, not musical excellence. But audiences were also at fault. They regarded opera as an evening's light entertainment and a means of flaunting their social status. Wagner wanted opera to convey ideas, explore human relations, portray life at its best and worst, and everything between. Artistic excellence could not be sustained commercially; it required fewer and better performances and must therefore be supported by state subsidies. Audiences would likewise have to change; they had to learn to treat opera-going as a transcendent aesthetic experience. Ideally the audience and the spectacle were to interact. Such were some of the notions that underlay proposals he submitted in 1846 and 1848 for the reform of the Dresden Opera where he was then a conductor. After his suggestions were brushed aside, he concluded that the problem was broader. A reform of the cultural world demanded a fundamental reform of society. When the wave of revolutionary insurrection sweeping Europe at the time reached Dresden in 1849, Wagner joined it.

The revolution was put down violently, and Wagner was forced to flee for his life, finding his way into exile in Zurich. There he immediately took up his pen, not to compose music but to write several meditations on art. A pervasive theme of these was that Western civilization had been in steady decline ever since the golden age of Greece and that only a social-cultural revolution could restore art and society to their previous glory. What is significant for a history of Bayreuth is that buried in these ruminations were the seeds of what later blossomed into an operatic festival.

In *Art and Revolution*, provocative in title and provocative in substance, he railed against the way art was the slave of mammon and had as a result become corrupt and hollow. 'Its real essence is industry; its moral purpose is the acquisition of money; its aesthetic pretext is the entertainment of those who are bored.'[4] Audiences were bored because they arrived at performances weary from the day's work, wanting to be amused rather than challenged to intellectual effort. What Wagner held up by contrast was the Greece of Aeschylus where the whole community, not just the social élite, attended artistic festivals and where the honour of participation, not money, was the reward. Although this may have been an idealization of ancient Greece, it none the less reveals what he envisaged as a model and the revolutionary nature of his vision.

His next essay, *The Art-Work of the Future*, discussed a proposed 'theatrical edifice of the future'.[5] Unlike contemporary opera houses, which were designed for social ostentation, class stratification and money-making, his ideal structure would be one where 'art alone gives law and measure, down to the smallest detail'. The auditorium was to be designed for the best possible optical and acoustical effects; everything that met the eye was to enhance a comprehension of the work on stage. Spectators were to be absorbed into the drama on stage while artists were to lose themselves in their roles. In this way the confines of the theatre would collapse, with the result, he maintained, that the public 'lives and breathes only in the art-work, which seems to become life itself, and the stage appears to be the wide expanse of the entire world'. In this brief passage, Wagner in effect defined total theatre. In so doing he declared his independence of a centuries-long tradition of theatre design and set down in generic terms the principles that guided his design of the interior of the Festspielhaus twenty-five years later.

'Small wonder', Thomas Mann once wrote, that the artist Wagner, caring for his art, had felt revulsion against 'the whole bourgeois culture industry of the time'. But the composer Wagner had a highly personal interest as well. His operas had serious intellectual content, requiring skilled presentation and a devoted audience. Although his two major operas up to then, *Rienzi* and *Fliegender Holländer*, had enjoyed successful performances, in his judgement they had been treated as so much artistic merchandise, not understood as consequential dramas. In 1848 he had begun a new opera based on the Nibelung saga. The longer he worked on it, the more convinced he was that it would be so novel and complex it could never be adequately produced—even if accepted—in conventional court theatres. It would also require an audience to enter into the work in the way a Greek audience had thrown itself into a performance of an Aeschylian tragedy—to see itself in the drama and to discover in it meaning for the individual and the universe. For Wagner what was vital was not simply the physical arrangements of a production but the psychological atmosphere of a performance.

This is why, despite the plethora of opera houses in Germany, Wagner wanted his own theatre where he could dictate his own standards of performance. Of course it was all a pipe-dream. To write an opera and have it performed was one thing; to conjure up a vast and unprecedented endeavour involving thousands of people and large amounts of money, and to bring that about, was quite another. Wagner himself was so dejected at times during those early years of exile that he could scarcely bring himself to work on an opera which, as he wrote in his autobiography *Mein Leben*, 'would never go further than the paper it was written on'.[6] Yet even then, as in the dark days to follow, he never lost hope—a completely irrational hope—that he would succeed. Because it absolutely had to be, somehow it would be.

Fantasy alternated with despair. To his close friend Theodor Uhlig, a Dresden conductor, he wrote in September 1850 that if he could raise 10,000 taler, he would erect a theatre out of 'boards and beams' in a meadow near Zurich. He would 'invite' the most accomplished singers and musicians, arrange for the best possible performance, permit all those who admired his work to attend without charge, have three performances one after another and then tear down the theatre and burn the score.[7] Leaving aside the *Götterdämmerung*esque finis, here were already the basic features of his grand design: a simple, functional theatre, specially selected artists, model performances and an audience of devotees, all coming together in a festival framework. What is of interest is not only how early the individual elements were fixed in his mind but the fact that they were all linked from the start.

Next he began giving thought to where his festival might take place. At this stage he was more concerned about the ambience of the site than its precise location. His initial ideas were set down in a letter, again to Uhlig, in October 1851. He reported that his 'Nibelung project' had expanded into three operas with a three-act prelude; the appropriate way of presenting such a work, he wrote, would be to produce it in the course of a week in a new opera house somewhere along the Rhine. What is implied here—performance outside an established operatic centre—was from now on an explicit desideratum. The vital element was isolation from the competing theatrical world. A month later he was emphatic that his new work could not be performed in Weimar— where his great promoter Franz Liszt had offered to put it on—or in any other German theatre. 'With my new concept I break entirely any link with our contemporary theatre and public; I break emphatically and forever with the formal present', he wrote to Uhlig.[8] His Nibelung work would require three years to complete and could only be performed 'after the revolution'. The revolution, he went on, 'must necessarily bring an end to our whole theatrical system; it must and will collapse, that is inevitable'. And on the ruins he would build his theatre—it was to be along the Rhine—and, after a year's preparation, there would be a four-day festival for his entire work. That, he said, 'will give meaning to this revolution'.

Then in January 1852 he added a new—or at least much more explicit—idea. In a letter to Liszt he declared that his Nibelung drama could not be performed in a large city with a metropolitan audience; instead it was to be done for those who appreciated his music in some 'beautiful quiet place' far from 'the smoke and disgusting industrial smell of our urban civilization'.[9] For a time he was again attracted to the meadow near Zurich. Encouraged by the success of a music festival held there in May of 1853, he later spoke to Liszt of his plan to erect a provisional structure outside the city for a *Bühnenfestspiel*, or stage festival—the term that later became a Bayreuth trademark. Some years after that, he even toyed with the idea of a performance of his Nibelung

Ring in a floating theatre anchored on Lake Lucerne—until he learned that sudden Alpine storms risked overturning it.

Were the outcome not known, this sort of daydreaming might have been considered excessively eccentric—in fact Newman remarked on its taint of cloud cuckooland. Quite apart from the complete lack of any funds or the slightest prospect of any, the opera itself—the project's whole raison d'être—had not even been written. Undeterred by such minor details, Wagner persuaded the eminent architect Gottfried Semper to abandon London in 1855 and to accept a professorial position in Zurich, bringing him nearby in case the hoped-for opera house ever became possible.

And in the late 1850s there were in fact several nibbles. The Grand Duke of Weimar offered to sponsor the première of the *Ring* and to construct a theatre in Weimar for it. For various reasons nothing came of this. Then the Germanophile Emperor of Brazil, Dom Pedro II, expressed interest in commissioning Wagner to write an Italianate opera and at the same time invited competition for the construction of an opera house in Rio de Janeiro for its performance. Wagner was willing to dash off an Italianized *Tristan und Isolde* and, as an enticement, sent the Emperor beautifully bound volumes of the piano scores of three of his operas. Semper entered the competition and submitted 'some marvellous plans which afforded us great entertainment', as Wagner wrote in *Mein Leben*.[10] The composer never had a reply, and the architect's proposal was rejected.

By now there seemed no alternative but to try an entirely new approach. Wagner decided to organize a considerably scaled-down version of a festival to be held in a large city, such as Paris, Vienna or Berlin, where he would be assured a large audience. With the *Ring* unfinished, it would be necessary to produce his other operas. The performances themselves would be held in a conventional theatre. With this proposal Wagner compromised every one of his original objectives, even cutting the sacred link between a festival and the *Ring*.

Accordingly, in 1859 he went to Paris in the hope of arranging a special two-month season for performances of *Tannhäuser*, *Lohengrin* and the première of *Tristan und Isolde* which he had just completed. Only *Tannhäuser* ever reached the stage. It was performed in 1861 and set off one of the greatest scandals in operatic history. In what was as much a political as a musical demonstration, a group of fops from the fashionable Jockey Club sabotaged the performance by creating such a din, with whistles and flageolets, that the work had to be withdrawn after the third performance. That was the end of the Paris scheme. Vienna proved equally impossible; there, despite years of effort, he failed to bring *Tristan* to the stage.

In 1862 Wagner published a foreword to his *Ring* text. In it he reverted to his original festival idea and spelled out for the first time, based on his talks with Semper, the main features of his proposed opera house and festival. The theatre, to be located in a small town, was to be a temporary construction made of wood and designed solely for artistic utility. To enhance the stage image and improve the orchestral sound, the auditorium was to be amphitheatrical in shape and the orchestra pit was to be invisible to the audience. The best artists from German houses were to be invited to perform, and great effort was to go into the production. The work itself was to be performed three times at a summer festival. Arrangements would be made to ensure that the audience did not attend in a state of fatigue after the work of the day and would be allowed long breaks during the performances. Wagner concluded the foreword by confessing that his dreams would be possible only if he could find a prince to finance it. 'Will this prince be found?'

The following two years were among the most difficult of Wagner's already difficult life. No opera house would stage *Tristan*, his work on the *Ring* and *Meistersinger* was stalled, his painful marriage came to a painful end, he was in poor health and his debts were so pressing that he eventually had to hide from his creditors. This was the darkest hour. But if determination had kept the festival idea alive, sheer good luck brought it to fruition. In the end Wagner did not find his prince; his prince found him. The eighteen-year-old Ludwig II, on succeeding to the throne of Bavaria in March of 1864, immediately summoned the composer to an audience. Ludwig had been a fanatical fan of Wagner's dramatic dream-world ever since attending *Lohengrin* three years earlier. And just a year earlier, he had read the portentous words concluding the composer's foreword to the *Ring* and decided that if ever it were possible, he would be the patron-prince for whom the composer was waiting. Wagner was on the run when the King's emissaries finally tracked him down. His dream of a *rex ex machina* had come true; it was, in his own words, 'an unbelievable miracle'.[11]

'Collaborators'—this is what Ludwig said that he and the composer would be, as they worked together to realize Wagner's dreams. These included productions of existing and projected operas, an opera house for the *Ring* and sacks of gold for Wagner. In return the *Ring* was to become the King's property. Ludwig could not contain his enthusiasm. On Wagner's recommendation he promptly engaged Semper as his architect and instructed him to design 'a large theatre of stone, since this incomparable work must have a worthy place to be performed'.[12] The building was to be completed in two and a half years. Although a monumental structure in Munich was far from his original intention, Wagner fell in with Ludwig's wishes. To Semper he made it clear that he would prescribe the principal features of the interior. The King shared Wagner's contempt for conventional opera houses and after discussions with his architect, Ludwig was nearly out of his mind with joy. 'Semper is designing the plan for our shrine. . . . Oh, holy day when the structure we long for rises before us! Oh, holy hour when your works finally become reality there!' he wrote to Wagner in early January of 1865.[13]

But by the end of that year Wagner had become apprehensive—concerned at the expense, the burgeoning public controversy and the ill-veiled opposition of court officials. He appealed to Ludwig to consider erecting a temporary theatre inside Munich's capacious Glass Palace exhibition hall. Here his visual and acoustical innovations could first be tested. Construction would be relatively inexpensive and could be completed within a year. Timing was now crucial to Wagner. Preparations for the première of *Tristan*—to take place in Munich in the spring of 1865—convinced him more than ever of the need for a theatre of his own. The rehearsals had begun in the small Residence Theatre. There it had been possible to stress the intimate, human nature of the drama, but the orchestral sound had been overwhelming. The opera was consequently moved to the larger Court Theatre, where the sound was attenuated but the characters became inaccessible. 'Oh, my invisible, deeply placed, marvellous orchestra in the theatre of the future!' he wistfully wrote to the King.[14]

Although Ludwig refused to bow to the strong pressure of his courtiers to abandon his grandiose theatre, he yielded to the extent of telling Semper also to prepare plans for a temporary theatre inside the Glass Palace. Now at last the composer's theoretical concepts were to go on the drawing board. His ideal theatre dictated a seating arrangement that offered the audience a direct, unhindered view of the stage. This simple principle marked a complete break with several hundred years of traditional horseshoe-shaped, balconied auditoriums. In fact it amounted to a revival of the classical amphitheatre—though, strictly speaking, not of the Greek theatre but its indoor Roman variant the *odeum*. Revolution or counter-revolution, it was a critical development in theatre history.

Semper's initial designs, adaptable to either of the projects, were completed by May. As a projection—or grandparent—of the interior of the later Festspielhaus, the plans are intriguing in their contrasts and similarities to what was eventually built. Semper's frame included such ornate features as a *fons scaenae* in the Roman style and a stately royal box flanked by an imposing row of Corinthian columns. The inner core incorporated Wagner's requisites, though, interestingly enough, Semper warned Wagner already at this stage that a sunken pit would make it difficult for a conductor to see both the musicians and the stage. A key interior feature and an important innovation was Semper's handling of the area between the front row of seats and the proscenium. By designing a second and wider proscenium in front of the narrow proscenium proper, the architect created, through the laws of perspective, an illusion of great depth—with the effect described by Newman in 1930. In this way there evolved what he and Wagner jestingly called a 'mystic gulf', a space which separated the 'real world' of the spectator from the 'imaginary world' of the stage. This feature became a vital part of the

Bayreuth theatre and of Wagner's whole concept of operatic staging. It was Semper's genius to have understood the composer's aesthetic vision and to have invented the means of achieving it.

Ludwig was as determined as ever to have his 'monumental theatre', and his dreams became grander and grander. A splendid new avenue, cutting a swathe through the centre of Munich, was to run from the royal palace to the Isar River, across a bridge to a terrace leading to the great theatre itself. He was enchanted at the prospect. 'I see the street, crowned by the magnificent structure of the future; people are streaming to the premières of the *Nibelungen* and of *Parcival*,' he wrote to Wagner. 'Prejudices vanish; amazement, heights of joy overwhelm everyone; all mankind will become brothers, wherever your gentle wings flutter! Do you see it my friend, do you not see it?'[15] From Semper, he asked for a plaster model as soon as possible.

By now the anticipated costs of the construction projects, an additional proposal for a school to train Wagnerian singers, along with Wagner's brazen fleecing of the King's treasury, had played into the hands of the composer's enemies at court. Scandal eventually ensued, and Ludwig had no choice but to ask his friend to leave Munich. So in December 1865 Wagner went for a second time into exile in Switzerland—albeit this time with a handsome annuity from the King. Although the Glass Palace project was quietly dropped for lack of royal interest, the King's passion for the original project reached new heights when in January 1867 Semper finally presented him with a model.

The finest opera house never constructed. Gottfried Semper's proposed theatre for a Wagner *Ring* festival in Munich was the architectural grandfather of the Festspielhaus. Semper presented his model to King Ludwig at a two-hour audience on 11 January 1867.

Ludwig gave immediate orders to begin preparations. A site was selected which responded, as far as possible in an urban area, to Wagner's desire to have his theatre in a quiet setting. Semper's plans, elaborating his Rio de Janeiro proposal and the Glass Palace designs, envisaged a huge structure. The harmony of the solid, dignified and serenely elegant exterior was reflected in the interior, with its marble floors, beautifully decorated foyers, galleries and reception areas, royal salons, niches adorned with statues of noted artists and impressive staircases. All this was pure Semper. It could not have contrasted more starkly with Wagner's notion of a temporary structure made of 'boards and beams'. Where Wagner's influence was felt was in the auditorium and stage, which adhered strictly to the composer's directions.

But the project was a monumental fantasy. While the unfortunate Semper was allowed to go on producing detailed plans, construction was postponed month after month as the King dallied. Wagner himself favoured delay—delay as a disguise for killing the project outright. The location could never have been to his liking. In principle he did not want his theatre in a city with its metropolitan diversions. And in practice he did not want it in Munich; there he had enemies, the King was bound to intrude and he would never be socially acceptable. But the problem was not simply the site, it was the structure itself. Unwittingly, Semper had put his finger on the problem when he once told Wagner that his operas were 'too grand and rich for a puny stage and wooden planks'.[16] For the composer all that mattered was the quality of a performance; a theatre was no more than a utilitarian shell. He did not want great architecture to detract from his operas or a great architect to detract from his own unique genius.

So the project died. Semper was treated disgracefully—he even had to threaten legal action to be reimbursed for the expenses of his years of labour—and he never recovered from the psychological blow. Yet his proposed theatre, considered by some architectural historians to be the finest opera house never built, lived on—incarnated in the Burg Theatre in Vienna and the splendid opera house in Dresden and leaving its mark on theatres in Prague, Altenburg, Stettin and even the Royal Albert Hall. Its outlines could be seen in countless other theatres from New York to Odessa but its amphitheatrical auditorium was imitated only once—in the Prince Regent's Theatre in Munich.

Ludwig now turned to constructing fabulous palaces and Wagner to composing. What would have been for any normal person a period of turbulence and tribulation was by the composer's standards a time of peace and happiness. In his comfortable exile at Tribschen on Lake Lucerne he completed *Meistersinger* and much of the *Ring*. But during these years he also stole a friend's wife and repeatedly quarrelled with the King. The wife was Cosima, daughter of Franz Liszt and since 1857 spouse of the noted conductor Hans von Bülow. She and Wagner had fallen in love in 1863; pretending to be the composer's secretary, she became his mistress and in 1865, during rehearsals for the première of *Tristan*, gave birth to their daughter, appropriately named Isolde. When Wagner was banished to Tribschen, she followed him, and there they had two other children, Eva and Siegfried. Only in 1870—following the death of Wagner's first wife and Cosima's divorce—could they marry.

Wagner's relationship with Cosima was the cause of one of a series of disagreements between the composer and the King. Wagner had blatantly lied to Ludwig about Cosima and when, by the autumn of 1868, the truth could no longer be concealed, Ludwig realized he had been duped. His confidence in Wagner never recovered. There were also open and acrimonious disputes over the operas. They bitterly disagreed over a Munich Opera production of *Lohengrin* in 1867 and two years later over Ludwig's desire to hold the première of *Rheingold*. Wagner wanted to produce the *Ring* as a single work; Ludwig wanted each part performed as it was completed. Wagner maintained that the work was his creation; Ludwig pointed out that it was his property. An indignant Wagner tried to prevent its being performed; an enraged Ludwig insisted, condemning the composer's 'dreadful intrigues' and threatening to stop his allowance. 'Do you want my work as I want it done, or don't you?' Wagner flung back.[17] Ludwig did not; the opera was performed and the next year the King commanded the première of *Walküre* as well, provoking a rerun of the earlier fracas.

These squabbles explain Wagner's growing desperation as the *Ring* neared completion. The prospect of having the work done piece by piece in productions dictated by Ludwig's mawkish taste horrified Wagner. Ludwig's wishes and Wagner's ideals had become incompatible. Collaboration was no longer possible. It was more than ever clear to Wagner that he had to have a theatre of his own, far enough from Munich to prevent Ludwig from interfering. And so it was on the evening of 5 March 1870 during a discussion of the subject with Cosima that, as she recorded in her diary: 'I tell R. he should look up the article on Baireuth in the encyclopedia; R. had mentioned this as the one place he would choose. To our delight, in the list of buildings we read of a splendid old opera house.'

As the entry makes clear, Bayreuth was already much in the composer's mind as a site for his Nibelung festival. He had retained pleasant memories of the town from a brief stop there in 1835. Not long after meeting Ludwig, he expressed a hope that the King might provide him with one of the royal pavilions there as a retreat. Some years later he even recommended it to the King himself as an alternative site for his own residence. Oddly enough, he seems in fact to have made up his mind even before visiting the town. In a letter to Ludwig in March 1871 he wrote that he had 'already chosen a site to be the showplace of our great artistic deeds'.[18] He declined to identify the town, except to say that it was in Bavaria and would not require the construction of a theatre.

When he and Cosima finally went there on 19 April they decided it was the right place, not only for a festival but also for their home. However, it was obvious at once that the theatre would not do. The Margrave's Opera House, designed in 1745 by Giuseppe Galli da Bibiena for the Margravine Wilhelmine, sister of Frederick the Great, was one of the finest baroque theatres in Europe and reputedly had the largest stage in Germany—in reality the stage was larger than the auditorium, which seated only around a hundred people. But in its size, design and elegance, the house was the very antipode of what Wagner sought. 'So we must build—and all the better', Cosima confided to her diary. The decision was a dreadful disappointment to Ludwig. While posing no outright objection, he let it be known that he could not be counted on for support.

The question often asked—why Bayreuth?—Wagner answered a short time later in a letter to Friedrich Feustel, a local banker. He had wanted a town that was small and that had no competing theatre, that was not a fashionable spa attracting an unsuitable public, that was roughly in the centre of Germany and that was in Bavaria and therefore enjoyed the protection of King Ludwig. Not only did Bayreuth meet these requirements, he wrote, it was itself a pleasant town and the surrounding area was attractive. Implied in the final point was the town's quiet situation and comparative isolation, which he had always seen as preconditions for a successful festival.

Wagner lost no time in moving preparations ahead, publicly announcing in May that the first festival would take place in the summer of 1873. The prominent Berlin architect Wilhelm Neumann, rather than Semper, was to design the edifice; Carl Brandt, the technical director of the Darmstadt Opera and the most famous theatre technician of his time, was to oversee the construction and Feustel was to be financial adviser. From Munich the composer retrieved Semper's designs, undertaking to use only those features that were his own intellectual property—the auditorium and stage.

Yet it was not until late in the autumn that he turned to the question of a site. First he asked the civic authorities to donate a plot, pointing out that while the festival would not make money, the town stood to benefit financially from it. Realizing that Wagner's enterprise would put their sleepy town on the map, the town council was only too pleased to oblige. Wagner's initial preference was to have both his house and the theatre situated on the edge of the Hofgarten, the royal park adjacent to the New Schloss in the centre of town. Although the site was satisfactory for his home, the water table of the parkland would not permit the construction of a theatre requiring deep foundations. Another proposal fell through when the owner refused to sell part of his tract, causing Wagner to take such offence that he threatened to go elsewhere. Baden-

Baden and Bad Reichenhall had already offered free sites and Darmstadt was willing to build him an opera house in place of its own which had just burned down. Undoubtedly he was bluffing, and in any case it all turned out for the best. The perfect place was soon found, on high ground—it came to be known as the Green Hill—overlooking the town. 'This spot is delightful, enchanting!' Wagner cried, on seeing it.[19] To Nietzsche he exulted: 'Finding Bayreuth was my instinct's greatest success.'[20]

After all the years of dreaming, the time had finally come to put theory into practice. The basics were outlined in a letter to Feustel. First, the theatre itself was to be temporary—'It would be all right to me if it were entirely out of wood . . . just strong enough to prevent it collapsing. So here, economize—economize, no waste.'[21] He left it, he added with a verbal wink and nudge, 'to the nation to erect a monumental structure'. Second, the machinery and staging must be the very best. 'Here *no* economizing whatever; nothing temporary, everything for the long term.' And finally, singers and musicians were to receive no payment, only reimbursement for expenses. 'Anyone who does not come out of esteem and commitment, I shall leave where he is.'

A little later he added specifics. The essential features of the interior were to be an invisible orchestra, an auditorium for an audience of 1500 with an unimpeded view of the stage and two galleries at the back, one for nobility and one above it for those who could not afford to pay for entry. The modest nature of the project was evident in the request for a construction permit, which asked for authority merely to build a temporary structure for the performance of a single work. In fact the opera house was often referred to simply as 'the Nibelung theatre' and that was how Liszt spoke of it on first seeing the site in 1872.[22]

Neumann generally followed these directions in drafting his initial ground plan. It was the direct descendant of Semper's designs and foreshadowed what was ultimately built. But like the Munich project, it was grand and costly rather than modest and provisional. Wagner rejected it. After that Neumann found himself so busy with projects in the capital of the newly founded Reich that he lost interest in a modest theatre in the provinces. Meanwhile inflation was raising building costs while contributions were very disappointing. With all the delays and worries, the proposed date for the festival already had to be postponed to 1874.

At this point there was another row with the King, now over the score of *Siegfried*. Completed in February 1871, by right it should have been presented to him then. When pressed to turn it over for performance, Wagner said he would sooner burn the score and go begging. His continued obstinacy—indeed his lies—eventually so hurt and angered Ludwig that he swore he would never 'under any circumstances' again help the composer.[23] Cosima recorded in her diary that it might be necessary to 'abandon the whole project, for we cannot succeed if the

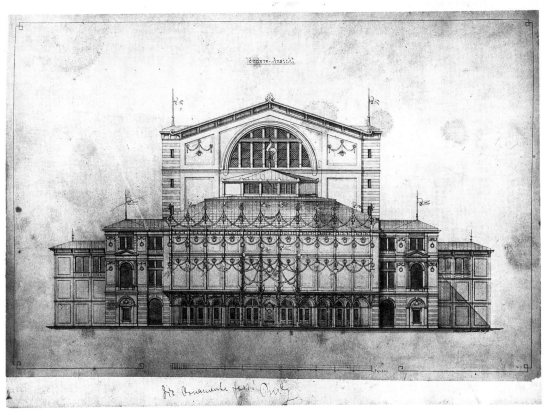

Otto Brückwald's initial design of the Festspielhaus exterior incorporated frills that were too elaborate for Wagner's taste and finances. Wagner's notation 'Die Ornamente fort!' is visible in the lower margin.

King himself is against us'.[24] As these and other problems mounted, she wrote indignantly: 'With all this, he is expected to compose!'[25]

Finding Neumann hopeless, Wagner replaced him at Brandt's suggestion with a young Leipzig architect, Otto Brückwald. His first plan—of May 1872—took up where Neumann had left off and outlined the edifice that was finally built. It adopted two ideas that harked back to the Rio and Munich projects: a convex front, which Wagner accepted, and large foyers and interior gardens along each side of the structure, which he rejected as extravagant. Frugality was now an obsession with Wagner, and he constantly admonished his architect to be ruthlessly economical and to omit even the most modest decorative frills. Typical is an exterior design of late 1872, showing garlands and other decorations on the front façade, which bears Wagner's handwritten command '*Die Ornamente fort!*'—away with the ornaments!

The ground-breaking ceremony took place on 29 April—almost precisely a year after the Wagners had first visited the town—and was followed the next month by the laying of the foundation stone. Construction then began. The building materials were all local: the stone was quarried in the area, the bricks made in town and the wood cut from the nearby Fichtel Mountains. Although workmen were on the job

42

The photograph at the time of the roof-raising ceremony on 2 August 1873 shows the bare timber frame of the stage, fly tower and roof. The brick inlay and masonry work of the exterior had just been begun.

every day of the year, including Christmas, progress was never rapid enough for Wagner, who constantly pressed Brandt and Brückwald to speed things along. As he observed his dream take physical shape, he had varying reactions—sometimes the structure seemed 'like a grave (the Pyramids)',[26] or 'the cross to which we are nailed';[27] at other times 'like a fairy tale in the midst of clumsy reality', in Cosima's words.[28]

The last great event before the building was finished occurred on 2 August 1873 with the roof-raising ceremony. Cosima grandly portrayed the scene in her diary:

> We set out at around 5 o'clock; strange ascent right up onto the scaffolding; the most wonderful thoughts; for the first time a theatre has been built for an idea and for an artistic work, says my father. The *Tannhäuser* march is played, and in place of the noble knights (or, rather, ignoble comedians dressed up as noble knights) genuine working people appear with a simple greeting; as the last hammer blows are heard, I feel that the march has received its true consecration. *Nun danket alle Gott* lifts up my heart as it is sung in the blue air of a glorious sky and a smiling landscape, sung after this victory; as my nervousness of the scaffolding disappeared, so also my timorousness in face of this bold undertaking. Faith raises our wings and fills us with joy!

In the meantime construction of Wagner's residence was proceeding. Financed largely by a gift from Ludwig, the structure was designed by Carl Wölfel, a Bayreuth contractor, based on an initial plan by Neumann, which in turn had incorporated a number of free-hand sketches by the composer himself. The two principal rooms were the *Halle*, the music room, which rose the entire height of the structure, and the adjacent *Saal*, the drawing room and library, which was the subject

A late nineteenth-century photograph of Wahnfried. The bust of King Ludwig II by Zumbusch was donated by the King in 1875. Visible on the left is the entrance to the Siegfried Wagner House, constructed in 1894.

of paintings, photographs and postcards in later years. In its functionalism, dignity and lack of pomposity, the structure was as expressive of Wagner as was the theatre itself. Enshrining a comment made years before to his friend Mathilde Wesendonck—'There is a voice within me yearning for peace, . . . for home'—he had affixed to the front of the villa plaques with the words 'Hier wo mein Wähnen Frieden fand—Wahnfried—sei dieses Haus von mir benannt', roughly meaning 'This house, where my dreams came to rest—Wahnfried—I name.' Above was a large painted graffito which Wagner intended as an allegory of the 'Art Work of the Future', showing Greek tragedy, German myth, music and the future.

With construction of the theatre under way, Wagner faced one supreme, remorseless difficulty—money. From the very beginning he had been vague to the point of indifference about the problem. Somehow it would all work out; then a prince would come along; then, when the prince had arrived and been jilted, other benefactors would be found. It seemed like human nature imitating Wagnerian art: Wotan tricking Fasolt and Fafner in the blithe assumption that Loge would set everything straight in the end. The all-important virtue of the Bayreuth enterprise was that it left Wagner completely independent in running his opera festival; the cardinal weakness was that it left him completely dependent on privately raised funds. He thought he could square the circle by finding a multitude of small donors. They would not threaten his autonomy and would preserve his original concept of a festival for 'friends of his art', as it was phrased.

And so was born the notion of patron's certificates, purchase of which would guarantee a seat at the forthcoming performances. They were priced at 300 taler (900 marks) and Wagner hoped to sell 1,000 of them, enough to finance the construction and an initial festival. Wagner societies were established to find patrons. It was an ingenious scheme but far ahead of its time. Fund-raising was then utterly unknown—it is still scarcely practised in Germany—and the idea failed to catch on. To most Germans it seemed like dealing in stocks—then considered a dubious activity—and had the unpleasant connotation of 'selling' culture by hawking 'shares' in Wagner. Only one or two of the innumerable German princelings bought certificates—because of the stigma of his revolutionary past, Wagner was convinced—and the biggest contributors were not even German: the Sultan of Turkey and the Khedive of Egypt.

By the spring of 1873, as work had progressed and contractors insisted on payment, the financial situation became desperate. With a mere 340 certificates sold, only a third of the 300,000 taler needed as a minimum had been subscribed. And prospects either for additional patrons or for additional donors were dim. The notion of a festival without charge for his devotees—one of the original proposals—now had to be abandoned. Tickets would be sold and the whole enterprise might have to be turned into a joint stock company. Wagner societies made public appeals to 'German honour' and Nietzsche penned an *Exhortation to Germans* calling upon his countrymen 'to support to the fullest extent possible this great artistic act of German genius'. Wagner himself wrote to an old friend: 'I am doing everything I can; if one thread breaks, I spin another.'[29] To Cosima, he was more blunt. Working at the time on the first act of *Götterdämmerung*, he remarked that Siegfried left Brünnhilde to go into the world and steal: 'since they must support themselves, he must wrest tribute from a number of kings'.[30] The 'king' whom Wagner now had in mind was the chancellor of the newly founded Reich, Otto von Bismarck. The composer had called on him in Berlin in May of 1872 and a year later sent him a copy of his proselytizing pamphlet *The Stage Festspielhaus in Bayreuth*.

Now, as then, Bismarck refused to rise to the bait. And so Wagner turned again to a real king. In a letter to Ludwig on 11 August he complained that those who had money were not interested in his festival, and those who were interested had no money. The aristocracy had lost its 'German soul' and was investing its funds in Jewish and Jesuit enterprises. He had done what he could through concerts and appeals, but it would be impossible to place contracts for the remaining work without a loan of 100,000 taler. He asked Ludwig to guarantee it. The King did not respond, but after considerable delay and several enquiries, Wagner received word from the Court Secretary, Lorenz von Düfflipp, that the monarch was now completely absorbed in his own building projects and would have nothing to offer. Unwilling to take no for an answer, Wagner appealed to the King for an audience. He was turned down. In January he launched yet another plea and received yet another rejection, this one at least with Ludwig's encouraging reminder of the saying *post nubila Phoebus*.

Turning his gaze back to Berlin, Wagner tried to interest the new Kaiser, Wilhelm I. The inducement was an offer to hold the first festival in 1876 and make it a celebration of the fifth anniversary of Prussia's victory over France. The Grand Duke of Baden, who was to act as intermediary, refused to forward the proposal. So at the outset of 1874, all hope seemed lost. To his redoubtable supporter Emil Heckel, Wagner wrote: 'Until construction work can begin again, I shall have the open sides of the Festspielhaus boarded up so that at least the owls will not be able to nest there.'[31] He seemed quite serious.

But suddenly the clouds did part and Phoebus appeared. Possibly with Düfflipp's encouragement, the Bavarian sun king decided after all to prevent the collapse of the project. 'No, no and again *no!*' Ludwig wrote on 25 January.[32] 'It should not end thus! Help must be given! *Our* plan dare not fail. Parcival knows his mission and will offer whatever lies in his powers.' What lay in his powers he did not say, though he ultimately agreed to an outright loan of 100,000 taler. The terms, however, were strict. Money raised from the sale of any further patron's certificates and half the proceeds of any fund-raising concerts which Wagner conducted were to go directly to repay the loan; in case of default, the collateral—the theatre and its contents—would become the property of the Bavarian government. Conclusion of the legal arrangements dragged on beyond Easter and, walking up to inspect the theatre on Good Friday, Cosima commented that it seemed like the ascent to Calvary.

Building could now proceed. A bit like Brunelleschi's reinventing the dome in 1420, Wagner, Brückwald and Brandt had to rediscover the classical theatre and adapt it to modern use. Semper had made a start, but his plans left many problems unsolved. Disposing of them was entrusted to Brandt, the person Wagner placed in charge of designing the interior. The difficulties Wagner had experienced in producing *Tristan* in Munich in 1865 had taught him that a middle way had to be found between sound and size on the one hand and sight and size on the other. With this presumably in mind, he and Brandt had extrapolated the requisite dimensions: a square space 35 by 35 metres. Into this area had to be placed a seating arrangement that ensured all spectators an unhindered view of the stage. These sight-line requirements limited the seating capacity to 1,345 seats in the auditorium proper, some 200 in the artists' gallery and a varying number—in the early days around 100 movable seats—in the so-called princes' gallery. The royal box was nothing more than the central loge in the princes' gallery. Curiously enough, a second-century *odeum*, later excavated in Athens, was virtually identical in size and shape, while the seating radius and rake of the auditorium were

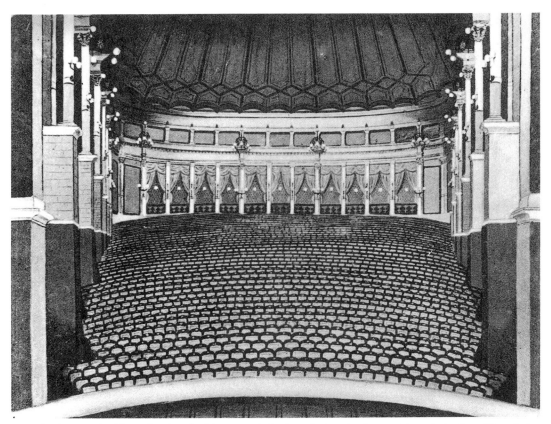

An early photograph of the auditorium, looking towards the draped princes' gallery and the artists' gallery. The velarium-like ceiling was painted by Max and Gotthold Brückner and the gas lamps were installed on the eve of the first festival in 1876.

subsequently discovered to be remarkably similar to those of the famous amphitheatre at Epidaurus.

By erecting a relatively narrow and fan-shaped, steeply raked amphitheatre, Brandt solved at once both vertical and horizontal sight-line problems—and solved them satisfactorily for the first time in the history of the proscenium theatre. The seating arrangement still left him with the challenge of reconciling a wedge-shaped amphitheatre with a square space. Semper had dealt with the dilemma by filling the empty corners with rich Renaissance ornament. Brandt disposed of it by throwing up six parallel pairs of receding proscenia. These not only hid the twelve doors which opened from the side vestibules into the auditorium but had the further effect of reinforcing the visual impact of Semper's double stage proscenium.

The surprising conclusion is inescapable. The Festspielhaus, so famous for its acoustics, was designed for optical effect and the excellent acoustics and sound quality were essentially fortuitous. Wood may have been used in the construction of the auditorium as much for acoustics as for economy. And the sunken pit was intended not just to hide the orchestra but to blend and moderate sound for the sake of voices. Even so, the

47

The auditorium as it has appeared since 1930 when a gallery, originally intended for the press, was constructed within the old princes' gallery. In the foreground, the orchestra pit as seen from the front of the stage.

hood, added at the last minute, was to block light from the pit while a sound damper was installed only in 1882. The primacy of the visual is therefore clear —Wagner the dramatist asserting himself over Wagner the composer.

The only serious error in design was in underestimating the size of the orchestra pit. On entering it the first time, Wagner realized it was too cramped for his Nibelung orchestra and directed that it should be deepened and extended further under the stage. When the alteration left the pit still too small, a further extension had to be made into the auditorium; two front rows of seats were in effect sacrificed for space to be occupied by the conductor and violins.

The stage itself, constructed entirely of wood, incorporated Semper's Munich design. But in a brilliant stroke, Brandt brought forward the first proscenium, making the proscenia of the stage and the auditorium equidistant, giving the illusion of an unbroken transition of arches from the auditorium to the stage. This Wagner characterized as the crowning achievement of the interior. Quite apart from architectural harmony, it not only created a new type of stage picture but also left an impression that the stage was larger and further distant ·than was actually the case.

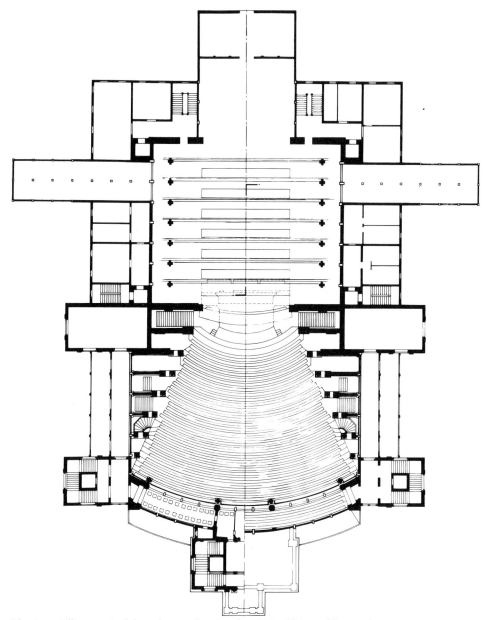

The Festspielhaus groundplan of 1876, showing the 1882 addition of the royal annex.

To accommodate the *Ring* epic, the stage was huge—roughly half the size of the entire structure. Although it only left room for very narrow fly floors, the fly tower was enormous, permitting rapid changes of scene. Picking up another of Semper's novel ideas, Brandt installed rows of gaslights around the entire interior of the second proscenium, allowing the stage to be illuminated not just from below but from the sides and above. It marked an important advance in the technology of the day.

The exterior of the Festspielhaus as it appeared when completed in 1875.

By the summer of 1875 the basic construction work was finished. Like an earlier creator, Wagner beheld what he had done and found it was very good. In spite of his hope that the body of the theatre would some day be replaced by an impressive structure of 'noble materials' and 'monumental ornamentation', he considered the auditorium and stage definitive, to be left unchanged when the grander edifice was built around it.

Wagner's opera house was the first proscenium theatre since the Roman era designed essentially to give a clear view of the stage. Yet by that very fact it was the most avant-garde theatre of its time and indeed for the next sixty or seventy years, when similar concepts began to influence theatre design. There was another paradox. The structure that set the world on its ears at that time was Charles Garnier's Paris Opera, also completed in 1875. Two more antithetical theatres would be difficult to imagine. Brückwald had been instructed to be as frugal as possible, Garnier above all to outdazzle the Vienna Opera. The Bayreuth edifice was as spare, plain and utilitarian as the Palais Garnier was grandiloquent and ostentatious. In the one an auditorium and stage were all, in the other they were an adjunct to a colossal staircase, sumptuous salons and splendid corridors, all in rich marble—the very epitome of the unoperatic opera house. The brick and timber Bayreuth theatre cost 428,000 marks, its Parisian sister 35,000,000 francs (28,000,000 marks)—in other words seventy times more. Garnier's stood as a symbol of the old order, socially and architecturally; Wagner's as a forerunner of the future.

The Festspielhaus was a monument to Wagner's imagination, practical sense, indestructible self-confidence and devotion to his genius. By any odds it should never have come about. Yet so great was Wagner's will that to look back over the evolution of the project is to sense something inevitable about it. What motivation, what inspiration could have been so powerful as to propel such an apparent chimera into reality? Ultimately it was the composer's obsessive, messianic conviction that the world must be redeemed through art, or more precisely through his music dramas.

His desire to transform theatre-going into an essentially eschatological experience dictated every detail of the festival—from the site and the architecture to what occurred on stage and even what happened off— and imbued it from the start with an aura of devotionalism. Wagner's aim was to generate an environment that removed spectators from the quotidian world and elevated them into the universe of his dramatic invention. The interior was therefore designed for the single purpose of converting stage illusion into dramatic reality.

He explained the process step by step in his 1873 essay *The Stage Festspielhaus in Bayreuth*. The starting-point was the need to focus attention, without the slightest diversion, on the stage and in that way to break down the separation of the stage and the auditorium. This required removing 'any sight of bodies lying in between'. That is why the hidden orchestra was the key feature and why the spectators were ranged in steeply ascending rows. The all-important need 'to frame the scenic picture', as Wagner phrased it, was achieved through the contrivances which Semper and Brandt had developed on the basis of his ideas.

Wagner had collected ideas for years. As a conductor in Riga from 1837 to 1839 he had been struck by several unusual traits about the small theatre there: a raked auditorium, an orchestra that was placed a full three feet lower than the stage and a dimming of lights during the performance. Then at a concert rehearsal in Paris in 1840 he had been deeply impressed by the effect when he sat in an area screened off from the main part of the hall and heard the music without being distracted by the sight of musicians. And through his admiration for Greek theatre he may well have been aware of the general dimensions of classical amphitheatres, such as that at Epidaurus. Such were the impressions that helped to form his notion of the ideal conditions for an operatic performance.

In his Bayreuth essay Wagner grandiloquently described the optical and psychological impact he intended to create for the spectator:

Between him and the picture to be looked at there is nothing clearly discernible, instead, only a shimmering sense of distance . . . in which the remote picture takes on the mysterious quality of a dream-like apparition, while the phantasmal sounding music from the 'mystic gulf', like vapours rising from the holy womb of Gaia beneath the Pythia's seat, transports him into that inspired state of clairvoyance in which the visible stage picture becomes the authentic facsimile of life itself.

No wonder Nietzsche called him 'a master of hypnotic tricks'.[33]

Although Wagner left the picture-frame stage intact, he not only broke the architectural mould of the traditional opera house, he initiated a transformation in the relationship between the spectator and the spectacle. The intent of his hypnotic tricks was as revolutionary as his architecture and, like that, looked at once back to the classical world and forward to the future.

With the construction of the opera house and the completion of the *Ring*—*Götterdämmerung* had been finished the preceding November—Wagner began to make plans for the forthcoming festival. King Ludwig had come to take a strong interest and asked for periodic reports. A brief excerpt from one of these shows how Wagner thought through every-thing, down to the finest detail, and how he laid down everything with Mosaic firmness:

> Every performance is to begin at 4 o'clock in the afternoon, the second act follows at around 6 o'clock and the third at around 8 o'clock, so that between each act there is an appreciable time for relaxation, which the audience should use to stroll in the park area around the theatre, to take refreshments outdoors in the charming neighbourhood, so that, thoroughly refreshed, they gather again—following the sound of the brass [fanfare] from the heights of the theatre—with the same receptivity they had for the first act.[34]

But even now, with success in sight, Wagner was not to have a moment's peace. An unending succession of financial crises continued to make his life an agony. To read about this more than a century later is painful and dreary; to have struggled through it day by day must have been a living horror. In fact it left him prey to a variety of illnesses as well as insomnia, nightmares and heart strain. Bills poured in for construction cost over-runs, for gas lighting, for furnishings for the auditorium and for costumes and stage decorations. There were also unanticipated expenses. One that Wagner found particularly vexing was the cost of transforming the approaches to the opera house from an appalling wasteyard into grounds suitable for a festival. When neither Ludwig nor the town of Bayreuth consented to help, an aggrieved Wagner gave back to the town the entire plot from the terrace to the bottom of the hill and reduced landscaping around the theatre to a minimum. As costs continued to mount, he several times asked Ludwig to forgo the income from future sales of patron's certificates. Sometimes the King agreed; sometimes he did not, and then Wagner had to conduct concerts. These tours always brought more applause than money. The situation became so desperate that Cosima even gave serious thought to pawning her own property. By the end of 1875 it once again appeared unlikely that a festival could be held.

With no more money to be squeezed out of Ludwig, who was himself almost bankrupt from his vast castle-building programme, Wagner had no choice but to make another appeal to Berlin, this time for a loan of 30,000 taler. The Kaiser seemed well inclined and referred the matter to Bismarck, who passed the request on to the Reichstag. When it appeared that public hearings were to be held, Wagner demurred. He was willing, he said, to bow to his emperor or to his chancellor but not to parliamentarians. Not only did he raise no money, but having turned to the Prussians he also offended Ludwig. By the time

A photograph of 1896 shows the so-called King's annex, added in 1882 in an unsuccessful attempt to lure King Ludwig to the première of *Parsifal*. In front of the Festspielhaus on the right, a restaurant; on the left a café.

the final rehearsals were to begin in June, Wagner was not in a position even to reimburse the singers and musicians for their expenses. Throughout that summer he lived a hand-to-mouth existence. A terse entry from Cosima's diary for 21 July tells the story: 'A good day for the box office today; 5,200 marks come in, enough to go on for two days.'

But it was not suffcient. For the nth time it appeared as though the festival would have to be cancelled; and for the nth time Wagner looked to Ludwig—this time for a small stop-gap loan. The King agreed and, along with the sale of some 2,000 tickets and a total of around 500 patron's certificates, there was just enough money for the Festival to take place.

The composer has been accused of double-dealing, of trying to play Prussia off against Bavaria. In fact he simply faced the plight of everyone with a great ideal and no money and drew the inevitable conclusion: the end being worth the means, he begged and borrowed where he could. Certainly he treated Ludwig shamefully over the years, and Ludwig responded with a forbearance that was downright saintly. Nothing save honour was lost. But what Wagner never compromised was the integrity of his art and for this he was willing to sacrifice everything else, including honour. 'Each stone', he said to Cosima of the Festspielhaus, 'is red with my blood and yours.'[35]

2

'The eternal work is done'
(*Rheingold*)

'Between the idea and the reality, between the motion and the act falls the shadow.' The problem posed by T.S. Eliot the poet was precisely what now confronted Richard Wagner the opera composer. In his case, bridging the gulf between inspiration and realization was not a solitary activity with pen and paper but a live endeavour involving hundreds of fallible, wilful human beings and a variety of art forms. And for Wagner personally the challenge was especially acute. On the one hand the intellectual cornerstone of the entire Festival enterprise was his belief that his works would regenerate German art, if not civilization itself. The premiss of this grandiose—even monomaniacal—notion was that the operas must be performed to perfection. With his own theatre, singers and musicians, he could no longer argue that the works failed to achieve their high mission because of flawed treatment at the hands of philistine impresarios and incompetently trained soloists. On the other hand, nothing like the *Ring* had ever been brought to the stage. Apart from the trial run of *Rheingold* and *Walküre* in Munich, there was nothing to go by.

The *Ring* endeavour marked an important stage in operatic history, the moment when an entirely new approach to operatic production was initiated. No longer was an audience to be served a performance with sets and costumes casually done up to suit the taste of the moment and with singers from the house repertory company. Now every aspect of the work was to be analysed down to the smallest detail and every detail was to be tailored to the purpose of the drama. Each singer was to be recruited for the role and trained in a new mode of singing and acting. Elaborate sets and a vast wardrobe of costumes were to be designed. Novel lighting and stage techniques were to be invented. Except for purely technical matters, the entire burden fell directly on Wagner's shoulders. Producer, stage manager, director, singing coach, orchestral adviser, final arbiter on sets and costumes—he was each of them.

The first problem was to recruit a cast, and in Wagner's case this meant finding for each role, however minor, a singer who was ideal in both voice and appearance. With the Festival already the talk of the musical world and the composer's prestige higher than ever, most singers were flattered to be asked. A number of years earlier, several vocalists had by chance died or gone mad after singing one or another Wagnerian role, giving rise to a widespread notion that performing in Wagner's operas could cause death or insanity. Fortunately no one appears to have been deterred by this scare. Rather the difficulty was that there were few, if any, singers who knew Wagner's operas. In fact, Wagner needed a new breed of soloist; only singer-actors could meet the novel and unprecedented demands of his roles. Given the centrality he attached to the drama, it is not surprising that he at first said he wanted 'actors who were also singers'. In the end he chose those with the best voices, and then spent endless hours developing their vocal style and training them to act.

Scarcely had the foundations of the Festspielhaus been laid when, in November 1872, he launched his search. After three years of trawling, he came up with only four soloists whom he considered naturals: Carl Hill for Alberich, Albert Niemann for Siegmund, Franz von Reichenberg for Fafner and Lilli Lehmann for one of the Rhinemaidens and Norns. But in Amalie Materna he had found a solid Brünnhilde, in Franz Betz an impressive Wotan, in Emil Scaria a promising Hunding and in Therese Vogl a fine Sieglinde. The main worry was whether Georg Unger could grow into the role of Siegfried. Not until the end of the summer of 1875 was the cast finally complete. Even so, Scaria and Vogl later dropped out; Vogl because of pregnancy and Scaria because Wagner refused him a large fee, since the others were performing for little or nothing. Josefine Scheffzky and Gustav Siehr were brought in as replacements; though the soprano was disappointing, the bass promised to be an eminent Hagen.

But there was a far broader problem. Here for the first time in modern history was an entire cosmology based on pre-Christian myth, a work on a scale as vast as those of Homer, Aeschylus and Sophocles and just as psychologically complex. To bring such a colossal work to the stage, Wagner faced not only the gulf between idea and reality but the inherent dilemma of opera: that being sung, it necessarily lacks realism, while being drama, it must create lifelike situations. For him, theatrical illusion was all. This even guided his selection of singers, ruling out anyone who did not look the role and benefiting those who did, even when the voice was questionable. Gladly would he have replaced Unger with Niemann, for instance, except that he could not bear the thought of a Siegfried who looked and sounded like his father Siegmund. Beyond the intent of mesmerizing his audience, however, he had little or no idea of how to translate his fantastic inner vision into flesh and blood staging within a proscenium frame. He hoped to solve the problem by finding assistants who would intuitively understand what he had in mind and be able to realize it in practice.

Even at its most elemental level, the challenge was unprecedented. What had to be put on stage was an operatic universe with a river bottom, subterranean cavern, rainbow bridge, forests, forge, rocky heights, royal hall and castle along with its population of giants, dwarfs, Rhinemaidens, ravens, flying horses, rams, serpent, talking bird, bear, toad and dragon, all to be finally consumed in a fiery cataclysm. Somehow this phantasmal creation was to be given palpable form by means of the pitiably primitive stagecraft of the time, with its elementary gas lighting, rudimentary stage machinery, fluttering painted backdrops and crude papier-mâché props.

Wagner never faced up to either the theoretical or the practical dilemmas that underlay the staging of his works, most acutely in the case of the *Ring*. How was illusion to be achieved through naturalism and how were mythical, symbolical and psychological dramas to be staged by physical means? Nothing could be simpler than to decree in stage directions that a character should ascend to a castle by walking across a rainbow. But how, except by the trick cinematography of a later age, was this to be accomplished? How, for that matter, was elaborate staging to be reconciled with his concept of sets as the *schweigend ermöglichender Hintergrund*—the silent, facilitating background? And what about the contrasting problem: how to deal with long scenes where the 'action' lay in the dialogues and music, while the singers were in near stasis?

Wagner knew only that he did not want conventional sets by a conventional stage designer. Instead in 1872 he commissioned a professional painter, the Viennese landscape artist Josef Hoffmann, to prepare sketches based on the *Ring* text. When Hoffmann submitted his drawings the following year, Wagner was favourably impressed, with the caveat that landscape effects had been emphasized at the expense of his dramatic intentions and that certain settings were too elaborate—specifically Hunding's hut and the hall of the Gibichungs. In 1874 these illustrations were turned over to Gotthold and Max Brückner, stage designers of the court opera at Coburg, to transform into scenery. At first the Brückners considered the drawings impractical and prepared to make wholesale changes. A tremendous row ensued, culminating in Hoffmann's dismissal. In the end, however, his originals remained the basis of the Brückners' decors and became some of the most influential designs in operatic history, setting the style at Bayreuth and elsewhere for over half a century.

As for costumes, Wagner again had a clearer idea of what he did not want—the traditional fanciful outfits depicted by German romantic artists—than what he thought might be appropriate. In the hope of getting something fresh and creative, he asked a Berlin costume expert, Carl Döpler, to do the designs. But instead of the 'inventive fantasy' Wagner had wanted, Döpler sought historical accuracy or at least plau-

The original staging of *Walküre*, Act III (*and see opposite*). Wagner's stage directions: 'To the right, a wood of fir trees. On the left, the entrance to a cave, forming a natural chamber; above it a rock rises to a high peak. In the rear the view is completely open; rocks of various sizes form the verge of a precipice which gives the impression of dropping steeply into the background. Occasional clouds, as if driven by a storm, drift past the edges of the rock.'

In illustrating this act, Hoffmann altered Wagner's directions by changing the wood into a single luxuriant fir tree, which he placed on the left, while positioning the Valkyries' rock in middle distance on the right.

sibility. Since no one had any notion what ancient Teutons actually wore, the conscientious Döpler combed the museums of Germany and Denmark for ideas, preparing 500 sketches of weapons and jewelry alone. When the costumes were made, his forty-one final designs were followed down to the last detail. In colour and outline they formed a harmonious unity. Cosima came to detest them, however, and complained in a much quoted remark that they made the singers look like Red Indian chiefs—an aperçu that would have raised the eyebrows of many a Red Indian chief. Like the Hoffmann-Brückner sets, Döpler's designs—with their winged and horned helmets, drinking horns, bear skins, cross-garters and sandals for men and their flowing robes, blouses of mail and shields for women along with the other fabricated Teutonic fashions—were models for Wagnerian productions for decades to come.

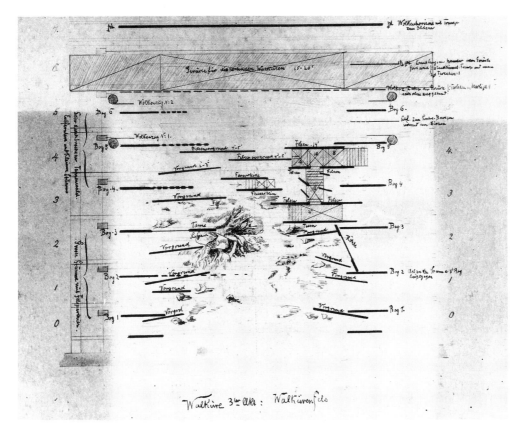

Hoffmann's illustration was the basis of this stage plan drawn by Fritz Brandt, son of the technical director of the Festival. His handwritten instructions specified a rock fourteen feet high, to be mounted by steps from the front and side. At the rear was a backdrop illustrating clouds, with a scrim to create an impression of lightning; further forward were gauzes to suggest scudding clouds.

No photographs were taken of the Bayreuth settings; however, photographs of a Leipzig production in 1878, with identical costumes and similar sets and stage plans, provide a good impression of the original. This scenic arrangement was maintained without essential change until 1952.

Döpler's costume design for Siegfried in *Götterdämmerung*,
1876.

Two full summers were devoted to preparations. The initial round of
rehearsals—which also functioned as auditions—began on 1 July 1875
in the hall of Wahnfried. These were solo rehearsals with piano accompaniment, usually played by Joseph Rubinstein and other members of
the so-called Nibelung Chancellery. As they proceeded, Wagner was
able to fill out the cast and to begin the gruelling job of coaching the
members on singing and acting. He had not only to train voices but to
tame egos so that the singers subordinated themselves to their role.
Niemann and Unger in particular caused endless, nagging worry which
possibly explains why Wagner later wondered aloud why he had ever
given his best roles to tenors. As a singer and actor, Niemann was
outstanding; but Siegfried not Siegmund was the role he wanted, and his
continual sulk poisoned the atmosphere. With Unger, the question was
simply whether he was up to the demands. Wagner convinced him that
the only chance of his becoming a heroic tenor was to withdraw from
any other engagements for a year and to dedicate himself full time to
voice study. He was to be taken apart both as a singer and as an actor and
reconstructed, as Newman has written, so that in the end he would be
'not only fictively but actually one with the character of Siegfried'.[1]

From this photograph of Georg Unger as Siegfried (1876), it is evident how meticulously Döpler's designs were carried out. The mail was gold, the cape bright blue.

Three weeks into the vocal rehearsals, the stage decorations for *Rheingold* arrived. The cast was in the opera house on the occasion and, after approving the sets, Wagner clapped his hands, turned to the Rhinemaidens and said, 'Let's hear something.'[2] The three singers scuttled onto the stage and, with an invisible Alberich joining in from the wings, they sang the opening scene of *Rheingold*. Their voices were the first musical sounds in the opera house, and both Wagner and the singers were delighted with the acoustical effect. Then on 2 August the orchestra, seated in the pit according to the prescribed arrangement, played for the first time. The results were all the composer had hoped for. 'That is just what I wanted,' he remarked; 'now the brass instruments no longer sound so harsh.'[3]

In assembling his orchestra, Wagner followed the precedent of the foundation-stone ceremony, choosing the best musicians from various opera houses rather than relying on a single established orchestra. To conduct, he turned to his faithful disciple Hans Richter. The rehears-

Charcoal drawing by Adolf von Menzel of Wagner on the Festspielhaus stage directing the 1875 rehearsals.

als—at an act a day—went on for twelve days. Cosima, Liszt and a number of invited guests, who accommodated themselves as best they could in a still seatless auditorium, looked on. Wagner himself sat on the stage at a small table, following the score by the light of an oil lamp, sometimes singing along, often gesticulating, occasionally beating time, at one moment admonishing Richter to be more flexible in his tempi, at another instructing a soloist on some point of acting or singing. Behind the quaint scene a revolutionary development in opera history was taking place. Serious acting, meticulous vocal work, impeccable music-making and elaborate staging were all forged into an artistic unity—in other words, modern *professional* operatic production was taking shape. And Wagner was becoming, as Hanslick labelled him, 'the world's first director'.

The second round of rehearsals began early the following May. The problems that now rained down on the composer were horrendous. Completion of the auditorium was so far behind schedule that the very sight of the interior left Wagner in utter despair. Managers of other houses denied their singers leave to participate in the Festival, relenting

only after long haggling. The Brückners' decorations were rarely delivered on time. Money problems mounted. The town was anything but
prepared for the influx of thousands of visitors. And there were all the
troubles, small and large, that bedevil the maiden voyage of any new
venture. Writing in his diary when the second year of rehearsals was just
getting under way, Richard Fricke expressed surprise that Wagner
'simply does not collapse'.[4] Fricke, a choreographer, worked closely
with Wagner the whole summer and recorded how the composer and
his assistants fought their way through the staging problems.

The most challenging of the four operas was *Rheingold*, especially the
opening scene. To create a realistic impression of swimming
Rhinemaidens, Carl Brandt had invented contraptions that suspended
the singers well aloft. These were anchored to triangular piers which
were shoved to and fro by stage-hands, directed by musical assistants
who kept the movements synchronized with the music. At first the three
singers flatly refused to be attached to the perilous vehicles, but Fricke
eventually talked them round and they managed beautifully. Other
expedients worked less well. The difficult transitions from river bottom
to mountain heights, from there to a cavern under the earth and then
back again to the heights, were camouflaged by great billows of colour-
lit steam produced by an old locomotive boiler, operated by a railway
machinist. Unfortunately the clouds of steam were so luxuriant that they
enveloped Hill, making it difficult for him to sing, and flowed into the
orchestra pit, causing the harps to lose pitch. For the Nibelung's hoard,
Wagner sent Cosima and Fricke into town to search out a tinsmith. The
forty-four objects they brought back included oil drums, pots, funnels,
cake pans, buckets, watering-cans and kettles. Such was stage illusion in
1876.

Another difficult scene, the Ride of the Valkyries, was managed by
having Döpler design and draw images on glass slides, which were
projected by a magic lantern onto the stage. Of the Nibelung menagerie,
it was the dragon in *Siegfried* which caused the most problems. All the
Ring fauna were manufactured in London, some of them with great
success. The *Rheingold* serpent was 'a masterpiece of fantasy and machinery', according to Fricke.[5] 'It opens its jaws wide, rolls its eyes in a
hideous manner and has a body covered with brightly shining scales.'
But the dragon arrived in sections, tail first and head last—its neck was
lost in transit, apparently misdirected to Beirut—and the unfortunate
monster aroused more pity than fright. In Fricke's opinion the whole
scene—props, dragon and Unger's acting—was 'not good enough for
little children'.[6] Without success, he begged Wagner at least to rusticate
the wretched beast. By far the most heated disagreement concerned
Brandt's handling of the final scene of *Götterdämmerung*. Although Fricke
insisted that it was impossible to choreograph and bathetic in its effect,
Wagner again allowed Brandt to have his way.

Wagner's real interest lay in directing—or, more accurately, in training the cast to sing and act. By all accounts his own talents were amazing. He was, Newman wrote in a lapidary passage,

> a far better conductor than any of his conductors, a far better actor than any of his actors, a far better singer than any of his singers in everything but tone. Each of his characters, each of his situations had been created by the simultaneous functioning within him of a composer's imagination, a dramatist's, a conductor's, a scenic designer's, a singer's, a mime's. Such a combination had never existed in a single individual before; it has never happened since, and in all probability it will never happen again.[7]

Thanks to Heinrich Porges, another chronicler of the time, a record survives of how the composer would throw himself into a role to illustrate the way it should be sung. Demonstrating to Materna, for instance, how to sing the scene in *Walküre* when Brünnhilde tells Sieglinde she will give birth to Siegfried: 'He placed the greatest importance on the delivery of the final words "A Wälsung grows in your womb." He himself sang them with truly thrilling force; in the tone of his voice there lay an expression of profound solemnity allied with prophetic inspiration, arousing in each of us shivers mixed with rapture.'[8] What he was trying to teach was not just beauty of tone and perfect voice technique but a feeling for the meaning of the words and an ability to express it vocally.

Angelo Neumann, himself a famous director, anticipated Newman in describing Wagner as 'not only the greatest dramatist of all time, but certainly the greatest stage director and character actor as well'.[9] In his theoretical writings, Wagner had defined good acting as the art of vanishing as an actor and reappearing as the character itself—a novel idea in the opera theatre of his time—and, according to Porges, he had a phenomenal ability to transform himself magically into any shape and to assume at a stroke any role in any situation. When writing her memoirs in 1913, Lilli Lehmann still vividly recalled how Wagner acted out the role of Sieglinde in the first scene of *Walküre* and concluded, 'Never yet has a Sieglinde known how to approach him, even approximately.'[10]

Fricke's diary entry for 18 June gives a good example both of Wagner's technique and of the remorseless way he drove himself. Despite a gum infection and fever that had kept him awake the night before, the composer insisted on directing the rehearsal of the second act of *Walküre*. He appeared with a swollen face and a voice so weak he had to ask Fricke to 'interpret' for him. But once the music began,

> Wagner forgot all his pain, ran up and down on the rocky heights, hobbled around and simply forgot himself. . . . It was highly interesting and amusing when Scheffzky, at the words 'Do not reject the outcast woman's kiss!' failed to throw herself passionately enough at Siegmund's neck. Demonstrating to

her how it was to be done, the tiny Wagner flung himself with one leap at
the neck of the huge Niemann, who nearly fell over, while his own feet at
that moment scarcely touched the ground. He then sang the passage in
question. . . .

Later on, he demonstrated how Hunding and Siegfried should conduct
the battle on the mountain heights. Fricke continued: 'Niemann turned
away: "Good God, if only he would come down; if he falls, it is all
over." But he did not fall; he clambered down, looking—with his
swollen face wreathed in cotton wool and a bandage—like a mountain
goat descending into a valley.'

Of the utmost importance to Wagner was finding the right balance
between the orchestra and the singers. 'The singers are the main thing,'
he said during a *Götterdämmerung* rehearsal. 'The orchestra accompa-
nies. . . .' Porges recorded that Wagner repeatedly stressed that the sung
words were the key and that the volume of sound had to be restrained
on their behalf: 'Never for one moment [were we] to forget that we
were dealing with a dramatic performance . . . and not a work of purely
symphonic art.'[11] As the rehearsals progressed he even tinkered with the
score—occasionally altering the vocal line, thinning out the orchestration and frequently changing the dynamics by replacing a fortissimo
with a forte, a forte with a mezzoforte and so on. He concluded with a
memorable simile which Porges noted: 'With his love of comparison,
the Master was often wont to say that the orchestra should always carry
the singer along as a rough sea does a small boat, without ever bringing
it in danger of capsizing, much less sinking.'

Wagner was renowned for drawing out of his singers their very best.
In part they simply wanted to please him, in part they were inspired by
his own infectious enthusiasm. But in striving for perfection, he could be
maddening. What he had insisted on one day he summarily retracted the
next. Sometimes the cast was at a loss to know what he wanted;
sometimes, one suspects, he himself was equally perplexed. On one
particularly trying occasion, as related by Fricke, he changed the tempo
of the orchestra and a passage of Brünnhilde's that previously he had
wanted performed slowly. 'He ran around in such terrible excitement
that it made one's blood run cold.' The day before he had been pleased
by Scheffzky's singing, now she could do nothing right. 'He turned
away from her in disgust,' Fricke wrote.[12]

Not surprisingly there were frictions and sharp words, lost tempers
and tears. On occasion he parried complaints with a sardonic comment,
as when the orchestra members grumbled about a draught. 'I composed
the opera,' came the reply, 'and now I am also supposed to close the
windows.'[13] But the more peevish the grievances, the more caustic the
retorts. The atmosphere was eventually so charged that outsiders were
rigorously banned so as to avoid public scandal. At least, as Newman has
recorded for posterity, there was

Amalie Materna as Brünnhilde and Cocotte as Grane, 1876. Fearing he would steal the show, Wagner excluded the horse from one of his best scenes, the Annunciation of Death in *Die Walküre*.

one model member of the company with whom Wagner had no trouble from first to last, one artist by the grace of God who did cheerfully and with the highest competence whatever was demanded of him, who never felt a single pang of jealousy of his colleagues, never considered himself slighted or underpaid, never whined, never stormed, never sulked, never threatened to throw up his part and return to the place from which he had come.[14]

This was the black stallion, Cocotte, presented by King Ludwig for the role of Grane.

With the final run-through of the third act of *Götterdämmerung* on 26 July, the rehearsals came to an end. Already Bayreuth was beginning to fill with guests.

There had never been anything like it in musical history and there could never be anything like it again. In the past, composers had paid homage to kings, now kings came in homage to the composer, as Wagner was not slow to broadcast. Among them were Kaiser Wilhelm, King Ludwig, Emperor Dom Pedro II of Brazil—who, in checking into a hotel, gave his name as 'Pedro' and his occupation as 'Emperor'—the King of Württemberg, the Grand Duke of Saxony-Weimar, the Grand Duke of Schwerin, the Duke of Anhalt and the Grand Duke Vladimir of Russia as well as sundry German princes, princesses, counts and countesses along with an assortment of Austro-Hungarian nobility. Anton Bruckner, Edvard Grieg, Peter Tchaikovsky, Saint-Saëns and Liszt were there as well as the managers and conductors of every German opera house and some sixty music critics.

One person who did not attend was Karl Marx. Travelling from London to Karlsbad in mid-August, he had planned to break his journey in Nuremberg, only to find that Wagnerians were occupying every hotel bed there and in all the other towns and villages of Franconia. After passing the night seated on a hard bench in a village railway station near the Czech border, he wrote to Friedrich Engels denouncing 'the Bayreuth Fool's Festival of the State Musician, Wagner'.[15] Wagner was no more a state musician than Marx was a state economist, but the philosopher's petulance was forgivable since he was known to suffer from carbuncles on his backside.

It was not just Marx who was incommoded by the lack of shelter; many Festival guests also found it difficult to find lodgings and even food. Of all the accounts of a day in the life of a Festival spectator, Tchaikovsky's was the most lurid. Within hours of arriving in Bayreuth, he reported that he had learned the meaning of the term 'struggle for existence'. He said he found people of all nationalities swarming through the streets foraging for something to eat. In restaurants anarchy reigned, and since there was not enough food for everyone, only by 'cunning stratagem or iron endurance' was it possible to find so much as a crust of bread or glass of beer. 'Cutlets, baked potatoes, omelettes,' he claimed, 'all are discussed much more eagerly than Wagner's music.'[16]

A few days after writing to Engels, a still querulous Marx complained to his daughter that wherever he went he was 'pestered with the question, "What do you think of Wagner?"'[17] His own answer was that the extended Wagner family was every bit as queer as the Nibelungs and merited its own tetralogy. It was not just in Karlsbad but everywhere in Europe—and not just in musical circles but, as *The Times* reported, 'among all the better classes of society'—that Wagner and his Festival were a main topic of conversation that summer.

But if no cultural event had ever aroused such attention, probably none had ever evoked such polemics. The denigration and glorification that long surrounded the composer personally had begun to envelop the Festival from the moment it was announced. To compose a fifteen-hour opera, construct a theatre solely for its performance and invite the world to attend was derided by some as vanity to the point of insanity. In 1872 a Munich psychiatrist, Theodor Puschmann, even published a text, *Richard Wagner: eine psychiatrische Studie*, which quickly went through two editions, claiming that Wagner was in fact clinically insane, suffering from 'chronic megalomania, paranoia, ambiguous ideas and moral derangement'. At the other extreme were those who looked upon 'the Master' as an unexampled genius combining the talents of Aeschylus, Shakespeare and Beethoven and who extolled the Festival as an artistic achievement unparalleled since ancient times. At any rate everyone agreed on one point—that, again in the words of *The Times*, 'the impending grand performance will offer one of the most exalted displays of dramatic art ever witnessed'.[18] By 1876 the Festival had been transformed from an operatic presentation into a Historic Event.

For one person, though, it remained purely opera. King Ludwig accepted Wagner's invitation to attend the *Ring* on the strict condition that he would see and be seen by no one. 'I am coming to be renewed and inspired by your marvellous creation and to refresh myself in spirit and heart,' he wrote, 'not to be gaped at by the curious or to offer myself as an ovation sacrifice.'[19] The dress rehearsal was therefore scheduled exclusively for him, with only the composer in attendance. Following the performance of *Rheingold*, however, Wagner persuaded the misanthropic monarch that the acoustics required an audience, and the other three works were accordingly heard by a full house. The performances went well—the vocal highlight was Niemann's Siegmund—and Ludwig clearly felt he had received an excellent return on his investment. 'Words are too inadequate for me to begin to express my enthusiasm and deepest thanks,' he wrote to the composer after *Rheingold*.[20] At the conclusion of the full cycle, he was moved to unimaginable heights of ecstasy and poured out his emotions in a long, rapturous letter, which included such passages as 'You are a god-man, the true artist by God's grace who has brought the sacred fire from heaven to earth to cleanse, sanctify and redeem it! . . . Never before have I been transported into such a state of inebriation, such unprecedented sanctity, so filled with such an unprecedented enthusiastic sense of joy.'[21]

A few days after Ludwig's departure the other royals arrived. To welcome the Kaiser, who delighted in being gaped at by the curious, Wagner and the entire orchestra and cast were present at the railway station along with civic notables. In greeting Wagner, the Emperor made two often quoted remarks. 'I never thought you would bring it off,' he said of the Festival[22]—back-handed praise that undoubtedly reflected the view of everyone except Wagner himself. And to this he added that he considered the event itself a 'national affair'—a comment that struck the composer as ironic, since, as he commented to King Ludwig, the nation had given no help at all. None the less the mere presence of the Kaiser, a simple old man without cultural pretensions, was a gesture of singular esteem for the composer.

Then at last, on 13 August, the Festival was ready to begin. Wagner wrote out his final word to the cast and posted it backstage: '!*Clarity!* The big notes will take care of themselves; the small notes and the text are the main thing. Never address the audience but only one another; in monologues always look up or down, never straight ahead. *Last request!* Be faithful to me, dear friends!' And to the wall behind the conductor he affixed an injunction to the orchestra: 'No prelude playing! Piano pianissimo—then all will be well.'[23] There the admonition remained for nearly a hundred years.

While the first cycle did not go as smoothly as had the dress rehearsal, it suffered no more mishaps than the average première. The scene changes in *Rheingold* were muffed. On one occasion the backdrop was raised too soon and revealed the rear wall of the stage and a group of stage-hands standing around in shirt-sleeves. Betz misplaced the ring and had to run into the wings twice during the Curse. At one point Brandt was so enraged he shouted at the stage-hands loudly enough to be heard in the auditorium. 'What remains of theatrical illusion now?' Fricke wondered.[24] Wagner was beside himself. At the end the audience cheered and called for him for half an hour, but he refused to appear. Instead he sat in his office utterly disconsolate, berating everyone except Hill. The remaining three operas were performed without serious hitches. At the end of the first cycle there was wild applause. This time Wagner joined the cast on stage and, in a brief speech, committed a celebrated gaffe: 'You have now seen what we can do. Now it is for you to *want*. And if you want, we shall have an art.'[25] The remark left everyone unsure just what had been produced if not an art. Wagner later apologized to the singers and musicians for an innuendo he insisted he had not intended.

Ludwig had been so profoundly affected by the preview that he entreated Wagner to make it possible for him to attend the final cycle. 'I appeal to you to isolate me in my box—literally by a wall—from all the rulers and princes who may attend and to prevent any of them, if necessary with police, from approaching me during the intervals,' he wrote.[26] Wagner was able to assure him that the philistine royals would all have left by then. So the King returned, and once again he and the composer sat alone in the centre box, entering after the lights went down and the orchestra began to play. At the outset of *Götterdämmerung*, however, the lights suddenly brightened; Feustel appeared on stage to thank Ludwig on everyone's behalf and to call the audience to join in three rousing cheers for the King. Then the theatre was darkened and the orchestra resumed. When the final curtain came down, some thought the theatre would come down too, so tremendous was the ovation. Eventually Wagner appeared on stage, and even the King came to the front of his box to join in the unending waves of applause. Graciously the composer praised Ludwig as sole benefactor and co-creator of his work; ungraciously he went on to say he hoped his endeavour was a step towards the establishment of a genuine German art—as though the German people had so far produced none. Wagner's tactlessness, Saint-Saëns remarked, was as enormous as his talent.

The performances of his great work left Wagner devastated. As the first cycle had unfolded, he saw mistake after mistake and the need for changes. 'Next year we will do it all differently,' he told Fricke.[27] The shadow had fallen between the motion and the act. During the next five years he flailed himself and others—and even destiny. The appearance of success and the enthusiastic approval of friends, he wrote to King Ludwig when the Festival was over, could not conceal the bald fact that 'I know now that I and my work have no place in these times of ours'.[28] His dejection ran so deep that only slowly could he dredge up his feelings even to share with Cosima. He wanted nothing more to do with those 'theatre parasites' Betz and Niemann, he told her. Brandt's staging had been a terrible disappointment. Richter did not get a single tempo right. And the first act of *Götterdämmerung* would have to be rewritten. 'R. is very sad, says he would like to die!' Cosima recorded.[29]

To relieve the depression he took himself and his family away to Italy. But there as well his conversations with Cosima always came back to 'the one dismal subject', as she couched it.[30] He told her that his overwhelming feeling during the third cycle was 'never again, never again'. He said he had 'winced so markedly that the King had asked him what was wrong, and he had then forcibly to restrain himself'. To the King himself he wrote despondently years later that he had given birth only to a very ordinary child of the theatre; he had constructed nothing more than an empty vessel. Even his dreams were poisoned. One of them reenacted a performance of *Siegfried*. 'Brandt, the lights are going out,' he shouted, waking himself up.[31] In 1878 he relented slightly in his essay, 'Retrospective on the Stage Festivals of 1876', in which he gave unstinting praise to Betz, Hill, Niemann and Siehr and wrote favourably of the three Rhinemaidens and Materna's final scene in *Götterdämmerung*. But in the same year he said to Cosima, 'It was all wrong!'[32] and later recited a long list of scenes that had not come off. Among these was the mountain-top in *Walküre*. Of it he said, 'I'll change that some day when I produce *Walküre* in heaven, at the right hand of God, and the old gent and I are watching it together.'[33] In that remark was the clue to all his bitter disillusionment. He had sought perfection and fell short. He had counted himself a king of infinite space and found that he was bounded in the nutshell of a stage.

Such were Wagner's despairing and acerbic views. How did others judge the performance? From around the world music critics had assembled, to sit in judgement and render their verdict. Indeed, the *New-York Times*, as it then called itself, well caught the mood in observing that 'much of the spirit of a jury with a prisoner on trial before them was exhibited'.[34] Interest in the case was awesome, chronicled in articles of such uncommon length that some were later compiled and published as slender volumes. Of the foreign press, none approached *The Times* and *Daily Telegraph*; the former began its reporting in June and during the Festival carried daily, often quite lengthy despatches. The *New-York Times* was not far behind, running its despatches as the lead article on the front page. The German press reported less frequently but even more voluminously. All in all, the operatic jurors would have fascinated experts on legal evidence by the way they filtered everything not just through closed minds but even, it seems, through closed eyes. They often could not agree on what appeared physically on stage, the time when the performances began, whether and when there had been applause or even on something as simple as the colour of the curtain— some said that it was yellow, others that it was red; according to some it had vertical stripes while to others the stripes were horizontal.

On one point at least everyone agreed. The Festival was not just the cultural event of the century, it was one of the great moments in cultural history. Even beforehand, Eduard Hanslick had written that if it came off, it would be 'one of the most remarkable events in the entire history of art and the greatest personal success of which any composer has dreamed'.[35] Tchaikovsky as well, for all his jealousy of Wagner, could not forbear referring to the Festival as 'one of the most significant events in the history of art'.[36] Echoing this, Edvard Grieg described it as 'an important new chapter in the history of the arts' and hailed the *Ring* as the 'creation of a true giant in the history of art, comparable in his innovation only to Michelangelo'.[37] Wilhelm Mohr, an influential critic who arrived in Bayreuth calling it 'cloud cuckooland', was by the end so overwhelmed that he found the impact equal only to that made on him by the 'two masters of all masters, Shakespeare and Beethoven'.[38] And in a nice figure of speech, Nietzsche likened the event to 'the first circum-navigation of the globe of the arts'. On and on in that vein went the comment.

Critics were oddly indifferent to the opera house itself. There were a number of comments on the 'democratic seating arrangement', the novelty of darkening the auditorium during the performance and the 'Wagner curtain', which opened like a camera lens so that the stage image would appear and disappear in an instant. Hanslick was one of the few to mention the sunken orchestra pit which, despite his reservations, he considered Wagner's most revolutionary innovation.

The new work itself received a thorough drubbing. 'It is no opera at all,' *The Times* declared. 'It is a play, the speeches in which are declaimed rather than sung, to orchestral accompaniment. . . .'[39] Hanslick was downright lyrical in his deprecation. The *Ring* 'will not be the music of the future,' he averred.[40] It was 'not an enrichment' but 'a distortion, a perversion of basic musical laws, a style contrary to the nature of human hearing and feeling. . . . There is music in it, but it is not music.' Instead of the usual choruses, duets, trios and so on, the singing resembled exchanges in a courtroom. There could be little doubt, he assured his readers, that the work was destined to fail. Along the same lines, Tchaikovsky confessed he was more impressed by the work's 'colossal dimensions' than by any musical quality.[41] Some lovely moments apart, he regarded the music as 'unbelievable chaos'. Similarly the *New-York Times* found the four operas 'unprecedented only in respect of the proportions'.[42] The critic went on, 'They have taught nothing new either in music, the drama, or as regards Herr Wagner himself. What

71

influence, immediate or remote, the bringing out of the cyclus at Bayreuth will exercise I am at a loss to understand.' Reflecting a broad French view, *Figaro* went further still: 'No, it is not a theatrical work; it is literally a complete hallucination, the dream of a lunatic, who thinks to impose upon the world a most frightful sort of art.'[43]

At the other end of the critical spectrum, Grieg commented: 'I cannot say that any part of the music is better than any other for it is all divinely composed and to pick out any one passage at random is to pick out a pearl.' Voice, he observed, played only a secondary part in the *Ring*, 'the orchestra is all'. The orchestration itself he found 'unbelievably well done'; indeed, he felt that Wagner's ability to describe scenes caused the spectator to be carried away by the effect and to overlook the lack of dramatic action. Among Grieg's favourite passages were the 'wonderful nature music' in *Siegfried* and Siegfried's Funeral March, which he thought was equalled only by Beethoven's Eroica Symphony.

Most critics shared Grieg's preferences, adding to his list Siegfried's Rhine journey, Brünnhilde's final scene and, above all, the songs of the Rhinemaidens, which were a favourite of everyone. *Siegfried* was the opera they liked most, *Walküre* the least, despite its highly admired first act. Many rated the final act of *Götterdämmerung* as the culmination of Wagner's art; but almost unanimously they accounted the second act of *Walküre* the great failure—'an abyss of boredom', in Hanslick's words.

Longueur was in fact regarded as a—if not *the*—grave weakness of the *Ring*. Never had anything been written that was 'so endlessly and wearisomely spun out', according to Tchaikovsky. Because it was impossible to understand the singers and the theatre was too dark to read the libretto, Hanslick complained, 'We sit there, helpless and bored, amid those endless dialogues, thirsting equally for clear speech and intelligible melody'. The composer Sir Charles Villiers Stanford sat behind Liszt during the performances and claimed that 'during the duller and uglier passages' the composer often nodded off to sleep.[44] Grieg too found some of the dialogues 'quite tedious'. Mohr defended most of this material as essential for the work's dramatic unity, but he also judged the second act of *Walküre* of greater musical than dramatic interest and thought that 'even to the musical ear it seems rather lengthy' and deserved to be substantially cut. In Hanslick's view the whole of *Walküre* could be dropped and, as for the rest of the *Ring*, 'every scene could stand not only the most extensive cuts but also the most extensive expansion'. Grieg thought the dialogue between Wotan and Mime in the first act of *Siegfried* should be trimmed; others recommended cutting back the Norns' scene. One of the few to defend the score as it stood was the Viennese critic Eduard Schelle, who insisted that the length of the work was essential to permit the orchestra to explore the psychology of the characters and situations.

No one even began to take the measure of the work, to have any inkling of its intellectual depth and breadth or to take seriously the notion that the *Ring* was music drama rather than conventional opera. Grieg recognized that the opera might have a significance 'outside its own sphere of music theatre'. And Mohr went so far as to liken Wagner to a painter, who depicted life not as it should be according to some higher ideal but as it was in its naked, sentient reality. Otherwise critics, like the rich and aristocratic audience, saw the work simply as an old-German romance about gods, whom they on the whole found boring and un-heroic, and humans, whom they by and large considered sympathetic.

In fact the characters were widely judged to be one of the principal flaws. Gustav Engels, a prominent Berlin critic, argued that because they were so unconvincing and remote from reality, there could be no dramatic catharsis and as a result the *Ring* failed. Hanslick also disliked the drama because of the characters. In particular he rebelled at the notion that Wotan—whom he referred to as an 'unctuous pedant' and 'this divine Night Watchman'—should be held up as a godly ideal for the German people. Others objected to the moral tone—the selfishness, brutality, cynicism and the like—and were specifically outraged by *Walküre*, with its mating of brother and sister. Even Mohr found this 'overpoweringly repulsive to the healthy sensibility' and all the more regrettable in what was sure to become an 'eminent national monument to the German spirit'. The critic for *The Times* went further still. In his view the 'matter was so objectionable to modern thought' that the very survival of the *Ring* was unlikely.[45] The objectionable matter in his opinion was not simply Siegmund's coupling with Sieglinde but Siegfried's marriage to the eldest of his eleven half-aunts. Such moraliz-ing was too much for one witty writer, Paul Lindau, who with tongue well in cheek examined the *Ring* text against the German penal code and showed, point by point, that Wagner's characters committed every crime in the book.

Critics had remarkably little to say about the music and voices. The most sweeping acclaim came from *The Times*. It found Richter's con-ducting excellent; the orchestra 'perhaps the finest ever heard'; the acting of an effectiveness rarely witnessed and, though the individual singers were not stunning, the ensemble was perfect.[46] Generous with metaphor, the writer likened the orchestral sound to 'an omni-coloured kaleidoscope' and more happily still to 'a wind that is always blowing, or a stream that is always flowing'. The *Daily Telegraph*'s critic was even more enthusiastic about the music-making; now for the first time he said he knew what an orchestra was fully capable of achieving.

Apart from the chorus, which was extolled, there was little agreement about the singing. Vogl and Schlosser (Mime) were considered out-standing, Materna was esteemed for her vocal power while Unger was dismissed as inadequate. Otherwise reactions contradicted one another. Nearly forty years later Lilli Lehmann still hailed Niemann as the greatest Siegmund ever, while in his memoirs Saint-Saëns berated him as already well past his prime. And so on it went through the cast.

The staging was judged both a success and a failure. On the whole Hoffmann's designs left a favourable impression—though not on Hoffmann himself, who was bitterly disappointed by what he saw at the première. 'Truly marvellous' is how Tchaikovsky described the sets; others singled out Nibelheim, Hunding's hut and Mime's forge for special praise. Certain innovatory special effects also went over well; the hissing steam and glowing red fires of Nibelheim, for instance, seem to have created a splendidly sinister atmosphere. Audiences were also impressed by the costumes; King Ludwig said they had left him 'extraordinarily pleased'.[47]

The failure was largely one of frustrated expectations. There had been so much talk beforehand about technological wonders and model performances that a let-down was inevitable. It was all the greater because the novel stage effects were what most often failed. The magic fire—gas jets, in fact—seemed neither magic nor fire. The rainbow bridge put Hanslick in mind of a 'seven-colour sausage'. The *Ring* zoo, especially the dragon, aroused embarrassment. The magic lantern slides portraying the ride of the Valkyries could be deciphered only by those close to the stage. As Fricke had predicted, the final scene in *Götterdämmerung* did not come off. The steam, tinted by coloured light, sometimes failed to obscure scene changes. And occasionally the transformations were not smooth, requiring the orchestra to slow down so that the music coincided with the action. Yet most critics indulgently took the same attitude that Samuel Johnson had about the dog which walked on his hindlegs: it may not have been done well, but the surprising thing was that it had been done at all. The production was creditable; what had been dashed was the hope of model performances. 'I cannot say that anything astonishing was presented to an English eye,' the *Daily Telegraph* commented.

It was unfortunate that Wagner began his Bayreuth venture with a work of such surpassing difficulty and that he did so at a time of low taste and primitive technology. The staging was an indigestible combination of literalism and romanticism. Grieg seems to have been the only one to put his finger squarely on the problem. By being so realistic and so obvious, he argued, the settings detracted from the drama. Far better would have been to make the audience 'use its imagination to create devils and demons within its own mind'.

Wagner had not created an operatic and architectural revolution to recount heroic sagas against a background of beautiful music. His aim was to propound ideas and, like the poet, he hoped that a great force would drive them like withered leaves to quicken a new birth. But innovative, independent and revolutionary though he was in other ways, when it came to staging he was the conventional man of his times, shackled by the traditions of Central European romantic naturalism. Grieg's point never seems to have occurred to him. That he faced a serious dilemma he knew. As early as 1854, when only just beginning to

Die Walküre, Act I: a favourite set at the première, is seen here in the Leipzig production (1878), modelled on the Bayreuth original.

score the already completed text, he wrote to his old Dresden friend August Röckel: 'I realize again how much there is, from the very nature of my poetical intention, that can be understood only through the music.'[48] But in 1872, as the *Ring* was nearing completion, he insisted it was not the music that expressed the drama, rather the drama that was the visual expression of the music. Hence the famous aphorism in his essay 'On the term "Music Drama"' that his dramas were 'acts of music made visible'. In staging the metaphysical by crude physical means, by relying on papier-mâché rocks, horned helmets, suits of mail and back-drops painted with naturalistic scenes, however, he clothed a timeless work in the garb of archaic romance, concealing much of its psychologi-cal, symbolic and mythic import. The medium obstructed the message. 'Fantasy in chains,' Nietzsche said.

None of this would have been of lasting importance had it not been for the fact that the *Ring* staging was assumed to have Wagner's impri-matur and was therefore not incidental to the work but as much a part of his conception as the score and the text. That was the fatal transfer-ence. And so great was Bayreuth's prestige that the 1876 settings and costumes were imitated in opera houses from St Petersburg to New

York and followed for the next seventy-five years—and in a few places, in outline, even today.

In another respect, however, the whole *Ring* enterprise had a tremendously salutary influence. The concept of model performances—of meticulously planned productions, of carefully coached soloists, of painstaking rehearsals, of an integration of music, acting, singing and staging in a cohesive production—along with such simple things as darkening the theatre and not interrupting a performance with talk or applause—in other words, serious opera in the conditions known in most houses today—began in Bayreuth that summer. In Newman's portentous words: 'From 1876 onwards for many years there emanated from Bayreuth a force that was to change the face not only of musical creation but of musical performance.'[49]

The pros and cons of the *Ring* and its performances were discussed at length in the culture columns of newspapers. But not just there. In Bayreuth's cafés and restaurants that summer the arguments were occasionally so heated that they erupted in outright brawls. In one of the more celebrated of these a critic from Berlin had his nose smashed in by a beer mug. Far uglier, however, was the intellectual bullying by Wagnerian fanatics. Even in a nation that took culture with exceptional seriousness, the Wagner craze was extraordinary. Beginning around the mid-1860s, there had developed a group of zealots claiming that music had scarcely existed before *Rienzi*, that such composers as Haydn, Handel and Mozart were of no account, that Bach and Beethoven were simply John the Baptists opening the way to the messiah, that Wagner was that redeemer and that he it was who raised music to the level of true art. By 1876 the Festival was already regarded as a sacred ceremony and the audience a community of worshippers. Non-believers were treated figuratively in the same way as the Berlin critic.

So it is not surprising that some who attended the première found the atmosphere was impossibly suffocating. 'Never in my life have I experienced such a sense of absolute regimentation as I have here,' Paul Lindau commented.

> It is an enthusiastic aesthetic absolutism with all the trappings of autocracy—service with pride to the supreme sovereign who rules and reigns without control; an anxious suppression of any sort of disagreement, which itself would be considered a lack of submissiveness; and the elimination of individual thought, which necessarily implies animosity because it is individual.[50]

Lindau described a state of mind on the Green Hill that never completely vanished.

One had gone to Bayreuth to attend an opera and had found a cult. Wagnerism had been turned into an ersatz religion and Bayreuth its holy place of worship. This was a critical development in the history of Wagnerian opera and of Bayreuth. In a society that was loosing its moorings as it underwent rapid industrialization and secularization, here was a new faith. Indeed, some Protestant Church officials regarded the Festival with considerable mistrust precisely for this reason, reproaching it for propounding a competing 'religion of art', with its own form of salvation.

But to the fanatics, Wagner offered not just a religion of art but a political ideology as well. In the wake of unification in 1871, Germany was awash with musings about national greatness, the 'German soul', the 'German spirit', 'national redemption', 'national salvation'. Wagner's dramas and prose writings had something to offer on all these topics. It was also perfectly natural to compare his struggles in launching the Festival with Bismarck's efforts in founding the Reich and to regard the success of 1876 as the cultural counterpart of the military and political triumph of 1871. Of course, making Wagner a conservative national hero required drastic cosmetic work, given the record of the composer's Dresden days. Nothing was easier. The line was simply taken that far from being a revolutionary, he was merely an idealist whose aim was not to reform society but to free Germany from the yoke of foreign influences. It is not difficult to see why Nietzsche suggested 'that a genuine Bayreuther should be stuffed or, better still, preserved in alcohol . . . with a label: "a specimen of the spirit in which the German Reich was founded"'.[51]

In this way the vital distinction between culture as an expression of national character and culture as an extension of nationalism was destroyed in 1876. From now on Wagnerian opera was treated by the zealots as uniquely German, the ultimate expression of the national spirit—fittingly enough for a composer who referred to himself as 'der deutscheste aller Deutschen', the most German of all Germans. This is why a critical gulf opened between the impact of Wagner's music and the influence of his dramas. As Nietzsche wrote of his countrymen in *The Wagner Case*:

> It was not with his music that he conquered them, it was with the 'idea'—
> the enigmatic character of his art, its playing hide-and-seek behind a hun-
> dred symbols, its polychromy of the ideal that leads and lures these youths to
> Wagner; it is Wagner's genius for shaping clouds, his whirling, hurling and
> twirling through the air, his everywhere and nowhere—the very same
> means by which Hegel previously seduced and lured them.

By the time the curtain closed for the final time in August 1876, the Wagnerian world had begun to mean something to Germans that it did not mean to non–Germans and Germans were already hearing the operas differently. Here lay serpent's eggs that, generations later, hatched to release ideological monsters.

The surprising news that the Festival had left a sizeable deficit reached Wagner in Italy. The cost of the whole venture—the construction of the theatre and all the expenses of the Festival—had amounted to 1,281,000 marks. Net income fell short by 148,000 marks. In addition Wagner owed the Bavarian treasury 216,000 marks from the 1873 loan. Not only did he now abandon hope of mounting a *Ring* festival the following summer, he even toyed with the idea of washing his hands of the entire enterprise by turning the theatre and the Festival over to the government either of the Reich or of Bavaria or possibly to some operatic entrepreneur. When nothing came of these ideas, he went off to London to conduct a series of concerts, hoping to earn enough to pay off the most importunate of his debtors. The concerts were a popular success but a financial flop, realizing but 15,000 marks.

By now Wagner was more embittered than ever. His dream of Bayreuth as a unique and independent institution—'a kind of art-Washington', as he once styled it[52]—had proved illusory. The nation had renounced him, so he would renounce it. Wahnfried was to be sold and he would emigrate to America. And yet, as in his years of Swiss exile, black despair alternated with wild, irrational hopes. At one moment he broached plans for festivals in 1880 (*Der fliegende Holländer, Tannhäuser* and *Lohengrin*), in 1881 (*Tristan* and *Meistersinger*), in 1882 (the *Ring*) and in 1883 (*Parsifal*). At another he considered holding a festival in Munich. Further schemes were mooted until the whole sorry financial business was finally settled in March 1878. An agreement, brokered through King Ludwig, provided that the Munich Opera would pay royalties on performances of Wagner's works until the debt was discharged.

Even so, Wagner abandoned his plan to restrict the *Ring* to Bayreuth until a perfect production could be mounted. He now released the work for general performances. The first of these took place in Leipzig in 1878, under the direction of Angelo Neumann, with staging and costumes modelled on those of the première. Four years later Neumann bought the entire Bayreuth 'Niebelung staging' from Wagner and set up an itinerant *Ring* opera company which performed in 135 opera houses from London to St Petersburg. Curiously enough, the original Bayreuth settings, which had caused Wagner so much anguish, eventually ended up in Prague, where they were still in service until 1927.

Wagner's new absorbing interest was his long-planned opera, *Parsifal*. The composition gave him deep pleasure, spoiled only by the prospect of what faced him in bringing it to the stage. 'Oh, I shudder at the thought, especially of the costumes—and grease paint!' he said to Cosima.[53] 'And when I think how these characters like Kundry are to be fitted out, my mind immediately goes back to those ghastly artists' balls; after creating the invisible orchestra, I would now like to invent the invisible theatre.' Then, with his usual sardonic wit, he added, 'And the inaudible orchestra.' Clearly he still could not purge himself of the mortification of 1876. 'My own deeds, creations and plans pursue me everywhere like fanged serpents, coiling around me and crushing me like a Laocoön. It was my misfortune to invent the notion of a Bayreuth ideal,' he wrote to King Ludwig early in 1880.[54] Some months later he said to himself—in Cosima's presence—'Bayreuth was utter folly.'[55] But even more than by the past, he was now tormented by the present. Trends in Bismarck's Reich—with its urbanization, capitalism, democracy, vivisection, meat-eating and emancipated Jewry—left him in despair. More than ever, the United States beckoned as a sanctuary. There he would inaugurate a new festival with his new opera. All he needed was lots of money.

Until then, he found solace in *Parsifal*. The opera, he hoped, would purify the world by bringing it to a state of Christian pity and renunciation. He spent most of 1880 in Italy working on the score. Ideas for staging the new opera took effortless shape. On visiting the gardens of the Palazzo Rufolo in Ravello, he immediately knew, as he wrote in the visitors' book: 'Klingsor's magic garden has been found!' He was accompanied on the trip by a new disciple, Paul von Joukowsky, a Russian-German painter. Wagner was so impressed by Joukowsky's sketch of the garden that he immediately asked the painter to do the scenery and costumes for his new opera. Some months later, Wagner visited Siena and was moved to tears by the interior of the cathedral there, saying it was the most impressive structure he had ever seen. Now he had found his temple of the grail. Joukowsky again did sketches and with these the inspiration for the second of two critical scenes of the opera was set.

While in Italy, another problem was solved with remarkable ease. Wagner had always intended *Parsifal* to be performed in Bayreuth alone and only for his patrons. In his desperation to liquidate the debts of the *Ring* Festival, however, he had agreed in the 1878 settlement to permit the Munich Opera to perform the work following its Bayreuth première. The prospect of a production outside Bayreuth appalled him, and already in 1879 he inconclusively raised the subject with King Ludwig. As the composition advanced, the issue became urgent. Writing from Siena, he brought up the matter unambiguously. He argued that the subject of the new work was too serious for performance in a regular repertory opera house where it would alternate with frivolous comedies. *Parsifal* was not an ordinary opera but a 'stage dedication play', appropriate only to Bayreuth. 'There and there alone may *Parsifal* for evermore be performed.'[56] The ever-obliging King unhesitatingly agreed that the work should 'never be desecrated by contact with any profane stage'.[57] The offending clause of the old agreement was cancelled, and with that issue resolved, Wagner was able to announce later in the year that a festival would be held in 1882 for performances of the new work.

Planning began shortly afterwards. To sing, he chose Hermann

Winkelmann for Parsifal, Materna for Kundry, Scaria for Gurnemanz, Hill for Klingsor and Theodor Reichmann for Amfortas, with alternates for the major roles. To conduct, he appointed Hermann Levi, assisted by Franz Fischer, both from the Munich Opera. To take charge of the staging and to direct the Brückners in realizing Joukowsky's designs, he again turned to Carl Brandt, despite a lingering sense of disappointment over his *Ring* work. To play, he accepted King Ludwig's offer of the Munich Opera orchestra, which he augmented with outstanding musicians from other houses. And finally, to entice King Ludwig to attend, he had a small annex added to the front of the Festspielhaus to provide a private entry and retiring salon.

Choosing Levi to conduct his 'sacred' work demonstrated both the depths and the limits of Wagner's anti-Semitism. That Levi was a Jew and the son of a rabbi galled Wagner. So even though himself an anti-clerical agnostic who despised the Christian church, he insisted that the conductor must submit to Christian baptism. Levi refused and from then on Wagner subjected him to unceasing, degrading torment. Following the dress rehearsal, Cosima recorded in her diary: 'To me he makes the remark that as a member of the orchestra he would not like to be conducted by a Jew.'[58] Yet the fact remains that he admired Levi and could think of no one better to conduct *Parsifal*. According to Felix Weingartner, he accepted Levi only because Ludwig would otherwise have withdrawn the Munich Opera orchestra, making the Festival financially impossible. But the assertion is not convincing. On the one hand Levi himself resigned a year before the performances as a result of a boorish insult by Wagner, offering the composer an escape if he had wanted one. Wagner persuaded him to return, insisting, 'You are my *Parsifal* conductor.'[59] On the other, the conductor of the première was so important to Wagner that he would not have had Levi unless convinced he was the best man to conduct. Wagner's art to this extent stopped at race.

One other important matter remained—financing. A Patrons' Association, founded in 1877 to raise money for a *Parsifal* festival, was now dissolved. The members had tried their best, Wagner told them, but it was clear that Bayreuth could not be funded in that way. The original idea of a festival for connoisseurs of his music had to be abandoned. From now on tickets were to be sold to the general public.

After another long sojourn in Italy during the winter of 1881–2, Wagner returned to Bayreuth in May to begin final preparations. There was little of the frenzy and vexation of 1876. Of course Wagner fretted about everyone and everything, was alternately pleased and displeased. He quibbled with this or that detail of the sets, complaining for instance that the colours of the magic garden did not go with his music. The costumes outraged him. In the end he did a sketch for the knights' caps and his daughter Isolde designed the Flowermaidens' outfits while Cosima oversaw the others. The rehearsals during the first three weeks

Parsifal (Hermann Winkelmann) and the Flowermaidens, whom Wagner wanted to look like singing flowers. 'Their costumes are tasteless, quite incomprehensibly tasteless, but their singing is beyond praise' (Felix Weingartner of the 1882 première).

of July went smoothly and Wagner was on the whole pleased with the results. The 23 soloists, the 107 orchestral players and the 135 choral members, having been given the score a year before, were all well prepared.

Most of the staging problems had already been ironed out the previous summer. The main technical challenges had again been posed by the transition between scenes—the ascent of Parsifal and Gurnemanz to the temple of the grail from the woodland meadow, the sudden disappearance of Klingsor's castle and the equally abrupt change of the magic garden into a wilderness. A plausible sound had also to be devised for the bells of the grail's temple. Brandt's outstanding innovation was the *Wandeldekoration* for the Transformation scene. This was a canvas backdrop, five times the width of the stage, on which the Brückners painted a landscape of mountain and woodland. Attached to rollers, it was scrolled across the stage to create the impression that Parsifal and Gurnemanz—though stationary—were ascending Monsalvat. The

A photograph of 1882 showing Joukowsky's temple of the grail on the Festspielhaus stage.

The original staging of Klingsor's castle in *Parsifal*, Act II.

mechanism was rather complex and, when first tested, the music concluded before the canvas had fully unrolled. Asked to stretch out the
score by four minutes, Wagner joked that having previously been
admonished to shorten his operas, he was now being asked to lengthen
them. When the problem persisted, he was less amused and grumbled,
'Now I suppose I shall have to compose by the yardstick.'[60] One of the
musical assistants—Engelbert Humperdinck, in fact—added a few transitional bars which did the trick. Several years later, when the mechanism was perfected, they were dropped.

The 1882 Festival began on 26 July. It drew an audience from all parts of
Europe and America and an estimable array of aristocrats, though only a
few minor royals. The critics were present in full force; Liszt, Saint-Saëns
and Bruckner were back, joined by Vincent d'Indy and Léo Delibes.
To Wagner's profound dismay, King Ludwig declined to attend, prefer-
ring to wait until the work was performed for him privately in Munich.

The performances were considered to have been just about flawless.
In a letter to King Ludwig, Wagner expressed his delight. 'The sets were
more successful than anything I have ever previously experienced'; the
voices were good; 'the scene with Klingsor's enchanted flowers was
quite unsurpassable'; and Levi's zeal 'I cannot praise highly enough'.[61]
Ironically, the main difficulty arose over applause. Wagner had wanted
no applauding or curtain calls to interrupt a performance—though he
himself had cheered the Flowermaidens—and this had at first been
taken as a request for silence even at the end of an act. With some
difficulty the misunderstanding was eventually corrected, though it left
a legacy of confusion that took over eighty years to settle.

Towards the end of the last of the sixteen performances Wagner
slipped into the orchestra pit and during the Transformation music of
the last act took the baton from Levi and conducted the final twenty-five
minutes of the opera—with tempi so slow that the singers and musicians
were stretched to the utmost. At the end of the performance, he seemed
well pleased. 'Until next year,' he is supposed to have remarked. 'I think
we can be satisfied,' Cosima wrote in her diary.[62]

This time the atmosphere in Bayreuth was different. There was less
excitement, but greater seriousness; sharp disagreements but fewer polemics. Since 1876 Wagner's public standing had risen still further;
opposition was on the defensive. One writer compared the situation to
Christians under Constantine: after being an oppressed minority, Wagnerians were now victoriously emerging from the catacombs.

The critical response was on the whole highly favourable. Some
gauged the new work to be the zenith of Wagner's artistry. Everyone
thought the score contained some of the most beautiful music Wagner
had ever composed. But there were impassioned disagreements over the
nature of the drama itself and whether the opera should be restricted to
Bayreuth. Indeed the great controversy that summer was whether the
drama had the 'sacred' character Wagner attributed to it.

On the one hand some critics considered the religious trappings either inoffensively symbolic, or so much mystical phonus bolonus or simply an embarrassment best ignored. On the other hand there were many who considered it a genuinely religious work but disagreed violently on what this meant. To Nietzsche it was a huge betrayal. Wagner had 'fallen sobbing at the foot of the cross', had 'transformed Christianity into theatre'. And of the work itself, 'What you hear is Rome—*Rome's faith without the text.*'[63] To others—Protestant theologians and laymen, especially—the grail scene and the foot-washing were a profanation and an impious step towards an art-religion. To still others it was a profoundly moving expression of German Christianity and as such was destined to make a vital contribution to the spiritual renewal of the German nation. But to Paul Lindau it was the Christianity of the Spanish Inquisition, sanctifying by burning heretics while a children's choir sings in praise of divine grace and bells toll on high.

The notion of redeeming the world, or at least Germany, through *Parsifal* responded to the broad and deeply German longing for national salvation. Writing in the prestigious *Neue Zeitschrift für Musik*, Wilhelm Tappert approvingly quoted a member of the audience: 'This is no longer theatre, it is divine service.'[64] To which he added the reservation, 'One must feel and think oneself German and Christian if one is fully to recognize the beauties of *Parsifal*.' And so, after the *Ring* had been pressed into duty for German nationalism, now it was *Parsifal*'s turn. Already Wagner's operas were being recruited for patriotic and racist purposes.

One of the chief recruiters was a Wagner acolyte, Hans von Wolzogen, who in 1878 had founded the *Bayreuther Blätter*, a publication intended for Wagner's patrons. Building on the composer's own *Kulturpessimismus*—his disillusionment with the modern world's political, social, economic and ethical development—Wolzogen used the journal as an ideological instrument to propagate a racist, anti-Semitic, chauvinistic, xenophobic and anti-democratic ideology. It would be difficult to find anywhere in the Western world in the late nineteenth century, even in the darkest corner of the French right, a publication so poisonous, so hate-filled, so spiritually demented. Naturally enough, to the *Bayreuther Blätter* what was important in *Parsifal* and the 1882 Festival was less the artistic aspect than what it regarded as the opera's message of German regeneration—that is, a Germany purified of Jews, liberals, democrats and indeed all modern influences.

The 'religious' debate apart, there was far more critical agreement than disagreement. The production was by and large highly commended. In the first act everyone was greatly impressed by the mechanical genius of the *Wandeldekoration* and overwhelmed by the golden splendour of Joukowsky's imposing temple. The final scene was considered one of Wagner's greatest scenic-musical feats and the three choruses were described as 'powerful', 'gorgeous' and 'magical'.

The magic garden in *Parsifal* Act II, designed at Wagner's direction with enormous, bright flowers, was criticized as not realistic. In a production otherwise considered sacrosanct, this scene was altered in subsequent years.

The reaction to the second act was more discriminate. Paul Lindau wrote that it was difficult to conceive of anything more beautiful and enticing than the music and the Flowermaidens' singing in the magic garden scene. Others agreed, Hanslick even considering it the greatest success of the opera. But almost no one liked the decorations or costumes. Wagner had insisted on having a garden that was not a fairy-tale spectacular but something almost surrealistic, with flowers so enormous that the Flowermaidens would seem to grow out of them, appearing as though conjured up by magic. Joukowsky did as bidden, but the result was the least satisfactory scene in the production—for that matter one that never ceased to frustrate his successors. As for the remainder of the act, the Parsifal-Kundry scene was generally recognized as the crux of the drama, though the act as a whole was variously judged to be convincing, baffling or even fundamentally untrue.

There were those who rated the third act the most beautiful of all and those who thought that it was a bit anti-climactic. In any case, the Good Friday music was a great favourite and the finale was considered 'dazzling', to quote Hanslick. A number of critics had been so moved at the end that they left the theatre in an inexpressible state of rapture. As he walked down the Green Hill after the performance, Felix

Parsifal, Act III: Amalie Materna (Kundry), Emil Scaria (Gurnemanz) and Hermann Winkelmann (Parsifal) at the culmination of the Benediction scene.

Weingartner—like so many thousands of others after him—seemed to hear Goethe's words, 'And you can say that you were present.'[65]

Indeed almost everyone felt the music had reached the greatest heights; some critics clearly had difficulty finding words to express how moved they had been. One considered the score as beautiful and affecting as any music ever written; another said that from the very first notes he had been transported into another world, drawn into an experience the like of which he had never known. *The Times* ventured the opinion that the choruses alone were sufficient to secure for *Parsifal* a permanent and unique place in the history of music. Poor old Hanslick, however, grumbled that the prelude was less impressive than that of *Lohengrin*, Kundry less convincing than the *Tannhäuser* Venus and the Good Friday music less inspired than the Midsummer Day music of *Meistersinger*. But even he agreed with the general view that such an achievement by someone Wagner's age was astounding and that the work was fresher and more modern than any by the youngest composers of the day. Most startling about the critical reaction, however, was what was not said. Even though the chromatic harmonies in some parts of the score took music to the fringes of atonality, no one seemed at the time

86

Photographed in 1882, the metal canisters which produced the sound of the temple bells in *Parsifal*; they were used along with a keyboard instrument constructed at Wagner's direction.

to notice. In fact some critics explicitly denied that *Parsifal* marked any development in Wagner's style.

Few warmed to the characters. Lindau commented that Wagner had no luck with any of his kings—Marke, Gunther or Amfortas. Critics on the whole found Klingsor somewhat disappointing, Kundry perplexing and Parsifal difficult to fathom. Gurnemanz was regarded as the one really human and appealing figure. Almost all the critics praised the singing. Scaria was the hero of the Festival. Materna was acclaimed both for her acting and singing while Winckelmann was felt to have done well with a difficult role. Apart from Ferdinand Jäger (Parsifal), critics had good words for the alternates as well: Marianne Brandt and Therese Malten (Kundry), Gustav Siehr (Gurnemanz), Anton Fuchs (Klingsor) and Heinrich Gudehus (Parsifal). The chorus, the orchestral playing and Levi's conducting were described as beyond praise.

This time Wagner suffered no post-parturition depression. Again, he fled to Italy—to Venice—but to escape the coming Bayreuth winter rather than a sense of failure. In fact he had few immediate worries. The Festival had been a financial success. Expenses had been kept to a minimum, thanks to King Ludwig's bearing the cost of the orchestra and chorus; income, with roughly two-thirds of the tickets sold, amounted to 240,000 marks, leaving a net profit of 135,000 marks. The performances also left Wagner with a feeling near to contentment. He had been generally pleased with the cast and asked most members to return for *Parsifal* festivals which he planned for the following two years. In an article for the *Bayreuther Blätter* he summed up the summer's experience with characteristic Wagnerian irony. Experienced theatre managers had asked him, he wrote, how it had been possible to create an organization capable of solving the tiniest problem and of putting on an impeccable performance—scenic, musical and dramatic—over, under, behind and in front of the stage. To this, he said, 'I was able to respond pleasantly that it was all due to anarchy, with everyone doing just what he wanted—the right thing. Clearly each person understood the entire undertaking and what it tried to achieve.'[66] His mood abruptly changed, however, and the article ended on the sort of black note that had initially inspired the opera. *Parsifal*, the composer concluded, had offered a

The Wagner family photographed on 23 August 1881 by Adolf von Groß on the steps of the garden entrance to Wahnfried. Behind: Blandine, Heinrich von Stein (Siegfried's tutor), Cosima, the composer and Paul von Joukowsky (seated); in front: Isolde, Daniela, Eva and Siegfried.

respite from 'this world of murder and robbery, which were organized and legalized by lying, swindling and hypocrisy'. It was his final malediction against a society now beyond his ken.

'With *Parsifal* stands or falls my Bayreuth achievement,' Wagner had written to Neumann.[67] Even at the time, however, Bayreuth rested on nothing so incorporeal. The Festspielhaus was not a memorial—like Beethoven's birthplace in Bonn or Mozart's 'Figaro House' in Vienna— but a living monument. In this it was no different from Shakespeare and his festival theatre established at Stratford in 1879. But Bayreuth was also a temple, a cult and an ideology. That in a word is why Wagner and Bayreuth had from the start a significance that Shakespeare and Stratford never acquired.

As to the future, Wagner wrote to King Ludwig of his plan to spend a decade producing each of his other operas, at which point his son, Siegfried, would be of age to succeed him. To Neumann, however, he had already written to say that he could foresee no one to succeed him and no prospect for a future Festival. Nor could anyone else. Sheer indomitable will had created the entire Bayreuth venture, and it was generally taken for granted that the enterprise would die with its creator. On 13 February 1883 the creator died.

3

'Here I sit, on alert, guarding the home'

(*Götterdämmerung*)

With a morbidity worthy of Queen Victoria and many another nine-teenth-century widow, Cosima sank into an emotional coma after her husband's death. For twenty-five hours she sat alone with his body. Then she cut off her hair and placed it on his breast as he lay in the coffin. For four days she had almost no food or sleep. Would she, Isolde-like, join Wagner in death? Had it not been for her five children, she would probably have done so. Instead she went into deep reclusion.

As the coffin was lowered into the vault at the foot of the Wahnfried garden, she looked on, arm-in-arm with her friend Adolf von Groß. The scene was symbolic. Groß had made all the funeral arrangements and was the person to whom Cosima now turned for support and counsel. A crucial figure in the 1878 debt settlement, he was the prototype of the successful banker: shrewd, far-sighted, discreet and cold-blooded. His devotion to Cosima was absolute, her confidence in him total. From now on she made no decision without consulting him; for the next thirty years he was Bayreuth's unchallenged éminence grise.

Wagner had left no will—perhaps because he had always had debts rather than assets—and by neither word nor deed had he entrusted any posthumous authority to his wife. This gaping legal vacuum left the future of the Festival in question. Not only that. Other composers had launched their artistic progeny into the world and left them to their fate. Wagner, however, had always tried to exercise the most complete control of every aspect of the lives of his musical offspring. Now, suddenly, they were without a guardian.

Cosima was scarcely in a position to claim custody. True, she had spent her entire life in a musical ambience, had worked closely with her husband and knew his mind better than anyone else. But all that was bound to count for little—especially with Wagner's cultist follow-ing—against the fact that she was a woman, a non-German by birth and someone without professional legitimacy. Accordingly she retired to Wahnfried and for over a year saw no one except her children and Groß.

The legend therefore developed of a grieving widow who wanted only to be alone with her anguish and who sat passively by until the Festival nearly foundered, when she reluctantly stepped in and rescued it. The truth is far different. Within days of Wagner's death she asserted herself to the extent of deciding to proceed with the 1883 Festival. At the same time she authorized Groß to take steps to have herself and Siegfried recognized as legal heirs to Wagner's property, including the Festspielhaus, and to have Siegfried declared to be Wagner's only legitimate child. Groß's legal creation amounted to a retroactive last testament, placing Cosima—and Siegfried after her—in an unassailable position as sole legal authority over Wagner's artistic estate. It was a preemptive act that settled everything before anyone else—such as the Wagner societies and other patrons who claimed a proprietary interest—could make a move.

She also lost no time in laying the foundations of a Wagner cult that became the mania of the rest of her life. Once back in Wahnfried, she made it her first concern to retrieve, at whatever the financial cost, every letter, document and manuscript that had ever been written by Wagner. She was determined to erase every wart and to highlight every creditable feature and thereby produce a magnificent, gilt-encrusted icon. And so she censored, altered or falsified any document that she felt sullied this hagiographic image. Thus began a lasting family obsession to possess and manipulate information about Wagner, his descendants and the Festival. Behind it lay a congenital paranoia which regarded anyone who was not a friend as an enemy, whatever did not flatter as hostile.

More important for a history of Bayreuth was Cosima's decision during that first year of her widowhood to restrict the Festival to Wagner's works—the composer's intentions were ambiguous—and to lay down a specific plan for the conduct of the Festival to the end of the decade. *Parsifal* was to be performed annually, and from 1885 on there was to be a new production every year—*Tristan* in 1885, *Holländer* in 1886, *Lohengrin* in 1887, *Tannhäuser* in 1888 and both *Meistersinger* and the *Ring* in 1889. To conduct, she evidently proposed to ask her former husband Hans von Bülow. At some point indeed Wolzogen sounded out Bülow about managing the Festival. There was also talk of Liszt to direct it. But the latter was too old and the former was not interested. In any case Groß soon brought Cosima down to earth about her ambitious but financially impossible plan for future Festivals.

Whatever her ultimate intentions, Cosima felt a lingering diffidence about openly asserting control. In 1883 she could allow the Festival to run under its own momentum, as a repeat of the previous season. She herself never set foot in the Festspielhaus. Scaria filled in as artistic director while Julius Kniese, a musical assistant in 1882, took charge of the rehearsals. Since that year's Festival was regarded as a requiem for

Wagner, the cast tried to do its very best. But behind the scenes, with no single authority, there were ugly problems. Scaria took too little responsibility, Kniese far too much. Self-appointed defender of the faith, Kniese branded as heresy whatever appeared at variance with the record he had kept of the previous year's performance. He bullied and offended the singers and sent Cosima hair-raising accounts about how the Festival was going to pot. Apparently motivated by the notion *après le déluge, moi*, he hoped to survive to triumph.

His primary target was Levi, whose position he coveted. Levi was a conductor in the twentieth-century mould, a Furtwängler sort—intuitive, interpretative, inspired. Kniese was a pedant, a prig and a precisionist. They quarrelled famously. And infamously. The ardently anti-Semitic Kniese did his best to humiliate the conductor and urged Cosima to get rid of him. 'Levi pretended to be hurt,' Kniese's memoirs stated, 'but he knew perfectly well and admitted that it had less to do with him personally than with his and his race's tragic destiny.'[1] Faced with a choice between art and anti-Semitism, Cosima in this case chose art. She let Kniese go at the end of the season.

Like her husband, Cosima needed Levi; and like her husband, she found his being a Jew nearly intolerable. In fact she is generally considered the more anti-Semitic of the two. Ernest Newman, otherwise a great admirer, commented that her letters to Prince Hohenlohe-Langenburg, published in 1938, 'might have been written yesterday by any leading Nazi'.[2] He added: 'The "Jew" leit-motive, combined with that of "Regeneration through Bayreuth", runs through these letters with the persistency of the "gold" motive in the *Ring*; the only difference is that Cosima repeats her leit-motives a thousand times without the slightest variation.' Despite her own bigotry, she faced down the tremendous agitation against Levi—and herself. At one point she challenged the protestors to subscribe to a statement that declared: 'Conductor Levi is morally unworthy and artistically unqualified to conduct *Parsifal*.' No one signed, and Levi stayed.

The 1884 season was another *Parsifal* Festival with essentially the same cast. To direct the rehearsals, Cosima now emerged from seclusion, or at least partially emerged. A curtained enclosure was constructed in the Festspielhaus, from which she listened and observed without being seen. Following the music with a piano score, she despatched a steady stream of comments and directions to Levi: 'if possible, more tenderly and the kettle-drums not so heavy'; 'to be played with reverence'; 'string playing not always precise'; 'not mysterious enough, somewhat flat'.[3] Levi took these quiddities in good measure, even praising Cosima's musical insight. Although Cosima's artistic and directorial talents have been debated, her handling of these rehearsals demonstrated not only a considerable understanding of her husband's work but a deftness in dealing with the musicians, performers and staff. Amateur or not, she asserted a convincing authority.

Her position was further strengthened by the success of the 1884 season. In the previous year there had been few reviews, probably because of the Festival's character as a memorial service. These latest performances, critics agreed, were a marked improvement, with singers, chorus and conducting more confident and impressive—or, as *The Times* said, 'if possible, still more excellent than before'.[4] German critics were, broadly speaking, divided into two camps. There were those who wrote with undiscriminating, unqualified praise and those who reported with discriminating, qualified praise; those who looked at the Festival through the optic of chauvinism and anti-Semitism and those who regarded it in non-ideological terms; those who regarded attendance as a pilgrimage and those who saw it as socially fashionable; those who condemned applause as a sacrilege and those who considered it appropriate. Again there was disagreement about the opera's character— whether sacred or profane—and about its restriction to Bayreuth.

Even the most obvious fact—that the institution itself had survived its creator—was cause for discord. For some the cup was half empty, for others half full. In the view of one German critic, for example, the Festival was now so well established that there was no longer anything special about it, that indeed the magic had already gone out of Bayreuth. *The Times* by contrast pointed out that there had been a widespread prophecy that after Wagner's death his works would lose their popularity and an empty Festspielhaus would become a monument to irrational vanity, a worthy pendant to the local insane asylum which crowned a neighbouring hill. Instead Wagner's fame was greater than ever, the Theatre better attended and the performances of even greater distinction.

Once the Festival had critically and financially survived two seasons, Cosima formally announced that she was assuming leadership. In music circles, where she was regarded as unqualified from every point of view, her decision was considered outrageous. Wagner societies objected so strongly that they even sent two emissaries to Bayreuth to register their veto. She declined to receive them. The Cosima Wagner era had begun.

Cosima's early years were not easy. A widespread belief persisted that the Festival was in crisis and would eventually disappear from the musical map. Opera-going at Bayreuth, the cynics maintained, was a novelty whose charm was bound to wear off. Attendance was in fact precarious and competition from other opera houses was actually increasing. Even those who were well disposed questioned whether an inexperienced widow in her forties could put on productions better than those staged by the great professional opera directors in such places as Munich, Berlin and Vienna. Cosima therefore faced unremitting pressure from Wagner societies and others to surrender control to a directorate or at least to accept artistic advisers.

Stability, consolidation, caution—such were what the Festival needed if it were to survive. Of that Groß was convinced, and as Cosima's professional superego, he made the decisions. Above all, he stressed that the Festival's artistic programme was mortgaged. Micawber economics were at an end; from now on Bayreuth was to tread the straight and narrow path of fiscal responsibility, expenditures never greater than income. It was Groß therefore who determined every aspect of the Festival's future format. *Parsifal*, exclusive to Bayreuth, was to be performed at every festival. But alone it could not pull in enough of an audience, so the repertory had to be expanded. There was to be a periodic 'rest year', to hedge against weak demand for tickets and to provide time to prepare new productions. Even the particular operas and the season when they were performed was decided with financial considerations in mind.

Cosima had no choice but to accept such advice. Though it pained her, she went along with Groß when he insisted that there could be no Festival in 1885 and even when he overruled her wish to do a production of *Tannhäuser* the year after that. With its small cast and relatively simple settings, *Tristan und Isolde*, Groß decided, would be the most economical to put on.

Despite her disappointment Cosima threw herself into the preparations with tremendous energy. In staging the opera, she began by studying the versions done under Wagner's supervision—the première production in Munich in 1865 and another in Berlin in 1876. Her own staging designs, executed by the Brückners, and the costumes, done by the Munich designer Josef Flüggen, were modelled on those of the Munich performances. The first act showed Isolde's heavily draped enclosure in the foreground, with the open deck of the ship at the rear of the stage. The second act was a precise rendition of Wagner's stage directions: 'a garden with tall trees in front of Isolde's chamber, to which steps rise on the side of the stage'. The third act portrayed a rocky height overlooking the sea. In the background was the silhouette of a castle on one side of the stage and a long fortification wall with a watch-tower on the other. In the desolate foreground was a linden tree, its branches extending almost the width of the proscenium.

In deciding to interpret Wagner's stage directions with pedantic literalism, Cosima established a mode of production not just for Bayreuth but for opera houses elsewhere. It was a style that perpetuated a staging orthodoxy with roots in the Baroque theatre and was now in its final flowering—or decay. It was elaborate, heavy, overripe and above all literal-minded. It was a nineteenth-century naturalistic drape over a universal drama.

None of the operas brought out this contradiction more blatantly than *Tristan*. Cosima herself glimpsed the problem, not with the sets but at least with the directing. In this opera, she wrote to Levi, 'where the most complex feelings are expressed in the music, there is scarcely any appropriate gesture without absurdity and scarcely any facial expression that equals the power of the music'.[5] Realism, she concluded, was the

Cosima herself drew the stage plans and wrote the instructions for lighting, props, colours and other details of her *Tristan* production in 1886. The basic division of the stage for Act I was followed for a century.

In Cosima's *Tristan* production, the dim lighting of the interior, the harmony of the colours—the rust-brown and dark reds of Isolde's apartment and the gold brown sails—along with the overall naturalism were highly praised.

In a photograph of the première production, Brangäne (Gisela Staudigl) shows Isolde (Rosa Sucher) a magic potion. Sucher's beauty and statuesque poses were said to have been an inspiration to painters and sculptors in the audience.

worst of all; a minimum of action, allowing the text and the music to convey the feelings, was the least bad solution.

As she produced it, the opera was less a drama of heroic passion than a chamber work of inner emotions. Everything about it was understated. The colours of the sets and costumes, along with the stage lighting, were subdued. The costumes themselves were remarkably plain for the time; in the second and third acts Isolde wore a completely unadorned white crêpe de chine gown. The orchestra's sound was dampened and the soloists' movements and gestures were as economical as possible. 'Only a small movement'; 'just one arm should move'; 'suggested merely by a movement of the head (not arms)'—so read some of her instructions. The point of this visual and orchestral restraint was to emphasize the introspective nature of the work and to subordinate the acting and music to the dramatic intent. With this, the cornerstone of the Festival's performing practice was formally laid: the drama not the music was paramount. Or, in Cosima's own phrase, 'The Bayreuth stage provides us drama transfigured by music.'[6]

Cosima's *Tristan* was a solid success. The staging, directing and singing were widely acclaimed. Rosa Sucher, who alternated with Therese Malten as Isolde, was the star of the Festival. Her warm voice, her mastery of the role and her own beauty left a stunning impression. Albert von Puttkamer, who in his book *50 Jahre Bayreuth* looked back over the Festival's first half-century, placed her Isolde on a level with Niemann's Siegmund and Scaria's Gurnemanz. Sucher was supported by Gisela Staudigl, in Puttkamer's judgement a classic Brangäne, and the two sang together in the following three years of the production. Fritz Plank as Kurwenal was regarded as the other outstanding member of the cast and now became a favourite Bayreuth singer. Heinrich Vogl, last seen in Bayreuth as Loge, received mixed reviews for his Tristan. He must have been overwhelming in the third act at least, since the *Frankfurter Zeitung* reported that his performance of the agonized Tristan was so realistic it made some in the audience flee the theatre in fright. Although reaction to Felix Mottl's conducting varied, *Tristan* became the Bayreuth opera for which he was most renowned.

The 1886 *Tristan* marked the moment when Cosima not only asserted control over an institution but also began to shape the whole mode of presenting Wagner's works. Here lay the origin of what was known as the Bayreuth style. Cosima did not see herself as imposing her own artistic concepts, but simply as carrying out her husband's intentions. 'There is nothing left for us here to create, but only to perfect in detail,' she said over and over. Others took her at her word and some condemned her out of her own mouth for shackling Bayreuth to the dead hand of tradition. In fact she was being slightly disingenuous. In perfecting the details, she was far more creative than she let on, imposing her will on the scores, conducting style, staging, directing and the mode of singing and acting. All this she did in the name of Wagner, but at times the Wagner was more Cosima than Richard.

That the composer gave primacy to the drama could be inferred not only from his theoretical writings but also from his remarks during the *Ring* rehearsals and, tangibly, from the design of the Festspielhaus with its sunken pit. On the question of whether music or text was more important in the drama or which came first in the creative process, he was contradictory; but that both were subordinate to the dramatic intention was beyond doubt. From this, all else followed—though whether it followed in precisely the ways Cosima dictated is another question.

'We have broken with opera,' Cosima proclaimed, 'and are obligated to reveal this break in the clearest possible way.'[7] The most obvious way was to emphasize the subordinate role of music and the secondary position of conductors. She therefore selected conductors who accepted her doctrine and she left them in no doubt that theirs was simply to follow orders. If she wanted a subdued reading of *Tristan*, for example, she did not want a conductor to give her an argument. So those who held independent views, who were considered concert rather than operatic conductors, or who were musicians—now a dirty word in Bayreuth—rather than musical dramatists were excluded. Least of all did she want musical assistants who had been close to Wagner in the early years of the Festival and who could assert their knowledge of the Master's intentions against hers. She expected submissiveness and, interestingly, had no difficulty getting it. The unctuousness, the humiliating servility shown by her conductors over the years verged on the masochistic. Felix Weingartner, a musical assistant in 1886, found Hermann Levi's self-abasement during a dinner at Wahnfried so degrading that he could not forbear taxing the conductor afterwards. 'It is easy enough for you in that house,' came the answer, 'Aryan that you are.'[8] Levi was evidently unaware that the Aryans behaved in exactly the same way. Of Mottl, for instance, Weingartner observed: 'His motto, too . . . was absolute submission.'[9] And so it was with all the others.

Cosima's decisive act was selecting Mottl, principal conductor of the Karlsruhe Court Opera, as her chief collaborator and in effect musical director from 1886 until 1903. Her choice raised many an eyebrow. In not inviting Hans von Bülow, she was forgoing the leading conductor and foremost Wagnerian interpreter of the time. While that was understandable for obvious personal reasons, her refusal to ask Hans Richter or Anton Seidl, one of Wagner's assistants from 1872 to 1876, aroused consternation and downright ill-feeling. Whether Mottl was invited because he was compliant or because he independently shared her views was never clear. In any case he became the great exponent of the Bayreuth style. The score he used in conducting the 1886 *Tristan* has survived and, indicatively, the marginal notes are far less about how the music was to be conducted than how the opera was to be directed.

A corollary of the Bayreuth approach was that the music must be inseparably linked with the action on stage—or, put another way, that the conducting was to come out of the drama not the score. This precept was again implicit in what Wagner wrote and in what he said during the *Ring* rehearsals, when he commented to Seidl, for instance: 'My dear friend, pay more attention to the stage, follow my staging directions and then you will infallibly find the correct way through the music.'[10] Since Bayreuth saw itself as a producer not of opera but of music drama, the ideal audience was one that would be unconscious of the music and would lose itself in the stage action.

Several important conclusions followed from this. For a conductor it meant that the volume of orchestral sound had always to be moderated for the sake of the audibility and clarity of the text. What was in any case fostered by the covered pit and the house acoustics, became an important rule in conducting. Mottl's *Tristan* score reveals how Cosima depressed the dynamics, substituted at one point two celli and double basses for all the lower strings and eliminated a cymbal at the end of the first act. Emphatic as ever, she once wrote to a singer: 'If anything must be sacrificed, it is the music that is to be sacrificed to the text rather than the text to the music. This is a point of principle and on this principle the Bayreuth stage rests.'[11]

Even more strictly regulated was tempo. For Wagner the key element of a performance was tempo, and this was to be both broad—he labelled *andante* (moderately slow) as 'the German tempo' to distinguish it from the faster French and Italian tempi that he disliked—and marked by 'omnipresent' variations. But how slow was slow and how omnipresent the modifications? In any case Cosima interpreted the general precept as meaning very slow and raised it to inviolable practice as the 'Bayreuth tempo'. It was enshrined by Mottl in the 1886 *Tristan*. Cosima had already gone through the score at the piano and set down the tempi as she wanted them. Her reasons have never been known. She may have felt that a slow tempo was necessary for her acting style. Or she may simply have been reinforcing the mood of solemnity and quasi-religious sanctity that she imposed on the Festivals.

A vital part of the Bayreuth style was the enunciation of the sung words. Again, this was for the sake of the drama—to express character, not simply to make the words comprehensible. Hence Alberich, Hagen and Klingsor had to sing their vowels and consonants differently from Wotan, Siegfried and Parsifal. But Cosima turned an obvious principle into a fetish. She took infinite pains to demonstrate precisely how she wanted words to be sung or at times 'more spoken than sung'. Consonants—given their relative frequency in German—were considered especially important. The resulting harsh declamatory style or 'hurling of masses of craggy consonants', as Newman put it, came to be derided as the *Bayreuther Konsonanten-Spuckerei*—the infamous 'Bayreuth bark'.

The Bayreuth approach also dictated that acting and gestures were to be draconically subordinated to the drama. This principle too could be traced to the composer's own words. 'Restraint in the movement of arms and hands,' he insisted. 'The more economy employed here, the more impressive will be the few gestures used on stage.' But Cosima went beyond enforcing restraint to regulating a singer's every movement, gesture and even facial expression.

Her injunctions were recorded by Carl Kittel, a musical assistant from 1904 and vocal coach from 1912 until 1939. The rules extended from a singer's never facing the audience down to the regulated movement of each finger, which was rehearsed until an entire scene could be run through without a miss. There were stringent rules for control of the eyes. First the gaze was fixed on a point on the ground five or six metres distant, with the lids almost closed; then the gaze was lifted almost to eye level and the lids slightly opened; finally the gaze was broadened and the eyelids were completely opened. Similarly, the palms of the hands had always to be held cupped and never extended flat toward the audience. And so it was with every role and each action.

In no other respect has Cosima been so roundly criticized or so strongly praised. Her critics maintained that she smothered all spontaneity and individualism. Lilli Lehmann accused her of turning her artists into 'soulless wooden dolls' whose 'everlasting "standing in profile" was carried to the point of mania . . .'.[12] But her admirers insisted that her acting style was her greatest contribution to the opera theatre of the time. More than anyone else she combated the old histrionics, the traditional show-acting, the star-dominated performance and made operatic singing and acting a serious art form.

Cosima's self-confidence in directing grew out of an acting talent ostensibly as great as her husband's. And as was said of him, she seemed able to turn herself into the very character she was portraying. Anna Bahr-Mildenburg, the most celebrated Kundry of her day, recounted how Cosima read her the text of *Parsifal* and, 'her lips scarcely moving, was at this moment someone quite different, left herself and was mysteriously transformed into Kundry'.[13] Similarly, Alfred von Bary, a leading Tristan in Cosima's later years, had an unforgettable experience when Cosima had to fill in for an indisposed Isolde and spoke the role at a piano rehearsal. He noticed that as soon as the music began, a complete change came over her. So overwhelmed was he by her movements, gestures and expression that he forgot himself in the scene. The rehearsal was the most rewarding of his life, he said, spoiled only by the thought that her talents would never be seen except inadequately through others.

Cosima had a right to be well pleased with the critical reception of her *Tristan*. The 1886 Festival had been openly regarded as her acid test. After it there could be no doubt that she was an effective operatic producer and manager. She rejoiced in her success and could scarcely wait for a repeat the following year.

Once again Groß brought her down with a bump. Success on stage had not been matched by success at the box office. The Central European aristocracy had turned up in goodly numbers—including the German Crown Prince, the future Kaiser Wilhelm II—but overall attendance was disappointing. The often repeated story that only twelve tickets were sold for one performance was no doubt myth; but as few as 200 showed up on some days and average attendance amounted to only 960. With the survival of the Festival at risk, Groß decided—to Cosima's deep dismay—that a Festival the following year was out of the question. And to make matters still worse, there suddenly emerged another and more direct threat to Bayreuth's existence—this one legal.

Following the death of King Ludwig in June 1886, the Bavarian government, in the person of Count Christoph Krafft von Crailsheim, summoned Groß to Munich and informed him that the *Ring* and *Parsifal* were now to be understood as belonging to the Munich Opera and that they might henceforth be performed in Bayreuth only with the permission of the new Prince Regent. When Groß countered by displaying

Ludwig's written waiver of his rights to the works, Crailsheim responded that since Ludwig had been declared insane, any agreement he had entered into was void. To this Groß rejoined that in that case Crailsheim's own appointment as Minister of the Household was equally invalid, making further discussions pointless, and that the matter was for the courts. His bluff called, Crailsheim backed off completely. An accord the following year declared Wagner's heirs to be owner of all the composer's musical works and texts and recognized Bayreuth's exclusive right to *Parsifal*. As an ostensible concession, but really almost a final tweak, Groß allowed Munich the rights to Wagner's early—unperformable—operas *Die Feen* and *Das Liebesverbot*. This was probably Adolf von Groß's finest hour, though not his last great moment.

With the way now open to a Festival in 1888, Cosima again wanted to put on *Tannhäuser* and was again overruled by Groß, who insisted that the Festival needed a festive opera to draw a big audience—*Meistersinger*. The work would fit in nicely with the mood of the country, in its exuberant nationalism and its search for historic roots. Once again, however, the choice ran directly counter to Cosima's whole Festival strategy of presenting original and impeccable productions that would show up the spurious, deficient versions elsewhere. In staging *Meistersinger* she had no choice, as she lamented in an embittered letter to Groß, but simply to duplicate the Munich première production of 1868 which Wagner had supervised and considered ideal.

Still, she was determined to do her best. 'You cannot believe how I worry about this production,' she wrote.[14] 'A good orchestra, good choruses, well and fine, but if the action on stage is not right, the performance miscarries even if they sing and play like angels in heaven.' Though both the sets and the directing followed the Munich model, Cosima made significant alterations. Instead of backcloths alone, she instructed the Brückners to produce a few cardboard props, minus some of the realistic detail. Costumes were designed for charm more than historical accuracy. Because of the great importance and difficulty of the choral scenes, she invited back Kniese, who now became chorus-master and one of her closest associates.

The Festival was an unprecedented success. For the first time every seat for *Parsifal* was sold and the demand for tickets to *Meistersinger* could not be met. The *Meistersinger* performances themselves excited wild cheering before the final notes sounded and went on long after. Most critics were equally carried away. Here at last was the true *Meistersinger*, exulted one writer; almost a new opera, wrote another; the performances demonstrated 'the real need for Bayreuth', raved a third. Some also commented with evident relief that it was possible for the first time to laugh inside the Festspielhaus. 'Anyone who witnessed the sheer jubilant enthusiasm for [*Meistersinger*] could scarcely believe his eyes when thinking back to the reaction at the première performance twenty years ago,' the *Kölnische Zeitung* remarked.[15]

The romantic naturalism and historical realism of Cosima's 1888 *Die Meistersinger*—seen here in the Meadow scene of Act III—responded to the nationalistic mood of the new Reich.

Yet, when it came down to it, critics were not greatly impressed with the singing. They considered Heinrich Gudehus a poor Stolzing and Theodor Reichmann a disappointing Sachs. There was also a consensus that Sucher, Malten and Kathi Bettaque, the alternate Evas, were creditable though not thrilling. And the smaller roles of Kothner, Pogner and so on and even the chorus were apparently disappointing. What saved the day were Fritz Plank and Carl Scheidemantel, the two alternates as Sachs, as well as Sebastian Hofmüller, who set a standard as David for years to come, and Fritz Friedrichs as Beckmesser. Cosima's transformation of the town clerk from the usual comic caricature into the serious figure Wagner had intended was considered a masterstroke. She was credited with having given the work a deeper meaning than ever before.

Above all it was Richter who carried the day. In this there was a certain irony. Cosima regarded the conductor with mistrust, if not misprision. He was too distinguished, too historically associated with Wagner, too self-confident to be requisitely deferential. Beyond that he was a mere musician and his tempi were unreliable—a view which she may have picked up from Wagner but which was shared by Bülow and Gustav Mahler. However, as the amanuensis of the fair copy of the score and conductor of the rehearsals for the Munich première, he was closely associated with this opera. To have passed him over would have caused scandal. So she invited him, even though, it is said, he accepted on the explicit understanding she would not interfere with his conducting. In the event he triumphed. His performance, Puttkamer said, 'will remain forever an unrivalled ideal'.[16] The music was in his blood, and throughout the entire performance he maintained 'an incredibly glorious fluidity'. In an otherwise not uncritical review, Paul Marsop, Paul Lindau's intellectual successor, commended Richter's reading as 'from the first to the last note rigorous and well-considered, with his tempi infallibly secure'.[17] This was no longer the Richter of the Nibelung festival, he wrote, but a surer conductor and one who was 'cooler and drier. For stretches he conducted as though for an English audience.' The *Kölnische Zeitung* also praised Richter's animated conducting, though describing it as characterized by 'good German tempi'.

The problem with the 1888 Festival was *Parsifal*. For the first time the work was conducted not by Levi, who was ill, but by Mottl. The jubilation among those who still resented a Jew's conducting this 'Christian' opera was spoiled, however, by Mottl's treatment, which was roundly and unanimously condemned. Critics complained that his tempi so dragged that the dynamics were distorted, tension destroyed and grandeur turned to boredom. The contrast was painful, not just to Levi's reading, generally considered authentic, but to Richter's relatively 'animated tempi' that year. It was widely assumed that Mottl, whom the critics respected, had bowed to Cosima's will. However, her biographer, Richard Du Moulin Eckart, related the intriguing story—*se non è vero, è ben trovato*—that so deeply disappointed had she been with his conducting that once, while in the semi-lucid state of her final years, she relived the performances and exclaimed, 'Faster, faster, my dear Mottl!'[18]

Parsifal notwithstanding, the Festival was a tremendous financial and critical success. At last there could be absolutely no doubt that the institution was there to stay. 'It consequently appears clear that this artistic enterprise, which only twelve years ago was treated with mockery and ridicule, is completely secure,' the *Kölnische Zeitung* commented.[19] Yet there were those who turned Cosima's accomplishments against her. Now that the venture was a success, some argued that it was too important to the nation to remain in private hands. Others condemned Cosima as a tyrant and an artistic dilettante, who had betrayed the Master's ideals. Conservatives denounced her for opening this 'unique German cultural site' to foreign influences. This was a reference to her having given the role of Parsifal to the Flemish singer Ernest van Dyck and, though it passed with less protest, the role of Magdalena to an American mezzo-soprano Edyth Walker. Even the normally sympathetic *Kölnische Zeitung* added its voice to the calls for her to resign or to limit herself to an advisory role.

The next year's Festival was musically the most dazzling ever, with

The great conducting triumvirate of Cosima's Bayreuth. From left: Hermann Levi (1839–1900), Felix Mottl (1856–1911) and Hans Richter (1843–1916).

Mottl conducting *Tristan*, Richter *Meistersinger* and, to everyone's enormous relief, Levi *Parsifal*. It was also an unprecedented social triumph. Appearance at Bayreuth was by now socially de rigueur, attracting precisely the sort of fashionable crowd Wagner had hoped to elude by holding his festival far from a chic resort spa. In addition to the regular contingent of German, Austrian and Hungarian aristocrats, this year's Festival drew the Prince Regent of Bavaria, the King of Saxony, the Queen of Rumania and the new German Kaiser and his wife.

Cosima harboured great hopes for Wilhelm II, envisaging him as Bayreuth's rich and powerful patron. And indeed he was a Wagnerian enthusiast—of sorts. What he delighted in was the Wagnerian kitsch that was so wildly popular at the turn of the century. His first motor car, for instance, was fitted with a horn that honked Donner's leitmotif from *Rheingold* while he himself was famously photographed dressed as Lohengrin, complete with silver winged helmet, and once entered Hamburg on a swan boat. As for the Festival itself, he was also an enthusiast—of sorts. After first attending in 1886 he had written to Cosima praising Bayreuth as 'the German Olympia'. And two days after becoming emperor in 1888, he had again written to express his deep interest in Bayreuth. But what interested him was not what he could do for Bayreuth—he declined to be the Festival's imperial patron—but what Bayreuth could do for German cultural supremacy. And so after gracing *Meistersinger* with his presence, he declared that Bayreuth exemplified 'the stunning victory of German art'.[20] The turn of phrase was revealing. Nationalism was creeping into the cultural discourse.

Among the notable commoners present that year was George Bernard Shaw, on the first of five visits as a music critic. His reports then and in later years were a typical Shavian mélange of detachment, iconoclasm and opinionated dogmatism—leavened by what never otherwise appeared in Wagnerian criticism: wit. Like Wagner himself, he held views on everything and held them exuberantly. Almost the only critic of his time to appreciate the revolutionary qualities of the opera house itself, he expressed amazement that it had no duplicate elsewhere and championed the construction of a twin in London. However, his assessments of the performances were at times brutal, and the more telling because he was not only a playwright and music critic but in a position to make a transnational comparison.

Bayreuth's productions, he maintained, were the product of 'scrupulous reverence for Wagner, thorough study, and reasonable care'—nothing less and nothing more.[21] They were not beyond what could be achieved elsewhere; indeed staging and orchestral playing were often superior in London. He even went so far as to argue that one was better advised to go from Bayreuth to London to hear Richter conduct than to go from London to Bayreuth to hear Levi. A few years later he was back with an even more ferocious put-down: 'The Bayreuth orchestra, judged by London standards, is not a first-rate orchestra, but a very carefully worked-up second-rate one.'[22] And as for the singing, it was at times 'simply an abomination'. Bayreuth singers did not sing, they shouted. At a performance of *Parsifal* the 'bass howled, the tenor bawled, the baritone sang flat, and the soprano, when she condescended to sing at all, did not merely shout her words, but screamed'. Shaw's criticism was subsequently endorsed by others, and even Wieland Wagner once said he had no doubt that Shaw was correct in asserting that more shouting went on at Bayreuth than anywhere else and that it was only necessary to bellow to be considered a Wagnerian singer.

Shaw was ultimately touching on the larger question of contemporary standards of musical performance. Some music historians confirm that the quality of orchestral conducting, playing and singing was lower in the nineteenth century than later, particularly from the 1920s on. Even at Bayreuth scores were apparently interpreted liberally and not always played accurately—indeed, they were not invariably without errors, as Toscanini found in 1930. Not only were musical instruments often of poor quality but members of the Bayreuth orchestra came from a variety of opera houses and not all were accomplished Wagnerians. Although Bayreuth was generous with rehearsals, there was not always time to train them to play well. Apparently all this was so much a part of the norm at the time that few minded or even noticed.

But Shaw's most devastating criticism was of Cosima herself, who 'sits on guard there' with 'no function to perform except the illegitimate one of chief remembrancer'.[23] Wedded to the past and lacking an understanding of directing, she sullied the operas with poor stage management and drastic overacting—the soloists 'making the most violent demonstration, striking the most overcharged attitudes' and 'attitudinizing on the stage' at times 'with unspeakably ridiculous effect'.[24] The reason for this? The very thing Wagner had rebelled against: the deadening hand of tradition. 'The whole place reeks of tradition—boasts of it—bases its claim to fitness upon it.'[25] The law of tradition was 'Do what was done the last time.' That, he said, was to invite death, and 'Bayreuth has chosen the law of death.' It claimed it had a monopoly on authenticity, 'or, as I prefer to put it, that it alone is in a position to strangle Wagner's lyric dramas note by note, bar by bar, *nuance* by *nuance*'. It was as though Shakespeare had left stage directions which had been blindly followed ever after. Wagnerian opera risked finding itself 'in the condition of Titurel in the last act of Parsifal'.

Shaw argued that a scene should be staged from the drama's inner meaning—allowing text, music and audience imagination to do the work—rather than from Wagner's arbitrary stage directions. Such was also the central point made around this time by one of the great stage reformers, Adolphe Appia. He had attended the 1886 *Tristan* and was appalled at what he saw. 'A living thing', he said, 'is being presented in an atmosphere without life.' He set down his reactions in *La musique et la mise en scène*, where he proposed a radical reform of the opera's visual presentation. Since *Tristan* was essentially a drama of emotional introspection in which the physical world was of little significance, stage clutter had to be reduced to a minimum. Spare sets would encourage an audience to concentrate on the nature of the work and to see it through the eyes of the protagonists. Appia therefore proposed a staging based on suggestion and even symbolism—almost abstraction—rather than historical verisimilitude. 'A few ropes of typical rigging' would suffice for the first act; an unencumbered stage—suggesting Isolde's sense of 'the cruel space separating her from Tristan'—for the second; a 'scorching sun' which sank slowly into the sea during Isolde's *Liebestod* for the third.

Some years later, when made aware of Appia's proposals, Cosima commented, 'Isolde's apartment, Tristan's view of the sea in Act III, the forest for Siegfried, everything, in sum, must remain just as it was set down by the creator of the drama.'[26] And that was that. For a time she apparently gave thought to having Appia as a costume designer and adviser on lighting. Nothing came of this. And when Appia subsequently sent her a complete set of staging proposals for the *Ring*, she told her friend Houston Stewart Chamberlain, who was well-disposed towards Appia, that she had looked at them in the hope of finding something useful. 'Unfortunately in vain,' she said, adding, 'Appia appears not to know that in '76 the *Ring* was performed here and consequently there is nothing more to be discovered with regard to staging and directing.'[27]

Cosima has been pilloried for this sort of closed-mindedness as much as for the conventionality of her productions. But the censure does her an injustice. When it came to operatic production, she was as much a child of her times as Wagner himself. In addition, she faced a constant struggle to maintain the Festival and her position as head of it. To have mounted controversial, avant-garde productions would have undermined both. And in truth she was being condemned for not doing what no other opera producer was doing. Most criticism at the time, moreover, was less for her rigidity than for her changes. Lilli Lehmann, for example, devoted indignant page after indignant page of her memoirs to all the alterations Cosima made in the 1876 *Ring* when she did her own production of it. That her productions were admired and imitated everywhere is perhaps Cosima's strongest defence. Change began to overtake the operatic world at the turn of the century, to be sure. Opera-goers and critics were beginning to reflect on the deeper meaning of Wagner's myths. In 1898 Shaw's *The Perfect Wagnerite* appeared. A masterpiece of social—and socialist—exegesis, it did to Bayreuth's interpretation of Wagner's texts what Appia wanted to do to the treatment of his staging directions. But endeavours to realize such novel ideas on stage did not go over at all well with audiences. Indeed, when Appia himself accepted Toscanini's invitation to stage *Tristan* more than thirty-five years later—at La Scala in 1923—the reception of his production was so unfavourable that it had to be replaced with an orthodox version. Shortly after that his *Ring* in Basel was discontinued after *Walküre* as a result of hostile audience reaction.

As jealous guardian of her husband's artistic heritage, Cosima had long had on her conscience Wagner's remarks shortly before his death that he still owed the world *Tannhäuser* and that it was the next opera he wanted to do at Bayreuth. With the financial success of the 1889 Festival and a rest year in 1890 to provide time for preparations, Cosima was at last in a position to stage the work. Here, finally, was her opportunity to do more than put a bit of polish on productions done elsewhere and approved by her husband. *Tannhäuser* was Wagner's most frequently performed opera, indeed in some houses it was presented more often than any other work in the repertory. It was commonly performed, however, as a loosely strung together series of solos and choral highlights. Now for the first time she was on her own, and she was determined not only to show the world the real *Tannhäuser* but to conduct the decisive battle in her campaign to perform the works as drama rather than as opera.

The effort she lavished on the production was amazing; no opera in history, probably not even the *Ring* première, was prepared with such care. For years she had given thought to this project. She read everything Wagner had ever written of any relevance. She tracked down whatever information was available on the productions which he had supervised in Dresden in 1845, in Paris in 1861 and in Vienna in 1875. She pored over the score and the scenic directions in the text. An art historian, an archaeologist and a literary historian—each eminent in his field—furnished professional counsel while other experts provided detailed advice on ornaments and the design and cloth of the costumes. She herself did exhaustive research in museums and libraries in Munich and Berlin. No fewer than forty-four proposals for Venus's costume alone were submitted. Cosima even gave a historic name and title to each guest at the song contest—of which there were fully 116—and then took professional advice about their appropriate order on entering.

The opera, as Cosima presented it, was less about Tannhäuser's fate than about the antithesis between Venusberg and the Wartburg, between the Dionysian ethos and the Christian spirit of the Middle Ages, between Venus and Elisabeth. 'We must create something magnificently classical in the opening scene,' she wrote to Mottl, 'and in the second part evoke the very soul of the Middle Ages. . . .' To highlight this contrast, she replaced the usual ballet with a remarkable Bacchanal, choreographed by the Milan prima ballerina Virginia Zucchi, with nymphs, sirens, naiads, fauns and the like. And in her most original stroke, she cast Elisabeth as young, innocent and naïve. 'Above all I tried to show, with the drama in mind, a virginal, childlike figure,' she explained, and Venus as 'the fullest evocation of womankind in her most demonic and enchanting power'.[28] What resulted was a Christian mystery play that Chamberlain said, with unintended ambiguity, was 'as holy a work as *Parsifal*'.[29]

To design the staging, Cosima approached the Swiss painter Arnold Böcklin, whom she had asked years before to do the designs for the *Ring* and *Parsifal* premières. Now, as then, he declined, with the result that she fell back on the Brückners. They translated Wagner's stage directions in their usual way, with realistic woodland scenes and the architecture of the hall of song in heavy romanesque style. The opening Venusberg scene was a bit of Victoriana at its frilliest. These settings must have been tremendously admired since they became the international norm for many years, with the Brückners themselves churning out duplicates in great number.

The production was lavish. In addition to the 116 nobles, there was a hunting party of 65 men, a pilgrims' chorus of 32 older and 40 younger pilgrims as well as 30 knights and a Bacchanal of 64 dancers. The hunting party had to do without horses, which were considered too distracting, but was allowed a pack of hounds, which were trained to do a great deal of barking. A daring element was injected when the production was revived in 1904, and Isadora Duncan performed in the Bacchanal. Her dancing barefoot and scantily clad on stage was risqué enough, but promenading around the opera house during intermissions,

Venus's grotto in the 1891 *Tannhäuser*. For all its frippery, Cosima's solution to this problematic scene went over well with audiences at the time.

again barefoot and now clad in a classic Greek outfit, caused scandal in the ultra-staid Festival atmosphere. What finished her at Bayreuth, however, was having vouchsafed to Cosima at dinner at Wahnfried that the Master's errors were as great as his genius. She was not asked back.

Cosima chose the Paris version of the score with its extended Bacchanal scene and gave it to Mottl to conduct. Her most important vocal selection was Pauline de Ahna, who later became Richard Strauss's wife, a young and fairly inexperienced soprano, to sing Elisabeth and an even younger and less experienced Norwegian, Elisa Wiborg, as her cover. Rosa Sucher was chosen for Venus. For Tannhäuser—often considered the most difficult of all Wagnerian tenor roles, with the possible exception of Young Siegfried—she selected Max Alvary, Hermann Winkelmann and Heinrich Zeller to rotate. Reichmann and Scheidemantel shared the role of Wolfram.

Conservative Wagnerians were appalled when this early 'romantic' opera, not considered in the same class with the mature music dramas, was included in the Bayreuth repertory. And that the *Paris* version, rather than the good *German*—Dresden—version had been chosen, was treated as a further provocation. For years the fundamentalists had taunted Cosima for her alleged artistic infidelity to Wagner's heritage.

109

Now they mounted their final challenge. 'How her enemies and pseudo-friends did all they could to discredit my mother with the public!' Siegfried Wagner wrote in his memoirs.[30] Predictions that the Festival's regular audience would stay away in protest proved entirely erroneous. Spurred in part by rumours of a fantastic Bacchanal, the 1891 Festival excited unprecedented interest, with seats so oversubscribed that tickets on the black market sold for three or four times their face value. By now Bayreuth was one of the world's biggest musical attractions and reinforced the enormous popularity of Wagner's operas elsewhere. 'The *Tannhäuser* year was the decisive battle. My mother triumphed,' Siegfried recorded. Chamberlain said it marked the 'turning-point in the Festival's history'.[31]

Yet paradoxically the production was anything but a success with the critics. *The Times* summed it up in one phrase: 'while excellent, it was not as good as had been anticipated'.[32] Chamberlain informed Cosima that of 300 newspapers, only one had reported favourably. As with the 1876 *Ring*, expectations had exceeded results and even critics well disposed to Bayreuth had to resist a sense of let-down. 'Some of the public had expected unprecedented marvels in the staging, following rumours for a long time of fabulous sums spent on costumes and settings,' wrote the prominent Berlin daily *Vossische Zeitung*; but when nothing unusual was produced, many felt they could see *Tannhäuser* just as well at home.[33] Cosima's belief that she had presented music drama rather than opera convinced few. And her attempt to interpret the work as a Christian mystery play went against the text and the popular conception of it.

All the same, almost everyone found one or another scene splendidly done, the Venusberg most of all. But the entry of the guests in the second act was generally considered absurdly mechanical and the final choral scene, which Cosima had intended to draw the dramatic elements together and underscore the opera's spiritual message, did not find broad approval. The singing also received mixed reviews. Puttkamer was unimpressed, particularly by the three Tannhäusers. By some accounts, Wiborg, who had to jump in for de Ahna at two hours' notice on the opening day, was the star of the Festival.

Cosima's next great labour was *Lohengrin*, which she produced in 1894. As with *Tannhäuser*, her aim was not simply to dust off older treatments but to revise the conventional approach to the work—a lyrical romance—and give the world a music drama. She had already spelled out her view of the opera to Levi some years before when she expressed her dislike of 'all that heraldic trumpery of double eagles and swans' which, she said, 'imposed such a fussy operatic quality on poor *Lohengrin* that it had been buried like an unfortunate corpse under a deceptive, fancy blanket so that all its devout piety was scarcely visible'.[34] The central point of her reinterpretation was therefore to emphasize the religious-mystical aspects of the story and present it as a clash between Christianity and paganism—even though this was anything but

Lohengrin, Act II (1984). The stage arrangement—seen here in Brückner's sketch—was designed for the deployment of the chorus, all-important in this act.

Wagner's own concept. The action was moved back to the more appropriate tenth century, which was also the period of the legend, rather than the usual thirteenth century, when Christianity was triumphant. In this way Cosima, so often chastised for her conservatism, fashioned a *Lohengrin* that contrasted strikingly with the usual jingoistic mise-en-scène of German opera houses in those pre-1914 years.

Wagner had written precise stage instructions for the 1850 Weimar première and Max Brückner—his brother Gotthold had died two years earlier—followed these with resolute literalness. The first act portrayed a meadow dominated by the 'mighty, old judgement oak' of the composer's directions and of German tradition. The prescribed silhouette of the citadel of Antwerp was no longer in the background, however; Wagner had later discovered that his visual image was historically wrong, and Cosima now omitted this detail. The second act took place in the courtyard of the citadel, with the knights' quarters at the back, the kemenate on the left and the minster, all in the Brückners' usual romanesque style, on the right. The bridal chamber of the third act was an ornate, heavily draped chamber in the Byzantine manner. The atmosphere of the entire production was heavy and solemn, no doubt reflecting the social mood of the time.

The 1894 Festival was organized to meet a new threat from Munich. Ernst von Possart, manager of the Munich Court Opera and an old antagonist of Wagner's, had never reconciled himself to Munich's ancillary position in the Wagnerian world and intended to move Munich to the centre by holding something very close to a festival—periodic, special performances of each opera. Even more provocatively, the first of these Munich 'festivals' was to commence in 1894 with a production of *Lohengrin* no less. Bayreuth's response was to try to beat the competition by offering a unique 'spiritual-mystical trilogy' that season—*Parsifal*, *Tannhäuser* and *Lohengrin*.

In the event, Cosima's *Lohengrin* was well received. No one appears to have been enticed to Bayreuth by the trilogy nor seduced away by the Munich performance, even though it was accounted by some to be superior. Chamberlain considered the production the greatest in Bayreuth's history. '*Lohengrin* is here not an opera but a *drama*,' was his ultimate accolade.[35] Shaw was back for the Festival and his strictures on the orchestra notwithstanding, he found the opera 'immensely more entertaining, convincing and natural than it has ever seemed before'.[36] Like the majority of other critics, he attributed the success to the stagecraft and the choral directing, along with the vocal excellence of the chorus itself. There was also wide critical praise for the beauty and historical accuracy of the costumes, though much of Cosima's other meticulous historicism went unappreciated.

The singing was rather disappointing. Ernest van Dyck was judged to have been miscast as Lohengrin. In Puttkamer's opinion the same was true of Lilian Nordica as Elsa. However, Demeter Popovici was considered a solid Telramund and Marie Brema's Ortrud was the surprise and success of the Festival.

Casting had in fact developed into a highly controversial issue, though for ideological rather than vocal reasons, and once again pitted Cosima against the conservatives. The Wagner phenomenon had by now spread throughout Europe and America like an epidemic. Every year Bayreuth became more international, with increasing numbers of British, Americans and French in the audience and a growing number of foreign soloists on stage. The situation was particularly eye-catching in 1894 since many of the principals were foreign: van Dyck, Flemish; Nordica, American; Brema, English; Popovici, Rumanian; Zoltan Doeme, Hungarian; and Wiborg, Norwegian—not to mention the numerous Austrians, who were not really accounted as foreign. The liberal papers commented on the foreign 'threat' with tongue-in-cheek remarks on what a change it would be to hear a German sing on the Bayreuth stage or find a 'German spoken here' sign in a restaurant. In their view Germans should have felt flattered at Bayreuth's attraction to a cosmopolitan audience. But for conservatives the situation was becoming intolerable. Was not the great purpose of this 'German Olympia' to bring about the regeneration of the Reich rather than to create an international meeting-place for snobs, enticed by foreigners on stage? Hence the paradox that some of the most fanatical Wagnerians were turning into some of the Festival's—and Cosima's—most unhappy critics.

Not surprisingly the conservative attitude towards Bayreuth was linked to an increasingly unpleasant nationalism and xenophobia that characterized the *Kaiserreich* as it approached its high noon. The mood was expressed with admirable candour in 1894 by the *Rheinisch-Westfälische Zeitung*, the daily paper of the Ruhr industrial establishment.[37] Asserting that the Festival had become a 'purely business enterprise' and 'a curiosity for rich foreigners', it complained that it was now 'ill-bred' to speak German in Bayreuth where 'French and English now dominate'. 'Except from the stage, scarcely a German word is to be heard'—here in the very place which Wagner had 'dedicated to the German spirit'. The Festival belonged to the nation, 'but foreigners now come with their arrogance and their money and shove aside the children of the nation', the article went on. An American millionairess had arrived with her own carriage and horses. Perhaps she had horse-racing in mind: 'In the mornings "handicap", in the afternoons *Parsifal!*' Instead of being the centre of German culture, as Wagner had intended, Bayreuth was a 'Babel', a 'boarding school for foreigners'. And as for Cosima: 'How the Master was angered when his wife preferred to speak to her father Liszt in French, which was in fact her native tongue!' She was a 'clever woman'. 'But half Magyar, half French she is hardly appropriate to hold a key role in matters of German art.' Because of her, 'foreign artists have been selected . . . for this true German institution'. 'They might be taught to sing and act, but who can instil in them the German mind, German sensibility?'

That article was nothing compared with what was being turned out by the so-called Bayreuth Circle. Formed around the *Bayreuther Blätter* with the original intention of propagating the ideas of Richard Wagner, the group had developed by the last decade of the century into a political sect dedicated to conservatism, nationalism and racism. Many of the Circle were publicists, and in their writings they described the Festspielhaus, for instance, as a 'glorious Aryan fortress' and a 'temple of art for the renewal of Aryan blood, for the awakening of the general consciousness of the Indo-German nation and specifically for the strengthening of a healthy Germanness'. The Circle took its place beside such contemporaneous organizations as the Pan-German League, the Colonial Society and the Naval Society in agitating for German expansionism in Europe and overseas. In such ways, Bayreuth itself was being transformed into a centre of an aggressive, chauvinist ideology and an instrument of German power—the Krupps of the culture industry.

On the issue of inviting foreign singers, Cosima was unrepentant. The need to cultivate a new generation of Wagnerian singers, as those trained by the composer went into retirement, was becoming acute. A planned new production of the *Ring* brought it to a head. Only three veterans of the première could be asked back: Lilli Lehmann as Brünnhilde, Marie Lehmann as a Norn and Heinrich Vogl as Loge. In looking for new talent, Cosima did not seek out stars. She wanted vocalists who were receptive to the Bayreuth spirit and to her guidance. Or, as Lilli Lehmann put it, 'All roads may lead to Rome but to the Bayreuth of today there is but one—the road of slavish subjection.'[38] To their nationality, Cosima was indifferent. Not, however, to their race. Picking up an axiom of Wagner's—'We have a German Reich of the Jewish nation'—she added a corollary: 'Now we want a German theatre of all nationals except for the "chosen people." '[39] Since her chief talent scout was Julius Kniese, she was not in any case likely to have been proffered anyone racially unacceptable.

To train new soloists, Cosima established a style training school, thereby realizing an old dream of her husband's for a Wagnerian conservatory. She placed Kniese in charge of musical training, while she herself gave instruction in dramatics and staging. Only seventeen candidates signed up when it opened in 1892 and, perhaps because of the stark regimen, most left before their training was finished. By 1898 only five students remained and the school eventually closed. But during its brief existence, it reared a number of highly talented singers—all of them young, inexperienced and entirely unknown. Several indeed came almost directly off farms.

One of these was Ellen Gulbranson, the first of the great Scandinavian sopranos. An awkward Norwegian farm girl, she became one of Cosima's finest creations. Arriving in Bayreuth with little or no experience, she launched her career as Brünnhilde. After each season she returned to her farm, leaving only to attend the next Festival. 'She puts her voice on ice in between times,' Mottl commented to von Puttkamer, 'that is why the organ is so well preserved.'

Another Bayreuth product was Alois Burgstaller, a farm boy who, after two insignificant roles in the 1894 Festival, sprang at the age of twenty-four into the part of Siegfried. Hans Breuer, the classic Mime of his time, and Otto Briesemeister, an outstanding Loge from 1899, were other notable alumni. There were any number of additional singers who were not products of the school but who were considered to have benefited from Cosima's training. Ernst Kraus, whom Puttkamer found negligible as Siegfried in Berlin in 1888, was transformed by Cosima into what he described as 'an incomparable Siegfried' at Bayreuth from 1899 to 1909. Even one of the leading singers of his time, Anton van Rooy, 'subordinated himself unreservedly to Frau Wagner's instructions', as Puttkamer phrased it, and she is credited with helping him to become an eminent Wotan.

Cosima also confronted a less acute but more sensitive problem with conductors. In 1889 a promising newcomer, Richard Strauss, appeared on the scene. A musical assistant that year and a rehearsal conductor in

1891, he impressed Cosima and Mottl by his slow tempi and his evident submissiveness. He played up to Cosima shamelessly. Angling for an invitation to conduct at the Festival, he wrote to Cosima: '. . . Yes, the Jews have come a long way with us. . . . Is it really too much when I say from the bottom of my heart "too bad"? So is poor *Parsifal* never to be let out of the Jewish torture chamber; why must the poor work suffer from the "services" of Levi?'[40] When Cosima invited him to conduct *Tannhäuser* the following year, he had to decline for reasons of health. But after then conducting the work in 1894, he was not invited back, and the friendly relations between the two came to an end. It is generally assumed that he fell out of favour because of his compositions. Cosima regarded their style as a betrayal of Wagnerian principles while Siegfried regarded them as dangerous competition to his own operas. 'A pig sty of pig sties', an embittered Strauss complained to his fiancée of the Festival.[41]

A second development was Levi's retirement, for health reasons, after the 1894 season. Before leaving Bayreuth, he penned an acerbic letter to Cosima about the degrading atmosphere in which he had worked for the last twelve years:

> I believe [ran one sentence] that everything centres on one point: I am a Jew and in and around Wahnfried it has become a dogma that a Jew appears a certain way, thinks and acts in a certain way and above all that a Jew is incapable of selfless devotion to anything; as a result everything I do and say is judged from this point of view and therefore everything I do and say is considered indecent or at least alien.[42]

In the meantime Siegfried Wagner, now in his early twenties, began his own conducting career. As a youth he had planned to be an architect. But in 1892, while travelling in the Far East, he decided that it was music to which he wanted to devote his life. Returning to Bayreuth, he studied under Engelbert Humperdinck, Kniese, Richter and Mottl. Assistant for lighting in 1891, musical assistant in 1892 and rehearsal conductor in 1894, he was appointed a conductor at the 1896 Festival. Even so, composing was Siegfried's greatest interest, and he turned out no fewer than thirteen operas, a symphony, a violin and a flute concerto along with a variety of lesser works. Composing was also his greatest failure. His first opera blazed brilliantly, then fizzled; the others were rarely performed outside provincial theatres.

In 1903 Cosima faced what she considered high treason on the part of the faithful Mottl, of all people. He had agreed not only to conduct in New York for a season but to be principal conductor at that arch-rival, the Munich Opera. That finished his Bayreuth career. With the removal of Strauss, the retirement of Levi and the betrayal of Mottl, Cosima fell back on Richter, who now became the pillar of the Festival. Two new conductors were inducted early in the century. One was Karl

Muck, an aspiring musical assistant since 1892; he was given *Parsifal* and became the successor to Levi. The other was Michael Balling, a musical assistant and violist in the Festival orchestra. 'Balling belongs to Bayreuth, both in his attitude and in his ability,' Cosima wrote to Richter, letting slip her order of priorities.[43]

With the passage of two decades, Cosima was ready to face the challenge of bringing to the stage a new production of the *Ring*. This time she had in mind not a reinterpretation but a resurrection, with the blemishes of the original smoothed over. Since the old settings and costumes had been sold, new ones had to be commissioned. Max Brückner painted the decorations and based them on the old Hoffmann designs, making them even more monochrome and more realistic in detail. Seeing the drafts in 1894, a delighted Cosima wrote, 'Your sketches express the most beautiful naturalism; everything is organic and is worthy of the great work of which it is part.'[44] One or two changes were introduced, also for the sake of realism—the Ride of the Valkyries was now performed by children on wooden horses drawn across the stage in front of a backdrop and Fricka's car was drawn by two live rams. However, advances in technology, such as the electrification of the Theatre eight years earlier, were scarcely exploited. As far as comparison can be made, the staging appears to have been little different from that of the première production.

With the costumes there were some marked alterations—hardly surprising in view of Cosima's outspoken discontent with Döpler's originals. This time Cosima turned to the German landscapist Hans Thoma, assisted by a Munich illustrator, Arpad Schmidhammer, who shunned historical models to design costumes that were practical to wear and relatively simple in appearance. Most female characters—in particular Erda, the Norns, Fricka and Sieglinde—were clad in plain gowns. Colours were toned down considerably and made more compatible with the staging.

Cosima put her stamp on the production in more significant ways, by shaping the conducting, singing and acting. From marginal comments in her piano score, it is clear how she sought to dampen the orchestra even in the most impressive passages, to train the singers to make their gestures in anticipation of the text and to downplay any lyricism. The stylization of singing and acting in this production earned Cosima more criticism, perhaps, than in any other—not just by those who might have had a *parti pris* but by bystanders such as Romain Rolland. 'Brünnhilde apart,' he wrote at the time, 'they all act in conventional tableaux vivants which quite appalled me and spoiled Bayreuth for me. . . . The hell with it! It is not worth coming to Bayreuth if one cannot experience—in these universal dramas—an uninhibited outburst of passion.'[45] But to all such complaints, Cosima had a pat answer, as recorded by Lilli Lehmann: 'You remember, Siegfried, do you not, that it was done this

A photograph of *Die Walküre*, Act III in the 1896 production shows how closely Cosima followed the original *Ring* staging.

way in 1876?' Whereupon Siegfried, who had been six at the time, would always respond, 'I believe you are right, mamma.'[46]

In contrast to 1876, the critics this time concentrated on the performance rather than on the work itself. By and large they found the whole greater than the sum of its parts. The *Vossische Zeitung* expressed as well as any newspaper the *juste milieu* of the critical reaction. The writer found the settings 'excellent in atmosphere and in beauty of conception', though no advance on Berlin's.[47] The Ride of the Valkyries was 'wretched' and the Magic Fire resembled 'garden fireworks'. However, the woodland scenes in *Siegfried* were 'poetic', the dragon was 'a masterpiece of stage technology' and the decorations in the first and last acts of *Götterdämmerung* were stunning. The weakest feature was the costumes, betraying Wahnfried's 'spirit of anti-artistic prudery'. Freia, for instance, looked upholstered rather than clothed. As for the singing, Carl Perron's Wotan was poor, Vogl's Loge 'a triumph', Brema's Fricka was adequate, Breuer's Mime and Friedrichs's Alberich were 'wonderful', the Rhinemaidens swam better than they sang, Sucher's Sieglinde was heartwarming but Emil Gerhäuser's Siegmund was inadequate, Burgstaller had a way to go before being a notable Siegfried and though Lehmann started well as Brünnhilde, she ended badly. As for the orchestra, it 'alone was worth a pilgrimage to Bayreuth'.

This account leaves out the sensation of the season, Gulbranson's

117

The stylized gestures of Cosima's Bayreuth are evident in the photograph of Marie Brema as Fricke in the 1896 *Ring*. The amber necklace was Cosima's own.

The 1896 Valkyries. 'I saw and heard *Walküre*, was delighted by what I heard and bored by what I saw' (Wilhelm Busch).

Brünnhilde. A pneumatic-shaped, ungainly actress, she had a large voice which, as Puttkamer said, effortlessly 'poured forth in radiant glory'. She was such a success that her alternate, Lilli Lehmann, left Bayreuth never to return and Gulbranson reigned as Bayreuth's sovereign Brünnhilde until her last season in 1924. Other critics were also more favourably disposed towards Burgstaller. Puttkamer found him an 'almost ideal' Siegfried: 'powerful, poetic, simple and unaffected'.[48] It was, however, a widespread view that he was at his best as Young Siegfried and perhaps even more outstanding as Siegmund, a role he took over in 1899.

Siegfried Wagner's conducting career began with both a bang and a whimper. The explosion came in the form of a letter Siegfried sent to a cultural journal, later published in the semi-official handbook for Festival audiences. In it Siegfried made uncompromisingly clear that authority in Bayreuth lay with the stage director and that a conductor had only to follow 'orders'. His own interest, he stressed, lay in the former; good conductors would always be available. This crass put-down of conductors made more a fool of Siegfried than of the profession and did not go over at all well in music circles. The whimper was his own conducting.

Richter, Mottl and Siegfried shared the conducting that summer, Siegfried doing the fourth of the five cycles. Among the public there was widespread resentment that tickets went on sale before it was clear who was conducting which cycle, since few wanted to hear the tyro. His performance, as far as can be told, was a flop. Strauss described it as 'horrible'. Years later an English Wagnerian wrote a letter to *The Times* describing it as 'without exception the most slipshod I ever listened to at Bayreuth'.[49] Unfortunately Siegfried's conducting improved little. Shaw and even Mahler praised it, and on occasion it reached splendid heights, as is evident from recordings. But more often it was lifeless, mechanical and of a narcolepsy-inducing languor.

Despite the Festival's astonishing successes, Wahnfried continued to suffer deep-seated insecurity—fears for Bayreuth's institutional hegemony and artistic primacy as well as concern for the fortunes, artistic and financial, of the Wagner family. '40 million, that is how much I need to give Germans a festival; perhaps sometime it will be given to me by a good soul, a Jew who wants to atone for the sins of his race.'[50] Thus Cosima in 1889. Although some concern sprang from plain Wagnerian paranoia, there was a genuine danger from Munich, where Possart was now having constructed for his 'Wagner festivals' an opera house based on Semper's original designs and named the 'Munich Richard Wagner Festspielhaus'. Bayreuth was in a weak position to fight back, being heavily dependent on the Munich Opera's support—for singers, musicians and production assistants—and therefore on Possart's good will. Groß argued tenaciously that Wagner's assignment of his operas to King Ludwig gave performance rights to the Munich Opera alone, not to any other house. The argument failed when legally tested, but eventually—

in part through the good offices of the Bavarian Prince Regent who was since 1888 the formal patron of the Bayreuth Festival—the parties reached an agreement much to Bayreuth's advantage. The new opera house itself was to be called the Prince Regent's Theatre. In any given year works performed in Bayreuth might not be performed in Munich and soloists who sang at the Festival might not sing in Munich. Bayreuth was consequently in a position to set the operatic agenda and to remove any risk of direct competition.

None the less, relations between the two establishments, far from improving, worsened. The immediate cause of friction was Possart's determination to perform *Parsifal* in Munich. This new danger happened to coincide with consideration by the Reichstag of extending German copyright from thirty to fifty years. Wahnfried made strong representations on behalf of *Parsifal*, due to come out of copyright in 1913. In May 1901 Cosima appealed to the Reichstag 'to honour the greatest of Masters by carrying out his last will'.[51] Her plea was strongly endorsed by Richard Strauss—possibly with a view to his own operas—but it gained little support and in the end what had come to be known as 'Lex Cosima' was rejected. Legislators could see little reason to make an exception for a single work by a certain artist, and they suspected—probably unjustly—that Wahnfried's interest was primarily financial.

With a dozen years still to go, Cosima hoped that *Parsifal* might yet gain legal protection. However, in 1903 a terrible blow fell when the Metropolitan Opera in New York performed the work with artistic support from Munich. There had already been several concert performances, but plans in London and New York to stage the opera had heretofore been dropped, out of consideration for Cosima. Wahnfried had used every possible legal and moral means to forestall this so-called 'rape of the grail'—from an appeal to the Kaiser to a civil suit in the New York courts. In New York itself the mayor and some clergy, who considered the opera blasphemous, were embarrassed. But since the United States was not a party to the Bern copyright convention, the efforts to ban the performance were fruitless. It was performed on Christmas Eve and during the following two years had no fewer than 354 performances around the United States. The German press whipped itself up into a frenzy of xenophobia, though probably less out of concern for *Parsifal* than for German cultural sovereignty. Cosima's revenge was terrible. Anyone associated with the production—including van Rooy and Burgstaller, among other important Bayreuth singers—was banned from the Festival and the conductor, Alfred Hertz, was never again invited to conduct opera in Germany.

With the new century—which coincided with the twenty-fifth anniversary of the Festival—Cosima completed her work, bringing last to the stage the first of his operas that Wagner considered suitable for Bayreuth, *Der fliegende Holländer*. Her decision to perform another early romantic opera not only angered the hardliners once again but caused apprehension even among some of her firmest sympathizers. As usual, she subjected the opera to her own mode of rigorous analysis. She studied reports of previous productions at Weimar in 1850 and at Munich in 1864 and procured from abroad books and illustrations bearing on every relevant aspect of Scandinavian architecture, interiors, dress and the like. On the basis of all this, she instructed Brückner on settings and the painter Maximilian Rossmann on costumes. Although she was now sufficiently self-confident to accept and reject from these sources what she wished, her naturalistic sets were essentially conventional. Entirely original, however, was her decision to give the opera dramatic intensity by performing it without a break, the scene changes carried out behind a curtain.

What made the visual impression a success was the stage management, which Cosima had placed in her son's hands. Through his skilled use of lighting, scrims, steam and colour, Siegfried was credited with stage images of great beauty, the final scene resembling a work of Turner, a painter he much admired.

For fully two years Cosima trained the singers. Van Rooy was the Dutchman; Emmy Destinn, Senta; Ernestine Schumann-Heink, Mary; Kraus and Burgstaller alternated as Erik; and Peter Heidkamp was Daland. Their singular success made the work more popular than it had ever been. The critical response was almost uniformly positive. The *Frankfurter Zeitung* headed its report 'Miracle of Light and Cloud'. A Berlin paper praised Bayreuth for 'the best directing in the world'.

The Wagner family around 1900. From left: Marie Gravina (Blandine's daughter), Daniela, Blandine Countess Gravina, Guido Gravina (Blandine's son), Siegfried, Henry Thode (Daniela's husband), Isolde, Eva, Cosima, Manfred Gravina (Blandine's son).

The Wagner dynasty prospered in these years. Thanks to Groß's astuteness, the Festival's capital reached the million mark level and a family fortune of four times that amount accumulated. Meanwhile the family itself grew. The two daughters of Cosima and Hans von Bülow were married—Blandine to Biagio Gravina, a Sicilian count, and Daniela to Henry Thode, an art historian. Cosima hoped, family legend had it, that her two Wagner daughters would make a musical match—to Anton Bruckner and Richard Strauss, indeed. Isolde did in fact marry a musician—Franz Beidler, who had come to Bayreuth in 1894 as a student of Kniese's. Considered quite promising, he was appointed musical assistant at the 1896 Festival. He later conducted in Moscow and Manchester and at Bayreuth in 1904 and 1906. In the latter year, however, there was a tremendous family dispute. Beidler, unwilling to recognize Siegfried as sole heir-apparent, wanted a more important role in the Festival for himself. Cosima supported her son to the hilt. He explicitly accused his brother-in-law of lacking the Bayreuth spirit—among other failings, he had not even read the Master's collected works—and banned him from entering the Festspielhaus again. *Hausverbot*, used against the singers in the New York *Parsifal*, was now imposed on a member of the family.

But Siegfried had his own problems. Although he fathered an illegitimate child in 1900, he was predominantly and promiscuously homosexual. Involved in one embarrassing scrape after another, he had repeatedly to be rescued by the faithful Adolf von Groß. Cosima knew nothing of this, and in any case the moment was approaching when Siegfried was to take over the Festival.

In 1906 Cosima produced an even more subdued version of her original *Tristan*, which was very well received. It was her last season. In December, while visiting her friend Prince Hohenlohe, she suffered several severe heart attacks. 'Destiny', according to Moulin Eckart, 'was knocking at the door, and it was assumed that the hour had come when she would follow the Master into the grave.' Instead she survived, though now entering what her biographer delicately described as 'that strange time when she lived between dreaming and waking'.[52]

4

'Oh, Siegfried! I was always yours'
(*Siegfried*)

'He who must renounce', Cosima wrote to Prince Hohenlohe, 'can learn to renounce.'[1] And difficult as it must have been, she scrupulously abstained from any further role in the Festival. For a time Siegfried discussed his plans with her, but she avoided giving any impression of interference, not even setting foot in the Festspielhaus until 1924—and then only to observe rehearsals of one act of *Parsifal* and one act of *Meistersinger*. Her life settled into a tranquil routine, and she could be seen as regular as clockwork walking arm in arm with her son in the Hofgarten or the streets of Bayreuth where she was regarded as an awesome, almost mythical figure.

After another heart attack in 1910, she grew increasingly frail and spent more and more of her time confined to her room in Wahnfried. Clad in a flowing silver kimono matching her ample silver hair, she was described as a 'white apparition' by many who caught a glimpse of her. Her eyesight deteriorated to the point of blindness, and she occasionally suffered from nervous prostration—periods of unconsciousness that might last for days, migraine attacks and hallucinations of hearing a military band. Her doctors forbade her to listen to more than brief snatches of music, and with the passage of time she lived enclosed in her own world of the past. Visitors taken to meet her in the early 1920s were embarrassed to find that she spoke about conductors and singers, long gone, as though they were still performing.

On the Green Hill everything went along as though there had been no change. With his experience as a director and stage designer, Siegfried was well prepared. And behind him was the full weight of Cosima's institutional legacy. The conductors and singers, the chorus master, technical director and chief vocal coach had all been chosen by her. A new position of dramatic coach was created and filled by Luise Reuß-Belce, a noted Bayreuth soprano and, more to the point, a protégée of Cosima's. Daniela took over Isolde's old position as costume

The apostolic succession: Cosima and
Siegfried following Cosima's retirement.

Siegfried and his assistants in 1914. Luise
Reuß-Belce on his right, Theo Raven (assistant director) at his far left. The others
were music coaches and stage assistants.

designer and Max Brückner continued to construct the staging. Everything ensured that the institution would run along the same old lines.

That was of course the problem. Bayreuth was in a rut. Elsewhere
stage production was beginning to be revolutionized by the theories of
Appia and the writings of the British stage designer Gordon Craig as well
as through experimentation with electric light. In Vienna, most notably,
Gustav Mahler and the stage designer Alfred Roller, head of the Vienna
Secession, were employing these new techniques to bring out highly
innovative and avidly discussed Wagnerian productions. Bayreuth was
being left behind, and the question widely asked was whether Siegfried
would modernize or leave things as they were. In 1907 he gave his reply.
'The right answer is not an either/or,' he said in a newspaper interview.[2]
Götterdämmerung could not be produced like an Ibsen play. What
worked in one opera house was not necessarily right for another. Craig's
ideas were marvellous but could not be applied everywhere. As for
Bayreuth, he concluded, the future lay in the new tool of electricity.

How could anything more have been expected? Crushed by a domineering matriarchy and indoctrinated since his earliest years in the
Bayreuth ethos, Siegfried was bereft of either the inclination or the
strength to shake off the weight of tradition. Intellectually, he never
went through an Oedipal phase; his parents' outlook remained part of
himself. He accepted his mother's productions as definitive even as he
treated his father's stage instructions as sacred.

Emotionally, however, he could not have been more unlike his father
and mother; he was soft, tolerant, genial and without a fanatical bone in
his body. The Bayreuth atmosphere therefore began to change. No
longer was there automatic hostility to new ideas and ways of doing
things. There was a willingness to experiment with new technical and
lighting equipment. The old crushing stylization of acting and singing
was less rigidly enforced. In his personal relations, Siegfried had a
winsome manner, rooted in his innate friendliness and modesty. The
mood in the Festspielhaus became more human, relaxed and sponta-
neous. A gentle monarchy replaced a stern autocracy.

The warm, familial atmosphere of those early days was nicely conveyed in a 1911 memoir by Anna Bahr-Mildenburg:

> Promptly at 9 o'clock Siegfried Wagner drove up in his carriage. Almost
> always dressed in plus-fours and yellow stockings, he walked among the
> artists in the best of humour, greeted each one with some pleasant, amusing
> comment, stood in front of the door and . . . called out, 'All right, folks, it's
> time, come along, come along', loudly clapping his hands and, with him
> leading the way, the whole assembly entered the Festspielhaus. . . .
>
> And then . . . one could observe and admire Siegfried in his element! He
> is the born director, tireless in his dedication, inexhaustibly energetic. . . . He
> never lost his patience. . . . No relaxing of attention, no day-dreaming, no
> imperfection was ever allowed; he expected everyone to do his best and with

this combination of uncompromising strictness along with an uncommonly kindly manner in guiding people along, he succeeded in getting everyone to accept his purposes and aims.[3]

Given Siegfried's own contradictions, it is scarcely surprising that his Bayreuth was a house divided. Whatever had been laid down by his parents was preserved unchanged out of a sense of strict filial duty. Whatever they had not explicitly ordained, Siegfried felt free to handle in his own way. So on the one hand everything from stage design to ideology remained frozen in the past; on the other, techniques such as lighting, colour and above all directing looked cautiously towards the future. The resulting inconsistencies were the great weakness of Siegfried's work.

In the years before 1914 Siegfried brought out three new productions. He based each on Cosima's originals while taking some account of contemporary developments. The first was *Lohengrin* in 1908. The settings, new except for the bridal chamber, were somewhat cleaner and less romanticized. In every scene Siegfried added colour, having disliked what he labelled the 'brown sauce' of the earlier production. More significantly, he made several important advances. Up to now Bayreuth had only used painted backcloths for its settings. In the second act

Siegfried's stage plan for the 1908 production of *Lohengrin* Act II rigidly followed the spatial organization set down by the composer and reaffirmed by Cosima.

Siegfried now replaced some of the old painted flats with a partially three-dimensional citadel. He also introduced a cyclorama, a curved backcloth providing a markedly greater sense of depth and theatrical illusion. It was used in the opening and closing scenes—the meadow on the river bank—with good effect.

Siegfried gave a great deal of attention to group choreography, especially important in *Lohengrin* as the most 'choral' of Wagner's operas. His skill, already apparent in his 1901 *Fliegender Holländer*, in moulding individuals into groups and integrating groups into the overall production, was now evident. Although spoiled at times by too much movement and gesticulation, group directing has been considered one of his outstanding talents.

Naturally those who had hoped that Siegfried would bring about a thoroughgoing change were disappointed. They criticized the interpretation for 'theatrical superficiality' and even 'mediocrity'; they found the directing 'conventional'; they likened the choral scenes to 'philistine gesturing' and panned the staging as the imitative work of an epigone. But praise surpassed criticism, with a consensus that he had forged a satisfactory middle way between the old and the new. He was credited with 'directing talent of the highest order' and an interpretation of 'fresh simplicity'.

Although Siegfried's conducting met either silence or disapproval, the singing was acclaimed. Albert von Puttkamer went so far as to maintain that the performances reached 'perhaps the absolute zenith offered at Bayreuth up to then' and offered 'a never to be equalled model for all opera houses'.[4] In his judgement Alfred von Bary was the greatest Lohengrin of his time and Lilly Hafgren-Waag, one of Siegfried's discoveries, for many years the best Elsa. The selection of Hafgren made clear that Siegfried intended to maintain Bayreuth's international casting. She was Swedish, and there were also several Americans in important roles—Edyth Walker (Ortrud), Allen Hinckley (King Heinrich), Gertrude Rennyson (alternate Elsa), Minnie Saltzmann-Stevens (alternate Kundry) and Bennet Challis (alternate Dutchman). Under its new director, the chorus was now more accomplished than ever. Hugo Rüdel combined the talents of an adept musician with the discipline of a Prussian drill sergeant to become in time a Bayreuth institution in his own right.

It was with his production of *Die Meistersinger* in 1911 that Siegfried achieved his great prewar triumph. Virtually everyone admired it, and virtually everything about it was admired. Although modelled on Cosima's 1888 version, the staging was now both simpler and more visually attractive. There were also several significant alterations. Siegfried moved the opening scene, in St Catherine's church, from the nave to a spacious assembly room, a much improved stage image that was copied elsewhere. And by installing a wide cyclorama, he gave the meadow in the final act greater depth and impressiveness. Daniela

Siegfried's sketch for the 1911 production of *Die Meistersinger*, Act I. 'I have never seen any stage picture that came so near to making you feel that it had a soul' (Ernest Newman).

designed the costumes, taking as her models various portraits by Dürer, Holbein and their contemporaries. The opera itself was presented as pure comedy, a mood reinforced by the elegant lightness of Hans Richter's reading of the score. Lilly Hafgren's Eva was the most impressive von Puttkamer could recall; he and others had high praise as well for the Beckmesser of Heinrich Schultz, another of Siegfried's discoveries. One of the few quibbles about the performance was that some of the acting was still in thrall to Cosima's hyper-stylization.

What most impressed audiences and critics was the directing. In particular they rated Siegfried's handling of the difficult riot scene of the second act a masterpiece. Indeed, the entire production had such a modern feel to it that Siegfried earned the reputation of being one of the outstanding directors of the German stage. Some enthusiasts compared him to Max Reinhardt, the theatrical genius just then becoming famous in Munich and Berlin, and the *Frankfurter Zeitung* went so far as to describe him as 'the greatest stage artist of the day'.[5] Prominent experts well outside the Bayreuth claque credited him with taking Bayreuth with one step into the contemporary theatrical world. The general glow of delight was clouded only by the knowledge that the second season brought to an end the conducting career of 69-year-old Hans Richter. Following his final performance, there was an ovation that was probably unprecedented since 1876. But it could not move him to appear on stage. 'Where the Master stood, it is not appropriate for me to stand,' was his only comment before leaving the pit for the last time.[6]

In 1914 Siegfried restaged *Der fliegende Holländer*. He spruced up the 1901 décor to make it more realistic and added some solid props and a cyclorama, lending the visual image a greater sense of depth and openness. He allowed the soloists unprecedented freedom to interpret their roles, giving the performance a certain spontaneity.

The weight of critical opinion was hostile to every aspect of the production. Siegfried's interpretation—as a music drama rather than a dramatic ballad—was judged to be flawed. His conducting was found stiff and languorous. The cast—Bennet Challis and Walter Soomer as the Dutchman, Barbara Kemp as Senta and Michael Bohnen as Daland—fared little better. Even von Puttkamer found them merely 'interesting'. One critic damned the production and the performance as scarcely worthy of a second-rate opera company. There were, however, some who found it powerful and convincing. 'We were all greatly thrilled,' Albert Schweitzer recalled years afterwards.[7] 'It seemed as though we were getting to know it well for the first time. And never did I hear the work so well conducted as by him. It was so marvellously simple and fluid.'

In the course of bringing out these three new productions, Siegfried also touched up *Parsifal* and the *Ring*, which were performed every season. In 1911 Brückner executed a new backdrop for the magic garden and Daniela designed costumes for Kundry and the Flowermaidens which were mercifully less absurd than those of the past. The sets themselves had badly deteriorated, critics describing them as 'unworthy', 'tasteless', even 'unbelievable'. The *Ring* decorations fared little better.

The singing in these two works ranged from magnificent to mediocre, leaving Siegfried with a reputation as an unreliable judge of voice. The leading tenor, probably the leading singer, of these years was Alfred von Bary, who sang—in addition to Lohengrin—the roles of Siegmund and Siegfried. Walter Soomer, outstanding both as singer and actor, was an excellent Wotan and also impressive as Amfortas and Sachs. Ellen Gulbranson continued to thrill audiences with her Brünnhilde, though her vocal powers gradually showed signs of decline. The Czech contralto Ernestine Schumann-Heink was celebrated as the best Erda and Waltraute of her time. Bahr-Mildenburg returned to sing Kundry from 1911 to 1914; her 'demonic' interpretation of the role turned *Parsifal* into a 'Kundry tragedy' and was long remembered with awe. But many important roles had inadequate singers, weakening the performances as a whole.

The conducting staff during this period—Richter, Michael Balling, Karl Muck and Siegfried himself—were all carry-overs from Cosima's day. Siegfried never challenged the old ideological, racial and other criteria, with the result that Mahler, Weingartner, Strauss, Arthur Nikisch, Max von Schillings and Siegmund von Hausegger, noted Wagnerians all, were not invited. In fact the only Bayreuth conductors of the highest rank in the first dozen years of the century were Muck and

Richter. Since festival programmes did not identify conductors, critics—whether in genuine or feigned ignorance of who was in the pit—were relatively impersonal in their comments. But that did not save Siegfried, who received some hard critical knocks. 'Unequal to tasks that require great style' was a fairly typical assessment—in this case of his *Lohengrin* in 1908.

Although there were fewer foreigners in the audiences during the early years of the century, Bayreuth retained its allure as a place of pilgrimage—socially, musically, ideologically. The pilgrims came from as far away as China and California. As usual the Central European aristocracy was present in force; scarcely ever did a princely house of Germany, Austria or Hungary fail to be represented. Czar Ferdinand of Bulgaria—a Saxe-Coburg by blood—was an invariable fixture, attending every Festival from 1882 until 1939. Verdi and Brahms apart, every European composer and conductor of importance showed up at least once, if only to attend *Parsifal*. No one with any cultural pretensions could admit to not having been there, and for well-to-do British and Americans it was an essential part of the continental grand tour, a stop on the way to the picture galleries of Dresden and Berlin. The British were always the most numerous among the foreigners, even warranting the spiritual ministrations of the Reverend D. Holland Stubbs, who held Anglican services three times on Sundays at the Central School. There were also large numbers of Americans and French. In 1909—a year in which Alban Berg, Virginia Woolf, Thomas Mann and Prince Rangoit of Siam were also there—roughly 250 British, 215 Americans and, greatly under-represented this year, 90 French signed the Visitor's Book.

Even in a nation where culture was of central and daily importance, the attention which Germans lavished in these years on Wagnerian opera and on Bayreuth was extraordinary. In part this was a measure of how far Wagner had by now eaten his way into the national consciousness.

> It is scarcely possible to exaggerate how deeply the last generation was spellbound by the influence of Richard Wagner, not so decisively by his music as by the gestures of his characters, by his ideas. . . . There is always someone—Lohengrin, Walther, Siegfried, Wotan—who can do everything and knock down everything, who can release suffering virtue, punish vice and bring general salvation, striking an exaggerated pose, with the sound of fanfares and with lighting effects and staging.

Thus Walther Rathenau, a Foreign Minister of the Weimar Republic, writing in 1918 of his prewar countrymen.[8]

But in larger part it was because the operas and the Festival had become embroiled in a tremendous ideological battle. The struggle was openly joined at the turn of the century, following an ever broadening conservative reaction against the entire social and ideological course of the recently founded Reich, with its industrialization, urbanization and Jewish assimilation. Tradition vs modernity—and behind that, art vs science—was perceived to be the issue in the great contest for the soul of Germany. The forces of counter-revolution took shape around a neo-romantic nationalism that harked back to antique Germanic concepts, expressed in a venerable and untranslatable Germanic vocabulary—*heldenhaftes Volkstum, Herrenvolk, Germanentum, Herrenmensch*—implying the uniqueness of the Teutonic race. No weapon could have been more convenient to combat 'moral decline' and to promote 'spiritual renewal', 'salvation' and 'a regeneration of the German soul'—such were some of the terms repeated over and over—than culture, or German culture, or German culture of a certain type. What began as a crank *Kulturkritik* developed almost overnight into an ideological rampage that translated Wagnerian opera into a national cultural religion with Bayreuth as its supreme place of worship.

To read what was being written about Bayreuth in the early years of the century is to enter a never-never land of a nationalism gone berserk. Even as rational and civilized a person as Hermann Bahr, the Austrian dramatist and husband of Anna Bahr-Mildenburg, published an essay on Bayreuth in 1912 that began: 'What is German, my heart never so strongly and firmly knew as here. This strangely deep and full-sounding word—German!'[9] He went on, 'And so someone who stands on this Hill of Sound will unhesitatingly be able to answer the question, "What is German?" He will point to this opera house . . . and say, "That is it!"' For Bahr and others like him, Bayreuth was not simply an emblem of Germanness; indeed, it was not simply or even primarily an operatic institution. And here, in their enthusiasm, the romantics soared into dithyrambic metaphor.

For Hans von Wolzogen, Bayreuth was 'not only a sanctuary, a place of refuge, but also a power station of the spirit' transmitting 'the electric power of idealism'.[10] For others religion was more apt. Thus Bayreuth was described as 'the new temple of the grail', 'a holy place of the German soul', a 'centre of artistic religion' from which the 'spiritually unworthy' were to be excluded. 'It stands with the prophets of the Old and New Testaments,' the *Vossische Zeitung* solemnly intoned, 'and with the greatest artists and philosophers of all times.'[11] The music critic Josef Stolzing-Czerny went further: 'As the Moslem sinks trembling to his knees at the sight of Mecca, so we Germans are moved when we behold the summit and end point of German cultural achievement.'[12]

With still greater imagination, the critic of the *Hamburger Nachrichten* portrayed Bayreuth almost as a cultural Lourdes, describing it as 'a holy place for the suffering and those seeking salvation', 'a source of healing' and 'a psychic spa with a splendid regenerative effect for the entire aesthetic, ethical and human complex of facts'.[13] The medical-surgical figure of speech appealed also to Hermann Bahr, who depicted Wagner as 'a doctor of the soul' whose works provided 'a dramaturgical cure'.[14] Attending opera in Bayreuth he likened to having 'one's skin removed and a new soul implanted'. And once the treatment began, no escape was possible: 'One really is taken by the scruff of the neck and is removed from his own world however much he may resist.'

Bahr was one among many to praise Bayreuth as 'the place to learn again and again to have confidence in Germanness, in German idealism and in German selflessness'. Far from being regretted, the decline in foreign attendance in these years was welcomed. 'Rich foreigners, especially English and American', Stolzing-Czerny sneered, preferred to take their Wagner in Munich because their 'parasitical existence' demanded the more luxurious accommodations available there. But since 'the Master's doctrine of salvation is so deeply embedded in the German people', he had no doubt that Bayreuth would manage just as well without them. This comment alluded to two special irritants to Bayreuth fanatics—Americans and Munich. The 'racism' in these circles was overtly more anti-American than anti-Semitic, Americans epitomizing, apparently more than Jews, the modern, commercial, vulgar world of money. Munich was a symbol of artistic competition. Even the notorious train service to Bayreuth was ascribed to the deliberate chicanery of Bavarian railway authorities to divert fans to the Munich Opera.

Had German Wagnerians taken leave, then, of their senses? Not all of them, of course, but the mixing of Wagner and political ideology was beginning to leave many people bewildered and aghast. Thomas Mann had his character Lodovico Settembrini, the idealistic humanist in *The Magic Mountain*, speak for them in effect with his remark, 'I harbour a political distaste for music.' The pregnant comment encapsulates the reaction—and plight—of the German liberal in the last years of the Second Reich. But it was the fatal error of the Settembrinis to think that conservative fanaticism would fall under its own obscurantist weight. Liberal music critics stayed close to their professional lasts, assessing artistry and ignoring ideology. Typical was the distinguished music journalist Paul Bekker. To him Bayreuth was not a shrine but an operatic institution to be judged like any other. Although he found much to praise over the years, he never tired of repeating the simple point that if Bayreuth was to be regarded as uniquely wonderful, its performances would have to be uniquely good. Time after time, however, he found that the Festival's uniqueness lay in a singular mixture of the superb and the mediocre. He accused Siegfried of being a slack manager—also a poor conductor—whose good intentions could not disguise his inadequacies. Bekker was one of the few critics of the time to warn against turning Wagnerian opera into a secular religion and Bayreuth into a haven of cultural reactionaries.

The conservative response to Bekker's reviews was not to contest his arguments—which were simply passed off as 'anti-Germanic' and 'anti-Aryan'—but instead to denounce him personally as a Jew whose 'inborn narrowness' had separated him from 'the spirit of the Folk'. He was accused of having 'overturned the altar' and of being associated 'with the boisterous international crowd against the masterpieces of the Folk, against Folk idealism and against national duty'. Here in embryo were the concepts and vocabulary that provided the breeding ground for German fascism. And now was the moment when artistic comment in Germany became overtly political and when music criticism was debased by *ad hominem* abuse.

Discussion of Bayreuth became frenetic as 1913 approached and the copyright on *Parsifal* expired. Only in Germany and only with Wagner could such an eventuality have ranked as a cataclysm. The amount of press attention was astounding, indeed is said to have exceeded in quantity everything that had been published about Wagner and Bayreuth since 1876. The issue was essentially symbolic. *Parsifal*-at-Bayreuth was a totem of German cultural supremacy, if not German supremacy *tout court*. Every city set up its 'Committee for the Protection of *Parsifal*'. There were stirring speeches, appeals and leaflets. The artistic community along with several princes and princesses were mobilized. Richard Strauss spent eight days in Berlin lobbying the Reichstag. The experience left him revolted by the very notion of 'idiotic universal suffrage', in his locution, which ignored the fact that one Richard Wagner 'is worth a hundred thousand votes and around ten thousand stableboys are worth one vote'.[15] Strauss as well as Humperdinck, Gustave Charpentier, Giacomo Puccini and Arturo Toscanini were among the 18,000 persons who signed a petition calling upon the Reichstag to restrict *Parsifal* to Bayreuth.

Various arguments were advanced on Bayreuth's behalf: moral—it was the composer's wish; practical—the Festival would eventually wither and die without its sole right to produce the work; aesthetic— only at Bayreuth could the work be produced correctly; even pseudo-religious—the Festspielhaus's unique mystical-spiritual character would protect the opera from desecration. Those who did not share such views were denounced as 'enemies of Bayreuth' and 'robbers of the grail'; they were warned that failure to reserve *Parsifal* for Bayreuth would mean the downfall of 'a centre of German-idealistic culture' and the triumph of 'Americanism or mercantilism in art'. Hermann Bahr confidently predicted the sacred work would be performed by 'every failed theatre and circus hack, with cuts, changes, insertions, a supplementary ballet and textual modifications of all sorts'.[16] In the same vein an article in the *Neue Zeitschrift für Musik*, which the author was at least too embarrassed to sign, railed at length against 'men with foreign blood', 'the unGerman democratic press', 'Americanization' and 'foreign-blooded artistic acrobats' before eventually arriving at the forecast that the opera would be liable to appear in the same theatres with 'Jewish brothel plays'.[17]

Somehow none of the zealots troubled to demonstrate that *Parsifal*

was unique in the Wagnerian canon, that Bayreuth was uniquely qualified to perform it or that there was any cultural virtue in depriving
Germans, except those who had the time and money to go to Bayreuth,
from seeing it. And since the law would not apply outside the borders,
the paradoxical effect would be that only German opera houses would
be banned from performing it. *Lex Parsifal* never even reached the floor
of the Reichstag.

It was not just the Festival that militant conservatives were now
claiming exclusively for themselves but Wagner's works as well. The
operas, they maintained, were innately and ineffably German and held a
meaning for Germans and aroused a response in them entirely different
from their effect on non-Germans, who in any case could not really
comprehend them. This line of argument received intellectual support
when in 1911 a noted Indologist, Leopold von Schröder, published *Die
Vollendung des arischen Mysteriums in Bayreuth* (The Culmination of the
Aryan Mystery in Bayreuth). The work, based on a serious study of
myths, reached the extraordinary conclusion that the highest artistic
expression of Aryan symbolism was to be found not in the ancient myths
but in the works of Wagner. Not only that, but 'through Wagner,
Bayreuth [had become] the ideal meeting-point of the Aryan peoples
who had been separated for 5,000 years'. The book was a treasure trove
for conservative Wagnerians.

So for the first time the operas were given an explicit nationalistic
gloss. The 1908 *Lohengrin* was praised by one critic for the way it
brought out the 'national-heroic character of the work' and how
it 'must have set ablaze the heart of every German in the audience and
have filled a Frenchman with admiration for the warlike manliness of
the Teutons with their ever-ready swords'.[18] By 1911, with nationalistic feeling perceptibly on the rise throughout the country, the
Meistersinger of that year unleashed a wave of chauvinistic feeling. The
work was construed as a particularly flattering self-portrait—'in its
innermost sense a typical German lofty, glorious gothic work of art'.[19]
The eminent critic Heinrich Chevellay found Sachs to be 'the personification of the true German character' and even the music itself to be
'specifically German'. Stolzing-Czerny also revelled in the opera's 'German mentality', its 'German depth' and its 'German humour', which, in
a racist twist, he contrasted with the 'crass materialism of those of
Semitic religions'.[20]

German power and hubris were running almost out of control in the
last years of peace, and the mood infected conservative music circles just
as much as it did industrialists, politicians and generals. Typical was an
article by Reinhold von Lichtenberg, a leading cultural historian, assessing the 1911 Festival. All three works—the *Ring*, *Parsifal* and
Meistersinger—reflected, in his view, uniquely German qualities, which
he identified as a strong sense of ethics, an admiration for heroes and a
longing for salvation. The *Ring* and *Parsifal* expressed 'the love of nature

and animals that is deeply rooted in the Teuton'—the swan and meadow in *Parsifal* as well as the bird, the horse and bear in the *Ring*. The works also taught lessons of political relevance. The tragedy in the *Ring* was due to the boundless avarice of the 'non-Aryan' Alberich; Wotan by contrast was blameless, interested solely in maintaining world order. Treaties were the cause of the gods' downfall; defeat could be avoided 'in the true German way', with the sword—'pure force against mean egoism'. Ominously he concluded: 'So we see in all the works of this cycle the final and victorious struggle of the Germanic ideal against foreign—that is, enemy—powers.'[21] Here, masquerading as music criticism, was the authentic voice of conservative Germany: paranoid, xenophobic and racist, exulting in Aryan blood, heroism and the sword. What is surprising is not that war broke out in 1914 but that Germany did not self-combust before then.

The 1914 season had opened on 22 July with Siegfried conducting his new *Holländer*. Though the weather was magnificent, the mood was clouded by the deepening international crisis. On 28 July Austria attacked Serbia and four days later Germany declared war on Russia. In his memoirs, Siegfried wrote:

> Of the twenty planned performances, only eight could be given, and those with difficulty. Already during the *Ring* performances disquieting rumours reached the Festival Hill, where, on this Island of the Blessed, one had otherwise avoided speaking of politics. After the *Siegfried* performance, all the Hungarian guests left, soon followed by the Austrians. The rows in the auditorium began to empty, or one saw in the place of foreign guests the owners of the lodgings where they had stayed. Still not believing in war, we tried to go on, until the actual declaration of hostilities put an end to it.[22]

At Muck's insistence *Parsifal* was performed on 1 August. With that, the lamps in the Festspielhaus, as those all over Europe, went out.

For the Wagner family the outbreak of war had the merciful effect of diverting public attention from a crisis that appeared to threaten Wahnfried's control of Bayreuth and Bayreuth's position at the centre of the Wagnerian world. The root of the problem was a dynastic dispute for power.

In December 1908 there had been an important development in family history, when Eva, her mother's secretary and ever-present companion, married Houston Stewart Chamberlain. Chamberlain, the scion of a British military family, was a fanatical Wagnerian, Cosima's close friend for many years and one of the most eccentric of eccentric Englishmen. His masterpiece, *Grundlagen des XIX. Jahrhunderts* (Foundations of the Nineteenth Century), was a two-volume interpretation of Western history in terms of racial struggle. The work was published in 1899 and, in the nationalistic and anti-Semitic mood of Central Europe at the time, was a sensation. To many, during an era of bewildering change, its theories of Aryan-German supremacy and Jewish menace seemed plausible and comforting. They gained Chamberlain a friend for life in a man looking for intellectual security, Kaiser Wilhelm II. They also had a formative influence on a vagabond Austrian water-colourist with aspirations to be an architect, Adolf Hitler.

With Cosima in retirement and Siegfried absorbed in running the Festival and composing operas, Eva and her husband took control of Wahnfried. Although increasingly incapacitated by illness prior to his death in 1927, Chamberlain transformed Bayreuth's passive nationalism and racism into an aggressive, crusading force. Under his influence the *Bayreuther Blätter* and the Official Bayreuth Festival Guide became oracles of militantly nationalistic, ardently anti-democratic and viciously anti-Semitic views. Together with Eva, he supervised the publication of Wagner's writings and built up a Wagner archive which was manipulated to suit his ideological purposes.

He also manipulated Cosima and the family estate, prompting Daniela to lament, 'Our misery began in 1908—with Eva's marriage.'[23] Central to Chamberlain's design was to keep power in Wahnfried. Crucial therefore was the permanent exclusion of Franz Beidler from Bayreuth and the preclusion of his and Isolde's son, born in 1901, from the Wagner legacy. When all of Isolde's attempts at conciliation with Cosima failed—Siegfried prevented her letters from reaching her mother—she believed that the only way to establish her son's legal position was to appeal to the courts. She informed her family in 1913 that unless acknowledged as Richard Wagner's daughter, she would initiate legal action resulting in 'a trial that would leave a lasting and indelible stain on the Wagner name'.[24] Rejecting Siegfried's offer of a substantial sum of money to drop the matter, she went to court. An ugly legal battle raised a risk that word of Siegfried's amorous affairs would leak out during the litigation. For years it had taken all of Adolf von Groß's skill to hush things up with courts and blackmailers. But there were ever-present threats of exposure. Maximilian Harden, the Jewish editor of the muckraking *Die Zukunft*, made a profession of destroying the careers of homosexuals and had Siegfried very much in his sights.

Faced with Isolde's litigation, the possibility of scandal and the fact that he was without an heir, Siegfried made the astonishing announcement in June 1914 that the entire Wagner legacy—the Festspielhaus and its operating funds as well as Wahnfried and its Wagner archive— was to be transferred to a 'Richard Wagner Foundation for the German People' to be managed by a board of directors under the chairmanship of the mayor of Bayreuth. Giving up everything that had been built up since 1876 was so amazing, so extravagant that it can only be understood as a gigantic ruse. Through one means or another the Festival would continue to belong to Wahnfried; in the meantime, the Foundation proposal diverted attention from the litigation and forestalled a potential disaster. So matters stood on the eve of the Great War.

In the summer of the same year Siegfried was introduced to Winifred Williams, a seventeen-year-old English orphan. Winifred's father had been a bridge engineer and after retirement a theatre critic and novelist, her mother an aspiring actress. Both died before her second birthday and, after being passed around among relatives, she was eventually placed in an orphanage. At the age of ten, she was sent to distant relatives in Berlin, Karl and Henriette Klindworth. Klindworth was a famous piano coach, a favourite pupil of Liszt's and a close friend of Richard and Cosima Wagner. Although Klindworth was seventy-eight and his wife seventy, they could scarcely have been more devoted to Winifred; they gave her a decent education and musical training. She was, as Siegfried wrote in his memoirs, 'brought up thoroughly German and in the Bayreuth spirit', though for the remainder of her life Germans always considered her to be English. Klindworth was regularly invited by Cosima to the season's dress rehearsals. In 1914 he took Winifred along and at tea one day at Wahnfried, she met Siegfried. For her it was love at first sight and for Siegfried there was an attraction that led to marriage in July of the following year. Although Cosima and her daughters would no doubt have preferred someone socially more distinguished, Winifred resolved their desperate fears about Siegfried's unmarried state.

To the young bride, Wahnfried must have seemed more terrifying than the orphanage. The mansion itself was a veritable museum and life in it followed the stilted routine of a minor court. The cast of characters was out of a gothic novel: a formidable dowager, venerated as though a

Wahnfried guests commemorating the thirtieth anniversary of Liszt's death in July 1916; from left: Hans von Wolzogen, Franz Stassen (the artist), Marie Pembauer, Josef Pembauer (the pianist), Siegfried, Winifred, Hans Richter and Eva.

sacred relic; two resident sisters-in-law, venomous in their hatreds; a brother-in-law, intellectually crazed; a husband who fled every morning to be alone in his garden house; a sister-in-law whose name might not be mentioned out of spite; and a long-deceased father-in-law whose name dare never be mentioned out of reverence. For Cosima time had stopped with her husband's heartbeat. Every chair, table, lamp, picture and book remained just as it was in 1883. Dusting these objects every morning was Winifred's sacred duty. The sisters made life hell for her, and though they soon left Wahnfried, relations among the three were forever hostile.

Beginning in 1917 and in quick succession thereafter, Winifred had four children: Wieland, Friedelind, Wolfgang and Verena. With that, the dynastic problem was finally resolved. It had already been half-settled in 1914 when Isolde's paternity petition was rejected on narrow legal grounds. The proposal for a Foundation was now silently dropped and Bayreuth remained secure in Wahnfried's grip.

In the economic privation and catastrophic inflation that followed the war, however, the Festival was left bankrupt. Between 1883 and 1913 Wahnfried had received over six million marks in royalties. However, the truncated 1914 season had depleted operating funds by a third and the postwar inflation wiped out the remainder—along with the family's savings. With the expiry of the copyrights in 1913, there was no further royalty income to help compensate. To keep Wahnfried and his family going, Siegfried had to go on concert tours and was even forced to sell several drawings and some of Winifred's jewellery.

It was not until 1921 that serious thought could be given to reviving the Festival. To raise funds Siegfried established a German Festival Foundation and, following the example of his father nearly half a century earlier, sold patron's certificates. Once again, the appeal was to crass nationalism: 'He who loves Germany and wants to do something for its recovery and its future as a culture-nation must come to Bayreuth's aid' was one of the less metaphysical slogans. Over 3,000 people signed up, including three royal has-beens—the ex-Kaiser, the ex-King of Bavaria and the ex-Czar of Bulgaria. Although an impressive five million marks were raised in this way in little more than a year, the sum was devalued by inflation and fell short of the amount needed to ensure Bayreuth's future. At this point Siegfried decided to appeal to rich Wagnerians in America. In January 1924 he and Winifred sailed to New York, on a two-month concert and fund-raising tour of the United States.

For Siegfried personally the tour was a reasonable success. American music-lovers, curious to have a look at the son of Wagner and grandson of Liszt, were disarmed by his modesty and amiability. Critics did their best to find something nice to say about his conducting—'not without excellent qualities' was the gentle phrasing of Olin Downes of the *New York Times*. Financially, however, the trip was a fiasco. On arrival in New York Siegfried said he hoped for contributions totalling $200,000;

After considerable persuasion, Cosima permitted Winifred to take this photo of her holding Wieland on his first birthday in 1918. The year before, she had celebrated his birth by playing a few bars on Wagner's piano which she had kept locked since his death.

on departure he spoke of having come to raise $75,000. In fact the tour realized an exiguous $8,000. It had been bedevilled from the start by reports, accurate in fact, that the Bavarian police had confiscated a $100 cash gift from an American friend of the Wagner family, which Winifred had donated to General Erich Ludendorff, the inventor of the stab-in-the-back legend of Germany's 1918 military defeat and now head of a radical right-wing party. Winifred was further said to be involved with the 'Nationalists' who had staged a putsch in Munich the previous November. Siegfried did his best to counteract the stories and gave the press a statement denying that funds for the Festival were being diverted for 'political purposes'. But the damage was irreparable.

Even though Siegfried's statement was true enough, it concealed his connection with a stratagem to help raise money for a radical new political movement headed by Adolf Hitler. Prior to a concert in Detroit, the Wagners paid a social call on Henry Ford. In the course of the conversation they—or more likely Winifred—induced Ford to meet Kurt Lüdecke, a man who was in the United States to raise funds for Hitler. It was hoped that the fervently anti-Semitic Ford would be

139

so impressed on learning about a rising anti-Semitic party in Germany that he would help with a sizeable donation. In the end Lüdecke was as unsuccessful as the Wagners in screwing as much as a penny out of the tight-fisted car-maker.

That episode was the merest hint of how deeply Wahnfried had been drawn into the orbit of Hitler's party. Already on the far right in the Wilhelmian Empire, the Wagner family had been appalled by the collapse of the monarchy and viewed parliamentary democracy and the liberal ethos of the Weimar Republic with loathing. Like many of their countrymen, they saw Germany as caught between twin menaces—a democratic and decadent West and an expansionist and bolshevist East—and looked to radical conservatism for a solution. As early as 1919 Chamberlain received at Wahnfried several persons involved with a nascent fascist movement in Munich. For Siegfried and the other Wagners, the ideal was a nationalistic, authoritarian regime headed by Ludendorff. Beyond that, Siegfried lacked any serious interest in politics and as head of the Festival avoided overt political commitment.

Winifred, however, was a Hitler fanatic. The fanaticism arose out of personal devotion to the man. She was not drawn to him by his violent anti-Semitism, which she did not particularly share, nor by his political movement, which she probably did not really understand and—like her sisters-in-law—joined only in 1926 at Hitler's request. But like many Germans, she found the postwar social and political 'disorder' intolerable and saw in Hitler an exciting, charismatic leader who would save the country. When they first met on a social occasion in Bayreuth in September 1923, she was immediately overwhelmed—hypnotized, like many others, by the famous blue eyes. She insisted that he must visit Wahnfried the next morning.

Before calling on the Wagners, Hitler paid his respects to the man who had been such a decisive influence on him, Houston Stewart Chamberlain. Chamberlain was too ill to say much but was so over-whelmed by what he heard and sensed that he was moved to write to Hitler a few days later. He had expected to meet a fanatic, his letter declared, and instead he had found Germany's saviour, the messiah of a counter-revolution. The widely publicized letter amounted to the first important endorsement of this minor demagogue in his scrabbling for re-spectability. At a moment of great discouragement and uncertainty, these words came, his biographer Joachim Fest has written, 'as the answer to his doubts, as a benediction from the Bayreuth Master himself'.[25]

And it was with the Bayreuth Master himself that Hitler next com-muned. At Wahnfried he was conducted by the Wagners through the composer's rooms and taken to his grave where he stood for a long time in silent homage. With tears in his eyes, so accounts go, Hitler said that Richard Wagner was the greatest German of all time and added, 'If I should ever succeed in exerting any influence on Germany's destiny, I will see that *Parsifal* is given back to Bayreuth.'[26]

Undoubtedly the Wahnfried visit was a sacred occasion for Hitler. 'At the age of twelve,' he wrote in *Mein Kampf,* 'I saw . . . the first opera of my life, *Lohengrin.* In one instant I was addicted. My youthful enthusiasm for the Bayreuth Master knew no bounds.' A few years afterwards he was stirred to his depths by a performance of *Rienzi,* Wagner's opera about the Roman tribune who restored the empire. 'That was the hour when it all began,' he is said to have remarked on meeting a boyhood friend in Bayreuth in 1939.[27] The comment is revealing, revealing of the fact that what appealed to Hitler was not the music as much as the heroics. And what heroics! Under a sketch he drew in 1912 of Young Siegfried, he appended the comment, 'Wagner's work showed me for the first time what is the myth of blood.'[28] *Blutmythos*—war and racial purity, already in 1912. A decade later in a public speech he explicitly declared that he revered Wagner because his works glorified the 'heroic, the Teutonic nature'. 'Greatness', he said, 'lies in the heroic.'[29]

As Hitler came to know more about the composer personally, he found in him a kindred soul, someone who had borne the same fears about Jewish ancestry, who had suffered a similar sense of rootlessness, who had also been buffeted by early failures and who even shared his views on anti-vivisection and vegetarianism. In the Social Darwinism and anti-Semitism of Wagner's political writings, Hitler found an ideology. And in the operas he found heroes, men like himself who were rejected outsiders battling against an entrenched social order. The idea of calling himself 'Führer' is thought to have been inspired by a passage at the end of *Lohengrin,* 'Zum Führer sei er euch ernannt!'— Accept him as your leader. Even *Mein Kampf* echoes the title of Wagner's *Mein Leben.* So Wagner evolved from idol to soulmate, inspiration and guide—'the greatest prophetic figure the German people has had'. And Hitler himself evolved from an ideological crackpot into the man who aestheticized politics to become supreme leader of Germany.

Five weeks after the Wahnfried visit, Hitler, Ludendorff and Hermann Goering launched the so-called Beer Hall Putsch. Their plan was to seize power in Bavaria and then, in imitation of Mussolini's march on Rome the year before, go on to Berlin. The coup collapsed with a few pistol shots; Hitler and Ludendorff were arrested and Goering fled to Innsbruck. Siegfried and Winifred happened to be in Munich at the time for a concert engagement. Neither saw any of the action but both were deeply shaken. Siegfried later visited Goering in Innsbruck while Winifred, back in Bayreuth, reported to a local Nazi party group on what she knew of the event. With reckless candour, she also wrote an open letter to the press giving Hitler Wahnfried's outspoken endorsement:

For years we have been following with the deepest personal sympathy and approval the constructive work of Adolf Hitler, this German man who, filled with the most ardent love of his Fatherland, sacrifices his life for his ideal of a purified, united national Greater Germany, who has taken upon himself the dangerous task of opening the eyes of the working class to the internal enemy and the danger of Marxism and its consequences, who has managed as no one else to bring people together as brothers, who has learned how to overcome implacable class hatred and who has given thousands upon thousands of confused people the welcome hope and firm belief in a revived, worthy Fatherland.

Thus ran one sentence.[30] 'We stood with him in time of good fortune, now we maintain our loyalty to him at a time of need,' the statement concluded. Winifred also collected food and clothing for the families of the men who had been arrested after the putsch attempt, and to Hitler himself she sent writing paper, giving rise to the bizarre story that *Mein Kampf* was written on Wahnfried stationery.

With such open support from one of the most famous families in the world, it is hardly surprising that Hitler was forever grateful. Nearly twenty years later he said to friends: 'It was not just the others but Siegfried as well who stood by me at the time when things were at their worst for me.'[31] And at the time he wrote to Siegfried from prison to thank everyone in Wahnfried for their moral support as well as for their work for his party in the recent election campaign. Bayreuth, he prophetically announced, was 'on the line of march to Berlin'; indeed it was the place where 'first the Master and then Chamberlain forged the spiritual sword with which we fight today'.[32]

So, while Munich and Berlin had yet to be conquered by Hitler, Bayreuth itself had already fallen in 1924. On reopening that year, the Festival turned into a veritable durbar for members of the now banned National Socialist party and its sympathizers. The Official Festival Guide had very little about Wagner's music but a great deal of radical right-wing propaganda. In its pages Wagner was described as the 'Führer of German art', a trail-blazer of nationalistic socialism and the enemy of Americanism and Judaism. The *Bayreuther Blätter* was by this time an undisguised pro-Nazi publication. Over the opera house Siegfried flew not the flag of the Republic but the old imperial banner—a clear, public renunciation of Weimar democracy. General Ludendorff, now out of prison, addressed an anti-republican rally in Bayreuth just prior to the Festival; he was an invitee to the dress rehearsals and an honoured guest at the performances. After the conclusion of the first opera of the season, *Die Meistersinger*, the audience stood in exaltation and sang all three verses of *Deutschland über Alles*. Aesthetics had now been politicized.

The liberal press and foreign guests were horrified. Siegfried awoke to a sudden sense of peril. From then on he forbade any overt connection between the Festival and Hitler or the National Socialists. The next year a large notice was displayed on the opera house declaring, 'The public is strongly urged not to sing at the conclusion of *Die Meistersinger*. Hier gilt's der Kunst!'—Art is what matters here! That slogan, a line from the opera itself, served from now on as a massive fig leaf. Overt art, covert politics. Only thus can the inconsistencies of these years be understood. When Hitler proposed to visit, and possibly even live in, Bayreuth following his release from prison at the end of 1924, Siegfried put his foot down. He later relented to the point of permitting him to attend the Festival the following year, but after that Hitler himself decided to stay away as long as he was an embarrassment.

Siegfried was poised between his instinctive nationalism and arch-conservatism and his equally innate tolerance and xenophilia. He was an artist but admired strong leaders, purportedly comparing Mussolini to Napoleon after meeting the Duce in Rome in 1924 and praising Hitler as 'a splendid fellow, the real soul of the German people'.[33] After declaring in 1925 that Bayreuth was to be kept 'free from any political influences', he—along with his three sisters and his wife—all became honorary board members of the Bayreuth League of German Youth, founded in part 'to inculcate a sense of the inseparability' of 'Adolf Hitler's cultural designs and the work of Bayreuth'. Further cementing a relationship with the burgeoning fascist movement, they later joined the National Socialist Society for German Culture and the German Fighting Union, dedicated to the overthrow of the Republic. In 1927 he permitted Hitler to attend Chamberlain's funeral and to provide storm-troops as pall-bearers. In his wartime table-talk Hitler reminisced that while the two of them had remained friends, Siegfried was 'politically passive' and 'somewhat in the hands of the Jews'.[34] In fact, Siegfried was above all politically naïve, and let himself be carried along—like many Germans at the time.

It was of course Winifred who maintained the connection between Hitler and Bayreuth. At her encouragement Hitler frequently spent the night at Wahnfried en route between Munich and Berlin. The visits were so secret that even Siegfried at times learned about them from the children. Hitler would arrive under cover of darkness, help put the children to bed and tell them stories of his adventures, which thrilled them. Winifred and her children were among the few whom he allowed to use his nickname 'Wolf'; he in turn called her 'Wini' and the children by their various nicknames. This warm, familial atmosphere was of enormous emotional importance to Hitler. Wahnfried was the home he had not known since childhood; Winifred was the wife he never married; above all, the children were the offspring he never had. In Wahnfried alone could he be himself. And since Siegfried and Winifred never had much time for their children—late in life Wieland complained that he had seen his father about ten minutes a day—they found Hitler more a father than their own. 'Uncle Wolf' clearly adored them and they him. As a child Wieland is said once to have remarked that Wolf should have been their father and their father Uncle. It is said that this is why in 1943 he named his own son Wolf Siegfried.

Winifred had little contact with other party leaders in those days. One

The Wahnfried brood—Wolfgang, Varena, Wieland and Friedelind—in 1922. 'We had a nanny for the children. My motto was: Nobody can look after Siegfried as well as I can, but somebody else *can* look after the children' (Winifred).

of the few who called was Josef Goebbels, who held her in high esteem. An entry in his diary about a visit to Wahnfried in May 1926 offers an intriguing account of his impressions of the family:

> A thoroughbred woman. They should all be like her. And fanatically on our side. Lovely children. We are all immediately friends. She complains to me of her worries. Siegfried is so spineless. Disgraceful! The memory of the Master should shame him. Siegfried also arrives. Feminine. Good-hearted. Somewhat decadent. Rather like a cowardly artist. . . . A young woman weeps because the son is not what the Master was.[35]

These political escapades had little or no impact on what happened inside the Festspielhaus on reopening in 1924. The problem there was in part practical. Musicians, singers and even conductors had to be found, a chorus and technical staff recruited and productions planned. The opera theatre itself and the old sets and costumes badly needed repairs. Funds were extremely limited. And the outlook for the Festival appeared anything but rosy. Wagnerian opera, regarded by the new

Varena, Wolfgang, Wieland and Friedelind in *Ring* costumes made by Aunt Lulu (Daniela). 'Dressing up in costumes and all that was really more or less for photographers, a bit of carnival, not a serious identification with Wagner characters' (Wolfgang).

generation as a remnant of the old order, had fallen out of vogue. And that mainstay of Festival audiences—the Central European aristocracy, princely houses and monarchies—had been swept away in 1918.

But the difficulty was also in part institutional conservatism. German theatrical staging was now in the throes of an enormously exciting period of change. From his travels—conducting concerts, overseeing the production of his own operas and recruiting singers—Siegfried was well aware of this upheaval. Some of the new work was incomprehensible to him. He was left compeletely cold by a remarkable expressionist production in 1929 at the Kroll Opera of *Der fliegende Holländer*, a production so disliked by conservatives that the conductor, Otto Klemperer, ultimately lost his position and the opera house itself was closed. However, he was so deeply impressed by a new production of *Lohengrin* in the same year at the Berlin Municipal Opera by Heinz Tietjen that he thought of inviting the dramaturge to Bayreuth.

Even more than when he succeeded his mother in 1906, Siegfried

Siegfried directing a stage rehearsal in 1927.

was therefore aware that Bayreuth was in danger of falling far behind the rest of the theatrical world. But he was helplessly in the grip of artistic neurosis. His aesthetic id, his deepest instincts, firmly held him back; his aesthetic ego, his experience of artistic change, drove him forward; his aesthetic super-ego, the Bayreuth tradition, stalled him from making a decisive choice. So on the one hand he wrote in the 1924 Festival programme: 'Bayreuth is not there for any sort of hyper-modern vogues. This would contradict the style of works which after all were not written and composed as cubist, expressionist or dadaist.' But on the other, he commented in a newspaper article some months later: 'We have always had our eyes open for all good scenic and decorative change.'[36] He praised the 'modern work' of the Dresden Opera and of Roller in Vienna, and concluded, 'This is the way in which we want to try to go forward.'

Not surprisingly, whatever Siegfried did was characterized by inconsistency and temporizing. His inner struggle can be seen even in his choice of conductors, one of the first issues he faced in reviving the Festival. The last of the original generation had died with Richter in 1916; their successors were the aging Muck and Balling. But there was no third generation that had risen through the Bayreuth ranks. Siegfried had not cultivated one before the war and the decade-long hiatus prevented any from emerging. This was a historic development: the unbroken tradition of a laying on of musical hands had come to an end. Never again was there a permanent conducting staff, born and bred in the Bayreuth style, devoted solely or primarily to the Festival. From now on it was necessary to look outside Bayreuth.

146

Before Siegfried lay the most glorious array of great conductors, German and foreign, that the world has ever seen. He could have had his pick. And in fact he was inclined, however cautiously, to bring in new talent. But in the end he was guided by whether the person fitted in with the Bayreuth spirit—meaning that they were politically no less than artistically conservative, were German, were not Jewish, were opera, rather than concert, conductors and above all were appropriately reverent towards Wagner and Festival traditions. As before 1914, this ruled out the leading conductors of the time. Klemperer, Bruno Walter and Leo Blech were unacceptable as Jews. Erich Kleiber was a modernist and Wilhelm Furtwängler a concert conductor; neither was deemed a committed Wagnerian. Arturo Toscanini, Sir Thomas Beecham and Willem Mengelberg were foreign. Richard Strauss, otherwise unexceptionable, was personally disliked by Siegfried. Even Balling was nearly ditched. As Siegfried complained to Muck, he was politically liberal, most of his friends were Jewish (he had also married Levi's widow) and he was rumoured to have subscribed to that 'radical' journal, Harden's *Die Zukunft*.

Nothing better exposes the state of mind prevailing in those years than excerpts from letters Siegfried wrote in 1925:

> Bayreuth is not simply 'performances' but a faith, which is doubly necessary at a time when cultural bolshevism threatens to destroy all traditions, all sense of style. . . .
>
> We must have men in the top positions who are not just good musicians but who know how to convey our way of thinking. Bayreuth is a prominent intellectual cultural centre; what matters is not simply a beautiful voice, beautiful décors etc. It is a self-contained whole that will only have an impact . . . if the top men are filled with a sense of this cultural mission.[37]

Consequently, on reviving the Festival in 1924 Siegfried fell back on Muck, Balling and Willibald Kaehler, an undistinguished musical assistant of Cosima's era. In a singular leap of imagination, however, he invited the young Dresden conductor Fritz Busch as well. It was all too symptomatic that when Busch wrote to introduce himself to Muck, to assure the senior conductor that their artistic views coincided, Muck replied that this was not of the slightest importance. What mattered, he responded, was whether Busch conformed to the 'Bayreuth way of thinking' and whether he would bring with him 'the unassuming humility and the holy fanaticism of the Believer'.[38] Predictably perhaps, Busch and Bayreuth did not mix. Finding the musical and vocal standards not what they should have been, Busch urged Siegfried to seek out better singers and to invite Toscanini. 'What was vexatious and even tragic', he recalled in his memoirs, 'was that Wahnfried turned a deaf ear to all this. . . . At my critical remarks and efforts at improvement obstinately repeated over and over again, they simply smiled.'

Busch decided not to return and the next year Balling died. In their place, Siegfried turned to Franz von Hoeßlin and Karl Elmendorff, men who fully met Bayreuth's conservative criteria. (Siegfried himself conducted only once in the inter-war period, taking one *Ring* cycle in 1927.) But finally in 1930 he was willing to break a tradition sacred not only to Bayreuth but to the political right wing. He invited Toscanini. Even his announcement was provocative; he had wanted to take this step for many years, he said, but had been prevented by 'the ruinous politics that spoils everything'. And to remove any ambiguity about what politics he had in mind, he praised the Maestro's refusal to conduct after fascists had heckled one of his concerts in Bologna.

The productions during these years were also marked by Siegfried's contradictions. To be sure he was greatly hampered by a lack of money. The 1924 season had to be financed on a shoestring. Singers performed without a fee; Kurt Söhnlein, the new stage assistant and successor to the venerable Max Brückner, volunteered his services and some of the operating costs were met by a loan from the Leipzig headquarters of the Richard Wagner societies. Not much more was possible than to dust off the old staging for the *Ring*, *Parsifal* and *Meistersinger*. From that year on, ticket sales were excellent, but even when they produced sizeable profits, Siegfried used the money for structural improvements—enlarging the depth of the stage, installing the latest lighting and other stage equipment and transforming the old Brückner backcloths into solid three-dimensional sets modelled on the previous visual images. With little left for new productions, the main works of the repertory were simply modified. Critics praised his taste, his sensitive use of lighting and his directing. However, they usually found his sets outmoded beyond what could be explained away by inadequate funds. 'Obsolescence modified by taste' was one of the less severe comments. The problem was as much a lack of nerve as a lack of money. Siegfried was a cautious remodeller, not an innovative builder.

The *Ring* underwent continuous, gradual revamping. Plastic rock formations were constructed in such a way that they could be assembled in various combinations for use in the entire tetralogy. Siegfried redesigned Hunding's hut to good effect and furnished the Gibichungs with a three-dimensional hall. He even ignored Wagner's stage directions in 1928 to provide the Norns with their own setting—an enormous fir tree against a wide sky. More novel was Siegfried's use of lighting and optical projection—to give the impression of waves in the opening scene of *Rheingold*; to create a sense of space, of fugitive clouds and of lightning flashes in *Walküre*; to lend magic to the forest scene in *Siegfried*; to cast cold moonlight over Siegfried's funeral procession and to annihilate Valhalla in *Götterdämmerung*. But there was no disguising the fact that all this was so much tinkering until an entirely new production could be mounted.

Far more problematical was *Parsifal*. The settings would soon be half

Siegfried's sketch of a new hut for Hunding in the 1928 *Ring* simplified the old sets and moved the door to front left from centre rear, giving better effect to Wagner's direction, 'Moonlight streams into the room and brightly illuminates the lovers'.

Hunding's hut on stage. Here in the final scene, photographed in 1930, Gunnar Graarud (Siegmund) and Emmy Krüger (Sieglinde). For Hans Pfitzner this new set was a desecration of Wagner's stage plan.

a century old; to many critics and spectators, they were now painful to behold. In 1926 Siegfried and Söhnlein sat down together and drafted sketches for a new production but in the end abandoned the project, feeling, in Söhnlein's words, 'we were committing a sacrilege'.[39] All the same, they altered the decors in the second act, giving Klingsor a new tower, the Flowermaidens new costumes and the magic garden a setting made of gauzes to which were attached blue and yellow flower petals. Söhnlein himself admitted that *Parsifal*, like the *Ring*, had become a stylistic mishmash. No one was very impressed with these touch-ups; the Flowermaidens appeared to one critic less as enchantresses than 'pupils from an old-fashioned ladies' school'. It was, incidentally, in the 1924 season that audiences for whatever reason abandoned the old tradition of applause after the second and third acts and initiated the practice of what von Puttkamer labelled 'contemplative silence'.

There were two new productions in these years. *Tristan* appeared in 1927. In a statement of intent that even Cosima might have found blush-making, Siegfried wrote to Söhnlein, 'I do not wish to alter the staging arrangements etc. that have been traditional since Munich in 1865.'[40] Yet what he produced was a remarkable transformation. All the basic features of the traditional staging were intact but now in simplified form. In the first act the mast, sails and most of the rigging were removed and Isolde's apartment was enclosed in an enormous light-green curtain. The stage was similarly cleared in the other two acts, and the new sets created a cleaner impression. More original was the emphasis on contrasts of lighting and colour, to give perceptible emphasis to the drama's contrast between the worlds of day and night—the first act in bright light, the second in obscure blue until the final scene which was brightly lit, and the third beginning in light and ending in darkness. Daniela also altered the costumes, depriving them of their conventional Germanic and Celtic character. Tristan, for example, no longer appeared in medieval armour but in a simple purple vestment. All this would have looked excitingly modern in the 1890s; in the 1920s it was hopelessly passé.

The other new work was *Tannhäuser*, the first since the 1891 original. For years Siegfried had dreamed of producing it. Postponed year after year for lack of money, it was eventually financed by a public appeal managed by Winifred as a gift for Siegfried's sixtieth birthday in 1930. Some 1,000 people, including the exiled Wilhelm II and the ever-faithful ex-Czar Ferdinand, contributed, and the fund eventually reached 127,000 marks, a handsome sum in those days. Although solicited with blunt appeals to patriotism—Bayreuth as 'the last bulwark of the German spirit'—the fund left Siegfried independent of the arch-conservative Wagner societies and free to stage the work as he pleased.

He set the tone in his initial instructions to Söhnlein, 'I agree to anything that contributes to the romanticism and poetry of the work.'[41] In designing the scenery the two men stripped away much of the fusty

Tristan, Act II, in the 1927 setting. With the entry of King Marke—and the world of day—the prevailing dark blue of the staging gave way to a brightly lit scene.

baroque detail of Cosima's production but still followed her outlines. Venusberg, modelled on the vast 'fairy caves' at Saalfeld in Thuringia, was done, as Siegfried said, 'in the voluptuous style of Rubens'. To drive home the contrast, the Wartburg scene was presented in 'the severe style of Holbein'. The hall of song was a solid gothic chamber in tones of gold. He also indulged in some eyebrow-raising operatic effects, giving the Landgrave's hunting party real horses as well as a pack of hunting dogs. Throughout, he resorted more than ever to his favourite techniques of colour and light and the use of scrims to achieve the shimmering, often indistinct effects he liked so much.

There were several novelties. Most daring was Siegfried's engagement of the avant-garde choreographer Rudolf von Laban to stage the Bacchanal. Another change was Siegfried's directing of the chorus, which marked a complete break with Cosima's stylization. Even the interpretation of the opera—presenting Tannhäuser not so much as a man facing a choice between sacred and profane love as an independent artist in confrontation with an uncomprehending society—was a basic shift from the old orthodoxy.

In retrospect, the *Tannhäuser* production has been widely hailed as having marked Siegfried's declaration of artistic independence. Winifred herself later rated it, along with the 1908 *Lohengrin*, her husband's

151

The Bacchanal scene of Siegfried's 1930 *Tannhäuser* was performed by Laban's dance troupe to suggest an orgy. Some found the choreography bold and exciting, others saw it as chaste gymnastics.

Daniela laboured for over two years on the costumes for *Tannhäuser*. That for Maria Müller (Elisabeth) was meticulously modelled on two famous Strassburg cathedral sculptures: the dress on 'the synagogue', the cape and clasp on 'the church'.

greatest achievement. At the time, however, the critical reaction was not warm. Of those who praised it, Ernest Newman was the most enthusiastic, ranking it as 'one of the two or three finest things of its kind' that he had ever seen.[42] 'The Bacchanal', he wrote, 'caught, for once, the spirit of the marvellous score. . . . The Hall of Song was mounted and managed as only Bayreuth, with its enormous stage, can mount and manage it; and the third act was set in a desolation of landscape and of light that of themselves struck a chill to the heart.' But the prevailing assessment was that the production marked a failed attempt to find a middle ground between tradition and innovation. Alfred Einstein, the famous musicologist, described it as 'a compromise, or let us say clearly and concisely: a stylistic monster'.[43] The trouble was, he said, that Bayreuth lacked the courage either to stick with the conventional or to mount something truly original.

Musically these years were on the whole outstanding. Critics found the orchestral playing superb and generally praised the conducting. One of the high points was Busch's 1924 *Meistersinger*. Muck's *Parsifal* was generally felt to have reached new heights of excellence, though in 1930 Ernest Newman complained that it dragged so painfully, especially during the Good Friday music, that it would not have been surprising 'to find that Good Friday had lasted until well into Easter Monday'. Newman also accounted von Hoeßlin and Elmendorff as 'efficient rather than dazzling'—a not uncommon opinion.

The great sensation was Toscanini's conducting of *Tannhäuser* and *Tristan*. The Maestro's intense devotion to Wagner—his intimate knowledge both of the scores and even of Wagner's writings—endeared him to Germans. But as the first foreigner and even more as an Italian, he put the conservative extremists in an embarrassing ideological position. They squared the circle, however, by following the example of Chamberlain, who had earlier designated Dante, Columbus and St Paul to be de facto Germans. Asserting that as a northern Italian, Toscanini had a good deal of Nordic blood in him, they claimed him as Aryan in reality. And so the comic irony: in assessing his conducting, the rightists were at pains to stress how impressed they were by the authentic Germanness of Toscanini's treatment of the scores while liberal critics were intrigued by its Italianate character. Alfred Einstein accordingly rejoiced in the way Toscanini extricated *Tannhäuser* from its traditional hazy German romanticism and gave the music 'the ultimate in clarity and precision'. The *Frankfurter Zeitung* lauded his *Tristan* for its razor-sharp rhythm, its control over romantic passion and its demonstration that shape is as important as expression. At the other extreme Paul Pretzsch acclaimed the 'genuine Wagnerian' quality of the conducting which he attributed to Toscanini's immersion in Wagner's works and Nordic links in his ancestry.

Casting posed its own difficulties. In reviving the Festival in 1924 Siegfried had to face down strong pressure from conservative Wagneri-

Siegfried and Toscanini in July 1930. The two men were fond of one another, but it took all of Siegfried's tact and fluent Italian to calm the Maestro's outbursts during rehearsals.

ans to exclude Jews and foreigners. 'It is a matter of complete indifference to us whether a person is Chinese, Negro, American, Indian or Jew,' he responded to one of them.[44] He not only put foreigners in some of the leading roles but now, for the first time at Bayreuth, Jews as well. He was also willing to take chances, inviting the little-known and relatively untried Lauritz Melchior, for instance, to sing both Siegmund and Parsifal in 1924. Although he was criticized, as he had been before the war, for accepting too many mediocre singers, the fault often lay with the managers of opera houses who refused to release the soloists Siegfried had requested.

Siegfried spent endless hours with his singers and was infinitely patient in coaching those, such as Melchior and Alexander Kipnis, who were poor actors. He also encouraged a change in vocal style in these years, away from Cosima's declamation and emphasis on enunciation towards a more lyrical approach, with stress on beauty of tone and purity of phrasing. Some have contended that his greatest contribution as head of the Festival was to allow soloists greater scope for spontaneity and personal interpretation.

The chorus, which Hugo Rüdel had to rebuild after the First World War, was again the world's best. It added lustre to every performance. Otherwise singing was the least reliable feature of these years; some soloists were rated as superb, some scarcely suitable for a provincial opera company. The Rhinemaidens might be excellent one year and the Valkyries poor; the next year it might be the other way round. Carl Cleving's Stolzing, said one critic, 'deserves all the Beckmessers in the world'. Sigismund Pilinszky's Tannhäuser was almost unanimously accounted a disaster; Rudolf Ritter was a forgettable Siegfried. Even in the above average year of 1930 Ernest Newman commented:

> Surely it would be easy to find better singers than some of those we have listened to during the last ten days. A few of them have style but no voice; others have a voice, of a kind, but no style; while others have neither voice nor style. . . . Moreover, more than one performance has come dangerously near disaster through the shortcomings of some singer or other. In the third act of *Siegfried*, Melchior had a lapse of memory, and for a time could only gesticulate; while Gunnar Graarud, the Siegfried of the *Götterdämmerung*, came so near to complete loss of voice in the last act that probably Hagen saved his life by killing him when he did.[45]

But if there were few performances in the twenties which excelled in uniformly outstanding singing, there were uniformly outstanding singers: Nanny Larsén-Todsen as Kundry, Brünnhilde and Isolde; Maria Müller as Elisabeth; Alexander Kipnis as Gurnemanz and Hagen; Emanuel List as Hunding and King Marke; Heinrich Schultz as Beckmesser; Frida Leider as Brünnhilde; Melchior as Siegfried and Tristan; Herbert Janssen as Wolfram; Rudolf Bockelmann as Kurwenal; and Friedrich Schorr as perhaps the greatest Wotan of all time. Adolf Hitler complained that he had been 'sickened' by the appearance at the 1925 Festival of 'that Jew Schorr'.[46] But in 1930 Josef Stolzing-Czerny, now music critic of the Nazi party newspaper *Völkischer Beobachter*, could not help himself: 'We, as always, honour the truth and declare that, regrettable as it is that the leading Germanic god should be sung in Bayreuth by a Jew—namely Friedrich Schorr—he offers a performance that in singing as well as acting is of the highest Bayreuth standard.'[47]

That comment was a symptom of the calamitous slide of music criticism—and the country itself—towards fascism. The trend had already been set in motion in 1914, with Wagner vicariously at the forefront. Cosima spoke for his disciples with embarrassing frankness when she commented to Hohenlohe that 'War seems to suit us Germans better than peace.'[48] Symptomatic was a book, suggestively entitled *Richard Wagner und der heilige deutsche Krieg* (Richard Wagner and the Holy German War), in which the Jewish historian Richard Sternfeld portrayed the conflict as a predestined step—foreseen in Wagner's operas

—towards German dominance in the world. But above all it was the Nibelung saga that, now firmly fastened in the German imagination, became a metaphor of the war and that provided the popular icons of German military prowess—above all, Siegfried with his invincible sword. The generals themselves made the connection explicit by mining the *Ring* for code names for their military operations—Operation Walküre, for example—and for the great defensive lines of 1918, such as the Hunding Line.

The collapse in 1918 was also translated into Wagnerian terms. With several generations of Germans conditioned to believe that the invincible Siegfried could only be destroyed by trickery and a stab in the back, wide sections of the public interpreted the military defeat in just that way. Here was the provenance of the infamous legend that Germany was brought down not on the battlefield but at home—'the warring German Siegfried was stealthily stabbed in the back' by a treacherous German parliament, as Hitler wrote in *Mein Kampf*. So, far from destroying aggressive nationalism, the defeat of 1918 endowed it with even greater potency among wide sections of the public. Interestingly enough, Carl Jung had predicted this development as a result of his psychoanalytical work during the war: 'In the dreams of Germans I treated then I could clearly see the Wotanistic revolution coming on.' God was dead, and what Nietzsche had done in philosophy, Wagner had done in music: each in his way had filled the gap left by the decline of religion with 'Germanic prehistory'. Jung concluded: 'Wotan the storm god had conquered.'[49]

And in conquering, he swept conservatives, especially conservative Wagnerians, steadily to the right until by the end of the 1920s most of them were firmly in the National Socialist camp. Political and ideological divisions were reaching their decisive phase. There was a tremendous resurgence of the *Erlösungsgedanke* — the notion of redemption — the preeminent theme of Wagner's works. The final Weimar years evoked powerful chiliastic yearnings, in which Wagner and Hitler together took the place of the messiah. First Siegfried's sword and then Hitler's swastika became right-wing symbols. The *Bayreuther Blätter* spewed out articles that were hate-filled, paranoid and carried away by a nationalism bordering on mental imbalance. The Official Festival Guide purveyed racist, proto-fascist propaganda in the guise of operatic comment. These anglers in the nightsoil of rightist ideology now claimed Wagner, Wagnerian opera and Bayreuth not just as exclusively German but as belonging solely to the radical conservatives. 'The incredible has occurred!' commented the *Frankfurter Zeitung*'s critic Bernhard Diebold in 1928. 'Since the war the right wing has elevated Richard Wagner to its special artistic culture-god.'[50]

Not only that, the content of the operas themselves was now Nazified. Stolzing-Czerny's reviews in the *Völkischer Beobachter* of the 1930 *Ring* cycle presented the work as a parable of the age. Fafner was a symbol of the indolent upper classes at the time of Wilhelm II which had failed to foresee the coming revolution. Hagen epitomized the politicians who had stabbed the German army in the back in 1918. Siegfried was 'a symbol of the young Germany which is now preparing to replace the remnants of the collapsing bourgeois-Marxist state and to erect a new Germany, the Third Reich'.[51] Bayreuth itself was described as a last bulwark — a favourite word — of true German values in opposition to 'modernism' alias 'expressionism' alias 'cultural bolshevism'. All in all it is small wonder that on attending the Festival in 1928, Hans Heinz Stuckenschmidt, now at the outset of his career as a noted musicologist, found that Bayreuth had been turned into an ideological institution. 'It stinks of swastika and reaction. Princes and generals come so they can be revivified by Germanic myths.'[52]

About the Festival itself the Wagnerian fundamentalists were utterly emphatic: absolutely no scenic alterations, no foreigners and no Jews. Consequently they were some of the harshest critics of Siegfried's artistic management. The composer Hans Pfitzner, himself a devout anti-Semite and National Socialist, led the attack. 'There is *one* opera house in Germany,' he wrote, 'that more than any other has the moral obligation to keep Wagner's creations completely untouched by these trends, to present the works as they were set down, that is, as they are: Bayreuth.'[53] He condemned the engagement of Toscanini and denounced Siegfried's modest alterations as 'vacillating half-concessions'. His views were echoed by the *Völkischer Beobachter*, which kept up a steady stream of abuse about the way Wagner's operas were being 'violated in the most evil way' and 'made the plaything of the most perverted scenic "reforms" '.[54] Eventually Siegfried himself was moved to complain about 'a certain type of hyper-Wagnerian who is almost more unpleasant than the opponents' of Bayreuth.[55]

The composer, conductor and critic Siegmund von Hausegger is a good example of a prewar conservative who moved steadily to the right until by 1928 he was an outright National Socialist supporter. From then on his music criticism was essentially an incantation of ideological slogans. Wagnerian opera, which grew out of 'the myths which slumber deep in the soul of the German people', he wrote, was being destroyed by 'big cities and technology'.[56] Bayreuth was a great 'bulwark', a 'beleaguered fortress' defending 'the German spirit' against the 'modern spirit', against 'technology', 'internationalization', 'cultural Bolshevism' and even the 'Diktat von Versailles'. To lay the words and phrases of this putative music criticism — with the paranoia and xenophobia implicit in them — side by side with the words and phrases of Nazi ideology is to find that the two are identical. An appeal by Pfitzner in 1926 for a legal ban on 'anti-traditional art' was the genuine, if precocious, expression of National Socialism in establishing the principle of politically unacceptable art and the need for state control of culture. These 'hyper-Wagnerians' did in the music field what the industrialists and bankers did in theirs in helping to destroy the liberal Republic and to prepare the way for the Third Reich.

By the end of the decade Siegfried seemed to begin awakening to the danger that was overtaking Bayreuth. Given the right-wing opposition to foreign singers and conductors, was his decision to invite Toscanini an act of political defiance? Was he coming to realize what was in store for Bayreuth and the German musical world if his wife's friends came to power? And was the clause in his will, transferring his entire estate to his children if Winifred remarried, intended to prevent any chance of his inheritance falling into the hands of Hitler?

Like Wotan, Siegfried was hopelessly enmeshed in bonds ultimately of his own making. But he at least was spared witnessing the destruction of his Valhalla. During a concert tour in England in January 1930 he suffered a mild heart attack. The next month he exhausted himself producing and directing the *Ring* at La Scala. In April, he was shattered by Cosima's death at 92. Preparations for that year's Festival were especially exasperating. Toscanini was a holy terror, raging at everyone and demanding changes in the orchestra and cast. Muck, furiously jealous at being upstaged by Toscanini, made rehearsals a daily misery, even threatening to resign unless Melchior were replaced as Tristan. Melchior in turn had to be discreetly invited to special rehearsals to help him learn his lines and persuade him to sing his roles without a cut. At the dress rehearsal of *Götterdämmerung*, Siegfried had a heart attack. After lingering for another three weeks, he died on 4 August, without having seen his *Tannhäuser*.

Siegfried was aware of his shortcomings and the disappointment he was to others — and no doubt to himself. Yet while his treatment of Isolde was unforgivable and his jealousy of Strauss and Beidler petty, his good nature usually triumphed. Instead of being embittered and malicious, he was usually the warm-hearted, defensive and ingenuous person he himself characterized in his little book of memoirs:

> My parents named me Siegfried. Well, no anvils have I smashed, no dragons have I slain, no sea of flames have I traversed. None the less, I hope I am not entirely unworthy of the name, since fear at least is not in my nature.[57]

5

'Thus evil enters this house'
(*Lohengrin*)

When Winifred sat down behind Siegfried's desk on the morning after his death, she in effect threw down a challenge not only to her sisters-in-law and the Wagnerian old guard but to the musical establishment at large. Siegfried's premature demise had created a highly anomalous situation. In the fullness of time artistic succession would have fallen naturally to Wieland as the eldest child. But in leaving everything to his wife—with the proviso that the opera house might neither be sold nor used for works other than Richard Wagner's—Siegfried had short-circuited strict dynastic succession. To the keepers of the sacred Wagnerian legacy it was unthinkable that a thirty-three-year-old woman—inexperienced, unqualified and English at that—should even for a moment contemplate managing Bayreuth. Winifred was an outsider, a usurper. She had to be stopped. Cabals were formed. More ominously, Karl Muck resigned. With his connection going back to 1892, he stood as the very personification of artistic continuity and authenticity. His withdrawal in the face of Winifred's pleas was a dreadful blow.

It was 1883 over again, but far worse. Like Cosima, Winifred held all the legal power; unlike Cosima, she could claim neither first-hand knowledge of the composer's intentions nor the loyalty of important musicians nor even the support of wise counsellors. But after surviving youth as an orphan and adulthood in a family like the Wagners, she was tough and she was canny. Having been at Siegfried's side since the Festival had reopened, she also knew how the institution worked. Her problem was a lack of professional legitimacy, and she recognized that without this she could not keep the Festival going. Credibility, she decided, was to be acquired vicariously, by turning over artistic and musical direction to professionals beyond cavil.

For her general manager, she chose Heinz Tietjen who, with the stage designer Emil Preetorius, had produced the 1929 *Lohengrin* that had so impressed Siegfried. As head of the Prussian State theatre system, which included the Kroll Opera and the State Opera of Berlin as well as the operas of Wiesbaden, Kassel and Hanover, Tietjen was the most important impresario in Germany. Bayreuth offered him the fulfilment of a passion that had possessed him since 1908 when he had written to Cosima of his dream of someday conducting there. He offered Bayreuth not only all the artistic and technical resources at his command in Berlin but his own remarkable talents as well.

Tietjen had worked his way up, both as a conductor and as a director, first in Trier and Saarbrücken and then in Breslau and at the Berlin City Opera, until he finally reached the pinnacle in 1927. He combined great professional ambition with a quality especially rare in the music world, great personal effacement. Although assessments of his conducting vary, no one ever doubted his solid expertise as a musician or his supreme competence as a manager. But with a lifeless exterior, an owl-like gaze and a notorious reputation for scheming, he aroused instinctive and almost universal mistrust. He was seen as a veritable Talleyrand, and what Napoleon had said of him—'You are a coward, a traitor, a thief. You do not even believe in God. You have betrayed and deceived everybody. You would sell even your own father'—was said in one way or another of Tietjen. Even those who testified to his kindness and dependability never seem to have had personal confidence in him.

At least he enjoyed the virtue of being equally mistrusted by the two extremes of the musical community. The conservatives would not forgive his collaboration with such dangerous avant-garde figures as Klemperer and Kleiber and accused him of turning the Berlin Opera into a 'stronghold of un-German spirit'. The avant-garde figures themselves could not forgive his selling them out when it became politically expedient and questioned his artistic integrity. The former feared he would tamper with Bayreuth's sacred traditions, the latter feared he would not.

Winifred at any rate came almost to worship him. For her, he was not just an artistic director but an omnicompetent manager, the most loyal of collaborators and the person she entrusted with the guardianship of her children. Her sentiments can be gauged from a letter to him at the conclusion of his first season at Bayreuth:

> When the enormous burden of responsibility for the continuation of the Festival fell upon me as a result of Siegfried's death, I was preoccupied day and night with the vital question: 'Where will I find the conductor-director who will be able to strengthen Bayreuth's artistic soul with a thorough mastery of the scores, the texts and the dramaturgical intentions of the Master? Where will I find the selfless assistant to allow me to accomplish my duty?'
>
> You, my dear Herr Tietjen, had already proven in decade-long artistic activity that you had this exceptional ability for the work; and our first

contacts brought the blessed recognition that you possessed not only the artistic qualities but also the human greatness which is necessary unreservedly to support and serve the work. The experience of this year's Festival reassured me that you are the Chosen One. Continue to help me in loyal cooperation and step by step educate my son Wieland in his life's work: the worthy successor of his father in the service of Bayreuth's mission.[1]

Finding a music director, however, was far more difficult and a problem Winifred never solved. The choice was between Toscanini, the most famous conductor in the world, and Wilhelm Furtwängler, the most celebrated conductor in Central Europe. Both were noted Wagner interpreters and both regarded Bayreuth as holy ground. Both were also notoriously vain, temperamental and dogmatic. As conductors, however, they were polar opposites. Toscanini regarded a score as inviolable writ, and he was fanatical in following it precisely as written down by the composer. For Furtwängler there was no final, objective score but only an imponderable creation requiring interpretation. Toscanini was a known quantity, the star of the 1930 Festival, an international attraction. Furtwängler was a complete stranger to everyone at Wahnfried. But another difference was undoubtedly decisive—nationality. For an Englishwoman, as Ernest Newman commented at the time, 'to hand over this greatest of all German national art-works to a foreigner would inevitably provoke an outburst of Chauvinism in Germany, to say nothing of the trouble Toscanini would meet from the German conductors engaged'.[2] So Winifred chose Furtwängler. Such was Toscanini's devotion to Wagner and his reverence for Bayreuth, however, that he was persuaded to return the next year to conduct *Parsifal* and *Tannhäuser*. Alas, instead of having the best of all possible worlds, she eventually had the worst. As Rudolf Bockelmann predicted at the time, 'Two popes in one house, that will lead to schism.'[3]

Winifred's first season, in 1931, began with an incident that was a portent for the whole sorry summer. En route from Berlin to Bayreuth to commence rehearsals, Furtwängler was nearly killed when his two-seater airplane crashed; miraculously he and the pilot escaped unscathed, if badly shaken. Arriving at the Festspielhaus half an hour late, the conductor found everyone more upset by his unheard-of lack of punctuality than by his close brush with death. This reaction was indicative of the Bayreuth state of mind that antagonized Furtwängler from the start. However, the mutual incomprehension went much deeper. The notion of being part of a team was alien to Furtwängler; he demanded complete and sole authority. In his view of opera, moreover, the music and therefore conducting and therefore conductors were supreme. As it became clear that this was not the view at Bayreuth, he wrote to Winifred suggesting he should withdraw. An old hand at dealing with temperamental artists, Winifred smoothed things over and he agreed to stay.

Planning the 1931 Festival (from the left): Alexander Spring (assistant stage manager), Furtwängler, Tietjen, Winifred, Toscanini and Carl Kittel. 'Furtwängler and Toscanini couldn't abide each other, and their dislike was fanned by Tietjen' (Friedelind).

Hardly had rehearsals resumed when Lauritz Melchior, Bayreuth's Tristan for the season, announced his intention of leaving Bayreuth at once. Whatever his reasons—he later invented a cockeyed story that was provably false—he got along neither with Furtwängler, who was exasperated by his lack of both vocal discipline and knowledge of the text, nor with Winifred, for reasons that have never been clear. In the end he remained, sang in two cycles but then broke his contract and abruptly left Bayreuth, never to return. He may have been put off by the reviews, some of which were devastating—'He shouts rather than sings,' was Hans Heinz Stuckenschmidt's comment.[4] In any case when Bayreuth made history on 18 August with the first worldwide opera broadcast—of that day's performance of *Tristan*—it was Gotthelf Pistor who sang the title role.

In the meantime a graver crisis had played itself out. At a memorial concert in the Festspielhaus for Cosima and Siegfried, Toscanini created a scandal. As far as can be deduced from the welter of conflicting accounts, he was offended that tickets to the concert were sold—he was conducting the season without a fee—and mortified at being relegated to conduct Wagner's minor Faust Overture while the main work, Beethoven's Third Symphony, was taken by Furtwängler. Following an incident or two at rehearsals, he broke his baton, bolted from the opera house and declined to conduct at the concert. Although the Festival itself continued without further incident, relations among Toscanini, Furtwängler and Tietjen remained poisonous. At the end of the season Toscanini informed Winifred he would not return, and he did so with considerable ill grace. Her letter of appreciation, enclosing as a token of gratitude Wagner's draft of the Flowermaiden scene from *Parsifal*, was returned unopened, under cover of his own letter which concluded, 'I leave Bayreuth disgusted and embittered. I came here with the sense of arriving at a genuine shrine and I leave a commonplace theatre.'[5]

Winifred's tribulations were not yet over and even though 1932 was a rest year, she had little repose. During the spring Furtwängler mastered his congenital uncertainties and resigned as music director. Contributing to the break were bad personal relations. Winifred found him a vain and insecure prima donna; he considered her—as he wrote in a letter and repeated even more brutally in a newspaper article—an upstart whose only qualification was her husband's will. The deeper problem was that Furtwängler thought he had been given complete autonomy in running the musical side of the Festival, including the selection of soloists, while Winifred insisted that final overall authority must rest with her. Some credited Tietjen with having played Iago to Winifred's Desdemona and Furtwängler's Othello. Certainly it was a ménage à trois destined to fail. But Tietjen did not create and could not have resolved the fundamental differences.

Within less than two years of Siegfried's death, Bayreuth had lost three of its most eminent conductors. These defections, along with the worldwide economic depression and the unsettled political conditions in Germany, damaged ticket sales to the point where the very future of the Festival was in danger. Winifred, who had never really reconciled herself to the loss of Toscanini, now recognized it as vital to win him back. Since Toscanini had a soft spot in his heart for Eva and Daniela, she worked through them. 'O kehr zurück, du kühner Sänger!' (Oh, come back, dauntless singer), wrote Eva, quoting Wolfram's words to Tannhäuser. 'All of Bayreuth's best friends join me in this heartfelt plea. . . .'[6] Willing to stoop to conquer—for the first but by no means the last time—Winifred herself journeyed to Toscanini's villa on Lago Maggiore and, after each had forgiven the other for past sins, Toscanini agreed to return to conduct *Meistersinger* and *Parsifal* in the coming season. The situation was saved.

Meanwhile political affairs were evolving in a direction with fateful consequences for the German musical world and in particular for Bayreuth. In January 1933 the National Socialists came to power and within a matter of weeks opera houses and concert halls were taken over by party louts who fired, harried or drove out Jews, leftists and other 'cultural bolshevists'. Although these activities were unorganized, the party—now the government—lost no time in declaring culture to be, in the revealing phrase, 'a weapon of the state'.

The target was any person or any art form that was considered Jewish, modern or leftist. In the music field, out went all such musicians, singers, pianists, conductors and managerial officials. Out went compositions by 'modernist' gentile composers like Berg, Bartók and Hindemith no less than works by Jewish composers such as Mendelssohn, Mahler and Schönberg. Out with twentieth-century opera went twentieth-century expressionist and experimental staging style. Out also went those who, like the Nazi mayor of Leipzig, were insufficiently appreciative of Wagner. Out even went unacceptable comment on Wagner—and out with that went Thomas Mann, banned from the Third Reich for his essay 'The Suffering and Greatness of Richard Wagner' with its reference to the psychoanalytic insights in Wagner's operas. No longer was opera an art form but a plaything of party leaders, to reflect their preferences, ideology and taste—or lack of it. In no time operatic staging was homogenized into a sort of Third Reich naturalism, and the productions and performances were designed to promote the official ideology. 'One Reich, one Folk, one staging style', went a saying at the time—mocking the official chant, 'One Reich, one Folk, one Führer'.

In this way every individual and every institution was 'coordinated', in the official euphemism, into the Third Reich. In overall control was a Chamber of Culture under Joseph Goebbels, himself now head of a Ministry for Public Enlightenment and Propaganda. With complete authority over all cultural affairs, the Chamber had sub-chambers for music, painting and the other arts. Membership was obligatory for anyone wishing to practise in his field and a chamber's decrees had the force of law. To the delight of the Nazis and to the dismay of their opponents, Richard Strauss agreed to head the Reich Music Chamber.

Such was the background of history's first great cultural blitzkrieg. The great strategist, as in later military campaigns, was Hitler himself. No other head of any great modern state was so fascinated by the arts as this reborn Pericles, as he thought of himself. 'For me politics is only a means to an end,' he would say. 'Wars come and go. What remain are cultural values alone.' Now all Germany was to be his opera stage and he the great impresario. The supreme hero in the new Reich would of course be Richard Wagner. Conveniently enough, the fiftieth anniversary of the composer's death fell on 13 February, and Hitler used the occasion to stage a grandiose memorial ceremony in Leipzig to which he invited Winifred and Wieland, members of the cabinet, the diplomatic corps and leading cultural figures—but excluding, as the party's newspaper *Völkischer Beobachter* snidely pointed out, 'the usual Jewish literary crowd'. The event was eagerly acclaimed by the already 'coordinated' press and reports emphasized that Hitler's presence signified the forging of a link between the new Germany and the spiritual legacy of 'her great son'. Within two weeks of becoming Chancellor, Hitler had appropriated Wagner and made him the jewel in the Third Reich's crown.

Goebbels, the great propaganda wizard, took over from there. Wagner was apotheosized in terms that soon became numbing clichés— 'the greatest music genius of all time', 'the fullest embodiment of the national ideal', 'the herald of National Socialism' and the like—while the press poured forth waves of similar panegyrics. Although Goebbels himself was no Wagner fan, the rousing third act chorale of *Die Meistersinger*, 'Awake! Soon will dawn the day', had always stirred in him, so he claimed, ecstatic feelings of nationalistic glory. Now he heard in it the sound of the party's triumph. So he proceeded to turn the entire opera into a Nazi anthem. What could have been more fitting than that the day which formally inaugurated the Third Reich, 13 March 1933, should begin with the convening of the new Reichstag and conclude with a gala performance of the work at the Berlin State Opera conducted by Furtwängler? And from then on it was performed on all important party and state occasions. Thus it came about that a work of profound warmth, joy and humanity, a work Shaw depicted as 'a treasure of everything lovely and happy in music', was shamelessly traduced in one of the great cultural crimes of the Third Reich.

The colossal anomaly is that just about the only person in the party who liked Wagner's operas was Hitler himself. For Goebbels they were merely a propaganda instrument. For the others they were an unpleasantness to be endured. And endured they had to be. Like many another fanatical music-lover, Hitler was determined that everyone should enjoy his favourite music as much as he did. An endearing example of his naïve enthusiasm was the occasion of the Nuremberg party rallies, when he always commanded a performance of—naturally—*Die Meistersinger*. The Berlin State Opera was brought in for the occasion, Furtwängler sometimes conducted and a thousand tickets were issued. On the first occasion the tickets were given to party officials. In his memoirs Albert Speer recalls that these men, 'diamonds in the rough who had as little bent for classical music as for art and literature', went instead on drinking sprees.[7] Infuriated, Hitler 'ordered patrols sent out to bring the high party functionaries from their quarters, beer halls, and cafés to the opera house'. The following year attendance was made a Führer command. But when the functionaries yawned and snored their way through the performance, even Hitler gave up. Subsequently he invited a more appreciative or at least a less overtly bored audience.

For the Wagner family and the Wagnerian old guard, the triumph of Hitler was very much their triumph. Wahnfried was for the first time opened to the public on the anniversary of Wagner's death. Article upon article appeared—Paul Bülow's 'Adolf Hitler and the Bayreuth Ideological Circle' was typical[8]—celebrating the marriage of Wagner and Bayreuth with Hitler and the Nazi revolution. The *Bayreuther Blätter* rose splendidly to the occasion—as well it might, for as Stuckenschmidt pointed out, 'If Bayreuth today stands under the swastika, we have Hans von Wolzogen and his publication to thank.'[9] The journal itself exclaimed, 'Now there is a Chancellor who loves Wagner, understands German culture, and who will not be afraid to deal with the Jewish question.' No longer a 'cultural island' in a hostile sea, Bayreuth would be 'a centre of German culture in a German-regenerated Germany'.[10]

In reality this was whistling in the dark. Bayreuth's future was far from clear in those early days. As an appalled Winifred soon became aware, party officials were lower middle-class cultural barbarians who hated the Festival, with its élitist and international tradition, performers, productions and audiences. The party press campaigned against its Jewish singers and the local Gauleiter threatened to 'smoke out that international crowd at Wahnfried'.[11]

Not until she arranged to meet Hitler in the Reich Chancellery on 1 April did she know for certain how matters stood. Then, in a cordial conversation, he assured her of his undiminished friendship and his unchanged devotion to Bayreuth. He acknowledged the hostility to Wagner within the party but maintained that he could best counteract it by personally attending the Festival each summer. Encouraging though the encounter was, it had no effect on the attitude of party functionaries—men who, when they heard the word culture, reached for their pistols. *Parsifal* was condemned as 'ideologically unacceptable' while the *Ring* was deprecated by the party ideologist Alfred Rosenberg as neither heroic nor Germanic. 'The powers of darkness are unremittingly at work and unfortunately with success,' Liselotte Schmidt, Winifred's secretary, wrote to her parents in May of 1933.[12] 'Systematically and very maliciously, impregnable Bayreuth has been robbed of its last support and the saddest thing is that the highest authorities will take no note. . . . Tietjen, who, God knows, is in the most difficult position, is treated shamelessly.' After the war Tietjen himself had his own bitter memories:

> In reality the leading party officials throughout the Reich were *hostile* to Wagner. . . . Germany believed and believes still in a 'Hitler Bayreuth' that never was. The party tolerated Hitler's Wagner enthusiasm, but fought, openly or covertly, those who, like me, were devoted to his works—the people around Rosenberg openly, those around Goebbels covertly; a great deal more could be said about this![13]

What saved Bayreuth from being 'coordinated' like other opera houses into the Nazi party machinery was not the Führer's passion for Wagner but his undiminished affection for Winifred. He never forgot her early support. 'I judge people', he commented to friends in 1942, 'according to how they treated us at that period of our struggle.'[14] At another time he singled out Winifred as one of the four women he most admired. Her name, cultural sophistication and English background also made her valuable to him in putting a respectable face on his regime. When British Foreign Secretary Sir John Simon visited Berlin in 1935, she was his partner at the official dinner in his honour. Hitler even besought her to find a way of inducing Edward VIII to attend the Festival in 1937. During Mussolini's visit to Germany in 1938, she graced receptions for the Duce in Munich and Berlin. Hitler and she had always agreed that

Hitler at Wahnfried; from left: Artur Kannenberg (Hitler's household steward), Wolfgang Wagner, Winifred, an adjutant, Hitler, Julius Schaub (an adjutant) and Wieland Wagner.

a war between Britain and Germany should be avoided. She therefore willingly acted as intermediary when Sir Nevile Henderson, the British Ambassador, hurried to Bayreuth in late July 1939 and asked her to arrange a meeting with Hitler at the Festival so that he might make one last desperate effort to stave off a German attack on Poland. Here friendship reached its limits, however; the Führer refused Winifred's entreaties to see Henderson or even share the family box with him at the day's performance.

That day's performance was *Walküre*, an opera which had left its serendipitous mark on history exactly three years earlier. At the outset of the Spanish Civil War, Hitler had received a request from Franco for German military assistance. The message was delivered to the Führer in Bayreuth, immediately after his attendance at *Walküre*. Hitler approved the covert operation and, with the music still echoing in his ears, gave it the code name 'Feuerzauber'—Magic Fire—the concluding leitmotif of the opera.

Because of his relationship with Winifred, Hitler went to Bayreuth each summer from 1933 to 1939. As Winifred's guest in the Siegfried Wagner House and in Ludwig's old box in the opera house, he attended every performance of the first cycle and usually returned at the end of the season for *Götterdämmerung*. Even in the summer of 1939 when preoccupied with negotiations for a non-aggression pact with the Soviet Union and final preparations for an invasion of Poland, he did not allow his consultations with generals and diplomatists to prevent his attending that year's Festival. These experiences enthralled him, moving him at times to weep and at times, as when Valhalla collapsed in ruins, to reach out and hold hands with Winifred. 'The ten days in Bayreuth', he later reminisced wistfully, 'were always my most wonderful time' and the end of each Festival was 'something terribly sad for me, as when a Christmas tree is stripped of its ornaments'.[15]

Having observed him during these treasured occasions, Albert Speer recorded in his memoirs:

> On these festival days Hitler seemed more relaxed than usual. He obviously felt at ease in the Wagner family and free from the compulsion to represent power, which he sometimes thought himself obliged to do even with the evening group in the Chancellery. He was gay, paternal to the children, friendly and solicitous toward Winifred Wagner. . . . As patron of the festival and as the friend of the Wagner family, Hitler was no doubt realizing a dream which even in his youth he perhaps never quite dared to dream.[16]

Winifred was consequently always able to count on the Führer's protection. Alone of private institutions in the Third Reich, Bayreuth remained beyond party control. Never were old staff replaced with party members. Winifred herself successfully repulsed Goebbels's persistent pressure to join one of the chambers of culture and prevented his Propaganda Ministry, which omnivorously swallowed every other cultural organization, from interfering in any way. More surprising still, she even persuaded Hitler to permit Jewish singers, such as Alexander Kipnis and Emanuel List, to continue to perform and, amazingly, to perform in his presence at the 1933 Festival.

The most remarkable sign of Bayreuth's independence was Hitler's acquiescence in Tietjen and his stage designer, Emil Preetorius, towards whom he doubtless felt an instinctive antipathy. Both had come out of that hotbed of 'cultural bolshevism', the Prussian State theatre system, and both had risen to their positions by the preferment of the Social Democratic governments of Prussia. Tietjen, with his diplomat father and English mother, had grown up in Turkey, Britain and Africa, was multilingual and an unmitigated cosmopolite. A long-time Social Democrat, he had a reputation in the waning years of the Weimar Republic of being anti-Nazi. During the Third Reich his enemies in the party tried to unseat him on the grounds that he had not only given preference to Jews and foreigners in selecting soloists but continued to be a close friend of prominent Weimar opponents of Nazism. Goebbels detested him and the Gestapo categorized him as 'politically unreliable'.

Undoubtedly Tietjen was an embarrassment to Hitler, and the two men appear to have avoided each other.

It was a bizarre constellation of forces that protected Tietjen in both Bayreuth and Berlin, his dual role having linked the two opera houses after 1930. At Bayreuth, he was shielded by Winifred. Friedelind Wagner recalled that her mother had constantly to resist Hitler's antagonism to him, stressing over and over that Tietjen was a great artist and absolutely indispensable to her. In Berlin his protector was, of all unlikely characters, Hermann Goering. Goering had been appointed Prime Minister of Prussia in April 1933; but since that position was now essentially ceremonial, Hitler compensated him and played up to his cultural pretensions by giving him authority over the Berlin State Opera. For Goering this was not just an agreeable hobby but a means of competing with his enemy Goebbels and the opera houses under his purview. Determined to outshine his arch-rival, Goering tended to place talent above ideology and gave Tietjen his full backing and left him largely free to do his job.

Even more obnoxious to authorities was Preetorius. A protégé of Bruno Walter and a close friend of Thomas Mann, Preetorius had been an active member of the Union to Combat Anti-Semitism and in 1930 had published an outspoken article attacking anti-Semitism and professing strong admiration for Jews—an article that had earned him a denunciation by the *Völkischer Beobachter*. He maintained his Jewish friendships through the years of the Third Reich, and in 1941 he— along with Winifred and Tietjen—tried to protect a prominent Dutch Jew who had been head of the Wagner Society of Amsterdam. In 1942 and 1943 he was intensively investigated by the Gestapo and the National Socialist party and found to be politically unreliable. What appears to have saved him was his international fame as a stage designer, Winifred's support and Hitler's grudging recognition of his artistic expertise.

Winifred's friendship with Hitler assured not just protection but positive assistance. And this became vital as the 1933 Festival approached. As a result of the government's anti-Semitic actions, Jews, who comprised a high proportion of the music-loving public in Germany, along with most foreigners not surprisingly lost their appetite for Bayreuth. So bad were advance ticket sales that the Festival faced financial ruin. In desperation Winifred went to Berlin, bearded Hitler and succeeded in cashing in—literally—on her old friendship. With the utmost generosity the Führer instructed party and government institutions from now on to buy large blocks of tickets and pledged a substantial grant to subsidize new productions. 'I considered it to be a particular joy', his table-talk records, 'to have been able to keep Bayreuth going at a time when it faced economic collapse.'[17] In guaranteeing the institution's finances with assured and ample funding for the first time in its history, Hitler made himself almost as great a patron as King Ludwig.

Indeed, at a Wagner memorial event at Neuschwanstein in 1933 he told the audience he regarded it as his mission to complete what Ludwig had begun. In so doing he at long last gave reality to Richard Wagner's dream of a Bayreuth recognized by the state as a 'national obligation'.

On only one occasion did Hitler's support for Bayreuth and the Wagners reach a limit. In 1934 when German copyright law was being revised, the question arose of giving special protection to Wagner's works. Richard Strauss took the lead, calling for an extension of seventy to a hundred years. Despite great effort on Winifred's part, Hitler decided he could not honour the promise made in 1923 to 'give back' *Parsifal* to Bayreuth by extending the copyright. Although Winifred later obfuscated the issue, from her remarks it appears that Hitler realized that the effect of banning it from other German opera houses would be to encourage Germans to see it abroad, where the copyright would not apply. The new law made no exception for Wagner's works and the long-standing hope of restricting *Parsifal* to Bayreuth was dashed for good.

Though Bayreuth benefited enormously from Hitler's favour and largesse—and would otherwise probably not have survived in its existing form—the institution did not entirely escape the damage that was inflicted on German musical life. The sacking of Jewish conductors, musicians and concert managers caused an international scandal and soon cost Germany some of the best talent of the day, German and foreign, Jewish and Gentile. Within a matter of weeks of the establishment of the Third Reich, such notables as Fritz and Adolf Busch, Bruno Walter, Otto Klemperer, Carl Ebert, Rudolf Serkin and Artur Schnabel left in fear or disgust.

Aghast at the plight of his German colleagues, particularly at the violence that prevented Bruno Walter from conducting in Leipzig, Toscanini informed Winifred he could not return to Bayreuth. He also let his name head a protest telegram to Hitler from prominent musicians in the United States, where he was then conducting. Poor Winifred was beside herself; having already lost Furtwängler, she now faced losing the world's most prestigious conductor and the Festival's greatest box office draw. In desperation, she telephoned Hitler and as Friedelind Wagner recalled the scene: 'From the half of the conversation that I heard, I gather that he felt very badly treated after he had generously permitted Mother to keep her Jewish artists.'[18] Although it could not have been easy for him, at Winifred's prompting Hitler sent Toscanini a courteous letter saying how much he looked forward to meeting the 'Highly Esteemed Master', as he addressed him, at Bayreuth that summer. With equal politeness combined with Italianate *sfumatura*, Toscanini replied that it would be a 'bitter disappointment' if 'circumstances' were to prevent his conducting at the next Festival.[19] Since circumstances did not of course change, he eventually had to write to Winifred:

The sorrowful events which have wounded my feelings as a man and as an artist have not undergone any change, contrary to my every hope. It is therefore my duty . . . to inform you that for my tranquillity, for yours and for everyone's, it is better not to think any longer about my coming to Bayreuth.[20]

With the Festival due to begin in a matter of weeks, Winifred was desperate and offered the position to Fritz Busch, now in Switzerland on his way into exile. Such was the spell of Bayreuth that even this stalwart opponent of National Socialism hesitated for a moment, until his sense of honour asserted itself. At that point Winifred saw no alternative but to ask Richard Strauss to fill in. This was awkward since he had been shunned by Wahnfried since 1894. But he now graciously consented— as he had agreed a short time before to take over the Leipzig and Berlin concerts of the banned Bruno Walter. Party leaders were overjoyed at his cleaning up another of their political messes. Walter himself saw a colossal irony on the part of a man who had composed a tone poem entitled *A Hero's Life*.

Toscanini's defection was only the first blow. It was followed by the refusal of some of the outstanding Wagnerian singers of the time to perform in Germany: not just Jews such as Schorr, Kipnis and List but such Nordic Aryans as Kirsten Flagstad, Kerstin Thorburg, Lotte Lehmann, Gunnar Graarud, Elisabeth Schumann, Frida Leider (after 1938) and Herbert Janssen (after 1939). Bayreuth reached its vocal acme during the 1930s, but had it not lost these singers, it would have scaled even greater heights.

A far more harmful consequence of Winifred's friendship with Hitler was the Nazification of Bayreuth which became, in Thomas Mann's famous phrase, 'Hitler's court theatre'. From the first summer, in 1933, what had been a Wagner festival became an outright Hitler festival. On arriving in the town, visitors were greeted by swastika banners hanging on every flagpole and from every house. Storm troopers crowded the streets and cafés resounded to the *Horst-Wessel-Lied*, the Nazi anthem. Shops that since 1876 had displayed illustrations and miniature busts and other souvenirs of Richard Wagner now featured photographs and mementos of Adolf Hitler. *Mein Kampf* replaced *Mein Leben* in book-shops. On settling into their hotel, visitors found their rooms well stocked with official propaganda, not only such operatic material as the text of Hitler's latest Reichstag speeches but also, as Ernest Newman discovered, 'a big book from which we learned, in three languages, that, far from the Jews being ill-treated in Germany, they were really having the time of their lives in that tolerant country'.[21] Then, in making their way to the Green Hill, they found that the street leading there now bore a new name, Adolf-Hitler-Straße. If it was the first cycle of the season, the street was lined with armed SS guards and tens of thousands of onlookers heralding—and heiling—the arrival of government and

party leaders, it now being socially obligatory for the prominent and the ambitious to put in an appearance.

In this atmosphere of Nazi festivity, Hitler himself saw a danger that the performances would be overwhelmed by political frenzy. So, on entering the opera house each spectator was handed a flyer with an instruction to abstain from singing the national anthem or the *Horst-Wessel-Lied* at the conclusion of an opera. The programme itself carried the admonition: 'At the explicit wish of the Reich Chancellor, it is requested that there should be no demonstrations inside the Festspielhaus that do not pertain to the works of Richard Wagner.' But between acts the Führer was the object of public acclamation and after the performance he was guest of honour at huge Wahnfried receptions that often went on till daybreak. 'At every turn and whether we liked it or not,' Newman complained, 'Wagner was being pushed into the background to make way for Hitler.'

Those words were written in 1933, when for the first time in Bayreuth's history, the Festival opened with Beethoven's Ninth Symphony. It was with this that Richard Wagner had celebrated the laying of the foundation stone of the Festspielhaus in 1872 and with this that Winifred—and Strauss, who conducted—now hailed the founding of the Third Reich. The season began with *Die Meistersinger*. During the first intermission Joseph Goebbels broadcast to the world directly from the opera house, telling listeners:

> There is certainly no work in the entire music literature of the German people that is so relevant to our time and its spiritual and intellectual tensions as is Richard Wagner's *Meistersinger*. How often in years past has its rousing mass chorus 'Awake! Soon will dawn the day' been found by an ardently longing, believing German people to be a palpable symbol of the reawakening of the German nation from the deep political and spiritual narcosis of November 1918. . . .
>
> Of all his music dramas the *Meistersinger* stands out as the most German. It is simply the incarnation of our national identity. In it is contained everything that conditions and inspires the German cultural soul. It is a brilliant compendium of German melancholy and romanticism, of German pride and German energy, of that German humour which, as they say, smiles with one eye and cries with the other. . . .[22]

It is impossible to understand these inflammatory words without appreciating how differently Germans and non-Germans had always reacted to Wagner's operas—for the latter they were an aesthetic experience, for the former they appealed to romantic and mythological feelings of Germanness and a deep yearning for redemption, replacing a

The Führer greeting the Bayreuth audience from King Ludwig's annex in 1934.

sense of paranoia and inferiority with an exalted conviction of uniqueness and superiority. Third Reich Bayreuth shamelessly exploited this phenomenon for its own purposes.

The Festival handbook itself was from 1933 on as much a Hitler as a Wagner publication, with issues containing a photo not of the composer but of the Führer as frontispiece. The keynote was struck in the 1933 issue by its editor, Otto Strobel, who praised Hitler as 'the creator of the new Germany', the agent of 'the spiritual and moral renewal of our people' and 'that other "most German of Germans"'. The following year's issue carried an article by the Nazi mayor of Bayreuth, presenting Wagner less as a composer than the forerunner of Hitler. 'Heil Germany! Heil Hitler! Heil Bayreuth art!' his article concluded. Putting a reverse twist on this idea, the journalist Karl Grunsky claimed in the same issue that many Germans had been converted to Wagner's music by reading *Mein Kampf*. In 1937 Grunsky was back with an article asserting that 'the reality of Folk and race' constituted a Copernican revolution in philosophy and that Wagner, more than any other cultural figure, had recognized this fact. On and on in this vein the writers went. These were the court jesters of Hitler's court theatre.

Nothing was easier for the National Socialists than to glorify Wagner and to use some of his music as party anthems. Yet the text of the operas—a few nationalistic passages in *Lohengrin* and *Meistersinger* apart—gave no support to Nazi ideology and in many respects stood in clear opposition to it. The best they could do was to try to put an ideological gloss on the operas. The results were painfully artificial, not to say laughable. An essay in the 1938 Festival handbook by Leopold Reichwein, a Viennese conductor, is an example. Why, he asked, was Wagner's music relevant to the times?

> Because it points to the future; because it teaches us hardness with Lohengrin . . . ; because it teaches us with Hans Sachs to allow art to be rooted in the German people and to honour everything German; because it teaches us like Siegfried to perform the liberating act without thought of the reward; because it allows us to recognize in the *Ring des Nibelungen* the terrible seriousness of the racial issue; because from beginning to end it sings high praise of Woman; because finally it shows us in *Parsifal* the only religion a German can embrace. . . .

Far more squalid was the ideological distortion of Wagner scholarship in these years with the intention of making the composer out as the great precursor of National Socialism. Control of information about Wagner—getting hold of as much as possible and then withholding as much as possible—was an honoured Wagner family tradition going back to Cosima's day. Only writers who would produce what the family desired—Glasenapp in his biography of Wagner, Du Moulin Eckart in his of Cosima, and Zdenko von Kraft in his of Siegfried—were allowed access to the Wahnfried archive. Winifred permitted a ray of scholar-ship to penetrate the secrecy by appointing Otto Strobel in 1932 to be head of the archive. Strobel began making historical documents available to scholars and published the full correspondence between Wagner and King Ludwig. Unfortunately, the publication had a coun-ter-productive effect. So angered was Eva Chamberlain by their frank exposure of Wagner's occasional high-handedness that she stipulated in her will that her mother's diaries must remain in a bank vault until thirty years after her own death—in that way punishing Strobel by making it impossible for him ever to lay eyes on the precious historic document. As a result this fascinating record was not available to the public until the 1970s.

To give further impetus to Wagner research, Hitler established in 1938, on the occasion of the composer's 125th birthday, the German Richard Wagner Research Centre in Bayreuth, with Strobel at its head. Its purpose, as stated by Strobel, was to correct the hostile picture of Wagner which Jews had allegedly created over the decades in revenge for Wagner's anti-Semitism. The Centre's first priority was to dispose of the awkward story that Wagner was the illegitimate son of Ludwig Geyer, who was believed—falsely—to be Jewish. Vast effort went into 'proving' that both Richard and Cosima had impeccably Aryan bloodlines. The Centre's fraudulent aims were further revealed when Winifred lobbied the state authorities for a ban on all publications about Wagner except those approved by the Centre. Anything 'unworthy', Strobel decreed, was to be 'forever prevented'.[23] Wahnfried's age-old dream ultimately went the way of the Third Reich itself.

With the apotheosis of Wagner and the glorification of Bayreuth as Germany's supreme cultural showpiece, it is easy to see why there took root in the public mind a symbiotic relationship: Wagner—Bayreuth—Hitler—National Socialism—Third Reich. To remove any doubt, Hit-ler himself was after quoted as having affirmed: 'Whoever wants to understand National Socialist Germany must know Wagner.' For him-self and his regime, such reductionism was a great political and cultural success; for Wagner and Bayreuth, it was a moral and practical disaster Leonard Woolf's comment in his memoirs—'Wagner was both cause and effect of [the] repulsive process which ended in the apogee and apotheosis of human bestiality and degradation, Hitler and the Nazis'—perfectly expressed a widespread view in left-liberal intellectual circles that has never entirely vanished.

A slightly different twist was put on this phenomenon by Carl Jung, who characterized Nazism as the first outbreak of epidemic insanity in history. In an article in the *Neue Schweitzer Rundschau* in 1936, he turned the tables on those who had Nazified Wagner by Wagnerizing Nazism. Taking up his Wotan theory where he had left off in 1918, he argued that central to understanding the Third Reich was to probe 'the unfath-omable depths of Wotan's character'. Wotan was the personification of a fundamental trait of the German psyche—'a restless wanderer who creates unrest and stirs up strife', 'the unleasher of passions and the lust of battle', 'a superlative magician and an artist in illusion who is versed in all secrets of an occult nature'. Jung concluded:

> The emphasis on the Germanic race (vulgarly called 'Aryan'), the Germanic heritage, blood and soil, the Wagalaweia songs, the ride of the Valkyries . . . the devil as an international Alberich in Jewish or Masonic guise . . . —all this is the indispensable scenery for the drama that is taking place and at bottom it will mean the same thing: a god has taken possession of the Germans and their house is filled with a 'mighty rushing wind'.

Despite the political distortions, Bayreuth in those years basked in the glow of unparalleled artistic splendour. With Tietjen and Preetorius, the Festival was for the first time in the hands of widely experienced professionals. And with Winifred's courageous support, Hitler's copious financing and the Prussian State Theatre system's matchless resources behind them, the Berlin team was able to proffer one memorable performance after another. Because of Tietjen's position in Berlin it was no longer necessary to organize each Festival more or less *ab ovo*; instead, singers and musicians were simply deployed to Bayreuth, which became known as 'Tietjen's summer theatre'. New productions were designed and in effect rehearsed in Berlin; then, when perfected, they were moved to Bayreuth. Frida Leider, who participated in this annual hegira for some years, portrayed the result: 'Tietjen's *Ring* in Berlin had already aroused a great deal of attention. But now [1933] on the ideal stage, with the Bayreuth atmosphere, the finest Wagnerian singers available, a superb orchestra and the Bayreuth chorus, his production reached its greatest heights.'[24]

And indeed it was Tietjen's most notable achievement to have raised the musical and scenographic standards to the consistently highest level in the Festival's history. The success was obviously far from easy under the political circumstances. A further complication was the intense competition, musical and political, that developed between Bayreuth and Salzburg after 1933. Both Winifred, backed by Hitler, and Toscanini, then the dominant figure at Salzburg, confronted all artists with a policy of 'Bayreuth *or* Salzburg', a policy which Winifred pursued even after Austria was incorporated and Salzburg 'coordinated' into the Third Reich.

In the vocal sphere, Tietjen successfully guided Bayreuth through a period of transition into its greatest era. Frida Leider replaced Larsén-Todsen as Brünnhilde, Isolde and Kundry; Maria Müller took over the roles of Eva, Sieglinde, Elisabeth and Senta; Margarete Klose became the new Fricka, Waltraute and Erda and also sang Ortrud and Brangäne; Martha Fuchs alternated with Leider in her roles; Rudolf Bockelmann replaced Schorr as Wotan and took on Sachs and the Dutchman; Franz

Völker followed Graarud as Siegmund and was outstanding as Lohengrin, Parsifal and Erik; Herbert Janssen succeeded Theodor Scheidl as Amfortas and was first rate in a variety of secondary roles; Helge Roswaenge sang Parsifal while Max Lorenz assumed the whole repertory of heroic roles—Siegfried, Parsifal, Tristan, Walther, Siegmund—and alternated with Völker as Lohengrin. Two other stalwarts were Jaro Prohaska, who alternated with Bockelmann in his roles while also singing Amfortas, Gunther and Kurwenal, and Josef von Manowarda, who took on Gurnemanz, Fafner, Hunding, Hagen, Pogner, Titurel, Heinrich, Marke and Daland. Two foreign singers appeared late in these years: Set Svanholm, a Swede who sang Siegfried and Erich, and Germaine Lubin, a French admirer of Hitler and vice versa, who sang Isolde and Kundry.

Sublime, as always, was the chorus. Though Rüdel retired in 1936, his successor Friedrich Jung maintained the traditional standard. The orchestra too was as glorious as ever, even after the Nazis came to power. 'Many of us expected', the *Manchester Guardian*'s critic wrote, 'that without Jewish string players the Bayreuth orchestra would be below its former level of excellence but . . . both the orchestral playing and the choral singing have been of the highest quality, electrifying in their precision and unanimity and of the finest subtlety of detail.'[25]

Most problematic was finding good conductors since, except for Furtwängler, all the best Germans had gone into exile and the sole foreigner willing to appear was Victor de Sabata, who conducted only in 1939. No season could match 1931, when both Toscanini and Furtwängler were in attendance. Critics, though not without cavils, were awed by each—and by the contrast between them. The ardour of Furtwängler's *Tristan* no less than the economy and precision of Toscanini's *Tannhäuser* and the classicism and tempi—the slowest in Bayreuth's history—of his *Parsifal* demonstrated more fully than ever, as *Le Temps* observed, what a variety of marvels were to be mined in Wagner's music. There were those, however, who remained convinced that Muck's *Parsifal* was not matched then or later. Certainly it was not in 1933, with Strauss's rendering of it, which caused a scandal. Having gone to Bayreuth with the intention of deflating the usual sacerdotal solemnity of the occasion, he speeded up the performance, lopping off no less than forty minutes from Toscanini's time in 1931. Few critics were impressed; Newman considered him 'merely second-rate' and unworthy of the Bayreuth orchestra. The following year Strauss conformed to Bayreuth convention.

In 1936 Furtwängler reappeared. He was Hitler's favourite conductor and it was almost certainly with the Führer's encouragement that he agreed to conduct both then and in the following year. But as in 1931, relations between him and Winifred frayed to breaking point, and at the conclusion of the second season she secured Hitler's approval to drop him from future Festivals. With jealousies in the Third Reich artistic

establishment more inflamed than ever, the dismissal not only humiliated Furtwängler but galled the regime's culture czar. Goebbels had
come to find Bayreuth's independence intolerable and Winifred's favour
with Hitler a cause of the greenest envy. In the secrecy of his diaries he
vented his animosity towards Winifred and Wieland and derided the
Festival as a 'family and clique affair' which should properly be taken out
of the Wagners' hands.[26] He had already sought to poison the Führer's
mind against the Festival by deprecating it as an Augean stable of
homosexuality, in need of ruthless cleansing. Now he argued long and
hard with Hitler against the exclusion of a conductor whom he not only
admired but found cooperative with his own cultural aims:

> I presented him with all the counter-arguments. It will be a heavy loss for
> Bayreuth. Tietjen is a sneaky intriguer. And now he is to conduct the whole
> *Ring*. Yes, with a woman in charge, poor Bayreuth! The Führer is her
> greatest protector.[27]

When it was to no avail, Furtwängler felt free to let Winifred know
what he thought of her:

> You are quite seriously of the opinion that there is no need at Bayreuth for
> a prominent musician of the first rank. You know little about the role which
> the music especially and therefore the conductor plays in Wagner's total art
> work; you are little aware of how deeply endangered is Bayreuth's position
> in the world today and why, here above all, only the best should be
> employed if Bayreuth is to have any reason to exist in the future. . . .[28]

This outburst, which even Goebbels found 'crass', angered an already
exasperated Hitler. Refusing the conductor's entreaties to meet to dis-
cuss the matter, he instead telephoned Winifred to express his sympathy
and support. And so Tietjen became principal conductor, assisted by
Karl Elmendorff and Franz von Hoeßlin. The appearance of von
Hoeßlin was illustrative of the anomalies of the Third Reich. He himself
was married to a Jewish singer and lived after 1935 in Florence; even so,
he had no qualms about conducting at Bayreuth and Winifred, despite
the official opposition to him, had no qualms about inviting him.

The greatest overall triumph of those years—and a legend in the
Bayreuth annals—was the *Lohengrin* of 1936, magisterially conducted by
Furtwängler and magnificently sung by Franz Völker and Max Lorenz
alternating as Lohengrin, Maria Müller as Elsa, Josef von Manowarda as
King Heinrich, Jaro Prohaska as Telramund, Margarete Klose as Ortrud
and Herbert Janssen as the Herald.

The critic of the *Neue Zürcher Zeitung*, who had attended performances of the opera for forty years, was overwhelmed: 'This new Bayreuth *Lohengrin* is in truth the "unique and indivisible miracle" which
Liszt recognized at its Weimar première. No praise is exagger-

The monumental and triumphalist character of the 1936 *Lohengrin* was evident in Act I. Costumes were designed for beauty, not historical accuracy; their colours added to the scene's impressiveness.

ated. . . . Wagner's deepest intent is here for the very first time reality.'[29] Hitler, said to have been moved to tears by the performance, was so impressed that he returned to attend two more times. He further offered the entire production—sets, singers, orchestra and conductor—to Covent Garden as a gift, in honour of Edward VIII's coronation. However, the monarch let it be known that pleased as he was by the gesture, it was hoped he would not be expected to attend, since opera bored him. With that and his abdication in favour of his brother whom Hitler disliked, the idea lapsed—to the enormous relief of Winifred and Tietjen, who found the notion wildly impractical.

Tietjen and Preetorius had equal success against even greater odds in staging the operas. The challenge was of historic proportions. Since Siegfried had made no fundamental changes in the staging, the Bayreuth repertory was still being produced essentially as conceived by Cosima. Revamping the lot was as urgent as controversy in doing so was inevitable. At the very outset Preetorius faced a critical intellectual dilemma. On the one hand the old romantic naturalism had been undermined by Appia and Craig. Preetorius recognized that a new approach was needed and, though he stopped far short of the expressionism of avant-garde producers, his 1929 *Lohengrin* at Berlin had marked an advance in Wagnerian staging. On the other hand the sheer weight of the Bayreuth tradition, fortified by the nearly palpable ghost

179

of Richard Wagner and his all too palpable stage instructions, posed a formidable obstacle to change. Standing by to forestall the slightest tampering with the sacred relics was the Wagnerian old guard, led by Daniela and Eva and the Wagner societies.

In an essay in the 1933 Festival programme, later elaborated in his book *Bild und Vision*, Preetorius candidly acknowledged his predicament. 'If anywhere in the world, it is in Bayreuth that Wagner's works must be done as far as possible in the way their creator intended.' And in any case, he insisted, the works could not simply be cut loose from their original moorings; a minimum of naturalism had to be retained to lend verisimilitude to the stage action and to comply with Wagner's highly expressive music, as in:

> the glimmering and shining of the forest leaves in the second act of *Siegfried*, the luminous moonlit night into which Siegmund and Sieglinde plunge, the waves in the depths of the Rhine, thunder and rainbow, the horse Grane, Lohengrin's swan, the reed from which Siegfried fashions his flute. Clearly these are all naturalistic elements and actions that must be rendered realistically, that cannot be transposed into the merely suggestive or ignored altogether.

None the less—and it was his key point—all Wagner's works are 'allegorical in the larger sense, archetypes of eternal phenomena'. The late romantic naturalism of earlier productions simply reflected the taste of the time and was not essential to the operas, indeed contradicted their fundamental allegorical spirit. Ideally the staging should aspire to timelessness. The trick lay in finding how 'to combine two demands which are a contradiction in terms: symbol and illusion, dream and reality, inner vision and outward nature—to make these things intermingle, to weld them together into one comprehensive scenic whole'. Preetorius argued that even though the pictorial element was more important in Wagnerian than in other operas, it was the music that carried the drama. Stage design dared never divert attention from that.

All this led to a greatly streamlined inscenation. The spacial layout remained essentially as Wagner had decreed, but sets were reduced to essentials, beards shaved off, Nordic headgear and similar paraphernalia scrapped or simplified and choreography altered. Costumes were much plainer and without any pretence at historical accuracy. Preetorius gave more importance than ever to lighting, which he described as 'the element which in its subtle power to change and create change is of all elements the one most nearly related to sound'.

The first of Preetorius's Bayreuth stagings were the *Ring* and *Meistersinger* in 1933. Stuckenschmidt could scarcely believe his eyes. At the very time the cultural clock was being turned back in Germany, he remarked, here were two productions 'with an entirely novel scenic dress, and executed in a fashion which departed completely from the

Although the fir tree and rock were in their accustomed places, Preetorius's 1933 staging of *Die Walküre*, Act III, with its cubistic rock, was his most controversial. In later years the fir tree was fuller and the rock flatter.

Bayreuth tradition'.[30] Ernest Newman, in a generally dyspeptic mood during that season, was at first taken aback by the bare sets of the *Ring* but found that he 'soon became reconciled to their gauntness' and came to like them best when they most eschewed the old naturalism.[31] In his last review before going into exile, Alfred Einstein had the highest praise for Preetorius, whom he referred to as the aesthetic and philosophic leader among stage designers. The *Meistersinger* settings he found especially successful. Almost everything was in its usual place, 'yet everything is new and suggestive'.[32] The *Ring* scenery he considered less satisfactory. But the fault here lay not with the designer nor even with the Bayreuth tradition but with Wagner himself, who lacked talent for stage design and whose instructions posed insoluble problems for later producers. In trying to respect Wagner's directions, Einstein felt, Preetorius had compromised his own art.

In point of fact the designer himself was never completely content with his *Ring* sets and costumes, and he continually altered them over the years. Bockelmann later quipped that during a decade of singing Wotan in this production, he had stood on three different Valkyries' rocks while clad in three different outfits. All the same, Preetorius was celebrated for the splendour of his visual images; certain effects, such as

181

the Valkyries' rock and Brünnhilde's fir tree, became famous optical leitmotifs.

Beauty, grace and harmony were traits of the other Preetorius stagings: *Lohengrin* in 1936, *Tristan* in 1938 and *Fliegender Holländer* in 1939, the first completely new version since 1901. Again, he simplified the traditional versions, though now he was decidedly less innovative in their replacements.

But it was Tietjen who carried these productions to full success through the flawless integration of staging, conducting, directing and singing into a seamless whole. Where he went wrong in the view of his critics was in exaggerating certain effects. Indeed, he did take advantage of Hitler's financial generosity to make the productions ever more lavish and the choruses increasingly monumental. The Gibichungs increased from a platoon (26) in Richard Wagner's time to a full company (101). Elsa and Lohengrin were attended by a suite of 300, with 70 pages bearing lighted candles. In 1882 Parsifal had to resist temptation by 24 Flowermaidens, while in 1937 as many as 48 turned out to seduce him. No fewer than 800 townsfolk frolicked in the meadow outside Nuremberg where previously there had been a hundred and something. And between 1886 and 1938, the crew of Tristan's boat increased from 22 to 38. Some found such pageantry overdone, even vulgar. The final scene of *Die Meistersinger* in particular was condemned—a small town fair transformed into a sort of Hollywood extravaganza à la Cecil B. de Mille, as one viewer commented. Tietjen always gave the unprovable but also unanswerable response that he did only what his predecessors would have done had the funds been available.

Tietjen's choral scenes were considered overstaged. The hypertrophy can be seen in Act III of the 1933 *Die Meistersinger*, characterized by Alfred Einstein as 'more Berlin than Bayreuth'.

The great accomplishment of the Berlin team was to have yanked Bayreuth out of the nineteenth century and pushed it into the twentieth. Though this did not amount to a revolution, it marked a vital evolution, the most dramatic break with an orthodoxy that had prevailed since 1876. Change was not limited to stage productions. On taking over in 1930 Winifred initiated a management style that also had the effect of opening the Festival to the contemporary world. Symptomatic was her highly controversial decision to abandon the Festival's aloof, if not hostile, attitude towards press critics by creating a press liaison office and having a press gallery constructed in the rear of the Festspielhaus auditorium. An even more striking break with tradition was her public declaration in 1931 that Wagner's scores permitted a variety of interpretations and that conductors would be welcome to express their 'artistic personality' at the Festival. Although the 'Bayreuth tempo' continued to prevail, Toscanini, Furtwängler, Strauss and Tietjen, whose fast-paced *Ring* amazed audiences in the late thirties, brought into performances an unprecedented measure of personal interpretation.

For the Wagnerian hardliners—most of them National Socialists and all of them fanatical opponents of change—the blow was especially cruel. At the very moment of their political triumph, they confronted cultural catastrophe. The music critics among them were in an impossible position; though press criticism was not formally banned until 1937, they could not publicly condemn productions applauded by their great leader himself. So they squared the circle by finding that the new political epoch had its parallel in a new artistic epoch, with nationalism triumphant in both. The new *Ring* was described as a 'glorification of German heroic will' and the new *Meistersinger* 'more German than ever'.

Outside the media, however, there was no restraint, and the attacks on Winifred, Tietjen and Preetorius were ferocious. No one was more appalled than Daniela, who was so sickened by what she had seen during the 1933 season that she poured out her heart in a letter to Preetorius:

> Let us be frank. Was it not an alien spirit that made us witness this year, to our astonishment and dismay, not only a complete disregard of the wishes and instructions of the Master but also something directly opposite in staging, direction and costumes etc.? . . . After each performance I wrote to [Tietjen] . . . with the despairing question: *Why?* Why all these countless changes that were no improvement? . . . Oh, Herr Professor, I could write down a whole litany of whys! . . . And what is Bayreuth if it is not the fulfilment down to the seemingly smallest detail of the will of the Master? Otherwise it has lost its reason for existence, its mission in the world; cut off from the hallowed tradition, it is no more Bayreuth.[33]

When it became known in late 1933 that the next work to be restaged was *Parsifal*—still being performed with the 1882 sets that were now so dilapidated that they caused audiences to wince and performers to fear bodily injury—opposition exploded. Eva and Daniela circulated a petition, phrased in the hieratic terminology of the fundamentalists, which declared that the original settings 'on which the eyes of the Master had reposed' possessed a 'timeless validity' and must be preserved without even Siegfried's alterations.[34] Eventually the '*Parsifal* petition' gained a thousand signatures, among them those of Strauss, Toscanini, Newman and the venerable ex-Czar Ferdinand. The petition circulated throughout Germany as a pamphlet and was accompanied by a wildly vituperative campaign against Tietjen and Preetorius, who were as a matter of course accused of being 'un-German' and 'under Jewish influence'.

Ignored by Winifred, the petitioners tried to turn the affair into a political *cause célèbre* by sending the appeal directly to Goebbels and Hitler. The Führer, according to Winifred, was greatly irritated and fully supported a restaging of the work. The petition was the last flickering of the power struggle between Winifred and the Wagner sisters. One fanatic, Adolf Zinsstag, head of the Wagner Society of Basel, never gave up. He carried on the campaign to such crazy extremes that he was warned in 1936 not to set foot in Germany again.

In thinking that Hitler would be sympathetic to their cause, the old guard had gravely miscalculated. Although he loathed modern art and expressionist stage design, Hitler was not conventionally reactionary. At this time in fact he was much under the influence of Paul Ludwig Troost, a respected Munich architect whose style was a severe neo-classicism that had a great influence on Third Reich architecture. And when it came to Wagnerian opera, Hitler happened to be a great admirer of Alfred Roller's work in Vienna. In his days as an aspiring artist, he had been politely treated by Roller, and his sketchbook of those years contains a drawing of the setting of the second act of Roller's famous 1903 *Tristan*.

So Hitler not only favoured an entirely new *Parsifal*—Winifred and Tietjen had envisaged a revision—but asked whether the staging might be done by Roller himself. Although Roller was ill and in his cups, Winifred was only too happy to oblige. With Hitler behind the production, she would be protected from the inevitable furore and accusations of ideological heresy.

There were yet other paradoxes in the *Parsifal* affair. After all the brouhaha, Roller's staging turned out to be little different from the sacrosanct original. The temple of the grail, the object of the old Wagnerians' deepest veneration, lost its cupola but retained the outlines of its forerunner. The magic garden was characterized by Winifred 'a disaster' and the whole production an embarrassment. The conductor of this new version was of course none other than the most famous signatory of the *Parsifal* petition, Richard Strauss. Nor did the paradoxes end there. For Winifred there was no alternative but to sound out Hitler about revamping Roller's fiasco. He agreed to a new production, and,

In his 1934 *Parsifal* Roller secularized the temple but left it rather formless. The contrast of the massive blue-green columns and the bright red knights' costumes enlivened the scene.

since Preetorius was more than happy once again to step aside, Wieland Wagner, just twenty, was invited to design new sets for the 1937 season. The result was another embarrassment. What Wieland produced was stylistically so retrograde that it clashed with everything else on the Bayreuth stage. Though innovative in projecting a film as background for the transformation scene, the work gave no hint that Wieland's was a powerful and original talent, full of promise for the future.

The *Parsifal* episode raises the question of Hitler's personal role at Bayreuth. Certainly the temptation to interfere must have been enormous. Hitler emerges from Speer's memoirs and diaries as someone whose dearest wish would have been to be an operatic stage designer and whose idea of heaven on earth would have been to live in Bayreuth, presumably as general manager of the Festival. What was a dream in the case of Bayreuth was reality in Berlin. There he spent endless hours working with his favourite stage designer Benno von Arent, who produced for him the grandiose theatrical effects that he found so bedazzling. The position of Reich Theatrical Designer was invented for Arent, and it is indicative that he not only created at the German Opera in Berlin productions appealing to the Führer's love of bathos and monumentalism but used the same techniques to decorate Berlin and other cities for state visits and official occasions. Hitler 'loved smashing effects', according to Speer, and smashing effects are what Arent gave him. His Nazified *Meistersinger*, produced under Hitler's personal supervision and with Goebbels's funding, had a third act finale distinctly

Wieland Wagner's 1937 *Parsifal* restored the temple's cupola and romanesque style. Done in stark red, gold and black, the stage image put some critics in mind of a luxurious Turkish bath.

resembling a Nazi party rally with its rows of banners and its crushing, regimented choreography. This is what Hitler would have liked at Bayreuth, and he repeatedly asked Winifred to take on Arent in place of Preetorius. But while she had been willing to accept the respectable Roller, she resolutely refused to have anything to do with Arent. Whenever the subject arose, Speer recorded, 'she pretended not to know what Hitler was driving at'.[35]

After the war both Winifred and Tietjen insisted that their independence had never been compromised. 'No one ever dared to try to interfere with me in any way,' Tietjen recorded in 1945.[36] 'Even the overall head of the Bayreuth Festival, Frau Winifred Wagner, allowed me complete freedom in all artistic matters. . . . Hitler himself never expressed any demands or wishes; we were *more* than sceptical of one another.' But did he and Preetorius trim their sails to catch the ideological winds? Could this explain the chorus of 800 in *Meistersinger* and the replacement of the cubistic Valkyries' rock of the 1933 *Ring* with something less expressionist in following seasons? It is highly unlikely. Tietjen's affinity for large choruses can be traced back to the 1920s in Berlin. And Preetorius was never content with his famous rock.

According to Friedelind Wagner, however, Hitler did in fact make occasional suggestions and these, she said, invariably 'gave Tietjen the jitters'.[37] One proposal harked back to Roller's *Tristan*, with its star-filled night sky that Hitler had seen in his youth and had admiringly sketched.

As Friedelind recalled, 'to avoid displeasing him by disregarding his scheme to light the sky in the second act of *Tristan*, with a moon and innumerable stars, Tietjen made the wood so dense that not a bit of the sky could be seen'. And in fact a critic commented of the production that 'the character of Preetorius's art was evident at its purest in the contrast between the extremely dense wood in the second act and the infinite breadth of the blue sea in the third'.[38]

The closest Bayreuth came to a 'political opera' was the 1936 *Lohengrin*, which coincided not only with the millennium of Henry the Fowler, the first German king and a character in the opera, but with the sixtieth anniversary of the Festival. More importantly, it was the year when the Olympic Games were held in Germany and foreigners were expected to return to Bayreuth for the first time since 1933—in fact fewer than a hundred showed up, mostly British and Americans. Finally, there was a personal element. Winifred, knowing how much the opera meant to Hitler, is said to have intended the new production—the first since 1908—as a token of affection.

To some observers the production was done in a spirit of Germanic triumphalism, with the tragic love affair between Lohengrin and Elsa being paralleled by a nationalistic call to arms, 'so that no one will evermore shame our land', as the King proclaims at the outset of the opera. The *Neue Zürcher Zeitung*'s critic was more explicit. In a report entitled 'Mythical-Political *Lohengrin*', he observed that the transformation of the

Was the dense forestation in Act II of the 1938 *Tristan* intended to foil Hitler's desire for a sky with a romantic moon and countless stars? The setting was Preetorius's most conventional.

swan, often considered unnecessary, here gained meaning: it represented the replacement of the old ethos with a Führer who was sent to protect the Reich. 'This secondary drama was now for the first time in Bayreuth consciously brought out.'[39] By contrast, any number of others, including opponents of the Third Reich, detected no political slant. Stuckenschmidt, who had been banned from writing in Germany after 1934, reviewed the performance for a Prague newspaper and had nothing but praise for every aspect of it.

From Winifred's correspondence with Hitler as well as Liselotte Schmidt's letters to her parents, it is clear that Winifred consulted Hitler on all important decisions. And after each performance the two of them returned to Wahnfried where they discussed the production long into the night. Still, when Bayreuth's productions are compared with those in other German opera houses in those years, the conclusion is inescapable that Winifred, Tietjen and Preetorius maintained Bayreuth's artistic independence, resisting both the reactionary tastes of the old Wagnerians and the overtly Nazified style that prevailed everywhere else in the Third Reich. They rejected outright proposals by party functionaries to include ideological frills, such as attaching swastikas to the Gibichungs' banners. And unlike many other opera houses of the time, Bayreuth did not hold special exhibits of a political nature nor was the interior of the Festspielhaus itself festooned with swastika banners.

The corruption of the Festival was on a different plane—in the overall pollution of cultural life in those years. In this context Bayreuth, far from keeping National Socialism out of art, provided it with its most distinguished aesthetic cover. Young Friedelind, who alone among the Wagners somehow never lost her independence of mind, observed this at first hand and found that it left her with an almost uncontrollable impulse to set fire to the place; instead in 1938 she fled, eventually finding her way to New York by way of London where she vented her feelings in broadcasts that mortified her family and, according to Goebbels's diaries, enraged party hierarchs. It was another exile, observing this from afar—Thomas Mann—who demolished the whole notion that it was possible to put on opera in the Third Reich without making propaganda:

> It was not right, it was impossible, to go on producing culture in Germany while all the things we know of were taking place. To do so meant palliating depravity, extenuating crime. Among the torments we suffered was the sight of German literature and art constantly serving as window dressing for absolute monstrousness. Strangely, no one seems to have felt that there were more honourable occupations than designing Wagner sets for Hitler's Bayreuth.[40]

6

'All that lives and soon must die'
(*Parsifal*)

Following the outbreak of war in 1939, Winifred took for granted that, as in 1914, it would be impossible to hold Festivals under wartime conditions. But when she prepared to close down the Festspielhaus, Hitler intervened and insisted that they must go on. To her argument that singers, musicians and stage-hands would be off fighting in the war, he replied that he intended to exempt artists from the military and asked her to provide him with the names of those in the music field to be excluded from service.

Hitler's determination to keep the country's opera houses and theatres open was meant to demonstrate the Third Reich's undiminished dedication to culture. But in the case of Bayreuth, he had a very special reason. At last he would be able to indulge his passion for having others—now tens of thousands of others—attend Wagner's operas. Beginning with the 1940 season, Hitler instituted what were called War Festivals, open no longer to the public but to persons known as 'Führer's guests'. These were members of the military and workers in war industries who, as a reward for their patriotic service, were to be taken to Bayreuth with all their expenses paid. Winifred and Tietjen were left in full artistic control, but otherwise the Festivals came under Hitler's personal direction. Administration was turned over to an Orwellian-sounding body, the party's recreation organization *Kraft durch Freude*, Strength through Joy. The key official of this institution, Bodo Lafferentz, was a fanatical Nazi—an officer in the storm troops, Hitler's praetorian guard, and a long-time party member. Known equally for his administrative skill and his political reliability, he was entrusted with several of Hitler's favourite projects. He avoided interfering in artistic matters, however, and in 1943 he became a member of the Wagner family by marrying Verena.

From the beginning there was something partly laughable and partly grotesque about the War Festivals. For the culturally unwashed party officials, with no love of opera—much less feeling for Wagner—they were simply an opportunity for cultural propaganda, and cultural propaganda of a particularly brutal and belligerent sort. The keynote was struck by Robert Ley—*Kraft durch Freude* was part of his bureaucratic empire—in inaugurating the first War Festival in 1940: 'We all know the old saying: "When the cannons speak the muses are silent."' But, he went on, 'in the new Germany lyre and sword belong together'.[1] This oxymoronic theme—destroying culture in the name of culture—was repeated by the Gauleiter of Bayreuth, Fritz Wächtler, to Festival audiences the following year. As German soldiers went from victory to victory in exterminating the 'Jewish-Bolshevist world enemy', he told them, German culture was being spread throughout Europe and the world. 'Kill for Wagner and the Fatherland' was roughly the message.

The propagandists also harped on the point that Bayreuth was for the first time open to ordinary people rather than to the rich, upper-class cosmopolites of earlier years, realizing at long last Richard Wagner's great dream of an invited audience attending the Festival free of charge. This attitude was in fact more revealing of the petit bourgeois resentments of party officials than of the composer's ideal—the whole purpose of which was to ensure the attendance of true connoisseurs of his works. Hitler's military-munitions worker audience was anything but that.

In this lay the innocent folly of the War Festivals. The guests of the Führer—those who attended were constantly reminded that such was their status—were in reality a captive audience. They had no choice but to attend and, as it were, to enjoy themselves like it or not. Transported in groups to Bayreuth in a Reich Music Train, they arrived at six in the evening and were marched in columns to barracks where they were quartered and then later marched to huge common halls where they were fed and provided with chits for beer, cigarettes and one operatic performance. The next morning they assembled at the opera house where they were given booklets on Wagner and his works and lectured about the opera to be given later in the day. Early the following morning they left, succeeded by another trainload of Führer's guests.

The arrangements for feeding and housing the throng were a shambles. The soldiers would undoubtedly have preferred to spend the time with their families and even the munition workers found the experience an ordeal. The comment of one harried worker to another, on emerging from the opera house to find it raining—'Now, on top of everything else, *this*'—was the sort of cynical anecdote that circulated at the time. As the war went on and audiences comprised ever larger numbers of wounded soldiers, the Green Hill took on a sadder and sadder aspect, resembling a hospital ward more than a joyous musical occasion. In all, some twenty to thirty thousand 'guests' a year attended each of the five War Festivals. With all the regimentation, the memory must have been less one of a night at the opera than a day on the parade ground with a musical interlude.

'Guests of the Führer' on their way to the Festspielhaus in summer 1940.

The sad face of the War Festivals: an audience during intermission.

Despite his crushing responsibilities in these years, Hitler took a keen interest in the Festivals. Winifred's letters to him make clear that she deferred to him for final decisions on every question—who was to sing, who was to conduct and what was to be performed. The main issue was the repertory, which was revised to suit the Führer's wishes and what he considered ideologically suitable for the audiences. For reasons never stated, *Parsifal* was banned throughout Germany after 1939, and Bayreuth complied. In 1940 and 1941 *Der fliegende Holländer* and the *Ring* were performed. The following year was limited to *Fliegender Holländer* and *Götterdämmerung*, though there was one full *Ring* cycle for wounded soldiers from the Russian front.

In early 1942 Winifred wrote to the Führer with ideas for new productions. *Tristan*, she remarked, would probably not be a good idea since the long third act narrative of the wounded Tristan about his suffering, loneliness and death would, as she put it, be too much of a burden for wounded soldiers in the audience. *Meistersinger* she thought would be preferable, even though she said she was aware that he wanted a new production of the work to celebrate the successful outcome of the war—this written less than two weeks after the German surrender at Stalingrad. Hitler approved the *Meistersinger* suggestion, and in that and the following year it alone was offered.

The ideological manipulation of the audiences was horrifying. What was discussed in the publications handed to them was not opera but 'the enemies of German culture', and these extended from the Bolsheviks in the East to 'the Jewish camarilla around Roosevelt' in the West. For those facing the Russian army, the slogan 'Wagner and Bayreuth' was said to epitomize what 'the most pitiless foe' wished to destroy. Men with the sound of battle still in their ears found that the operas made clear what was at stake. The essence of the *Ring* was ultimate German victory; the collapse of the world at the end of *Götterdämmerung* made it possible to envisage the new Germany taking shape. Soldiers were assured that, having faced death themselves and seen it all about them, they would find meaning, as no other audience, in the second act of *Walküre*, with its allusions to the death and transfiguration of war heroes. *Meistersinger* audiences were told that the work would fill everyone who saw it with a sense of the sacred mission of German culture, inspiring them to return to the battle front or factory with renewed enthusiasm to destroy the 'international plutocratic-Bolshevik conspiracy'. To commemorate the occasion, they were given a venomously anti-Semitic tract in the form of a souvenir book, *Richard Wagner und seine Meistersinger* by Richard Wilhelm Stock.

Audiences were not the only conscripts. Singers and conductors were also in effect inducted and ordered into operatic action. Under these circumstances Furtwängler returned and conducted in 1943 and 1944. Other conductors included the old stand-bys: Tietjen, Elmendorff and, in 1940, von Hoeßlin. They were joined by two newcomers with only an attenuated connection with Bayreuth: Hermann Abendroth, who had studied conducting with Mottl, and Richard Kraus, an assistant at Bayreuth for several years in the late twenties and early thirties. With the same casts as those of the thirties, musical standards—except for the chorus—were as high as ever.

Apart from a freshened-up version of *Rheingold* in 1940, *Meistersinger* three years later was the only new production of these years. At Tietjen's invitation, Wieland designed the staging and gave it a traditional, realistic treatment, a retrogression reflecting both his own conservatism at the time and a determination to dissociate himself from Preetorius, whose work he despised. Because of the manpower shortage at this stage of the war, the mammoth chorus of the old production was decimated and had to be filled out, no doubt thanks to Lafferentz, with members of the 'Viking' Division of the SS. Now, with storm troopers singing on stage and sounding the introductory fanfares from the balcony, Third Reich Bayreuth sank to its moral nadir.

Tietjen had turned to Wieland rather than Preetorius to design the *Meistersinger* sets in the hope of bolstering an armistice in a rancorous war between them. Over the years, Tietjen's relations with the Wagner children, especially Wieland and Friedelind, had become increasingly strained. His seemingly complete domination of Winifred aroused deep,

In his 1943 staging of *Die Meistersinger*, Act I, Wieland Wagner gave a literal interpretation to Wagner's stage directions.
Left SS troops sounding the fanfare from the Festspielhaus balcony.

no doubt partly Oedipal, resentments on Wieland's part. At first these were more personal than professional. For although it had always gone without saying that Wieland would succeed his father and grandfather, he himself was uncertain about his own intentions. He had no particular musical talent and what interest he took in opera was in designing sets; even this he did not with models but with painted sketches. His first settings were designed in 1937 for a Lübeck Opera production of his father's opera *Bärenhäuter*. The following year came not only Tietjen's commission to revise Roller's *Parsifal* at Bayreuth but also invitations to design the decors for Siegfried's operas in Antwerp, Dusseldorf and Cologne. However, when Tietjen then offered to take him on at the Berlin State Opera so he could learn about opera management from the ground up, Wieland spurned the offer.

Once the war began Hitler gave orders that Wieland should be permanently exempt from military service. He had always revered the boy as Richard Wagner's descendant and future head of the Festival. In 1937 he had ordered his release from paramilitary duty and in later years treated him as a sort of national monument, to be protected from harm. When both he and Wolfgang were expelled from the Hitler Youth for insulting the head of the organization, there were no unpleasant repercussions.

Wieland was therefore probably unique among men of military age in the Third Reich in being free to do what he wanted. And what he wanted at that stage was not to be an opera impresario but to pursue his childhood delight in painting. He consequently went to Munich to study. During his second year there, in 1940, he met Kurt Overhoff, a composer, conductor and Wagner expert, who fascinated Wieland with his explanations of the inner meaning of Wagner's music. Under Overhoff's tutelage and with the encouragement of his fiancée Gertrud Reissinger, he started to take a greater interest in opera. But as his interest grew, so did his suspicion that his mother and Tietjen had denied him this sort of training as a way of blocking him from his heritage as head of the Festival. Some sort of showdown evidently occurred in the summer of 1940 when Winifred agreed that both Wieland and Wolfgang should begin training in Bayreuth and that she and Tietjen would retire in five years, the event to coincide with the dedication of a new Festspielhaus.

The construction project was the result of a brainstorm which Hitler had in the mid-thirties. In his view the Festspielhaus was far too small and unimposing. His ideal of an opera house was Garnier's Paris Opera, and on his triumphal visit to Paris in June 1940 it was the first building he visited. In 1936 Hitler raised the subject with Preetorius, and after the latter said he thought the idea was a poor one, Hitler never spoke to him again. Winifred, aware that outright opposition would be counterproductive, humoured him and spent endless hours over the years hearing him out on his grandiose ideas to create a Festspielhaus that would be one of the great cultural sites of the world. The town itself was one of a number of German cities to be reconstructed and endowed with a great new civic forum, enormous meetings halls, a stadium and the like. Crowning it all, the Green Hill was to be turned into an acropolis with a huge new opera house as its parthenon. Smashing effects again.

Eventually Hitler was persuaded that because of its acoustics, the core of the building should be retained. The somewhat scaled-back final plan incorporated the existing auditorium in a vast complex. At the centre was a greatly enlarged stage with spacious accommodation for singers along with offices and workshops, while flanking these were two meandering wings to house a museum, archive, lecture hall and restaurant. The result was a cold, neo-classical maze of typical Third Reich architectural kitsch which probably reflected Hitler's not so subconscious desire to absorb Richard Wagner and Bayreuth into himself or perhaps to project himself onto them. The new house and the Wieland–Wolfgang era were to be inaugurated with a new production by Wieland of *Tannhäuser*.

But when construction was postponed, Wieland suspected Tietjen rather than the war for the delay until Hitler put him straight. Distrust turned into implacable hatred. In the summer of 1941 he complained to Goebbels and at least twice discussed his desire to oust Tietjen in

Hitler's proposed new Festspielhaus, designed by the architect Rudolf Emil Mewes, was to be inaugurated at a 'peace festival' celebrating Germany's final military victory. With the outbreak of war, construction was stopped.

conversations with Hitler. Tietjen, by this time thoroughly exasperated, played his trump card. He offered to resign. Faced with the withdrawal of the resources of the Berlin Opera—which meant nearly all of Bayreuth's soloists and musicians—and knowing that he was in no position to run the Festival on his own, Wieland realized his bluff had been called.

An uneasy truce ensued until Goebbels solved the problem by appointing Wieland chief operatic producer—with Overhoff as music director—in Altenburg. This Saxon town had a remarkably fine opera company, and there Wieland launched his career. Fired by the challenge, he went to work with a passion. In little more than a year he mounted productions of the entire *Ring*, Weber's *Freischütz* and his father's *An allem ist Hütschen schuld*. At the same time he accepted outside commissions: *Walküre* and *Götterdämmerung* in Nuremberg and *Die Meistersinger* in Bayreuth.

Of all these the Altenburg *Ring* was most important. It stimulated Wieland for the first time to give the work independent thought and devise ways of staging it that expressed Wagner's intentions rather than his directions. According to Overhoff, the catalyst was Wagner's essay *A Communication to my Friends*, which recommended ridding the stage of whatever was not strictly necessary. Here began the deconstruction of

197

the operas that was to become the hallmark of postwar Bayreuth. The stage images, while still realistic, were simplified. Lighting, which had begun to fascinate him, was used to replace solid objects and to intensify physical and psychological impressions. Wieland at this point still viewed the stage through the lens of traditional realism and continued to see the gods as the same old nineteenth-century Nordic deities, even if he relieved them of some of their armour. But his approach to staging was clearly in transition.

Wieland was also occupied with plans for the repeatedly postponed Bayreuth 'Peace Festival' to celebrate Germany's final military victory, and this brought him into continued contact with Hitler. The Führer himself attended the Festival only once during the war. In August 1940 on his way back to Berlin after the conquest of France, he ordered his train to Bayreuth so he could go to the day's performance—*Götterdämmerung*, as it appropriately turned out. Contacts and visits between the Wagners and Hitler continued to the very end, however. Not long before the July 1944 attempt on his life, Hitler visited Wahnfried, saying as he left, 'I hear the rustling of the wings of the victory goddess', a remark that struck even Winifred at this phase of the war as so barmy that she traced it to the effect of the injections he was being given by his quack doctor. Although it was the last time he and Winifred met, they stayed in touch by letter and telephone. Even after the July plot, while everything around him was sinking into ashes and rubble, Hitler had Bayreuth so much on his mind that he asked Winifred if it might be possible to hold the Festival in the summer of 1945. She replied affirmatively.

The Wagners typically had their minds on themselves. In January of 1945 Wieland sought out the Führer in his Berlin bunker to ask his help in arranging for publication of a new edition of the scores, texts and piano versions of Wagner's works. Astonishingly enough, Wieland returned only a few weeks before the final collapse to plead with Hitler to place in safekeeping in Bayreuth a cache of Wagner manuscripts that had been presented to him on his fiftieth birthday in 1939 by a group of industrialists, who had purchased them from the descendants of King Ludwig. These were the original scores of *Die Feen*, *Das Liebesverbot* and *Rienzi*, original copies of *Rheingold* and *Walküre* and the orchestral sketches of *Der fliegende Holländer*, *Götterdämmerung* and the third act of *Siegfried*. Hitler refused to give them up, insisting they were safe where he had hidden them. It is assumed that they were destroyed in the final days of fighting.

In the course of the war, while other German cities were being mercilessly bombed, Bayreuth had been ignored by the Allied air forces. As hundreds of bombers regularly flew past to drop their bombs on other targets, Bayreuthers invented various theories to explain their luck—Friedelind had persuaded Roosevelt to spare her home town; British and

American Wagnerians had intervened and so on. In fact the town did not enjoy any immunity; neither the Festspielhaus nor Wahnfried nor any other historic structure was included on the Allied list of protected buildings. The simple reason was that the town lacked any military significance. Alas, it had a small railway yard and though this was without any importance by April 1945, the Anglo-American war machine mindlessly targeted it to pave the way for invading land forces. The American air force hit the town with four raids—on the fifth, eighth, tenth and eleventh. Together these were so destructive—over two-thirds of the town was destroyed—they left Bayreuth the fifth worst damaged city in Bavaria, proportionately even worse than Munich. Although the final raid wiped out most of old Bayreuth, it was in the first that Wahnfried was hit.

Early in 1945 Winifred had begun removing items of historic importance from the villa. Richard Wagner's library was stored with a friend in a nearby village; paintings and archival material were placed in the basement of the Winifred Wagner Hospital in Bayreuth. But when she tried to take away historic furnishings, a Gestapo official intervened, accusing her of 'defeatism'. Consequently the bomb that fell on Wahnfried, wrecking much of the back of the house—the famous Saal and the old nursery—destroyed Wagner's desk and other personal relics, though not the Steinway that had been presented to him in 1876. Wieland and Wolfgang, now living back in Bayreuth, quickly spirited away as much as possible of the remaining property as well as what had been stored in the hospital, secreting the things in the family's summer house on Lake Constance and in Winifred's weekend cottage at Oberwarmensteinach, about twelve miles outside Bayreuth, where Winifred herself now withdrew. After the raids, civil order lapsed—British prisoners-of-war and displaced persons roamed the streets at will—and the Festspielhaus was broken into. Costumes were stolen and it is said that for miles around German refugees could be seen in the garb of characters from one or another opera.

Fortunately the Wehrmacht decided not to defend the town, which an American armoured column entered on 14 April. With it went a *Baltimore Sun* correspondent, who reported:

> Many of the tankers had never heard of Bayreuth before. Many of them said they had never heard of Richard Wagner. A few of the older ones seemed to recall a connection between the man and the town, and a major from Boston had a hazy recollection of 'some sort of a summer music festival, something like the one they have in the Berkshires, isn't it?'

The correspondent and a patrol of scouts were the first Americans to reach the Festspielhaus. White cloths fluttered from the old royal entry; Paul Eberhardt, Tietjen's lighting director, greeted the men in English. He was assured the building would not be harmed. 'The big summer opera house was empty, dusty and completely deserted,' the *Sun* reporter found. 'Its red fire hose had been unreeled, presumably for any emergency that might arise during an air raid. Its stage was shut off by the great curtain of corrugated tin.' Some three weeks later, on the day the war ended, Joseph Wechsberg, then Technical Sergeant Wechsberg, en route through Bayreuth, decided to have a look at the opera house about which he had heard so much. A stage door open, he went inside and found himself on stage, in Hans Sachs's workshop, in place for rehearsals for the 1945 season. The fire curtain was now raised, and Wechsberg sat down in Sachs's chair and sang his *Wahn* monologue to an empty auditorium, empty except for a carpenter who had been roused by the sound and came to listen.

After the war the American Military Government confiscated the property of prominent National Socialists and supporters of the regime. The Festspielhaus, Wahnfried and all Winifred's other property, except her houses outside Bayreuth, were taken over by the army. The opera house was used for religious services as well as for plays, operettas and shows to entertain the troops. The Siegfried Wagner House eventually became headquarters of the local Army Counter-Intelligence Corps. Wahnfried was left to moulder, though occasional parties and dances were held in the garden. Winifred and many other Germans were

Flyer for a performance for American forces in the Festspielhaus.

PROGRAM

BAYREUTH
SYMPHONY ORCHESTRA

*Music You Love
To Hear*

GUEST CONDUCTOR
MR. PAUL LINCKE

CONDUCTING
ORIGINAL COMPOSITIONS

Wednesday 12 Dec. 1945
19.30 hours

WAGNER FESTSPIELHAUS
BAYREUTH

As many as 500 Sudeten German expellees were housed in the Festspielhaus in late 1946. A refugee agency had offices in the restaurant and the chorus rehearsal hall for another four years.

outraged by the 'desecration' of these sacred sites and the story was repeated over and over that soldiers had actually been seen jitterbugging on Wagner's grave. Typical of the high dudgeon was a report in the *Stuttgarter Zeitung* regaling readers about the Americans' 'excesses' and their 'political anti-Wagneritis' and the horror of having '*black* occupation troops quartered in the Festspielhaus'. Black soldiers were an anathema to Winifred especially and though there were very few of them, she for evermore spoke as though the American occupation forces were almost entirely black—'black soldiers danced in the Wahnfried garden with blonde German girls', 'black soldiers plundered the Festspielhaus' and so on. In any event the opera house soon proved impractical for the army's purposes—'a white elephant', the local commander called it. The Americans stopped using it in July 1946 and four months later transferred it in trust to the city of Bayreuth.

What was for the Americans a white elephant, was for the Germans a decaying albatross. For a time it served as a reception centre for Sudeten Germans expelled from Czechoslovakia; after that the city authorities had no idea what to do with the building. They did not know what it should ultimately become or how it should be used in the meantime or in what way, if at all, the Wagner family should be involved. All that seemed clear was that the Festspielhaus could not be employed for its original purpose. The Wagner family had been disgraced, the Festival desecrated, the operas traduced, the old Wagnerians discredited and Wahnfried exposed as the Valhalla of German culture, morally corrupted and physically in ruins.

Since the opera house was one of the few public buildings not destroyed by the bombing, however, the idea was raised of using it for films or variety shows. The mayor, Oskar Meyer, persuaded his colleagues and the American authorities to restrict it to serious concerts, recitals and operas. And so for the only time in history it was possible to hear how such works as *La Traviata*, *Fidelio*, *Die Entführung aus dem Serail* and *Madama Butterfly* sounded in the Festspielhaus acoustics.

As a concert hall, the Festspielhaus soon ran the city so far into the red that a solution had to be found to what had become the highly contentious issue of the institution's ultimate future. That it should eventually be resurrected for an annual Wagner festival was fairly clear by the late autumn of 1946. Proposals to use it for the premières of contemporary operas, for performances of music by Nazi-persecuted composers or, along with the Margrave's Opera House, for a more loosely structured festival of the Salzburg type, never gained much support. The practical problem revolved around ownership and management.

To help him find a solution, Mayor Meyer had wanted to set up an advisory committee of Wagner experts and those members of the Wagner family who had not been discredited by the Third Reich. Wolfgang was invited but declined. Wieland at first anticipated that the institution would be taken over by Friedelind, possibly sponsored by the American military, which disliked the idea of Winifred's reviving the Festival. However, when Meyer contacted Friedelind in America, she did not reply. Busy at the time trying to start her own opera company in New York, she later told an interviewer, 'I was officially asked to reopen the Festival . . . but when the time will come for reopening it, who can know? Perhaps in ten years. . . .'[2] Meyer also wrote to Franz Wilhelm Beidler, Isolde's son and a noted opponent of National Socialism. He responded with an elaborate plan to create a 'Richard Wagner Foundation' to take full responsibility for the opera house and the Festival. Expert advisers were to include the likes of Ernest Newman, Alfred Einstein, Arnold Schönberg, Paul Hindemith and Arthur Honegger; the honorary president was to be Thomas Mann. Although Beidler's trial balloon never got off the ground, the concept of a foundation to manage the Festival enjoyed influential support. High officials in the Bavarian government in particular were convinced that the Festival could never disavow its Nazi past as long as the Wagner family was in charge.

For a time the Wagners themselves were uncertain and divided. 'It has become clear to me that our family can no longer continue on its own with the Festival,' Wolfgang wrote to his brother in 1947.[3]

Wieland and Wolfgang in the Wahnfried rubble.

Wieland himself thought at one time that it might be necessary to hold the Festival outside Germany, in Switzerland or Monte Carlo. The great complication was Winifred. By the terms of Siegfried's will, all the property belonged to her. But under Allied denazification laws she was heavily incriminated, falling into the category of 'major Nazi offender'. She was charged with having been one of Hitler's most fanatical supporters and of having turned 'Richard Wagner's legacy' over to the Nazi party for propaganda purposes. She had also sought to profit personally in such despicable ways as asking the head of the SS in Prague, the infamous Karl Frank, to give her furniture confiscated from Czech Jews who had been put in concentration camps.

Like all the others, she held herself blameless. 'I have done nothing wrong in my life,' she wrote to a friend in 1947. 'I more or less remained faithful until the bitter end, only because I knew this man [Hitler] to be kind, noble and helpful. It was the man and not the Party that held me.'[4] But desperately worried by the prospect of a long prison sentence, she thought she might escape punishment by regaining her British citizenship through remarriage. 'I am looking for an Englishman who is the right age for me,' her letter went on. 'I am not that old and not that ugly, not to have that even chance.' What eventually saved her was testimony that she had tried to help certain Jews, homosexuals—Lorenz and Janssen—and other persecutees and in some cases had succeeded. In July 1947 she was reduced to the category of 'less incriminated' and although she avoided imprisonment in a labour camp only because she had committed no acts of violence or brutality, she was still subject to extremely harsh disabilities.

While appealing against the sentence, she realized by now that the Festival could not be revived if she were in control. Some months later she told her sons she was prepared to turn over her authority to them. In the meantime, however, the Bavarian government had come to the view that the Festival should be directed by an international council whose members, in addition to Thomas Mann, were to include Bruno Walter, Sir Thomas Beecham, Paul Hindemith and Richard Strauss. By mid-1948 a clear battle line had formed—on one side Winifred and her sons, the town of Bayreuth and the Bavarian Social Democrats in favour of the family's retaining control; on the other, key officials in the Bavarian government, the conservative Christian Social party and managers of the main West German opera houses who for their various reasons wanted the Wagners out. In a way the historic rivalry between Bayreuth and Munich had been revived.

Then, suddenly, Winifred threw a spanner into the works by suggesting that she and Tietjen should after all take over again. The denazification programme was running out of steam and she evidently anticipated that her sentence would be eviscerated. Such is what happened in December 1949, when her punishment was reduced to a period of probation and even that was to be forgiven if she irrevocably withdrew from the Festival. This she then did the following month. 'I solemnly swear', her statement went, 'to withdraw from all participation in the organization, administration and leadership of the Bayreuth Festival.'[5] To avoid family squabbles and to keep Friedelind out, the legal arrangements were crafted in a way that left Winifred with all her rights under Siegfried's will while delegating management of the Festival to her sons, to whom she leased the Festspielhaus and Wahnfried. Although there were those in the Bavarian government and beyond who strongly felt that Winifred's revised sentence and her withdrawal did not really absolve the Wagner family from culpability, the trusteeship was finally ended and in April 1950 the theatre and the Festival's assets were turned over to Wieland and Wolfgang.

The challenge facing the brothers could scarcely have been greater. Not since the Thirty Years War had Germany been so devastated. The town of Bayreuth itself was still a shambles and overflowed with refugees from the East. Accommodation for visitors was scarcer than in 1876. The Festival was bankrupt and the opera theatre was in urgent need of repair. The costumes and sets had either been plundered or lay in storage in a salt mine beyond reach in the Russian zone. There were neither singers, conductors, musicians nor a chorus to fall back on. Political resentment against the brothers lingered on, as did doubts about their professional abilities and intentions. And of course there was the problem of Wagner himself.

Germans had now to come to terms with a Wagner of their own making, a Wagner that responded to iniquitous national traits and nourished them, a Wagner that never existed outside their country. Hence the oddity that though Wagner's operas continued to be performed in London and New York during and after the war, and were performed again in Paris from 1946, not until the autumn of 1947 was any German theatre willing to risk putting one on and only in the early 1950s were they fully back in the repertory. The *Ring* was considered especially hazardous, both artistically and ideologically; the small theatre in Coburg was the first to venture it, in 1950, and only later did the large city operas follow.

From the start Wolfgang and Wieland agreed on a division of labour corresponding to their differing backgrounds, temperaments and talents—Wieland's in stagecraft, Wolfgang's in management and finance. After being discharged from the army in 1940 as a result of a wound suffered in the Polish campaign, Wolfgang had been taken on by Tietjen at the Berlin State Opera as a trainee. With this experience and a clear bent for administration, he was able to lay the practical foundations for a new Festival.

Money was the main problem and the prospect of raising the necessary amount must have seemed remote. The 1948 currency reform had left each German with a mere 400 marks and the celebrated economic miracle was not yet under way. With no assets, no cash, uncertain prospects and a compromised institution, Wieland and Wolfgang faced the bleakest financial prospects. Although the German tradition of government support for the arts was as strong as ever, the Bavarian authorities were at first not disposed to help and Bayreuth civic officials simply had no money to offer. There was, however, strong interest in industrial circles in getting the Festival going again. Among conservative nationalists and ex-Nazis—and some not so ex—it was Wagner rather than Bach or Beethoven, Goethe or Schiller who was to be the guiding ideological light, pointing the way back to good, old-fashioned Germanic values. One of their number was a dubious character who in his earlier years had been a freelance thug. Gerhard Roßbach was one of Hitler's earliest collaborators, commanded his own unit in the Free Corps—the paramilitary group that had tried to undermine the Weimar Republic—and was a principal in the 1923 Munich putsch attempt. He had helped to organize the storm troops and, after the 1934 purge of that body, retired from the profession of violence and went into business. A man with musical interests, he now made himself the catalyst of a fund-raising effort on behalf of the Festival.

And so it came about that in 1949 a Society of the Friends of Bayreuth—a reincarnation of the old patrons' associations of 1871 and 1921—was founded, selling membership for donations. The Society not only provided crucial seed money but lent the brothers equally vital respectability in conservative financial circles. In return they were to maintain silence about the past. This was a defining moment for postwar Bayreuth. Not only was there to be no accounting, there was also to be no repenting. Nothing could have been more telling than the fact that at the conclusion of the Society's first plenary meeting, Winifred appeared and was given an ovation.

But, as in the distant past, the patrons' support was not nearly sufficient; money had to be scrounged from public and private sources. 'In the year before the beginning of the Festival,' Wolfgang later said, 'I travelled around for a total of six months; I chalked up nearly 40,000 kilometres on my motor-cycle, going from pillar to post.'[6] As an earnest of intent, the family also offered to sell manuscripts from the Wahnfried archive, including the score of *Tristan*. Despite lingering scepticism on the part of Bavarian and other officials about the institution's past and the brothers' abilities, Wolfgang's target of 1,483,157 marks (a meagre £126,000 or $360,000) was finally reached in the autumn of 1950. It came from the Bavarian government, the Bayreuth city administration, private donors from now-reviving German industry, radio licensing fees and anticipated ticket sales. In the end it proved unnecessary to sell any manuscripts.

Once funding was secured, it was formally announced that the Festival would begin in 1951, with performances of *Parsifal* and *Meistersinger*. Later, despite the obvious financial and political risks, the *Ring* was added. Orders for tickets—a quarter of them from foreigners, with large numbers of French and Americans—were so encouraging that the number of performances was increased to twenty-one. The *Ring* surprisingly proved to be the greatest draw. The brothers also initiated closed performances for the Friends of Bayreuth and, to counterbalance the rich industrialists, a similar one for trade unionists. At the end of the first season, the financial balance sheet, despite a small deficit, was so close to Wolfgang's projection that he won great respect for his financial savvy.

In the meantime, preparations were going ahead on the artistic side, and these fell to Wieland. 'It must be obvious to you', Furtwängler wrote to him, 'that this task will be a heavy one, particularly in these difficult times, and that you, having up to now given the "outer world" no indication of your ability, will be subjected to the most stringent examination.'[7] True enough, but for Wieland it was imperative not just to establish artistic credibility but to break completely with the artistic past. He therefore excluded in principle conductors, singers and other veterans of Third Reich Bayreuth; only Kurt Palm as costume director and Paul Eberhardt as lighting expert were taken back. A new choral director had to be found and, on the recommendation of the up-and-coming young Aachen Opera director Herbert von Karajan, he appointed Wilhelm Pitz. The indefatigable Pitz travelled throughout East and West Germany, visiting 38 opera houses and listened to over 800 singers before making his selection. Some 1,500 musicians—many of them Festival veterans—offered themselves, and they too had to be auditioned.

Finding soloists of the requisite distinction at a time when Germany was still recovering from the war was an intimidating task. Wieland asked around widely, studied press reviews and—lacking funds to go further abroad—visited opera houses throughout Germany. He first turned to Kirsten Flagstad for the key role of Brünnhilde; she declined but recommended Astrid Varnay, whom Wieland accepted without an audition. Flagstad also advised starting off with new, younger singers, which was in any case inevitable since most of the previous Bayreuth generation had retired. He therefore had to run the risk of taking on, even for the principal roles, singers who in many cases were unknown and untried. Gradually a solid team was built up that formed the core of early postwar Bayreuth. Besides Varnay it included Martha Mödl, Wolfgang Windgassen, Paul Kuën, Hermann Uhde, Ludwig Weber and Gerhard Stolze.

Recruiting conductors was more critical than at any time since the early days of the Festival. They would set the musical tone literally and figuratively while at the same time going a long way towards establishing the Festival's artistic credentials. Inviting exiled conductors would have been too much of a provocation; even so, choosing among the autochthons was a nightmare. Except for Hans Knappertsbusch, whose quarrel with National Socialist authorities cost him his position as music director of the Munich Opera in 1935, all the leading German conductors—Furtwängler, Clemens Krauss, Karl Böhm and Karajan—were politically malodorous, not just because they had stayed in Germany rather than fleeing but because they had personally profited, by taking the positions of those who had been driven into exile, or had to some extent collaborated with the Nazi regime and explicitly endorsed some of its political aims. The past of these conductors troubled few Germans, but it was not a good advertisement for the Festival abroad.

What did concern Wieland was a conductor's musical style. On the one hand he needed to give the Festival firm artistic ballast, which argued in favour of traditional conductors. On the other he wanted to avoid anyone who had been associated with the old Bayreuth or with conventional German musical tradition. His preference was for what he called 'Latin conductors', and he arbitrarily baptized anyone as Latin who had the lightness of touch he desired, such as the Austrians Clemens Krauss and Karl Böhm. They had been admired by Strauss, who was admired by Wieland. Why? Because Strauss had broken the Bayreuth tradition in 1933 with his ultra-fast *Parsifal*. Yet Levi's 1882 performance took four hours and four minutes, Strauss's four hours and eight minutes. Wieland also ignored the Latin Toscanini, who in 1931 went to four hours and forty-eight minutes.

Not only was Wieland tendentious, he was also driven to wild inconsistencies. To stress the break from the past, he would have liked to build a team around non-traditionalists such as Krauss and Karajan. But to disarm the sceptics and ensure the Festival unequivocal musical respectability with its conservative constituency, he needed solid tradition. So he invited Furtwängler to be chief conductor, while at the same time recruiting Karajan. Karajan was poison to the older man, however, and as a consequence Furtwängler agreed only to inaugurate the Festival with a performance of Beethoven's Ninth Symphony. Even then—and as always with Bayreuth—he wavered: '. . . said "yes" three times and "no" five times and now definitely "yes" on the understanding that 1951 would not be a Karajan Bayreuth but a Richard Wagner Bayreuth.' So read the record of a meeting of the Society of the Friends of Bayreuth.

Wieland had already signed on Knappertsbusch who, as an unofficial assistant to Hans Richter in 1911 and 1912, was as much a part of Bayreuth orthodoxy as it was possible to be. This then ruled out Krauss. He had taken Knappertsbusch's post at Munich in 1935, and Knappertsbusch therefore refused to appear in the same opera house with him. The sum result was that Wieland had to make do with Knappertsbusch and Karajan alone for all twenty-one performances. Fortunately the two men worked well together; Karajan was highly adept at rehearsing musicians, which Knappertsbusch did poorly.

In the end it was the productions and the aesthetic and intellectual concepts behind them that were bound to make the difference. These were Wieland's responsibility, and only slowly did he grow into them. In 1945 he was as devastated psychologically as his country was physically and morally, his benumbed state evident in photographs of him in front of the ruins of Wahnfried. The ruins also told their own tale, and Wieland decided to leave the villa unrepaired, 'as a sign of destiny and the beginning of a new era'.

A few days before Bayreuth fell to American forces, Wieland moved his family to Winifred's summer house at Nussdorf on Lake Constance in the French occupation zone. And there he lived for the next three years, years he called his *schöpferische schwarze Jahren*, creative black years. The blackness came first: facing up to the collapse of everything in his life up to then. The stages of his subsequent transformation are not known; neither then nor later did he openly go beyond such brisk epigrammatic utterances as 'After Auschwitz there can be no more discussion of Hitler.' Even this opened an unbridgeable gulf between him and his mother and presumably Verena and Lafferentz. What he began doing in these years was what many other Germans were doing at the same time: looking back in history to find where things went wrong, to see what was good in the past and should be cultivated and what was bad and had to be jettisoned.

In his years of enforced isolation, Wieland discovered entirely new intellectual and aesthetic worlds, worlds that had been closed to him in Wahnfried. There, virtually no book or picture or music or idea con-

ceived after 1883—and only certain ones before then—had been allowed to penetrate. Even more exciting were those that had been
outlawed during the Third Reich—his intellectually formative years.
One can imagine with what wild surmise Wieland suddenly looked
upon the universe of Freud and Jung, Picasso and Klee, Adorno and
Bloch, Moore and Lipchitz. At the same time he made the acquaintance
of Mozart, a composer admired but not heard in Wahnfried. The effect,
he remarked to Overhoff in 1946, was 'the reward of a lifetime for
which I gladly bear all the unpleasantness of the past year'.[8] Another
revelation to him were the Greek dramatists, whom he found that his
grandfather had discovered at the same age. 'I was transformed into a
Greek in those "creative black years"—a Homer fan, if you like,' he
later said.[9] From these readings, of Aeschylus in particular, he became
aware of the great similarities of Greek and Nordic myths. Then in the
spring of 1947 he went through several months of intensive studies with
Overhoff. Together they took the scores of several operas apart,
Overhoff explaining the musical-psychological elements of each.

In later years, when asked about the influences that had formed his
concepts of opera production, Wieland was cagey. He had an obsessive
need to believe, or to have others believe, that his ideas sprang full
blown from his own brain, telling the French musicologist Antoine
Goléa, for instance, that he was an autodidact and had never had a
proper artistic education. Sometimes he acknowledged a vague debt to
Craig and an even vaguer one to Appia, Roller and a few others. Before
the Festival began he broke with Overhoff, who had dared question one
of his *Parsifal* designs, and soon thereafter relegated the unfortunate man
to the status of non-person, someone whom he had never known. As for
Preetorius, he rarely let the name pass his lips, and then only to denigrate
his 'Japanese tea garden style'. Wieland disparaged his originality, poking
great fun, for instance, at the famous Valkyries' rock of the 1933 *Ring*.
The antipathy was not so much artistic; Wieland started out from the
same premises that the older man had set down nearly two decades
before. Basically it was symbolic; Preetorius was a personification of the
Third Reich Bayreuth against which Wieland was rebelling with all his
might.

Rebellion was one powerful impetus. Another was a realization that
to salvage Bayreuth, it was necessary to salvage Wagner—not from
Nazism, since Wieland did not see the works themselves as tainted by
the past; rather, the composer had to be resurrected aesthetically and
intellectually. After the Third Reich it was impossible to look at him in
the old way. It had to be shown that the operas had something to say to
a postwar, post-nuclear world. 'Bringing the works to life' was the
central aim of the new Bayreuth.

The creative black years concluded with Wieland still working his
way through the welter of ideas picked up from others and the thoughts
percolating in his own mind. There was no single moment of afflatus, no

sudden epiphany when all the ideas swirling around in his head came together in a cohesive pattern. Instead there was a slow and, as it turned out, an unending evolution, a continuously unfolding creativity. In those early years he did not say much publicly, but several themes emerge from what he did say. He stressed that more than any other opera theatre, Bayreuth would have to prove itself through the quality of its performances. He emphasized that Bayreuth's traditional style of production was to be the basis of his new work. But at the same time he made it clear that the Festival dare not become a museum and must offer productions consistent with the contemporary artistic outlook. And, finally, he insisted that it was vital for Bayreuth to reach the new generation. Some of these objectives were mutually exclusive, betraying either his own confusions or his desire to appease various opposing constituencies, notably right-wing patrons and left-wing intellectuals. What is interesting is how quickly his order of priorities shifted, every step leading away from tradition in the direction of innovation.

In his earliest public comments—in 1950, to the Munich *Abendzeitung* and the *Jahrbuch der Musikwelt*—he appeared at pains to emphasize his commitment to Bayreuth orthodoxy: 'In its continual effort for a faithful presentation [of Wagner's works], there developed in the Festspielhaus a type of linguistic, musical and scenic representation that was commonly called "Bayreuth tradition". This tradition will also be the basis of the forthcoming renewal of the Festival.' Then he added, almost pianissimo, 'The Festspielhaus is by its nature not a theatre museum, bound to the past, but belongs to people of today, that is, to everyone for whom Wagner's art will be a new experience.'

Scarcely a year later, on the eve of the Festival, it was the latter theme that was now played fortissimo. In an essay entitled 'Überlieferung und Neugestaltung' (Tradition and Innovation) in the Bayreuth *Festspielbuch*, he wrote: 'The transition from fidelity to change is inevitable.' Each Bayreuth production over the years had marked an advance in style; never had there been permanence. Every age had its own way of looking at things.

> The conventional picture that has congealed over the past decades may still happily remind the old, ultra-loyal and distinguished veterans of the secure and happy days of the era of their youth; but for the generation on this side of the quantum theory and nuclear research, it has no value. For this generation, it would be a dreadful risk to confuse appearance with reality, to sacrifice the permanent in Wagner's work for the incidental.

These simple words, at once a declaration of independence and a statement of commitment, marked Wieland's first move towards a new approach to the staging of Wagner's works. Here, deeply buried, were germs of ideas that he spent the rest of his life developing—that culture was not a realm apart from society, that works of art expressed social concepts unintended by their creator, that the moral essence of the operas was universal and was valid no less in daily life in the twentieth century than in a mythical or fairy tale setting. As such they betrayed the first glimmerings of the influence of leftist philosophers such as Theodor Adorno and Ernst Bloch, to whom Wieland was now turning for intellectual inspiration. In fact, had he known of it, he could easily have endorsed the old Frankfurt Institute's definition of art as 'a kind of code language for processes taking place within society, which must be deciphered by means of critical analysis'.

It was in his determination to reach the postwar generation that Wieland faced the most delicate problem of all: how to free Bayreuth from its disastrous past, its long years of reactionary politics and anti-Semitism. Through men like Adorno and Bloch, both Marxists and Jews, Wieland hoped to reach those who had never been at home in Bayreuth. But here he was playing a zero-sum game: the more innovation, the less tradition; the wider the opening to the left and Jews, the less space for traditionalists and erstwhile National Socialists. How was an open confrontation to be prevented? The answer was simple: a veil was to be drawn across the past. On the reopening of the Festspielhaus in 1951, posters were displayed, signed by both Wieland and Wolfgang, declaring: 'In the interest of the smooth conduct of the festival we kindly request that discussions and debates of a political nature should be avoided. Art is what matters here!' So out was trotted the old slogan, 'Hier gilt's der Kunst!' Another fig leaf for another era.

The German press followed a similar line. Articles anticipating the Festival spoke of anything but the institution's recent past, or the past at all. Eyes were on the future. And here a startlingly new theme was sounded. No longer was Bayreuth played up as the emblem of German, much less Aryan or National Socialist, cultural supremacy. Now it was to be 'a bridge between nations on the basis of a common cultural experience' and a 'path to a genuine understanding outside the realm of politics'. Bayreuth's civic authorities picked up the point, decorating the town for the first time with the flags of other countries. This was a new Festival, a new Bayreuth, a new Germany.

Understandably enough, the overall cultural mood in the country at this time and for the next decade or so was conventional, restorative and cautious. Germans wanted continuity and reassurance; they were not looking for innovation or experimentation. In the case of Bayreuth the great question was whether the Festival would be able to reach anything like the old artistic standards. While there were vague hopes, there were few expectations. Certainly nothing out of the ordinary was anticipated.

7

'Marvel upon marvel now appears'
(*Meistersinger*)

The reopening of the Festival on 30 July 1951 with a performance of *Parsifal* must rank as the most important operatic event in Germany since the première of *Wozzeck* in Berlin in December 1925. From the moment the performance began that afternoon it was apparent that a sacred Wagnerian rite had been rigorously secularized. By the time it ended, no doubt remained that the old orthodoxy in interpreting and staging Wagnerian opera had been irreparably shattered.

Although it eventually came to be considered one of the century's greatest operatic productions, at the time this *Parsifal* left the audience stunned, some in rapture, some in anguish. Because of the hallowed custom of devout silence at the conclusion of each act, no one was irreverent enough to vent either sentiment. But critical opinion was outspoken.

> This was not only the best *Parsifal* I have ever seen and heard but one of the three or four most moving spiritual experiences of my life.
>
> Ernest Newman, *Sunday Times*

> What the Master's grandson has conjured up for us is a symphony in darkness, a formless and—with its renunciation of individual dramatic relationships and its unremitting symbolism—ultimately a boring spectacle of shapes and shadows.
>
> Hans Schnor, *Westfalen Blatt*

> Bayreuth has risen again: the mystique around Bayreuth is no illusion. Wagner still lives; his message has not died.
>
> Bernard Gavoty, *Figaro*

> We cannot disguise our fear that Wagner's timelessness seems to be called into question when such of his works as *Parsifal* . . . are presented as nothing more than oratorios and optic-melodrama.
>
> Heinz Joachim, *Die Welt*

The strength of the reaction was not surprising. To have revolutionized the most tradition-bound operatic work at the most tradition-
bound opera house, before an audience of the most tradition-bound
opera devotees, was bold indeed. That this was accomplished—or
perpetrated—by a grandson of the Master himself was the last thing
anyone anticipated, or forgave. Of course only a grandson would have
dared.

What amazed the audience was less what it saw than what it did not
see. In place of the sumptuous, Constable-like woods and rippling lake
of the conventional opening scene, there was an all but empty stage.
Even the background depicted no road ascending Monsalvat to the
castle of the knights of the grail but merely hinted at a forest through
which sifted the gentle morning light. The walk to the castle led not
through rocks and woodland but across a barren desert. And, in the final
scene, the celebrated temple of the grail, with its solid pillars,
cosmatesque pavement and ornate romanesque cupola, had been sup-
planted by a dark, almost dream-like interior, betraying four stark
columns and on a dais a plain round table and bench. In the second act,
Klingsor's old magic castle, with its sinister battlements and its tower
stocked with necromantic appliances, had simply vanished; now all that

The opening scene of Wieland's 1951 *Parsifal*, with Amfortas (George London), Gurnemanz (Ludwig Weber) and
Kundry (Martha Mödl). Key stylistic features of New Bayreuth are evident: light and shadow rather than solid sets, a disc
defining the acting area, plain costumes, indeterminate time and place.

The occult and sinister world of Klingsor in *Parsifal*, Act II. 'The visible action in this mystery play is merely allegorical; the main characters are not specific individuals but symbols of human types' (Wieland Wagner).

could be seen in the bleak obscurity was the evil magician's head and shoulders at the centre of what appeared to be a huge spider's web. When the scene shifted to the magic garden, rather than the 'tropical vegetation, luxuriant flowers . . . battlements of the ramparts, which are flanked by projecting portions of the castle (in rich Arabian style) with terraces', as prescribed in the composer's stage directions, there emerged a scene devoid of any object or decoration except a tenebrous, pastel backdrop, which in later years resembled a canvas by Jackson Pollock. The Flowermaidens had no flowers, just as the flowery meadow was neither flowery nor a meadow. There was no swan in the first act and no dove in the third. Klingsor had no spear. What else was missing was impossible to know in the dim lighting. When Hans Knappertsbusch, who had conducted, was asked by an outraged spectator how he could have had anything to do with such a production, he replied—only partly in jest—that he had assumed during the rehearsals that the settings were yet to arrive.

Parsifal was followed by the *Ring*, which caused a similar shock. Although it was concrete rather than suggestive and had realistic components, the production also represented a radical break. To be sure, such familiar sights as Valhalla, the rainbow bridge, the ash tree in Hunding's hut, the Valkyries' rock and Mime's forge were still there, but none as they had been seen before. Otherwise the traditional ornaments, props and costumes were gone; what replaced them suggested a saga not of Nordic but of Greek gods. This impression was much intensified in the following years as Wieland ruthlessly rid the production of any remaining naturalistic elements until by 1954 he achieved a stylistic harmony. The central stage feature was a novelty: a disc—at times more a circle of light—on which the drama was played out. As a technique it consciously reincarnated the *orchestra* of the Greek theatre; as a symbol it embodied the ring itself. In the course of the opera the round platform altered its shape and disposition, regaining its original unity only at the end when, in a greenish light, it lay, restored, in the depths of the Rhine.

Both *Parsifal* and the *Ring* were performed the first year without opening the curtain. Instead the scene was revealed by gradual illumination which gave audiences an exciting illusion of being participants in an unfolding drama. The essence of the new stagecraft was to leave the viewer almost unlimited scope to fill in the picture suggested by the

The Awakening scene in *Siegfried* was one of New Bayreuth's most sublime stage images. In this 1954 performance Siegfried was Wolfgang Windgassen and Brünnhilde was Astrid Varnay, who sang the role during the years 1951–67.

music, a technique that was a paramount trait of what came to be known as New Bayreuth.

The following season Wieland turned to *Tristan*. Convinced that the traditional stage clutter distracted attention from the principals and deprived the psychological drama of its impact—precisely the view expressed by Appia more than half a century earlier—he staged the work in a completely abstract style which focused attention on the two protagonists. The first act showed neither sail, rigging, mast, wheel, nor even a single sailor, but only a glimpse of the outlines of a deck, a huge tarpaulin and a simple couch (without so much as a pillow). That was a scene of Babylonian excess, however, compared with the remorseless austerity of what followed. The love duet took place on a bench in a darkness-enshrouded cosmos. All that could be detected were the heads of the two lovers in a blue-black infinity. And in the last act, the familiar landscape with Tristan's castle, the lime tree and the bed under it, the view of the rocky Breton coast and the sea beyond were replaced by an unidentifiable site of monumental emptiness, of irredeemable bleakness. The overall visual asceticism was reinforced by banishing the crew and royal courtiers from the stage, allowing only the principals to appear, and by the spareness of the gestures and the statuesque appearance of the seven main characters. In other respects as well, the directing was innovative. In the first act, the moment the lovers drank the potion, rather than standing motionless, they ran together in a frenzy of liberated libido. In the final act, Tristan sang his first lines while on his back while Isolde died not transfigured on his breast but standing with her arms outstretched.

With these three productions Wieland had set in place the defining characteristics of New Bayreuth—a circular acting area, the use of light to link music to movement and colour, the simplification of costumes without any suggestion of a specific time or place, the transformation of characters from pseudo-human beings into symbols and the stripping away of sets and gestures inessential to the conceptual core of the work. The aim was to deprive the operas of their traditional Germanic character and to establish a new relationship of staging, music and acting. The abstract style demonstrated that as silence is an essential element of music, so emptiness can be a vital part of staging. In fact, Wieland once attributed the spark of inspiration for his approach to the chance discovery of the passage in Cosima's diary which recorded Wagner's statement that having created the invisible orchestra, he wished he could invent the invisible theatre. In Wieland's view, what was all-important was the central dramatic idea; anything immaterial or distracting or obfuscating had to go. In practice he decided that this required discarding virtually all the old staging and staging practices. *Entrümpelung*—clearing out the attic—is what the process was sometimes aptly labelled. But that was merely the negative side. The key to his work was the use of staging as a tool to enable—or force—an audience to see an opera in an entirely new way.

Entrümpelung reached its zenith in Act II of Wieland's 1952 *Tristan*. Ramon Vinay and Martha Mödl were the highly praised principals in the 1952 performances.

In turning to *Tannhäuser* in 1954, Wieland took his first step into a further creative phase. This was the first new treatment of the work since 1930 and its first performance since Toscanini had conducted it in 1931. Once again the old naturalistic props were banished and the acting simplified. But this time rather than leaving the stage bare, he emplaced a sequence of highly stylized expressionist tableaux which demonstrated his painterly approach and betrayed a clear debt to Paul Klee.

In a highly evocative—and equally provocative—opening scene, the two worlds of the drama were juxtaposed. On the left was Venusberg as an abstract cavern formed by concentric circles of golden light. On the right, at the foot of a huge cross, lay Tannhäuser. Choosing the way of the cross, he emerged not into the conventional sun-bathed valley with its view of a distant Wartburg but into a stark, disciplined world, manifested in a background of flat planes of gold, a colour symbolic of the Middle Ages. The meadow was represented by nothing more than a floorcloth with a floral design in pastel green. In the second act the hall of song in the Wartburg was laid out geometrically; the background planes were surmounted by friezes suggesting gothic entablatures while

The hall of song in the 1954 *Tannhäuser* looked like a chess board, with Elisabeth (Gré Brouwenstijn) the White Queen and Tannhäuser (Ramon Vinay) the Black Knight. Here the Landgrave (Josef Greindl) inaugurates the song contest.

the stage floor looked like a chessboard, on either side of which were ranged four straight rows of seats for the Landgrave's guests at the song contest. The performers were positioned and moved almost like chessmen. Equally novel was the deployment of the chorus, both of the pilgrims and of the Landgrave's guests. It was no longer the chorus of a European opera but that of a Greek drama—a seemingly solid block of sculpted figures, impassive as statues and moving with regimented, brigade-of-guards discipline. The opera concluded with an amazing transformation of the conventional pilgrims' chorus into a flat pyramid of haloes glowing in the dark like an apparition of several hundred golden Greek icons.

Wieland was sometimes taunted with the charge that he was producing oratorios in costume and that the logical culmination of his approach would be to present the operas in concert performances. So when it was announced that *Die Meistersinger* was next on the agenda, there was great anticipation—and apprehension—about how this grand old favourite would fare. Unlike *Tristan* and *Parsifal*, here was a work rooted in a specific milieu and period. Had not Wieland himself written in his 1951 essay 'Tradition and Innovation' that, in contrast to Wagner's other

218

works, '*Die Meistersinger* calls for a certain naturalism, imposed by a historically fixed time, a geographical place and human beings of flesh and blood'?

On being unveiled in 1956, the production was considered worse than the worst that had been expected by those who expected something bad. Not only was the break with a well-loved tradition more blatant than ever and the New Bayreuth style more brazen, but this version was also an outright affront to nationalistic sentiment. The visual impression might best be viewed through the relatively benign eyes of the critic of *The Times*:

> Wieland Wagner's production of *Die Meistersinger* has set musical Germany by the ears. Tradition, honoured in the setting of the first act, has been rudely shaken in the second, and in the last act laid in the dust.
>
> *Die Meistersinger* was the last bastion of the old orthodoxy in Wagnerian production; now it too has surrendered to the onslaught of the new style. 'Meistersinger ohne Nürnberg' has been the reaction of many German critics and connoisseurs. . . .
>
> The setting [of the first act] recalls late medieval German art in an individual and delightful way. It is realistic and functional, but also original and a joy to the eye.

The celebrated second act of the 1956 *Die Meistersinger* which Wieland said he staged with 'the romantic irony of a Shakespearian midsummer night'. To some it was a scandal; to Walter Erich Schäfer, the 'solution of the century'.

In the second act the heads begin to roll. In place of the traditional narrow street there is a small, kidney-shaped space in the middle of a blank stage, cobbled like a road and overhung by a vast ball of leaves and flowers, a kind of world elder-tree, attached to the earth by no visible means and floating in a sky of intense midnight blue. Walther and Eva cannot hide 'unter den Linden', because there is no linden. . . . Hans Sachs, deprived of his workshop, must sit on a bench not 10 ft away from them. . . . The setting, though impractical at times, has an arresting beauty of its own, and it allows Wagner's midsummer eve magic to work its potent spell on the mind of the listener, and evoke the Nuremberg which the designer has avoided.

The final scene is the oddest. Gone are the festival meadow, the guilds, the trumpeters, the coloured streamers, and the people arriving in boats. A section of a great yellow stadium is shown, with seats steeply raked at the back, from which the people, uniformly dressed, watch, as at a circus or baseball game, the stylized dances in the arena below. As a spectacle, it has a kind of aseptic splendour. . . .

The mood of the audience, according to press reports, soured more and more from one act to the next. The final scene was the most shocking, without any sign of dear old Nuremberg in the distance.

The notorious 'lecture hall' amphitheatre of *Die Meistersinger*, Act III. In design and mood, more an oratorio than a festive celebration. In the foreground: Hans Hotter (Sachs), Gré Brouwenstijn (Eva) and Wolfgang Windgassen (Walther).

Hence the jibe that Wieland had produced a 'Mastersingers without Nuremberg'. When the curtain fell, the Festspielhaus witnessed booing for the first time in its history. For the Wagnerian fundamentalists and the political conservatives—mostly the same people—the production was a travesty of Wagner's creation. Even worse, by rubbing audiences' noses in the fact that the Nuremberg of the mastersingers no longer existed for reasons all too clear, it was a political mortification.

The music critic of *Die Zeit*, Walter Abendroth, who in his National Socialist days had praised the 'imperishable Germanness' of the 1934 production, was not surprisingly outraged and asked in a widely quoted article: 'Who will defend Wagner in Bayreuth?' The right-wing German Party even dared to resurrect the term 'decadent art' to discredit the production. The second highest official in the Bavarian Justice Ministry complained that it went beyond the limits of free artistic expression and labelled it a scandal that the Festival received public financial support.

But it was Moritz Klönne, head of the Friends of Bayreuth Society, who exposed the real issue in a private letter to Wieland. 'Bayreuth is a sacred German cultural shrine,' he wrote, 'and *Die Meistersinger* is Wagner's most German work. All your romantic internationalism cannot change any of that.' Here was proof if any was needed that the sentiments of the old guard had not changed in a century, that nothing had been learned and nothing forgotten. Klönne did not stop there, however; he also provided an inventory of the traditional settings that he and the Friends wanted to see restored to the stage. If they were not put back, he concluded ominously, their links to Bayreuth would be broken and they would go elsewhere for their *Meistersinger*. Wieland replied with a contemptuous wave of the epistolary hand. He had decided from the start that if the political and operatic right wing wanted to use Bayreuth as its cultural nesting-place, it would have to do so on *his* artistic terms. It was the classic Bayreuth trade-off.

In 1958 Wieland turned to *Lohengrin*. The inspiration for his interpretation, he said, came to him on discovering that the opera had been composed when his grandfather was reading Aeschylus. This led him to conclude that Wagner looked at the opera through the eyes of a Greek dramatist. Wieland's resulting production was widely considered his most harmonious and beautiful, a series of mythological dream pictures alluding to what Thomas Mann characterized as the 'silver-blue beauty' of the music. The curtain opened indeed to reveal a scene in sapphire and silver with the knights and nobles of Brabant and Saxony arranged, motionless, in a tiered semicircle. There were no sets as such; the great judgement oak and that most famous of all opera props, the tug-boat swan, were reduced to elegant decorations. Stylized choreography was a key feature. Movement was kept to a minimum and the chorus, strictly regimented, witnessed and commented on the action, just as in a Greek drama.

In the second act, rather than the conventional battlements of the

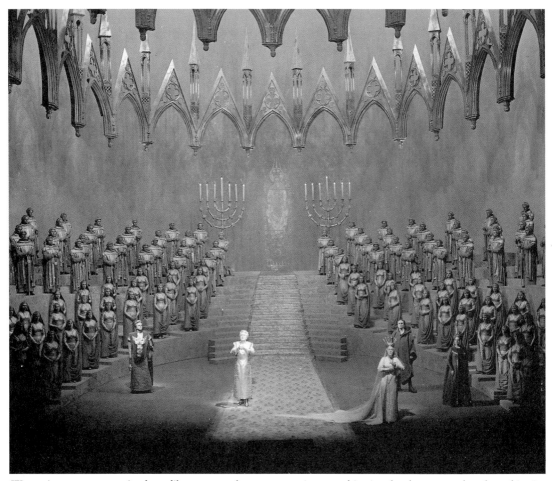

Wagnerian opera as a static, dreamlike mystery play, concentrating on subjective development rather than objective action, reached its culmination in Wieland's 1958 *Lohengrin*.

great Pallas, the minister and the kemenate, all that could be seen were the simple outlines of a church interior with a dimly lit stained-glass window and the mere outlines of gothic arches. The bedchamber scene of the final act was handled ironically with a small bridal chorus de- scribed by a critic as 'lily-carrying, white robed pre-Raphaelite virgins in the soft art nouveau of a Rossetti or Burne-Jones'.

Lohengrin marked the culmination of a second phase of Wieland's evolving style. It was distinguished by the use of the stage as a *geistiger Raum*—an imaginary space—by a chorus whose dress and movements were uniform and which was amphitheatrically deployed facing the audience, by simple decors enhanced by the imaginative use of radiant colour and light and by sets that made subtle references to place and time.

When he finally came to the *Fliegender Holländer* in 1959, Wieland adopted yet another style, taking a step back—or forward—towards a post-modernist realism that typified some of his final work. The disc, the Greek chorus, the symbols and stylized movement of earlier productions were now abandoned. In their place were a real ship with nautical accoutrements, real spinning wheels propelled by unattractive, big-bosomed girls and thrilling choreography for the sailors. The costumes—so far as they could be seen in the penumbral gloom of the dim lighting—were a joyous riot of styles and colour. For the first time at Bayreuth the work was performed with the original, harsher Dresden score, without Wagner's later revisions of the orchestration and without the addition of the redemption motif at the end. In place of the romantic apotheosis, Senta vanished into darkness and the Dutchman died on stage. Precisely because of the difficulty of staging the opera effectively, Wieland had long looked forward to tackling it. The result was considered by critics as a revelation, the greatest production of the work ever staged at Bayreuth. The conducting by Wolfgang Sawallisch, along with the singing by Leonie Rysanek and George London, left audiences, including Wieland himself, with a sense of having assisted at a historic performance.

With this *Holländer*, Wieland had completed his treatment of the entire Bayreuth canon. Although Siegfried's will restricted performances in the Festspielhaus to these seven works, Wieland toyed with the idea of adding *Rienzi* and even operas by contemporary composers such as

In *Fliegender Holländer* the realistic outlines of Daland's vessel dominate the stage, against the sinister background of the Dutchman's ship. The powerful choreography of the sailors' chorus heightened the visual impact of the sets.

Carl Orff. However, after producing *Rienzi* in Stuttgart in 1957, he concluded that the work was too cumbersome for Bayreuth. And the notion of doing works by Orff was dropped as his infatuation with those operas lost its ardour. His experimentation with the works of other composers was therefore confined to other opera houses. At Bayreuth, in what turned out to be the final six years of his life, he started redoing his original productions.

First, in 1961, was *Tannhäuser*. Though the basic structure of the earlier version was retained, there were important changes of detail and atmosphere. Venusberg was no longer a cavern. Venus herself now stood immobile beneath an object vaguely resembling an enormous hornet's nest. The valley below the Wartburg was a bleak area punctuated by a huge cross and stylized trees while the hall of song had become a gilded abstract space. Stage movement was greatly altered; the nobles, though clad alike, were no longer regimented and the pilgrims' chorus appeared in three straggly groups. What made the production a sensation was its 'black Venus', the twenty-four-year-old soprano Grace Bumbry. For most in the Festival audiences, a black singer at Bayreuth was considered a disgrace, an outrageous provocation. Next, they supposed, Hans Sachs would be a Chinaman. And as if that was not enough,

The symbolic monoliths in the 1962 *Tristan* were like Rorschach blots. Was the stela of Act II a phallic shape, Brangäne's watchtower, Tristan's gravestone, a gigantic owl? Was it protective or threatening?

Maurice Béjart's dance troupe emulated a sex orgy in the Bacchanal that *The Times* described as 'a combination of Wagner, Place Pigalle and Henry Miller'. This was a production which Wieland altered substantially in subsequent years.

With his second version of *Tristan*, performed every year from 1962 until 1970, Wieland achieved the high point in his symbolic style. Although the stage was almost as bare as in the earlier version, each act was now dominated by a great monolith, created by Wieland in the style of Henry Moore. The power and mystery of these totemic shapes—erotic and phallic on the one hand and suggestive of the Celtic origins of the story on the other—was heightened by the effect of the lighting, in strong shades of greenish-yellow, blue and red. Most remarkable was the second act, in which the lovers stood throughout, at the base of an imposing stela modelled on a stone in Cornwall which carried the inscription 'Here lies Tristan, Marke's son'. The earlier version, by banishing the sailors and royal courtiers, highlighted the self-obsession of Tristan and Isolde and their indifference to the outside world. Now, both the crew and the royal retinue were brought into the first act, to demonstrate that the pair could not escape the intrusion of society. The production has been considered by many critics as Wieland's most nearly perfect. The performances in seven successive seasons, with Birgit Nilsson, Wolfgang Windgassen and Karl Böhm at the height of their powers, were among Bayreuth's greatest. As Böhm himself commented in his memoirs, the soloists 'sang with such indescribable beauty that the entire orchestra and I were carried along with the stream of sound, and I suddenly had the feeling, "If you do not watch out you will be swept away"'.[1]

Wieland was in the full stride of his self-confidence and sense of mission when he turned again to *Meistersinger* in 1963. If the earlier treatment portrayed mastersingers without Nuremberg, this version lacked both Nuremberg *and* mastersingers. The staging showed Wieland at his most eclectic, taking ideas from sources as varied as Shakespeare, Brecht and Bruegel. He introduced startlingly new techniques; the chorus, for example, was now a collection of individuals, moving with the lack of coordination typical of crowds. The production was both an imaginative venture into realism and an adventurous essay at parody. It was arguably much closer to real life in the real Nuremberg in the sixteenth century than any version ever before staged.

The last remnants of the traditional approach to the work had vanished. All three acts were staged as though inside an Elizabethan theatre, with a wooden gallery and wooden floors as a permanent setting. There was no church, song school, Nuremberg street or shoemaker's house, much less a great meadow. Sachs's studio was a sales booth for shoes and Sachs himself was less a patrician tradesman than a shabby cobbler. The mastersingers, in one critic's view, looked like 'a philistine glee-club of country yokels' and the apprentices like 'dirty guttersnipes'. The mid-

Act III of the 1963 *Die Meistersinger*. As in his previous version, Wieland shunned the traditional solemn entry of the guilds; instead he staged a satirical frolic, masterfully choreographed by Gertrud Wagner.

summer's night brawl was a lethal riot, concluding with the Night Watchman stumbling over prostrate bodies. The great festive scene in the meadow was an unruly pageant of earthy vulgarity rather than a solemn occasion on which German art was revered. Nothing irritated Wieland more than the traditional ceremonial entrance of the masters, which reminded him of the Nazi party rallies; so in this version, as in the earlier one, there was no procession of the guilds. Such light-hearted slaughtering of such sacred German cows made this production in some ways Wieland's most revolutionary. It was certainly his most controversial, booed as nothing before in Festival history.

While 'he really went too far this time' had long been a common complaint of the traditionalists, there was by now a suspicion going well beyond those ranks that Wieland was out to shock—if for no other reason than to attract attention and sell more tickets. The charge was unworthy—and one that especially infuriated him—but shock he did, and was no doubt pleased to do so since it admirably suited his purpose of forcing spectators to rethink the operas. Consequently, when he unveiled his new *Ring* in 1965, public anticipation ran so high that there were said to have been more critics present than at any other postwar musical event, except possibly the reopening of the Vienna Opera a decade earlier.

After Henry Moore had declined to design the sets, Wieland did them himself and the result was the epitome of his abstract and symbolic style. Valhalla was there, but in the form of a towering and menacing wall, marked by criss-cross lines. There was a gold horde but, when piled up, it took the shape of a female idol. The Giants had no clubs; Donner had no hammer and in any case there was no rock for him to strike. Of Hunding's hut there was no sign, and the object with skulls on it could be inferred to be an ash tree only because it was on stage when the curtain opened on the first act of *Walküre*. The sets for *Siegfried* and the first two acts of *Götterdämmerung* were totemistic and megalithic objects that looked as though they might have come from a science-fiction film studio. There was an equally stark break with the past in the singers' movement and gestures, or lack of them. Alberich made no attempt to seize the gold. Wotan and Fricka slept standing up. Fasolt was never struck, much less pummelled to death. The drinking horn was never broken. Gutrune's brief solo scene in the third act was entirely deleted. Siegfried was given no funeral procession and Brünnhilde no funeral pyre.

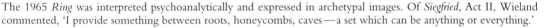

The 1965 *Ring* was interpreted psychoanalytically and expressed in archetypal images. Of *Siegfried*, Act II, Wieland commented, 'I provide something between roots, honeycombs, caves—a set which can be anything or everything.'

This was an interpretation that completely wiped away the past and created a sort of tabula rasa that was left for the spectator to fill in. Clues to the meaning were provided in the symbols. Wieland said the production was partly inspired by his discovery that Wagner's original score was marked with mysterious ciphers and hieroglyphs; his own archetypal images were their scenic counterpart, challenging a viewer's imagination. More obviously than ever, this was not opera as an evening's diversion but opera with a didactic purpose.

In relaunching the Festival in 1951 Wieland had several objectives. There was the obvious one of achieving the highest possible musical and vocal standards. Another was to liberate the institution itself from its artistic and political past. But above all he wanted to show that Wagnerian opera was a living and ever-changing art form that went beyond marvellous sound and spectacle, that it was in fact great drama with potent meaning for the contemporary world. How this was to be accomplished was far from clear when he began and had to be worked through, opera by opera. And with each opera being staged according to its own dramatic and musical individuality, a uniform style never emerged.

Although Wolfgang did his own productions from time to time in these years, it was Wieland who was the pathbreaker—'a born theatrical revolutionary', his brother called him. What he put on stage—strange to say of an institution as old as Bayreuth—was in most cases only the third Bayreuth production of the work, having been preceded merely by the Cosima-Siegfried and Tietjen-Preetorius versions. Small wonder that breaking that degree of continuity caused offence. Wieland once said he regarded every new production as 'an adventure in the quest for an unknown goal'.[2] Step by step he had to feel his way ahead, and he did so with considerably more travail and self-doubt than was apparent in his overtly confident productions and his often imperious and intolerant demeanour. Everything—style, techniques, concepts and even an understanding of the operas—evolved as he went along. But as he went along, his work was increasingly assured and uncompromising. It was also resolutely cerebral, seeking to reach the mind more than the senses, the intellect more than the emotions. It was instructive rather than entertaining, disturbing rather than satisfying.

With the quality of the music and voices generally assured, the staging was what arrested attention, made the news and received the plaudits or caused a rumpus. Well into the fifties critics were still uncertain whether New Bayreuth was just a flash in the pan or whether it marked a permanent change in the way Wagnerian opera was interpreted and produced. The answer came production by production. From the start there were always those for whom Wieland could do no wrong and those for whom he could do no right. The overall critical reaction, however, was enthusiastic. His work was admired for its imagination, clarity, strength, inner integrity, unity. It was both a revolution and a revelation. Even the most hostile never denied that his productions were quite often surpassingly beautiful and unforgettably thrilling, beyond anything seen up to then on an operatic stage. 'Here for the first time in my experience was a *Tristan und Isolde* in which stage, orchestra, singers, conductor, costumes, lighting, in fact all the elements that go to make up an operatic production, were merged into a unity such as Wagner could only have dreamed of,' wrote a critic of the 1952 production.[3] And this was fairly typical. Many who at first attacked, later returned to surrender. One critic who had been 'dismayed' by the 1956 *Meistersinger*, for instance, went back later and found it 'the truest and most beautiful production of the opera that one could hope to see'.[4]

But there was always plenty of opposition and some of it was as fanatical as it can be only in Bayreuth. The opponents made the same embittered complaints—indeed were some of the same people—as in the *Parsifal* fracas of 1934, the only novelty being that epithets like 'Jewish-influenced' and 'cultural Bolshevism' were no longer used, at least publicly. The hostility also demonstrated that even now no less than in prewar Germany every artistic act was a political act and that artistic conservatism and political conservatism still went together, indeed remained different sides of the same coin. It was symptomatic that when Dietrich Fischer-Dieskau—in Bayreuth to sing Wolfram in the 1954 *Tannhäuser*—was invited to tea with Winifred Wagner, he listened in appalled silence as she condemned her son and Picasso, while praising Adolf Hitler. For the Bayreuth old guard a portrait should have an eye, a nose and a mouth as God created them, just as a production of *Die Meistersinger* should have a Nuremberg as Wagner conceived it—and just as Hitler should be properly appreciated. In the mechanics of their little grey cells, art and ideology were inseparable. Here at least they were right.

Wieland's most extreme opponents—many of them unreconstructed National Socialists—formed a group around the composer Hans Pfitzner. They saw *their* Wagner being traduced, and they intended to put a stop to it. The fanaticism was evident in everything from the title of their organization, 'The Society for the Faithful Presentation of Richard Wagner's Dramas', to their activities, which included acts of sabotage on the stage, the furious circulation of pamphlets and the initiation of legal action to have the old productions—and by this they really had in mind those prior to 1914—declared 'national monuments' and restored to the status quo ante: with Wotan's eye patch and the Valkyries' armour, Brünnhilde's horse and Brangäne's torch, King Henry's judgement oak and the battlements of Tristan's castle on down to Lohengrin's wooden swan boat, Siegfried's bear and ye gables of olde Nuremberg.

At the same time there were some rational critics and opera-goers who also found fundamental fault with Wieland's work. According to their main contention—and it was the same charge levelled against Appia and Preetorius—Wagner's music as well as the stage directions *require* a inscenation of a fairly specific kind and these had been blatantly ignored. Wagner knew what he wanted, it was argued, and violating his explicit instructions amounted to a wilful alteration of his works. Moreover, replacing the grand old versions with cold-blooded, expressionist and symbolic stage images—sometimes with nothing at all—deprived the operas of much of their romantic beauty and pageantry, their historical atmosphere and individualized characterization. In Carl Dahlhaus's generic summation of the complaints: 'The aesthetic maxim that tampering with the letter of a work of art will necessarily damage the spirit was extended in the Bayreuth tradition from the verbal and musical text to include the staging as well.'[5]

Wieland's adversaries accordingly took offence that such of Wagner's precepts as his famous 'last request' that singers should not face the audience and his rule that soloists and chorus should behave like real people in a contemporaneous social situation had been outrageously flouted in *Tannhäuser*, *Lohengrin* and *Meistersinger*. They were appalled that the musically and visually impressive transformation scene in the second act of *Lohengrin* was played to a blank curtain. And they considered just about everything in the *Ring* productions a violation of the composer's directions. As late as 1978, a New York critic was still lamenting Wieland's baneful influence and longed for

> a *Ring* in which the scenic and acting directions were carefully observed, where skies were blue when they should be, the sun shone when it should, and trees had branches, one in which curtains rose and fell where the composer's music as well as the words say they should. . . . Tinkering, tampering and modernization are unnecessary; they merely tend to weaken the work.[6]

Not only did these mid-twentieth-century productions get the settings wrong, according to this view, they did not match the style and character of Wagner's nineteenth-century, high-romantic music. Hans Knappertsbusch himself was so pained by the dichotomy he felt between the *Parsifal* score he was conducting and the scene he was observing on stage that he resigned after his second season. Of a catalogue of instances where the score was inconsistent with, or indeed falsified by, the production, the end of the second act of *Lohengrin* was cited as a small but clear case. Just as Elsa is about to enter the minster, the stage directions have her turn to look back, and as her glance falls on Ortrud, the orchestra thunders out the Warning motif. The glance is significant and the motif impressive. Wieland cut out Elsa's glance, needlessly depriving the scene of an important musical and dramatic point. Most distorted of all, even in the opinion of friendly critics, was nothing less than the whole of the 1963 *Meistersinger*. 'With the music constantly, if vainly, giving the lie to the production it was a sorry proof that it takes a producer of genius to make the real mistakes' was one sour comment.[7]

The gravest charge was that Wieland eventually became so wilful that he even meddled with the music—deleting or cutting and pasting bits in *Der fliegende Holländer*, *Tannhäuser*, *Lohengrin* and *Götterdämmerung*. Perhaps there were occasional weaknesses in Wagner's scores, it was argued, but they were the composer's mistakes and not for anyone else to correct. That such a thing was done at Bayreuth was all the more shocking. 'The basic fault—and it is perhaps the most serious one that an opera producer can commit—seems to be that he has placed visual spectacle before the music: he has imposed his own designs on the music, and the designs do not fit,' grumbled one critic.[8] 'It is Richard Wagner who draws us to Bayreuth; his grandson has no duty other than that of being the composer's humble servant.'

Capping it all, there were any number of anecdotes to the effect that Wieland had no interest in Wagner's music, that indeed he hated it, as indeed he hated Wagner's dramas and that the way to his heart was to be anti-Wagnerian. Of his experiences in Bayreuth under Wieland, Dietrich Fischer-Dieskau claimed, 'If a singer wanted to have his way about something, all he needed to say was that the Master did not want it that way, and it immediately became part of the production.'[9] Perhaps Wieland believed, subconsciously at least, that denazifying Bayreuth required some de-Wagnerizing of the operas.

Wieland had little patience with critics, whom he regarded as so many pesky neo-Hanslicks, and even made a fool of himself by trying—unsuccessfully—to ban one of them from the Festspielhaus. What is remarkable, however, is that he anticipated most of their complaints and even answered them—in his 1951 essay—before they were made. Like Appia and Preetorius before him, he insisted that opposition to change was not fidelity but pedantry. Cosima's error was not that she established a strict style but that she considered it final and unalterable. The development of electric lighting alone had swept away a whole world of past stage techniques. Opposing change, he wrote, 'is to transform the virtue of fidelity into the vice of rigidity'.[10] To the assertion that the changes amounted to artistic treason, his answer was *inszenieren heißt interpretieren*—any inscenation amounts to interpretation. Cosima, Siegfried and Preetorius interpreted no less than he. True masterpieces are capable of the most varied treatment. The sole criterion of loyalty is whether a production conveys or betrays the meaning of the music and the drama.

And that led to his second counter-argument: the traditional sets falsified the score and Wagner's dramatic intent—precisely Appia's point. 'The stage can at best offer only an imperfect image of what the orchestra in the mystic gulf triumphantly conveys to our ears without any need for visual manifestation,' he maintained. 'No highbrow theories nor pseudo-philosophical tracts on the problem of Wagnerian staging, no debates between the fanatics of tradition and those who want innovation for its own sake will—or should—alter this fact.'

In any case, Wagner's original staging was behind the times, his argument continued, and the times themselves were regressive. The stage instructions were merely hints of the visionary images in his mind. 'The zealots of tradition cling to every comma in the Master's stage directions as though the perfect realization of the work depends on these alone. But how far did the productions of 1876 and 1882, though under Wagner's personal direction, deviate from his own sacrosanct instructions!'

> What must he have thought when he saw the airy rainbow of his imagination reduced to a fusty, rickety bridge? And what of those utterly inadequate creations of his inner vision? The demon Klingsor turned into a bourgeois magician; the arch-fiend Kundry corsetted in a flowery evening gown with a train; Fafner the wild serpent, almost degraded to a comic figure.

He therefore considered his grandfather's stage instructions no more sacred than his writings on vegetarianism. In disregarding Wagner's 'last request' to singers not to face the audience, for example, he told his biographer Geoffrey Skelton: 'The Swan chorus is one of the finest choral pieces Wagner ever wrote, and I find it horrible when this whole piece is sung towards Lohengrin standing at the back of the stage, just for the sake of conventional stage realism.'[11] Wieland was fond of quoting Liszt: 'Der Buchstabe tötet den Geist', the letter kills the spirit.

It was obvious to him that the Nordic and Teutonic bric-a-brac and costumes, along with the old realistic style of acting and choreography, had to go. For one thing, the attempt to simulate nature and to mimic the customs of a past era inevitably failed. 'Scenes like the cosmic catastrophe of *Götterdämmerung*, the spring night in *Die Walküre*, Brünnhilde's Annunciation of Death or the *Rheingold* thunderstorm—to cite but a few examples—can never come even close to having a visual impact to equal their musical expression.'[12] For another, the old productions had the effect of turning the operas into fairy tales, into entertainment rather than commentaries about life here and now. They at times falsified the music and blunted the dramatic intent, indeed they created a barrier between Wagner's creation and the real world. Wieland's personal experience in his youth—seeing Hitler sit through the *Ring* and not realize that it was about himself and his Reich—may well have been reflected here.

In placing the operas in an essentially timeless cosmos, he hoped to shift attention away from the incidentals to the essence of the drama. Such was no more than Wagner himself had intended in taking myth as his mode of dramatic expression: 'What is unique about myth is that it is true for all time and its content, despite its intense concision, has relevance for every age.'[13] For this reason Wieland presented some of the works essentially as mystery plays, with an entirely different staging and logic from that of realistic opera. At the same time he stressed that no production could ever be definitive; it could only hope to kick a stone or two out of the path that measures what Busoni called 'the distance which separates us from the essence of music'. Each era, he said, will have its own Wagner.

Behind the problem of staging lay the issue of the relationship between the visual image and the music. 'Wieland and I discussed hour upon hour', Wolfgang Sawallisch once said, 'how to transpose the music onto the stage—about which figure a musical theme referred to and what had to happen on stage to correspond to it, so as to make visually clear why Wagner had written this theme.'[14] Wieland knew the scores better than many conductors, Sawallisch went on, and what the music expressed aurally need not, in his judgement, be expressed again on stage. In the second act of the 1956 *Meistersinger* the symbolic hint of the elder tree sufficed because the whole atmosphere of the scene had already been described by the music.

In his early years Wieland gave primacy to the score, but later he reverted to the Bayreuth convention that the drama is supreme. By the early 1960s he therefore argued: 'All composers who wrote for the opera theatre began not with the music but with the concept of a theatrical work. The music is secondary because without the dramatic idea it would never have been written. The idea begets the music which therefore is only one but not the dominant component. . . . The scene, the idea, is paramount.'[15] Wieland therefore started with the basic psychological elements of the drama and built his production around those. 'My settings abstract essential meanings not from the stage directions, but from the scenes themselves.'[16] When the music and scenery were out of step, those like Knappertsbusch wanted the staging to change; Wieland insisted that the music had to conform. It is easy to understand why some accused him of being more a producer of theatre than of opera—a charge Nietzsche had made against Wagner himself.

With music, text and staging subordinate to the dramatic concept, conventional effects sometimes had to be sacrificed. Doing the transformation scene in *Lohengrin* with the curtain down had been dictated by two considerations that he explained in a BBC interview.

> The whole scene carries far too little weight. That is one reason. The other is that, according to Wagner's stage directions, several things happen during the transformation: the gate is opened, maidens go down to the well (it used to be done that way in Bayreuth once), water was scooped up, a whole lot of men come in. And what do they do? In the good old German way they clap each other on the shoulder, they shake hands. And none of it has anything at all to do with *Lohengrin*.[17]

For the same reason he came to feel justified in tampering a bit with the scores themselves—*Tristan und Isolde* alone he considered so perfect as to be inviolable. The first occasion was in his initial production of *Tannhäuser* when he rejected the usual Paris version in favour of his own collage of the Paris and Dresden scores and then altered somewhat the instrumentation of the former. He further deprived Wolfram of one of his lines in the same production and in *Lohengrin* dropped a choral passage from the final act because of its dramatic weakness and its noxious nationalism. But it was in his 1965 *Ring* that Wieland created his own great drama by deleting Gutrune's brief scene between Siegfried's funeral march and the return of Hagen with Siegfried's body. As he explained to Geoffrey Skelton,

> It is not strong enough dramatically to follow the funeral march: only Hagen's reappearance can do that properly. After the funeral march it really is immaterial to hear Gutrune asking Brünnhilde if she is awake and then discovering that she has gone down to the Rhine. By cutting the scene we achieve a considerable tightening of the whole act.[18]

Though he did nothing without the most careful thought, he was never content with the result and constantly modified it. Sometimes these were self-initiated corrections of what he recognized as mistakes; at other times they were to placate those critics who were, as he said, without imagination. With *Parsifal* he added light and touched up the staging, especially in the second act; he rid his first *Ring* of all its naturalistic elements; in the original *Meistersinger* he sketched in rooftops, gave back Sachs his workshop and provided a distant view of Nuremberg; in both productions of *Tannhäuser* he made changes throughout. Those critics *with* imagination, however, usually regretted most revisions as a compromise of the integrity of the originals. The most notorious example occurred in 1960 when Knappertsbusch refused to conduct *Meistersinger* unless the 'amphitheatre' in the third act was replaced with a conventional festival meadow. What Wieland fashioned in response—or revenge—was such a visual calamity that few mourned when this otherwise much-loved production was taken out of the repertory after the next year. Wieland regretted that attention had been focused so intently first on *Entrümpelung* and then on his handling of stage directions and the music. Exchanging German for Greek gods, replacing naturalistic props with abstract settings, tampering superficially with the scores were mere means to an end. Far more important was what he put in their place. And this often seemed lost in the furore.

One of Wieland's notable innovations was the *Scheibe* or disc. It not only gave focus to the stage picture and the action but also had symbolic significance. It was introduced in 1951 with the *Ring*, where it was both a staging device, giving the four operas a visible unity, and a symbol of the universe. The idea was imitated in other opera houses, often with results that he found embarrassing. Other techniques included walls, critical in certain productions, and steps, an adaptation of the famous

'Jessner-stairs' developed in the 1920s by the expressionist theatrical producer Leopold Jessner. These were employed in amphitheatrical form, most notably in the 1956 *Meistersinger* and in *Lohengrin*. In the former production they were laid out in such a way as to create the impression of a mirror image of the Festspielhaus auditorium. With a huge disc seemingly between the two amphitheatres, the Festspielhaus audience almost became participants in the performance. Equally cunning was his integration of the stage floor itself into a production. Taking advantage of the sharp rake of the auditorium, which makes the stage floor visible to an audience as in no other opera house, Wieland raised floor decorating to a fine art.

In giving shape and dramatic force to the operas, physically and conceptually, Wieland narrowed the focus on the main characters and events. This was an important reason for the austerity of the sets. It also explained, for instance, the absence of the crew in the 1952 *Tristan*, the framing of the first version of the *Ring* as a series of duologues between male and female characters and the emphasis on Ortrud and Lohengrin to the derogation of Elsa and Telramund. Wieland also radically altered stage movement, which he regarded as not as much a matter of deploying bodies as a mode of dramatic statement. Singers were no longer required to follow the traditional Bayreuth convention of coordinating their gestures with the music, and choruses no longer mimicked conventional social behaviour. The chorus, regimented into a highly stylized Greek chorus, virtually became a part of the settings.

Regarding costumes as dramatic rather than decorative in function, Wieland gave them as much thought as he did settings. 'The colour of a costume is as important as the sound of a violin,' he once commented.[19] On another occasion he said of his *Lohengrin*, 'I have sought to carry over the architecture into the figures, into the costumes.'[20] Dress had both to define a role and fit in with the overall production. In most cases this required a complete break with the past. In some operas he presented the characters less as real people than as symbols. In *Tristan* the dress divulged no indication of rank; the two principals could have been almost anyone, anywhere, at any time. In the *Ring* the treatment was especially drastic. 'We do not want any German gods any longer, only human beings,' Wieland said.[21] He achieved this more clearly in the second *Ring*; in the first production Wotan, Brünnhilde and Fricka, for instance, would easily have passed for Greek sculptures. He also emphasized that costumes had to suit the individuality of the soloist. The basic pattern for Isolde in the 1962 production was altered ten times; then different versions had to be created for the two sopranos alternating in the part, Birgit Nilsson and Astrid Varnay.

But the central element in Wieland's staging technique was lighting. Although Bayreuth had since Siegfried's time laid great emphasis on light and colour, it was from reading Gordon Craig that Wieland became convinced of their full potential. 'Light is for me the great

Wieland's 'de-Germanification' of the *Ring* was apparent in costumes as well as sets. Here Wotan (Hans Hotter) and Brünnhilde (Martha Mödl) resemble Greek sculptures rather than Nordic gods.

magician,'[22] he told Antoine Goléa, and he quickly became a master of the technique. His lighting technician he considered no less important than his conductors, and he once remarked to Joseph Wechsberg in evident pride, 'Our lighting scores are as complicated as the musician's scores, and we have a lighting staff of 20 men.'[23] Yet for all the resulting subtleties and glories, he at times frustrated his audiences by the obscurity in which he drenched the stage. One critic wryly suggested changing programme credits from 'lighting by . . .' to 'darkening by . . .'.

Wieland used lighting the way Richard Wagner used music: to clarify and amplify the dramatic action and to create atmosphere and mood. He was intrigued—as his grandfather had been late in his life—by the relation of colour to music. Sawallisch recalled the long discussions they had about *Lohengrin* and how to express in colour the very clear, bright and radiant sound of A major. In working together on *Der fliegende Holländer*, they found passages, particularly in the second and third acts, where the right colours were difficult to fix. 'We used a colour catalogue. The original [Dresden] score of *Holländer*, with its rough orches-

236

tration required appropriately harsh colours. I said to Wieland, "If the staging is dominated by a particular colour which in my opinion does not correspond with the music, it is very difficult to conduct to it. . . ." He agreed.'[24] The two men worked together night after night, Sawallisch said, until Wieland, with a smile, would ask whether a certain colour suited the conductor and he felt able to conduct the corresponding music.

Wieland's great collaborator was his lighting technician Paul Eberhardt, and they would sit together for hours while Wieland played passages from the scores and Eberhardt at the lighting panel tried to find the colour appropriate to the music. Their joint struggles with the medium were commemorated in Wieland's letter of appreciation on Eberhardt's retirement in 1966:

> Year by year, day by day, often night by night—I think back with pleasure at the times when at dawn we would take leave of one another [at the stage door], exhausted and completely colour blind—we sat in the winter cold of the auditorium, feebly warmed by electric heaters, while we discussed and tried, again and again, to find the nuances of a green or blue, a filter mixture or the precise relation of the music to a lighting transition.[25]

For Wieland, as for his grandfather, no detail was too small, no aspect of a production too irrelevant to engage his attention. But nothing was ever considered completed, ever found satisfactory; always there was a search for something new and better. Yet each element—sets, lighting, costumes and so on—was for Wieland merely a means to his supreme aim: to elucidate the moral of the dramas. Not since the operas had been composed had anyone given them such deep and original thought, and as time passed his endeavour to reach the intellectual core became an obsession.

He began by putting aside every production, every accepted idea of the past. Out with the old sets and theatrical conventions went the old ways of looking at Wagner. Then he dug as deep as possible. He picked up ideas with intellectual omnivorousness, adapting them to his own purposes. He pondered Wagner's texts, scores and prose writings, not just to know what the composer wrote but what he *meant*. A voracious reader, he also turned to other sources—as varied as Freud and Jung, Brecht and Aeschylus, Adorno and Bloch—that might offer additional insights. He also looked back not just to Craig and Appia but to such innovative productions as the 1929 *Fliegender Holländer* by Jürgen Fehling, Ewald Dülberg and Klemperer at the Kroll Opera and a January 1933 *Tannhäuser* commissioned by Tietjen and carried out by Fehling, Oskar Strnad and Otto Klemperer at the Berlin State Opera, a production closed under National Socialist pressure after four performances. As he thought his way into the drama, it began to stage itself. The main thing was to get the characters clearly fixed, he always said, then the rest fell into place.

In a sense the process was psychoanalytical. This was not simply because Wieland looked at the operas through the lenses of Freud and Jung, but also because he never stopped peeling off the onion-layers of the myths in an effort to reach their core. Sometimes he was criticized for a Germanic over-intellectualization. And it is true that he was very German in his probing, his agonizing, his philosophizing. But there was also an important personal and political angle. The scrapping of the old interpretations was ultimately a purging of his own past and of Bayreuth's past. Expunging history was a deep psychological and artistic need for Wieland. His aim was to create a new Bayreuth—and even a new Wagner—free of the old Germanness with its nationalism and romantic sentimentality.

So if there was digging, there was also constructing, and the overall concept was applied to every aspect of each production. And every aspect was designed to draw the spectator into the inner meaning of the work. As he explained to Geoffrey Skelton:

> In the second scene of *Rheingold* I no longer show the distant vision, the blue sky, the ground covered in flowers, but present the abstraction of Wotan's lust for power in the form of a mysteriously threatening, skyscraper type of building. The citadel is the symbol of Wotan's destructive will for power. . . . The tree in *Die Walküre* is not just any tree, but the tree in which Wotan has plunged the sword. . . . This is where the fate of the world is decided. . . . I present a tree that has a sort of totem quality: hence the skulls hanging on it and the mysterious signs carved on it. This tree must impart a sense of awe: it can't be just a nice straightforward ash tree.[26]

The result was as moving and powerful to some as it was incomprehensible and outrageous to others. In either case, if a spectator emerged from a performance the same person who went in, it was not for Wieland's lack of trying.

Parsifal was perceived in essentially psychoanalytical terms, as a drama expressed in symbols and archetypes. The actions were not objective events but allegories, the characters were not specific individuals but symbols. 'Strictly speaking, the staging is nothing more than an expression of Parsifal's state of mind,' he remarked in a letter to Knappertsbusch.[27] At its core was a contest between Amfortas, who sought to maintain absolute chastity in the realm of the grail, and Klingsor, who ruled through hatred, magic and luxury. Both worlds were contrary to nature, and their symbols—the spear and the grail— were sexual, indicative of the division of the world and the need for reintegration. Kundry was the mediator between the two realms; Parsifal eventually destroyed the unnatural character of both and joined them.

Wieland explained all this in the 1951 Festival handbook, with an elaborate schematic design, 'Parsifal's Cross: A Psychological Diagram'. The schema placed the action within four poles, mother ('goodness'),

Klingsor ('belief in nothing'), saviour ('divine paternal spirit of all-embracing love') and Titurel ('pure faith'); their symbols were the swan, the spear, the dove and the grail. The horizontal line contrasted Kundry and Amfortas and compared the main features of their psychological state through the course of the opera. The vertical line recorded the developments in Parsifal's psychological evolution. At the centre of the two lines was Kundry's kiss, the explosive spark of the drama. It transformed Parsifal and left him, in Kundry's word, *welthellsichtig*, worldly-wise. Now he understood the link between sexual desire and Amfortas's wound, comprehended Amfortas's guilt and recognized the need to absolve it. At last he was 'wise through pity'. With this wisdom he broke out of the bonds of egotism, entered the community of the suffering and offered deliverance.

In this way Wieland sought to wring out of the story the quintessence of its psychological significance, just as Richard Wagner had wrung out of his music the quintessence of its emotional feeling. In fact, Wieland held that there was a certain psychoanalytical flavour about the music itself, not only in its search for explanation, clarification and discovery but also in its move from hyper-romantic density towards a style that opened the way to Debussy and the atonalists. In demolishing the traditional interpretation of the work as an ersatz religious service with Christian undertones, he said he wished to demystify and demythify it. Hence the bareness of the stage and the general obscurity of the lighting were intended to shift attention from 'real' events to the psychological realm.

But all too soon he realized that what his production was trying to say was not what many people wanted to hear. Audiences remained firm in their perception of the opera as a Christian mystery and went on shushing anyone who tried to applaud at the end and continued demanding a Parsifal who made a sign of the cross before Klingsor's castle, just before it collapsed. 'No matter how maladroit and infantile all that business is and how completely it destroys theatrical illusion,' he remarked to Goléa in exasperation, 'it simply does not dissuade the public from believing in miracles, in mystery. *That* is the atmosphere of Bayreuth against which it is impossible to fight.'[28]

The secularization of *Parsifal* was followed by the demonization of the *Ring*. Given the Teutonism of conventional productions and the attempts by nationalists and National Socialists to claim the work for themselves, Wieland's version was bound to be a statement not just for Bayreuth but for Wagner and in a way even for Germany. The wounds of the past were still so painful in German society, especially among the Wagnerian dogmatists, that it took no little courage in 1951 to launch an assault on this Everest of the Wagnerian landscape. In effect his treatment of the work amounted to a catharsis for himself and a penance by Bayreuth for its honoured place in the Third Reich.

Wieland saw the work not as a Germanic heroic epic but as a Greek tragedy, with Wotan as Zeus, Siegfried as Heracles and the Wotan-Brünnhilde conflict as the counterpart to that of Creon and Antigone. Given the close similarities between Nordic and Greek mythology, he had made a distinction without a difference, but that very fact exposed his determination to dismantle the *Ring* as a Germanic saga. This reassessment only did the opera vastly overdue justice. Presenting it as a timeless tragedy in the style of Aeschylus and in his second version as a universal moral drama in the manner of Schiller and Brecht, he removed it from the narrow realm of Teutonic heroes and gave it a Shakespearean universality. 'The *Ring*', he told Geoffrey Skelton, 'is the mirror which Richard Wagner holds up to humanity. "This is how you are," he says, "and this is what will happen to our world if humanity does not radically change." '[29]

That was only the starting-point. The clue to his interpretation was the conflict between the female qualities of order and love and the male qualities of aggression and will to power. In this way he stressed, more uncompromisingly in his second production, the work's political character, indeed its evil political character, its virtual equation of politics with evil. It is impossible to understand Wieland's treatment of the *Ring* without appreciating how much he was reacting to his own political trauma. At times his feelings burst out during rehearsals, as when he told a Waltraute whom he was coaching to think of Valhalla as Hitler's bunker, with Hitler inside knowing that the end is near and intent on pulling the whole world down with him. Ultimately Wieland was railing not just against National Socialism but against a state of mind that exists to some extent at all times and in all places. Like his grandfather he was dealing with the raw material of human motivations—power, ambition, aggression, oppression—which, unless controlled, lead inevitably to destruction.

Wieland's reassessment was also original in its desolate portrayal not only of the characters but even more in his handling of the drama, which went from a grey pessimism in the first *Ring* to a black nihilism in the second. Wotan was no longer Ernest Newman's 'god who is caught in a web of his own careless weaving', much less the traditional 'distinguished old gentleman with white hair who strides over the stage singing solemn melodies', in Wieland's ironical phrase.[30] Here he was the great villain, the incarnation of the ruthless will for power, a proto-Hitler. It was he who initiated the whole cosmic catastrophe by disturbing the natural order, symbolically violating the world ash tree to make a spear. This act had set in motion sacrilege after sacrilege: selling Freia to the giants, duping Alberich, allowing his own son Siegmund to be slaughtered. Then, 'as is always the way with dictators', he said to Antoine Goléa, the god was unwilling to recognize that the end was near and tried, through Waltraute, to extract the ring from Brünnhilde in a last attempt to regain power. At the end, 'like an Adolf Hitler before the deluge, Wotan prepared a more or less heroic suicide, felling the world

ash tree and disposing of the pieces around Valhalla, awaiting a spectacular death by flames, a death that will come to him as a criminal plainly
responsible for his crimes'.[31] The first *Ring* production ended with a lone
firefly circling the stage, showing that life had survived. At the end of the
second there was nothing.

In his lust for power this Wotan was the archetypal male. His
antithesis was Brünnhilde, the archetypal female whose all-embracing
love guided her every action. The natural order which Wotan upset, she
reestablished. Within this framework, all the other characters were
secondary, though Wieland gave them an immense amount of thought,
with deep psychological insight. Even Siegfried now emerged almost as
a passive bystander, the opponent of Wotan but no longer a great heroic
figure. The one true male hero was, significantly, Siegmund; he was
heroic because he was a rebel, a defier of the gods. The others were seen
in a political light as well. Alberich, a fascist and slave merchant, made
Nibelheim the first concentration camp in history; his techniques of
anonymity (the tarnhelm) and fear (the ring) were typical of dictators.
Mime was a supreme liar, a mini-Goebbels; his technique was poison.
Hagen, possibly a Himmler, also used poison but with more success,
another figure of absolute evil. To Wieland the end was in the beginning, and he expressed this visually at the culminating moment of
Rheingold when the gods marched not up but down to Valhalla across a
blood-red rainbow bridge. It was as though he had in his mind's eye
placed a transparency of the *Ring* over the historic record of the Third
Reich.

The ultimate phase in Wieland's 'de-Germanification' of Bayreuth
and of Richard Wagner's works was his treatment of *Die Meistersinger*,
the main victim of German chauvinism. Wieland had come to loathe, as
he once said, the imbecile Teutonism, bourgeois *Gemütlichkeit* and
bombastic nationalism under which it had been buried. It was this work
that he personally most associated with Third Reich Bayreuth, just as
Nuremberg was the place most overtly linked to the Nazis—as the site
of the party rallies, the place where the 1935 race laws had been
promulgated and the location of the war crimes trials. Liberating the
opera from that incubus was his personal and artistic mission. He
accomplished it in two stages.

The first production was political only in the negative sense that it
stripped away all traces of nationalism and presented the work as a very
human parable about the creative act of genius. To leave the audience
in no doubt as to his didactic purpose, Wieland explained his intentions
in a programme note, entitled 'Here a Child Was Born'. The father, the
progenitor of the creative act, was Walther, the 'ecstatic dreamer and
unruly revolutionary' who epitomized Wagner himself. For his
'child'—the original inspiration—to become a masterpiece, it needed an
inspiring example from the past (Walther von der Vogelweide), a wise
teacher to show that dreams without reflection and enthusiasm without

control do not produce art (Hans Sachs), a woman to arouse the latent creativity of male eros (Eva), a snobbish opposition (the guild members), a provocative adversary (Beckmesser) and finally a bold patron (Pogner). Along the way there was bound to be a public outcry and a bit of the madness that Wagner personally considered essential in the creative process (the midsummer's night riot). Blithely unaware of all the fuss were most contemporaries (the Night Watchman). Taking life as it came were the simple townsfolk (David and Magdalene). At the end the supreme judge in such matters (the people) was united with the genius in the name of art. Such, he said, was Wagner's 'little art theatre'.

Utterly different from this cerebral approach was Wieland's second rendition, which combined parody, satire and comedy. It had been inspired by his growing conviction that between the traditional romantic version and his previous interpretation there was a third way of looking at the work, the way in which he believed Wagner had more or less conceived it—as a Shakespearean comedy. Wieland placed the action in a vulgar, materialistic society and portrayed the characters with a mixture of cynicism and persiflage. No longer was Sachs a venerable sage but an old cobbler; no longer was Walther a creative hero but a down-at-the-heels aristocrat happy to marry into money. Eva was the selfish child of a rich man; her father, more interested in his wealth than in his daughter, was anxious to marry her off under the cover of art. Beckmesser was attracted less by Eva's beauty than by her dowry. The mastersingers themselves, a rather shabby lot, took on airs as they put on their robes. And the people of Nuremberg were a rough, pre-capitalist proletariat. It was not surprising that such a debunking caused an unprecedented explosion of outrage. It was Wieland's least popular production.

Entirely different was Wieland's treatment of the four earlier operas. His starting-point in both productions of *Tristan* was to throw out the traditional version of a soppy, if tragic, love story and to present the opera as a bleak epic about the deadly power of eros and thanatos. Central to both versions was the sharp focus on the two lovers and their unfolding psychological state. 'The innermost hidden motive which dictated all the decisions of both Tristan and Isolde', Wieland wrote in a programme note, 'was nothing less than the death wish, a passion for night. Undoubtedly they loved one another, but each loved the other only from his own standpoint, not the other's.'[32] At the same time he developed a parallel theme: the inevitable clash between sexual freedom and social oppression.

> All passion is a threat to the established order and represents a fatal danger to society. Richard Wagner himself remains so objective that through Marke he sets against the dreamers—for whom happiness, society and morality no longer exist and who regard love as their destiny, the ideal and supremely beautiful mystery—the indisputable realities of the world: power, renown, honour, loyalty, chivalry and friendship.

Wieland approached Wagner's three romantic operas more or less as a group, seeing in them a common theme: the man—the outsider—searching for personal salvation through the love of a pure woman. In the case of Tannhäuser he summed up his conception in a programme note:

> In *Tannhäuser* the 'evil principle' to be overcome is not eros as such but the typical masculine selfish egotism in contrast to feminine self-sacrifice and unquestioning devotion. The tragedy of *Tannhäuser* is the general one of man in the Christian era, who is conscious of the division between mind and instinct and seeks to find the way back to his original divine-human unity.[33]

But by the time he came to do his second production he saw the work in more overtly religious terms in which, as he said, 'the themes of repentance, of representational sacrifice, of redemption and of the insuperable differences of *eros* and *religio* are worked out from the standpoint of western Christianity'.[34]

Lohengrin, for all the originality of its staging, was the least novel in concept. While presented as a parable of the outsider without escape from his social isolation, the opera had as its central theme the question of the true nature of love. It was because he found it difficult to bring such stereotypical figures as Telramund and Ortrud to life that Wieland took liberties in his staging of the second act. He also placed the emphasis on the contrast—and contest—between Lohengrin and Ortrud, relegating Elsa and Telramund to the periphery. The bridal chamber scene was treated as the critical element in the drama since it was only then that the issue of the essence of love came to a point. Because there can be no anonymity in love, Elsa's question about Lohengrin's identity destroyed them both. It was essentially a replay of the various classic myths where the mortal destroys happiness by casting his gaze on the divinity, and many critics sensed about it the solemnity of a Greek tragedy.

In *Der fliegende Holländer* Wieland gave the theme—exile, sacrifice, love and redemption—a less sentimental treatment than was traditional. The Dutchman at first appeared more a spectre than a person; through his acceptance of the selfless and unconditional love of Senta, he became completely human. Senta herself was portrayed as naïve rather than obsessed; Daland was presented as a personification of materialism and avarice, which is no doubt why, with his red and white striped trousers, blue jacket and stovepipe hat, he was dressed to resemble Uncle Sam. The interpretation was a middle way between a tragic ballad and a sentimental romantic opera. 'Now has he done things', a critic commented, 'which no one before him ever imagined, but to the last he has explained the *Flying Dutchman* better than anybody else.'[35]

Such was, in a few words, how Wieland conceived of the operas. Although much of his interpretation either did not come through to audiences or was emphatically rejected, he left a concept of Wagnerian opera at least as thoroughly revolutionized as the staging. By the time of his death he had made it impossible for those who had experienced his productions to see Wagner's works in the old way.

The 'new Wagner' was neither nationalistic nor fairy-tale opera; it had no old Nordic deities or any other type of superhuman hero, providential saviour, valiant knight, proto-Führer, Chosen One. Gone were sentimentality, *Gemütlichkeit* and happy endings. Instead there was opera as living and universal drama. It was opera inspired by the same sources which had inspired Wagner: Aeschylus, Calderón, Shakespeare. But it was also opera that looked to psychoanalysis for an insight into character and to Marxism for an understanding of social dynamics. This Wagnerian opera had lessons to teach, above all that power tends to corrupt and that absolute power corrupts absolutely. It found its creative urge, as had the composer himself, in the exploration of the nature of love. Its interpretive axis was the conflict between the male will for power and the female desire for order. It was operatic drama whose profound impact grew out of its inner strength and integrity. That this sort of opera should have been developed in Richard Wagner's own sanctuary gave it particular meaning and authority.

'The Richard Wagner Festival', a critic wrote in 1958, 'has turned into a Wieland Wagner Festival.'[36] Although intended as a comment on the sensation caused by Wieland's productions, the remark could just as easily have been a reference to his omnicompetence. He developed the concept, designed the staging, sketched the costumes, chose the singers and conductors, coached the performers and directed each of his productions. Behind the scenes, however, there were others whose help was vital. Above all, Wolfgang relieved him of the enormous burden of financing and administration, which left him free for his work not only at Bayreuth but also at Stuttgart—the 'winter Bayreuth', where he developed the prototypes of his later Bayreuth productions—and many other opera houses around Europe, with a repertoire extended from Gluck and Beethoven to Strauss and Berg. His wife Gertrud did the group choreography. Wilhelm Pitz maintained the chorus at its usual heights. Curt Palm, whom Wieland had worked with in his 1937 *Parsifal*, remained wardrobe master, though other designers were brought in for the *Ring* and certain other productions.

The music, like the stage, was to be rid of anything distinctively German or traditional or solemn. 'Forget the way it was done in the past,' he constantly admonished singers and conductors.[37] 'What is the point of going in a new direction on the stage', he remarked, 'if the music is done in the spirit of the previous century.' He wanted orchestral sound that was characterized by the lightness, clarity, delicacy, transparency and fast tempi which he associated with his so-called 'Latin conductors'. Choral sound was also to be lightened. The voices of the

Flowermaidens, for example, were to seem, he said, 'Debussy-ish'. His final advice to Wilhelm Pitz on the *Parsifal* men's chorus exposed his horror of the conservative mentality in art as well as in politics: 'No unnecessary crescendos and decrescendos, no marcatos, everything mystical but not German and not Christian Democratic.'[38]

Finding and keeping conductors was his main headache. He continued to be torn between what he wanted and what was expedient. He started out with Knappertsbusch and Karajan, who conducted splendidly. However, both resigned after their second year; the former because he could no longer stand Wieland's staging of *Parsifal* and the latter as a result of personal and professional differences. With Knappertsbusch gone, it was possible to have Clemens Krauss, who took his place in Bayreuth history for having conducted the fastest *Parsifal* in history up to then, knocking twenty-three minutes off Strauss's 1933 gallop through the score. When Krauss died shortly before his second season, Knappertsbusch took pity on Wieland and returned. Although the two were Bayreuth's odd couple—given their deep and enduring artistic differences—Knappertsbusch was from then on in effect chief conductor until his death in 1965. The *Parsifal* he gave audiences year after year made him a worthy successor to Levi and Muck.

There were two other mainstays in those years. Joseph Keilberth conducted the *Ring* and several other operas from 1952 to 1956, when Wieland peremptorily showed him the door. The other, Wolfgang Sawallisch, arrived in 1957 and left before the 1963 season as a result of a disagreement over casting. The first 'Latin' conductor to arrive—in 1955—was the Belgian André Cluytens, whose light sound received a mixed reception from the critics. Similarly, Böhm's treatment of the 1965 *Ring*, described by Wieland as 'Wagner via Mozart', did not meet universal critical approval. Most of Wieland's other conductors were solid, old-style Wagnerians: Eugen Jochum, Erich Leinsdorf, Rudolf Kempe, Ferdinand Leitner, Josef Krips and Robert Heger. Even Heinz Tietjen, in an amazing act of reconciliation, was invited back to conduct *Lohengrin* in 1959. Two others were invited for 'political' reasons. As a deliberate snub to the Wagnerian old guard, Paul Hindemith—persona non grata in the Third Reich—was asked in 1953 to conduct Beethoven's Ninth. And Otto Klemperer, who had last conducted a Wagnerian opera in Germany in 1933, was engaged for *Meistersinger* in 1959, though he had to withdraw after a tragic accident.

Although it included most of the outstanding conductors of his day, Wieland constantly chafed at his orthodox conducting staff. In the hope of getting the transparent textures and 'fresh interpretations' he always talked about, he sought out a number of young, then largely unknown conductors—Lovro von Matačič, Lorin Maazel, Thomas Schippers and Berislav Klobucar—though after a single appearance he asked none of them to return. In 1966 Wieland at last found his ideal musical collaborator in Pierre Boulez, who had never conducted a Wagnerian opera and who was as sceptical of tradition and as willing to experiment as Wieland himself. Wieland told him to conduct *Parsifal* with 'fresh ideas'. 'It was as though', the music historian Egon Voss has written, 'the 1951 *Parsifal* production had to wait until 1966 to receive the musical interpretation intended by Wieland Wagner.'[39] The way finally appeared open to Wieland's dream of a completely secularized *Parsifal* with music à la Debussy.

Less problematic were the singers, though they were initially not easy to find and in principle Wieland avoided anyone who had previously sung at Bayreuth. True to an older Bayreuth tradition, he was at first less interested in finding international stars than in cultivating new talent, younger singers who could be moulded to suit his requirements. Like Wagner himself in 1875, he wanted to develop a new type of singer—the singing actor, the acting singer who used his brain as well as his voice. 'Our singers', he once said, 'must know the meaning not only of the music but of the words. They must be able to express every nuance with as little gesture as possible and give just the right volume of voice. And they have to give up egocentric mannerisms.'[40] He became very angry when singers responded to the music by a gesture to correspond to a leitmotif or accent. 'The music says everything!' he would exclaim.[41]

There was another—sometimes overriding—criterion if one was to sing at Bayreuth: an ability to get along with Wieland Wagner. Although deeply loyal, Wieland could be irascible, quixotic and ruthless. Anything that annoyed him, however small and unintended, could result in a fall as vertiginous as Lucifer's, with no hope of ever singing at Bayreuth again. Dietrich Fischer-Dieskau learned only years afterwards from a third person that he had been summarily dropped because of his unwillingness, while singing Wolfram, to wear a hunting hat—a hat which made it impossible for him to hear so he could adjust his voice. Bayreuth thus lost one of the finest postwar baritones. It was similar with Keilberth, who also never knew how he had erred and who was offended ever after.

Over the years Wieland built up a troupe of singers second to none. To his original group—Mödl, Varnay, Kuën, Stolze, Uhde, Weber and Windgassen—he added Birgit Nilsson, Anja Silja, Leonie Rysanek, Gré Brouwenstijn, George London, Theo Adam, Kurt Böhme, Hans Hotter, Gustav Neidlinger, Ramon Vinay, Jess Thomas, Thomas Stewart, Josef Greindl, Eberhard Waechter, Erwin Wohlfahrt and Martti Talvela. Foreign singers came in unprecedented numbers, though some of the more exotic—Maria Callas, Leontyne Price, Nicolai Gedda and Mario del Monaco—could not be lured to Bayreuth.

Just before the 1966 season began Wieland fell seriously ill. He spent the summer in a Munich hospital, unable to attend that year's Festival. In October, suffering from lung cancer, he died. His last hours he spent discussing, as best he could, a new production of *Tannhäuser*.

The previous spring Wieland had been awarded *Pour le mérite*, a national honour founded by Frederick the Great and presented by the government to the most intellectually and culturally esteemed figures in German life. In this case the award was in recognition of precisely what Wieland had sought to achieve in reviving the Festival: the liberation of Wagner's music from its association with the Third Reich and a demonstration of its timelessness and universality. By showing the way to new productions and new interpretations, he had opened the door for other opera houses to follow in his path and, in so doing, inspired a renaissance of Wagnerian opera around the world.

8

'It's mine and I'm keeping it'
(*Götterdämmerung*)

For a second time in its history Bayreuth was shaken by an unexpected and premature death. Now the overshadowed younger brother, the Wagner who was always ignored, the operatic producer whose creations were scorned, the man who described himself as 'an odd duck, whom no one ever took seriously',[1] suddenly found himself sole and supreme head of the Festival. And for a second time the succession had the effect of a coup d'état, setting off another blazing dynastic row.

Over the years relations inside the Wagner clan had been increasingly strained by differences extending from the personal to the political. By far the deepest rift was between Wieland and Wolfgang. After a cooperative start, their association had degenerated into rivalry and eventually into irreconcilable animosity. For his brother's productions, Wieland had only contempt. 'That sort of thing simply should not be allowed to happen in Bayreuth,' he said of Wolfgang's 1960 *Ring*.[2] By the same token Wolfgang ridiculed his brother's reputation as a theatrical genius and derided his work as a sacrilege against Richard Wagner. 'Because he gave more offence, people said he was the greater. What nonsense!' he told an interviewer years later.[3] Relations between the two families had inevitably followed the same downward course; wives and children were not on speaking terms and Wolfgang's son and daughter were forbidden to attend their uncle's impious productions. The situation was further complicated in Wieland's case by years of estrangement from his wife and profound political and artistic differences with his mother. Adding to the tensions, the notorious anti-Nazi exile Friedelind returned to Bayreuth in 1953. It was made clear that there was no place for her in the Festival, though with Wieland's encouragement she ran master classes at Festival time. Only Verena managed to keep her literal and figurative distance from the internecine combat by having withdrawn with her family to Nussdorf on Lake Constance and never returning.

Each unhappy family, Tolstoy said, is unhappy in its own way. The Wagner way could not have been more Wagnerian. After a lifetime of feeling inferior and humiliated, Wolfgang suddenly had his opportunity for vengeance. And Hagen-like, the moment his brother's back was, as it were, turned, he drove in the spear. He destroyed the models of Wieland's productions and, in what the German press referred to as a 'pogrom', sacked almost everyone who had worked with him. From then on he did whatever he could to dismantle Wieland's reputation, both professional and personal. He belittled his brother's role in getting the Festival restarted after the war. He repudiated the notion that his brother had revolutionized Wagnerian opera. He complained that because he himself had forgone the chance of also producing an opera in 1951, Wieland had stolen the limelight. Merely because his own work had followed in time, it was considered inferior in quality. And rarely did he lose an opportunity to assert that Wieland had been a Nazi. Although party files hold no record of Wieland's having joined the party, the fact is that at the 1938 Festival Hitler had simply decreed that Wieland, having reached majority, was a member of the party. And in any case, Wolfgang himself had joined the Reich Theatre Chamber.

The spear also came down on Wieland's widow Gertrud. When she asserted a claim to her husband's share in the Festival, Wolfgang confronted her with the agreement which he and his brother had made in April 1962, providing that in case of the death of one of them, the survivor would be sole head of the Festival. She and her family, he let her know in no uncertain terms, were out. They were out of the Festival and out of Wahnfried. When Gertrud protested, an unsympathetic Winifred responded, 'After the forester dies, the forester's family has to leave the forester's house.'[4] Friedelind as well was out, Wolfgang having made it impossible for her to go on with her master classes in Bayreuth. She removed herself and them to Yorkshire.

While the family feud provided audiences with entertaining intermission gossip, the Festival itself went smoothly on its solipsistic way. The second half of the sixties in fact enjoyed a number of excellent performances, thanks to the continuing success of Wieland's famous productions of the *Ring*, *Tristan* and *Parsifal*, with their outstanding casts and conductors. But as in 1883, 1906, 1930 and 1951, there was widespread uneasiness about the future. The issue was the same as before: concern about artistic standards. No one doubted that Wieland's death marked an abrupt end to the most exciting chapter in Bayreuth's history. And highly competent though Wolfgang was as a manager, it was far from clear that he was the commanding figure needed to maintain Bayreuth's position as the world's leading music festival and the supreme interpreter of Wagner. Above all, there was scepticism that his own productions could fill the gaping void left by Wieland.

The record was not encouraging. Although the brothers had started from the same general artistic premisses and had used essentially the same

Although the simplicity and stylization were overtly New Bayreuth, Wolfgang's 1953 *Lohengrin* was otherwise conventional. In Act I Lohengrin (Wolfgang Windgassen) bids farewell to the swan, as Elsa (Eleanor Steber) looks on.

techniques, what they put on stage was unmistakably different. Wieland's had the mark of genius; Wolfgang's, the sign of workmanship. Wieland soared; Wolfgang plodded. Wieland had blazed a new path; Wolfgang appeared to have no clear sense of direction. Inevitably, two brothers producing the same operas on the same stage were compared, and one had to be found inferior. That was the curse that stalked Wolfgang from the start.

He began in 1953 with *Lohengrin*, which he staged with the utmost simplicity. The opera opened and ended with a stage that was barren except for enormous stylized tree trunks flanking the two sides. In the second act the scene was overwhelmed by towering, even oppressive walls, more reminiscent of a Sumerian fortress than of a medieval Brabantine citadel. Although there were a few traditional features—an old-style swan appeared in the bright white light of heavenly miracle and the duel between Lohengrin and Telramund was conducted with realistic swords—the production and directing otherwise shunned naturalism. The economy of staging was matched by the stark simplicity of the costumes and the spareness of movement of the soloists. The chorus was arranged in massive, rather inchoate groupings. This was a demilitarized *Lohengrin*, the Saxon and Brabantine men wore neither helmets nor armour and held few spears and only one banner. The focal point of the drama rested on Ortrud and Telramund, an interpretation greatly emphasized by the outstanding singing of Astrid Varnay and Hermann Uhde.

By combining some New Bayreuth techniques with prewar tradition, the production was neither naturalistic, symbolic nor abstract, yet bore traces of all three. Baffled by the combination, Stuckenschmidt politely characterized it as an indefinable synthesis. Although conservative critics rather liked the result—'exceedingly distinguished' and 'nobly proportioned' were some of the comments—the general response was decidedly cool. It was this unfavourable reaction that Wolfgang traced to his late start as a producer. 'People had already been beguiled by my brother and thought that when a second person came along, he had to be bad.'

Der fliegende Holländer, which followed in 1955, was done in the same styleless style—in this case rigid simplicity, mixed with some good old-fashioned naturalism. The sets were plain to the point of frugality and shunned all the old folkloristic detail and nautical paraphernalia. The stage was dominated by the sea, which in the first act gleamed a vivid greenish blue and at times heaved to the point of seeming almost to spill over into the auditorium. The Dutchman's ship, a shadowy projection with the customary black mast and blood-red sails, flickered across the stage, to reappear in the last act as a permanent fixture until it vanished into nothingness at the end. Daland's living room, although conventional in its outlines, was stripped almost bare; bathed in bright sunlight, it left an impression of clarity and order. The characters appeared in simple, realistic dress and acted with equal simplicity and directness: the spinning maidens were maidens who spun, the drunken sailors were sailors who were drunk. Senta was an ordinary country girl, not a supernatural heroine; the Dutchman was a doomed sailor, not a demonic superman.

Varnay and Uhde teamed up again and once more were the musical highlight of the production. In its lack of pathos and heroics, the interpretation reflected the New Bayreuth approach. A few observers were enthusiastic. 'That rare thing, a perfect opera performance,' asserted one. But most complained that it had nothing new to say, that the lighting and direction were unexciting and that the spectacle was imposed on the drama instead of growing out of it. At no point, commented *The Times*, did the production 'by grouping, gesture or lighting, deliver a blow to the solar plexus such as we experience in [Wieland's] productions'.[5]

Two years later Wolfgang turned to *Tristan und Isolde*, producing it in a visual atmosphere of lead grey and darkness to mirror the mood of gloom and doom. Visually it was a cousin of Wieland's earlier work. In the first act a flat, austere tarpaulin divided the stage—the foredeck—

with Isolde's cabin in the foreground and a glimpse of the stern visible through a small opening. The love duet took place in near darkness and in the final act a streamlined wall and simple couch were the only décor. The theme of the production was that Tristan and Isolde existed in a world apart, a world closed to all but their most trusted attendants, Kurwenal and Brangäne. Their magic space was symbolically denoted by a circle of light, from which others were excluded. A bleak loneliness, Wolfgang himself said, underlay the action, giving way only rarely to passion.

The prevailing critical reaction was hostile, even devastating. What overall concept guided Wolfgang? asked Joachim Kaiser. His answer: 'There is none. It is impossible to find any principle explaining the varying degrees of abstraction and emptiness.'[6] He brought to the drama 'no new ideas, only a foggy disenchantment'. Critics found in the musical treatment, however, a chamber opera of unusual effectiveness. In his highly successful Bayreuth debut, Wolfgang Sawallisch—at thirty-five the youngest person ever to conduct there apart from Siegfried Wagner—provided a reading of the score that was 'beautifully clear in rhythm and texture, rich in sonority, marvellously paced but emotionally restrained and in the last analysis architectonic rather than poetic', in the words of *Opera*'s William Mann. The only warmth in this refrigerated production—which indeed concluded with the stage covered with snow, suggesting the eternal winter of a world without love—came from Birgit Nilsson's singing, which initiated her eventual apotheosis as one of history's greatest Isoldes.

Wolfgang's 1957 *Tristan* was visually his least successful, Act I dismissed by Joachim Kaiser as 'less a ship than a psychotherapist's office'. Seen here, Birgit Nilsson (Isolde), Wolfgang Windgassen (Tristan), Grace Hoffman (Brangäne) and Gustav Neidlinger (Kurwenal).

Wolfgang's architectonic approach to the 1960 *Ring* is apparent in the Gibichungs' hall in *Götterdämmerung*, Act I. Wieland's abstract symbolism has been ostentatiously replaced with symbolic naturalism expressed in rough three-dimensional sets.

Next came the *Ring* in 1960. Wolfgang overwhelmed the stage—and the audience—with a huge plate, which was irreverently termed, among other things, a giant crumpet, a Dutch cheese, a collapsible saucer. This was both the site of the action and the central symbol, representing at once the ring and the universe. The disc was ingeniously tilted in various ways, raised and lowered, broken up into as many as five segments which were themselves canted and folded, until in the end the whole resumed its original shape as a new world dawned upon the ruins of Valhalla. In its concave form it stood for peace, unity, order—the world of the gods. Convex, it implied evil—the world of the Nibelungs. So, when inverted, it became the roof of the Nibelheim underworld; raised it was the lofty platform from which a feathery rainbow bridge led to another slice signifying Valhalla; broken in two, the rear half was raised to form the back wall of Hunding's hut; split again later, a raised portion formed the rock on which Brünnhilde was put to sleep; hoisted

253

onto two rough pillars, it was the roof of the Gibichungs' hall; and so on. Technically the device was a tour de force, intended both to lend the stage greater three-dimensionality and to unite symbolism and stage realism.

Technology apart, the production was conservative—as compared with Wieland's first *Ring*, downright reactionary. It reinstated much of the old-fashioned Nibelung paraphernalia: swords, spears, drinking horns, Hunding's hearth and Mime's forge. And it restored Wotan to his honoured place as a tragic hero, victim of his own human weaknesses, who had to sacrifice those whom he loved until he eventually destroyed himself and everything around him in the hope of creating a better world.

The production had an excellent cast, which in the first year included Birgit Nilsson and Astrid Varnay (alternate Brünnhildes), Hans Hopf (Siegfried), Jerome Hines and Hermann Uhde (alternate Wotans), Wolfgang Windgassen (Siegmund), Aase Nordmo-Loevberg (Sieglinde), Grace Hoffmann (Waltraute), Otakar Kraus (Alberich) and Gottlob Frick (Hagen). Rudolf Kempe's conducting was widely acclaimed.

But the music could not save a production that was otherwise roundly condemned, by German critics especially, as a palpable flop. Wolfgang had put so much effort into the engineering that he had neglected the other aspects of the production. His directing and stage management were judged to be inept: the Rhine gold and the Rhinemaidens were effortlessly within Alberich's reach; the rainbow bridge led not towards but away from Valhalla; Fafner was a couple of puffs of unconvincing smoke. The realistic props clashed with the symbolic and abstract background. The lighting, though at moments impressive, was usually nothing more than delicate modulations of Stygian darkness. And the costumes—Siegfried's, according to one spectator, was more suitable for centre court at Wimbledon than a primeval forest—were unattractive as well as inappropriate. All that many critics found memorable about the production was Wolfgang's feat in making an intrinsically exciting drama boring. The *Frankfurter Allgemeine* expressed a widespread view in dismissing it as 'Not worthy of Bayreuth'.

The failure of the 1960 *Ring* brought to a head the anxieties about Wolfgang's work that had been deepening for years, not only among music critics but also within the Wagnerian inner sanctum itself. These apprehensions were expressed in a private letter at the time from Joachim Bergfeld, head of the Richard-Wagner-Gedenkstätte, the Wagner archive, to the editor of the *Baseler Nachrichten*, who had written to express his fear that Wolfgang's productions were having a disastrous effect on Bayreuth's reputation. Reciprocating the concern, Bergfeld replied that some of the leading music critics had stayed away that season to avoid having to comment publicly on a production they took for granted would be poor. But bad as the *Ring* was, he went on, Wolfgang's three previous productions had been even worse, inferior to what was being done outside Bayreuth. Particularly weak was the directing. Even friendly critics, he remarked, saw Wolfgang's style as a step backward, and they found it all the more regrettable that a *Ring* of this standard should replace Wieland's. Yet despite the criticism, Bergfeld wrote, Wolfgang himself was firmly convinced that his productions were better than his brother's.

To the head of the Society of the Friends of Bayreuth, Bergfeld wrote even more frankly. It was painful, he wrote, to witness how Wolfgang's productions were destroying Bayreuth's standing. This assessment was not just his own but that as well of the critics of the two leading German newspapers, the *Frankfurter Allgemeine* and the *Süddeutsche Zeitung*, in whose opinion Wolfgang's work was no better than what was being done by minor opera companies. But the graver problem, Bergfeld went on to say, arose from the fact that Wolfgang was determined to develop a style different from Wieland's and as a result he was undermining the Festival's artistic integrity. In her 1949 agreement, Winifred had given her sons equal rights; but in the long run, Bergfeld observed, either one of them would have to leave or they would have to reach a new division of responsibilities.

Against this background it can be imagined what a staggering blow was Wieland's death to the Festival's admirers and, given Wolfgang's record as a producer, what deep apprehension it created about the institution's future. There was nothing for it, however, except to put as good a face as possible on the situation. Some critics comforted themselves with the thought that after the frenetic excitement of the previous fifteen years, a period of decompression might not come amiss. Others saw benefit in a shift of attention from the visual to the aural, which Wolfgang had defined as one of his aims. Then, too, there was hope that on his own Wolfgang might develop into a better producer and director. His 1967 *Lohengrin* was therefore considered something of a test— unfairly, since it had been on the drawing board for several years.

There was a marked architectural tone about it. In place of the disc, the scenic leitmotif was an octagon, usually a multiplicity of them. But far from being coldly geometrical, the overall impression of the staging was lavish and colourful. Once again Wolfgang tried to combine the simplicity of New Bayreuth with tradition, symbolism with realism. The meadow scene which opened and closed the opera was dominated by two towering pendants of art nouveau foliage on either side of the stage, inspired by the decorations on the doors of St Zeno's in Verona. At the appropriate moment the image of a swan appeared, its plumage vastly magnified and projected onto the clear blue horizon of the cyclorama. In the second act, an overpowering clinker wall with stylized, romanesque references towered over the scene and formed an impressive backdrop for the movements of the large chorus. The bridal scene

Further reversing New Bayreuth style, in his 1967 *Lohengrin* Wolfgang employed three-dimentional sets in the old Bayreuth tradition: 'I can only say that romanesque, with its down-to-earth simplicity, seemed to me the most appropriate mode of elucidating the work'.

took place on a bench under an outdoor vaulted arch, itself modelled on the east portal of Pisa cathedral. Except for this 'moorish garden pergola', as it was referred to, the staging was on the whole praised. The costumes—the Saxon and Thuringian nobles in red, the Brabantine nobles in blue-green and the women in blue—also added a certain architectonic solidity, though to some they appeared ungainly. Wolfgang interpreted the opera not as a conflict between pairs of characters but as a contest between Lohengrin and the world he vainly yearned to embrace. What Wieland had presented as a neo-Greek mystery play in oratorical style was returned to the fairy-tale world as a medieval romance about human beings and supernatural intervention.

Musically this *Lohengrin* was well received, although its première year had faced near catastrophe when Sándor Kónya, the Lohengrin of the season, was taken ill a few hours before the second performance. He was replaced in subsequent performances successively by James King, Jess Thomas, Hermin Esser and Jean Cox. Five Lohengrins in eight performances set a Bayreuth record. Most of the rest of the cast— Heather Harper (Elsa), Grace Hoffmann (Ortrud), Donald McIntyre

(Telramund) and, in his Bayreuth debut, Karl Ridderbusch (the King)—
sang well, encouraged by the lyrical conducting of Rudolf Kempe. In
the following year there was only one German singer in the cast, so far
had Bayreuth's internationalization gone.

Back to mid-sixteenth-century Nuremberg was where Wolfgang
took audiences with his centenary production of *Meistersinger* in 1968. It
was a realistic, a human, a warm Nuremberg, a Nuremberg as *deutsch*,
though certainly not as *echt*, as Hans Sachs himself could have wished. At
the same time it was ideologically no less than visually a conservative
production. Wieland's debunked Mastersingers were rehabilitated and
the settings marked a jubilant return to romantic naturalism.

The curtain rose to reveal a large wooden-framed hall; that it was an
ecclesiastical space could be deduced only from the purplish light shining
through the (presumed) stained glass windows. The second act could
almost have been modelled on Cosima's Nuremberg of 1888, except
that the sets were now transparencies lit from behind. Sachs's room in
the third act had both a transparent wall behind and an invisible wall in
front. The final scene in the meadow was relatively orthodox, except for
the trees, which were outlined on pasteboard. Ingenious it was but, in
the view of most critics, gimmicky. 'Toytown,' said one, of the settings;
'Broadway-medieval,' said another, of the costumes.

There was praise for Wolfgang's directing. His handling of the Midsummer Day fête was particularly successful, presented as a joyous,
popular Franconian holiday, with folk-dancing and city pipers, with

Modelled on an illustration in the famous Nuremberg *World Chronicle* of 1493, the sets of the 1968 *Meistersinger* have
rough woodcut contours. In the final scene of Act II xenon-light projections dissolved the walls, a metaphor of the
disintegrating medieval order.

Wolfgang's 1970 *Ring* was a hybrid: a bit abstract, a bit concrete, a bit symbolic and a bit naturalistic. Again the disc was the central staging technique. Seen in the Awakening scene of *Siegfried*, Jean Cox (Siegfried) and Berit Lindholm (Brünnhilde).

pantomimes and acrobats and the guilds showing themselves off, all culminating in the song contest. Wolfgang emphasized the humanity of the opera, which he saw as the story of an emerging bourgeoisie, which had its faults but was basically proud and decent, and a German culture, which had its faults but was rich and glorious. In a later touch meant to bring out the irenic mood of the interpretation, Beckmesser was not banished at the end but remained on stage to participate in the joyous conclusion. Here was opera as entertainment, intended to titillate the eye and the ear. Eva (Gwyneth Jones) was nicely sung, but if the critics could have had their way, she would certainly have been awarded to Sachs (Theo Adam) on the basis of his singing rather than either Walther (Waldemar Kmentt) or Beckmesser (Thomas Hemsley) for theirs. The conducting was shared by Karl Böhm and Berislav Klobucar.

In 1970 Wolfgang restaged his *Ring* of ten years earlier. His reincarnated disc was by now such an exhausted scenographic cliché that it prompted one observer to wonder how stage designers would have managed had Richard Wagner stuck to his original title for the opera, the *Gold of the Nibelung*. Again the disc epitomized a united and peaceful world. And once again, in parallel with the unfolding drama, its five basic parts moved and leaned at various angles, broke apart and came together in varying shapes until, with the final notes of the score, it closed in its pristine form, a symbol of expiation and hope for a new world—though whether that world was to be a utopia or another of the same was unclear. In this new version Wolfgang used the disc with greater subtlety and dramatic effect. He was more daring with light and colour, creating an impression at times abstract, at times realistic, at times symbolic. Light, water and fire in vivid moving projections were synchronized with the music.

Wolfgang produced the work neither as metaphor nor as myth and depicted the characters neither as heroes nor as symbols. Following the example of G.B. Shaw, his *Ring* was a worldly drama of highly fallible human beings. It shunned any political message, however; Siegfried, for example, was not a proto-revolutionary challenging the established order but simply a young man fighting for the woman he loved. Although a marked improvement on its 1960 predecessor, this *Ring* neither offended nor enraptured. The audience was no longer challenged to ponder archetypal symbols or social messages but was left to sit back and enjoy straightforward opera theatre.

Musically the weak point in the first year was Horst Stein's conducting. Although critics liked moments and even whole scenes, most contended that he had failed to grasp the full measure of the work. The principal vocalists—Thomas Stewart (Wotan), Berit Lindholm (Brünnhilde), Jean Cox (Siegfried), Helge Brilioth (Siegmund), Gwyneth Jones (Sieglinde) and Karl Ridderbusch (Fasolt, Hunding and Hagen)—were by and large judged to have acquitted themselves adequately or better.

In 1975 Wolfgang turned to *Parsifal*. The final performances of Wieland's classic had been held two years earlier. Although the production was by then a pale shadow of the original, some ardent admirers wanted to preserve it as a memorial to its creator. Wolfgang reacted with understandable horror to this latest twist in the opera's tortured history, and so after 101 performances in 23 successive years—the 1882 original had been performed 205 times in 27 Festivals—the production went into retirement.

Wolfgang's version retained the structural outline of Wieland's staging, including the circular temple of every production since 1882. But the mood and overall impression were vastly different. What Wieland had merely hinted at through abstraction and the veil of a twilit dream world, his brother made concrete and suffused in romanticism and colour. Wolfgang perceived the theme of the drama as the knights' inhuman self-denial and their search for personal perfection. As a result of their fanatical asceticism and élitism, they lost their original dedication to a life of compassion. The brotherhood was on the point of dissolution

Wolfgang's 1975 production of *Parsifal* signalled the end of New Bayreuth. Act I was as luxuriant and vivid as Wieland's was austere and monochrome.

when Parsifal, the outsider made wise through pity, enabled them to re-embrace their original ideals. In this version Kundry did not die at the end, presumably implying that the female principle was no longer to be excluded from the world of the grail.

Critics were beguiled by some of the staging, the woodland scenery especially. A good many of them, however, considered the production badly flawed by Wolfgang's recurrent problem, incompetent stagecraft. The *Neue Zeitschrift für Musik* compiled a veritable catalogue raisonné of directing blunders—beginning with the flight of the wounded swan in the first act down to the movement of the knights at the end of the last. The singing enjoyed a better response. René Kollo's Parsifal, Hans Sotin's Gurnemanz, Franz Mazura's Klingsor and Bernd Weikl's Amfortas were well received, though the assessments of Eva Randova as Kundry varied widely. Horst Stein's conducting, one critic remarked, lay between Knappertsbusch's romanticism and Boulez's simplicity.

Wolfgang had inherited an operatic institution that, thanks to his brother, was the most exciting and admired in the world. But after only a few years of his solo control, there was a widely shared feeling in the international music world that Bayreuth was in serious decline. Germans in particular feared that this historic flagship of national cultural life—the one German cultural institution known and esteemed around the world—was dangerously low in the water. Artists and conductors were jumping off what they sensed was a sinking boat. Better performed and more innovatively produced Wagnerian opera was being offered in other houses in Europe. 'Wolfgang Wagner has now used up all the credit Wieland had amassed over the years,' said one critic. 'Bayreuth is in the doldrums,' charged another. 'Why should the state finance such stuff?' asked a third. 'Bayreuth Sinks into Mediocrity'; 'Bayreuth's Struggle for Its Artistic Existence Has Begun'; 'Can the Festival Survive?' cried some of the newspaper headlines.

In a private commentary, Joachim Bergfeld summed up, as he had ten years earlier, the fears among Bayreuth insiders. He began by observing that the entire authoritative German press had expressed the deepest concern about the Festival's future. He said he fully shared the misgivings, as did other friends of Bayreuth. The Festival had been in crisis ever since Wieland's death. For four years Wolfgang had tried to run the Festival on his own, without competent assistants. Though critics respected Wolfgang as an administrator, they had no respect for him as a director and scenic designer. As long as ticket sales were good, Wolfgang's position was impregnable. But Bayreuth faced two dangers, Bergfeld concluded. One was increased competition from Salzburg. Karajan had promised never to challenge Bayreuth with an entire *Ring* at Salzburg; but he had vowed in 1952 never to do Wagner at all in Salzburg and had broken his word. The other was a further decline in artistic standards if outstanding artists declined to participate in the Festival.

Bergfeld's fears were anything but hypothetical. Already the year before, Pierre Boulez had said in an interview with the Munich *Abendzeitung*, 'I shall conduct *Parsifal* next year, but what should keep me there after that? Bayreuth is no attraction any more. To conduct there, simply to conduct, is of no interest. Wieland, with whom I wanted to do so many things, is dead, and what goes on there today under the word directing is quite astounding.'[7] Other conductors— Böhm and Kempe—had already left; some big names, such as Georg Solti and Rafael Kubelik, kept their distance. In the absence of a stable conducting staff there had been a series of temporary or inadequate conductors—Berislav Klobucar, Silvio Varviso, Lorin Maazel, Hans Wallat. Orchestral playing had become uninspired and even sloppy. Singers were at times forced to shout against overheated playing; on occasion it was they who salvaged a performance. Famous soloists— such as Nilsson and Bumbry—declined to return and others were impossible to recruit. Although Bayreuth had traditionally run occasional risks with newcomers, it was now a house where even principal roles were being taken by debutants. Often they were relatively successful. But no longer could one go to Bayreuth with the certain expectation of hearing eminent Wagnerian singing.

In short, singers, conductors, critics and much of the Wagnerian laity had no respect for Wolfgang as artistic director of the Festival. His most visible shortcoming was his staging. Up to the 1970s the 'newest' productions in the repertory were the oldest: Wieland's orphaned works—*Tristan* and *Parsifal*, supervised by Wieland's close collaborator Peter Lehmann, and the *Ring*, overseen by Bayreuth's great Wotan of the fifties, Hans Hotter. Wolfgang's productions had been no match. Though critics had loyally praised individual elements, in truth they could see in them no identifiable style and no maturation in artistic techniques. The productions were neither old-fashioned nor avant-garde, neither concrete nor abstract, neither original nor conventional. As a result what came across on stage lacked the stamp of any special conviction. Part of the problem was that they lacked a driving intellectual concept. 'I want to stage my *Ring*, not interpret it,' Wolfgang once said.[8] Wieland had regularly enraptured or enraged his audiences and in either case left them overwhelmed; Wolfgang pleased them or disappointed them but in either case left them underwhelmed. Because he was himself unintellectual and conservative, he emptied the operas of their moral and social content. As a result he deflated them.

Most surprisingly, Wolfgang somehow managed, despite his long years of experience in Berlin and Bayreuth, to be a consistently poor director. He left loose ends, inconsistencies and ragged edges. All too often the whole was less than the sum of its parts. Performances consequently lacked the strength, the tension, the sheer panache of what Wieland had accustomed audiences to expect on the Festspielhaus stage. Bayreuth was losing its fizz.

Overtly Wolfgang was imperturbable, even in the face of tough questions from interviewers. To criticism of his productions and directing, he simply answered that the Festivals were regularly sold out. To complaints that he could not attract top singers and conductors, he responded that Bayreuth was an ensemble company and he could make do with singers with small voices because of the Festspielhaus acoustics. To assertions that his work was inferior to his brother's, he countered that Wieland had been well regarded only after his death. But underneath the bravado, Wolfgang knew that the Festival could not go on as it was and that he could not continue on his own.

The serious threat to Wolfgang's control of the Festival was less the deepening disquiet over his artistic leadership, however, than the legal complications resulting from the situation inside the Wagner family. After Wieland's death relations among the members had become ever more venomous. In a comment that a delighted German press quoted widely, Nike Wagner, one of Wieland's daughters, once described the family as this ancestral tribe, this many-headed, thousand-footed monster that pon-derously rolls through the corridor of generations. . . . A diffusely expanding family hydra, a selfish, pretentious mass with prominent noses and thrusting chins. An Atreus clan, in which fathers castrate sons and mothers smother them with love, in which mothers cast out daughters and daughters defame mothers, in which brother harms brother and brothers rise against sisters just as sisters rise against brothers, in which daughters are disowned and daugh-ters-in-law are pushed aside, in which men are feminine and women masculine and in which a great-grandchild nibbles on the liver of another great-grandchild.[9]

The reason the family acrimony posed a grave practical problem was that Siegfried's will left the entire Wagner estate, after Winifred's death, equally to the four children or their heirs. Winifred's 1950 agreement delegating her managerial authority to her sons, along with their own 1962 agreement on the succession, were merely transitional arrange-ments. Upon Winifred's death the terms of Siegfried's will would come into force and the legacy would then be divided among Verena, Friedelind, Wolfgang and Wieland's children. Wolfgang's position would be in jeopardy and the institution immobilized.

Since Winifred was three years older than the century, legal chaos loomed. So Siegfried's proposal in 1914 to turn the Festival into a national foundation was in effect revived, this time in earnest. After several years of negotiations an agreement was reached between the Wagner family and various German government authorities to transfer the entire Wagner estate—the Festspielhaus, Wahnfried and the Wagner archive—to a foundation, the Richard-Wagner-Stiftung Bayreuth. To this Foundation the family gave without remuneration the Festspielhaus, its adjacent land and its auxiliary buildings. Wahnfried was donated to the town of Bayreuth, which now leased it permanently to the Founda-tion and transformed it into the Richard Wagner Museum. The Siegfried Wagner House was sold to the town, which incorporated it into the Wahnfried property. The archive had been separately sold for 12.4 million marks (£2.3 or $5 m.) to the federal, Bavarian and local governments, which presented it 'on permanent loan' to the Founda-tion. The Foundation leased the Festspielhaus to the director of the Festival, whose operational autonomy was 'guaranteed'. The executive of the Foundation was a board of directors comprising eight members: the federal government and the government of Bavaria each with five votes; the four branches of the Wagner family with one vote each; the Society of the Friends of Bayreuth with two votes; and various other local governments and foundations with two votes each.

Where did these arrangements leave the Wagner family and its historic enterprise? By preserving it as an autonomous institution for the performance of Wagner's works, the agreement gave the Festival that 'national' status of which Richard Wagner had dreamed. And by pro-

viding state authorities as well as the Friends of Bayreuth with representation on the board, it indirectly ensured financial support, realizing
another of the composer's aims. But in vesting the authority to choose
a Festival director in the board, the agreement brought the Festival as a
private, dynastic institution to an end. In return the Wagner family
received little, apart from money. They were given a few votes on the
board and a commitment that the board would look first to the ranks of
the family for a candidate to be head of the Festival. Were no member
considered suitable, the director was to be chosen by a three-man expert
commission which itself was to be selected from among the directors of
the operas of Berlin, Munich, Vienna, Hamburg, Stuttgart, Frankfurt
and Cologne. When the terms of the Foundation came into force in
1973, Wolfgang Wagner was unanimously selected to be director of the
Festival—a predetermined outcome of the whole scheme.

The Wagners' agreeing to establish a Foundation was a rare instance
of familial accord, but it did not diminish the acrimony or the competition over the succession. In the summer of 1976, however, there was
a sudden reversal of alliances. After divorcing his wife of thirty-three
years, Wolfgang married Gudrun Mack, a Festival secretary. He fired his
daughter Eva, whom he had taken on as an artistic assistant following
Wieland's death, and placed his son Gottfried under the customary
Wagner form of excommunication—*Hausverbot*—in this case a legal
injunction not to enter the family home or the Festspielhaus. What was
now taking place on the Green Hill was not Wagnerian but soap opera.

To complete his break from all the rest of the family, Wolfgang
proclaimed to the press and the annual meeting of the Friends of
Bayreuth that there was 'not a single person named Wagner' who was
suitable to succeed him as head of the Festival. With that, he united the
entire fourth generation against himself. This was now such a titillating
scandal that it stirred even the most serious German newspapers to give
it full-page coverage. Some regarded the family feud ironically, comparing it with the blacker stories in the Old Testament, or a particularly
nasty Grimm fairy tale, or a Shakespearean tragedy unfolding in 'Bay-
reuth-upon-Avon'. Others were less amused. 'During a century in
which Bayreuth had long ago forfeited its key role as a Wagner centre,
the firm Wagner & Co., divided as it is, should vanish from the
management of the business,' grumbled *Der Spiegel*. 'Less the pity. From
an artistic point of view, 100 years in Bayreuth was quite enough.'[10]

That rumpus was as nothing, however, compared with the scandal
that had exploded the previous year—in this case over Bayreuth's
political past. The subject was one that had been strictly taboo.
Throughout the postwar period everything possible had been done to
conceal, repress, falsify and simply wish away that past. In itself this state
of mind was not surprising; secrecy had always been an automatic,
obsessive reflex—almost a genetic trait—of all Wagners. Already in the
late nineteenth century there were widespread complaints about

Cosima's *Geheimniskrämerei*—secrecy for secrecy's sake. But never had there been so much to be secretive about as there was after 1945, not simply Bayreuth's association with the Third Reich but its close association with the ideology that led directly to it.

Despite the break with the past artistically, there had otherwise been no denazification of the Festival. Far from it. As if nothing had happened between 1933 and 1945, the first issue of the official *Bayreuther Festspielbuch* included one article after another by persons who had been devout, believing and practising National Socialists, who had been joyous Nazifiers of Bayreuth and who, one might have thought, had disqualified themselves for ever from any connection with the Festival— such people as Paul Bülow, Hans Grunsky, Zdenko von Kraft, Hans Reissinger, Otto Strobel, Oskar von Pander and Curt von Westernhagen. On the conducting staff that first year were the compromised Furtwängler and Karajan. To sculpt a large bust of Richard Wagner to be placed in the garden outside the Festspielhaus, whom did the Friends of Bayreuth commission? None other than Arno Breker, Hitler's favourite sculptor and someone who had executed the most grandiose of his commissions—including an identical bust of Wagner that had stood in the Führer's study. Symptomatic as well were Wolfgang's destruction of Mewis's model of Hitler's proposed Festspielhaus and the systematic omission from Festival listings of the celebratory performance of Beethoven's Ninth in 1933. And, just as much as in the past, the Festival was the ideological-cultural rendezvous for the right wing.

It was the age-old arrangement since the days of Wolzogen. The Wagners would produce what they liked on stage while the archconservatives might feel at home on the Green Hill and treat the Festival as their annual assembly. In its contradictions Bayreuth was a microcosm of the Federal Republic itself—a state where democracy and social welfare flourished but also a state where Nazis were not seriously purged from any profession, where concentration camp commanders and participants in mass murder went scot-free, where judges who had passed thousands of death sentences remained on the bench and where, in short, the desire to forget, and even to forgive, was overwhelming. The town of Bayreuth itself had a similarly mixed record. Although the citizenry were predominantly Social Democratic, there was a powerful rightist minority which in the mid-sixties gave the neo-Nazi National Democratic party some of its strongest support in Germany and was influential enough, for example, to prevent until 1988 changing the name of the street which Hitler himself in 1936 had dedicated as Houston-Stewart-Chamberlain-Straße. Bayreuth bookshops were too frightened of reprisals from the Festival authorities to sell Friedelind Wagner's memoirs or Fred Prieberg's *Musik im NS-Staat*, a book about musical life in the Third Reich. Like Kafka's castle, the Green Hill loomed intimidatingly over the town below.

There were any number of people who recoiled in distaste. Theodor Heuss, the Federal Republic's first president and a man untainted by National Socialism, regarded Bayreuth as a symbol of the unreformed Germany and refused to attend the Festival either when it reopened or at any other time during his ten-year term of office. Wieland himself soon found the right-wing, crypto-Nazi Wagnerians intolerable. 'I would like to know what Richard Wagner did to deserve all these ultra-nationalistic secret societies and Germanic women's organizations and all the others who swarm around the Green Hill,' he said on one occasion. 'We must break once and for all with this old nonsense.'[11]

By the early 1960s, with the change of generations and increasing national self-confidence, German society began facing up to the past. In Bayreuth, however, the façade was kept intact until it was undermined, paradoxically enough, by a number of articles and books written to celebrate the 1976 centenary. Most startling was a work by Michael Karbaum, a scholar who had been commissioned to prepare a semi-official study of the Festival's first hundred years. The first outsider to dig around in the Wahnfried archive, he described and documented how deeply Bayreuth had been involved with the German radical right since the late nineteenth century and with National Socialism from its inception in 1919.

Wolfgang Wagner was appalled at these 'indiscretions', as he called these disclosures, and blocked publication of the book for several years, allowing it to come out only after it had been bowdlerized. A little later Peter Pachl, preparing a sympathetic biography of Siegfried Wagner, was denied access to the Festspielhaus archive and later dedicated his biography to 'Wolfgang Wagner whose obstructionism first put me on the right track'. Summing up the common experience, one writer remarked, 'Wolfgang Wagner declines to see scholars, refuses access to the Festspielhaus archives and family papers and has even destroyed some documents. I suppose I might act the same way if my mother had been one of Hitler's best friends, but his behaviour makes scholarly work impossible.'

In all this, Wolfgang was acting in the best Wahnfried tradition: controlling and manipulating information and granting access to the files only to someone who could be trusted to write what was desired. Once asked by the *Frankfurter Allgemeine* what quality he most prized, Wolfgang answered 'Verschwiegenheit'—a word whose meaning lies between secrecy and discretion. Therein lay the crux. Wolfgang was not compromised by Nazism, was not anti-Semitic. Rather, like most Germans of his generation, he simply wanted to bury and forget the past. If atonement there was to be, it would be silent and by indirection— through his irenic opera interpretations, for example, and by engaging Jewish conductors to be the core of the musical staff.

In the end the person who blasted the biggest hole in the façade and who did so in the most mortifying possible way and in full view of the international public was Winifred Wagner herself. For her the past had never been forgotten or repented. In a report in the American army newspaper *Stars and Stripes* in the summer of 1945, Klaus Mann wrote that he had travelled the length and breadth of Germany since the collapse and had found but one person who acknowledged admiring Hitler and the person was a woman of English birth. During the years that had followed her sense of self-righteous innocence achieved a grotesque grandeur. When asked by Furtwängler how she tolerated the appalling calumny heaped upon her, she said that it was so totally unwarranted that it left her completely untouched. Furious at the injustice of the disabilities imposed on her, she gave as her return address 'in exile'. Correspondence to friends was closed with '88'—referring to the eighth letter of the alphabet and meaning 'Heil Hitler'. Hitler himself was referred to in her circle as 'USA'—*unser seliger Adolf* (our blessed Adolf). And she held court to legions of old, equally unreconstructed Nazis. When Wieland's children told her of seeing films of concentration camps, she responded, 'That is all falsified, all misrepresented.'[12] Wieland had opposed her move back to Bayreuth in 1957. Eventually he relented, but on observing that she constantly entertained her old Nazi cronies, he had a wall constructed between Wahnfried and the Siegfried Wagner House where she lived. The wall, she later said, hurt her even more than Wieland's operatic productions—and those she royally loathed. Not only were they hideous to see, she maintained, their claim to being revolutionary was bogus; it was Siegfried who had shaved off the beards and rid the stage of obsolete bric-a-brac.

Wieland had imposed a certain restraint over Winifred's public activities. After his death, she was more shameless than ever in displaying her Nazi sympathies. She took Edda Goering, daughter of the Air Marshal, Ilse Hess, wife of Rudolf Hess, and relatives of other high Nazi officials to sit with her in the family box in the Festspielhaus. To celebrate her seventieth birthday in 1968, she invited many of the same, along with a niece of Himmler's and the head of the neo-Nazi National Democratic party, to a gala dinner at a public restaurant. In the political and moral ambiguities of postwar Germany, no one took much notice.

Her antics finally exploded in scandal in 1975 when she gave a five-hour television interview to the off-beat film producer Hans Jürgen Syberberg. Feelings bottled up for thirty years came pouring out. Now for the first time since 1945 someone spoke publicly and unashamedly—defiantly—with undiminished affection for Hitler. Her words were like the freely associated murmurings of an analysand on a psychoanalyst's couch. They fascinated, not just because they were the views of an intimate friend of Hitler's but also because they were the ventriloquized voice of numberless Germans and Austrians.

About postwar Bayreuth itself, she was by turns discreet and outspoken. Wieland himself had been a great trial to her. She could not understand why he had renounced Hitler as he had. After all, he owed his life to him; some gratitude was certainly due. As regards the Festival productions, she had been 'ordered' to keep quiet, but the warning had been unnecessary since she had intended to follow Cosima's example. Privately, however, she had objected furiously to what Wieland was doing. He had simply 'pulled down' all the splendid work of Tietjen and Preetorius. When he had cleared the stage and relied on lighting for his effects, she assumed it was for lack of funds; later she was amazed to learn that this had come to be considered a 'style'. Nor did she like the way social commentary and politics had been injected into the operas; in her day, one had simply produced art. And what pure joy working in the Festspielhaus had been then! Artists dared not ask for more than a modest fee; there were no unions to interfere. 'And everybody kowtowed, naturally.' During the war, when Hitler gave the orders, the orchestra, the soloists, the technical personnel were all in place. 'It was simply an ideal situation.'

Establishing that sort of discipline was part of the reason Hitler had been so popular in Germany, she insisted. He had restored 'order and cleanliness'. But had he not also caused a world war? Well, the outbreak of the war, she said, was 'regrettable'. But 'everyone, every reasonable person had to recognize that with the huge number of enemies surrounding Germany, one upon the other, such a small country simply could not survive and a catastrophe had to come'. And the Jewish question, had she discussed it with Hitler? 'With him never. Quite honestly, I never considered myself sufficiently competent about these things.' About Hitler personally, her central point was that he had a good side, and this was the only side of him she knew. 'I shall never disavow my friendship with him; I cannot do it. . . . I am able, I mean, perhaps no one understands, but I am able completely to separate the Hitler I knew from what he is accused of these days.' But can one do that? 'Yes, yes certainly. I can. . . . The part of him I know, so to speak, I treasure as much today as before.' All restraint now gone, she added, 'If Hitler came in the door today, for example, I would be just as pleased and happy as ever to see him and to have him here, and the dark side of him, I know that it exists but for me it does not exist because I do not know that side.'

With those terrible words and the worldwide scandal they caused, Wolfgang asked his mother to stay away from the Festspielhaus for a time. Of course she had merely articulated a view shared to a greater or lesser extent by many Germans and Austrians, including those in the music world—the Furtwänglers, Strausses, Böhms, Karajans—who believed that there had been nothing culpable in their own behaviour and that the Third Reich and its consequences were like an earthquake or other natural disaster, a cataclysm for which no one was responsible rather than a boundless moral catastrophe which they had sought to beautify with their music. The scandal was less that Winifred held these views than that she dared to express them openly. Even Wolfgang acknowledged that she had merely articulated publicly what many others thought privately.

Whatever remained of the great wall of silence after Winifred's bravura performance was demolished the following year by Walter Scheel, President of the Federal Republic. As the guest of honour at the centenary celebration in the Festspielhaus in July 1976, Scheel addressed the specially invited audience of Wagnerians and devotees of Bayreuth. Instead of the politely conventional—and conventionally evasive—address that had been expected, President Scheel gave his listeners a brief but scintillating lesson in German intellectual history during the preceding hundred years. In the course of this he demythologized Wagner and Bayreuth and—in the nicest possible way—shoved the audience's noses in the institution's ideologically odoriferous past, the responsibility for which he laid squarely on 'those who were responsible for Bayreuth, who still thought that Bayreuth was only a place of culture without noticing that it had long since become an instrument for evil policies'.[13] Thomas Mann himself could not have put it better. Nor could he have improved on the President's conclusion: 'Bayreuth's history is part of German history. Its mistakes are the mistakes of our nation. And in this sense Bayreuth has been a national institution in which we are able to recognize ourselves. . . . We simply cannot erase the dark chapter of German history and of Bayreuth's history.'

Winifred had been told not to attend the ceremony and did not hear these words. But how did those in the audience—such as Karl Böhm—who had been fervent supporters of Hitler and his Reich, react? They were enraged. A nonplussed Wolfgang Wagner put away his own prepared remarks and instructed Böhm to conduct the musical portion of the festivities without further delay.

The head of the German state had faced up to the past. But not the head of the Bayreuth Festival. Wolfgang bravely struggled to keep some remnants of the façade intact. He was so opposed to Syberberg's film, once it was completed, that a publisher dropped plans to publish the text—'so strong was the pressure from Bayreuth', Syberberg later wrote. For similar reasons a Munich cinema that had shown Syberberg's earlier films refused to screen this one and the Federal Republic's Foreign Office declined to provide copies of the film to German cultural institutes overseas.

Not until 1981 did Wolfgang produce another opera, now his second version of *Meistersinger*. The settings of the first two acts were more old-fashioned than anything he had ever done, bearing in fact a striking resemblance to Wieland's 1943 production. And there were none of the innovative frills of his earlier treatment to lend the stage pictures any

The homely settings and costumes of Act III of the 1981 *Meistersinger* were transformed into marvellous spectacle to life by Wolfgang's directing. In this photograph of the 1986 performance Kothner (Jef Vermeersch) bids Beckmesser (Hermann Prey) to begin the song contest.

novelty. The finale of the third act was the most successful. It took place on a stage that was almost empty except for an enormous tree, a tree in fact modelled on a 300-year-old linden in the Franconian village of Limmersdorf. Around it the festive crowd frolicked and danced and then settled down for the song contest. Of the skyline of a distant Nuremberg there was no sign; what had created such scandal and pain in 1956, now passed unnoticed. Wolfgang managed this scene even more skilfully than earlier, and for many it was not merely the high point of the production but the best thing he ever did.

This was the opera Wolfgang most enjoyed producing, and the one he kept for himself to produce. His new treatment was even more benign than the earlier one. 'He brought *Die Meistersinger* down from the lofty heights of artificial idealization and alienation,' Erich Rappl, the Festival's most experienced critic observed, 'and back to the soil of his native Franconia, and he strove to bring the plot to life in such a natural and human way that there could be no more talk of nationalist emotion.' Wolfgang also presented the characters as much younger than usual: Eva and David as teenagers, Walther in his early twenties and

Sachs and Beckmesser as forty at most. He de-emphasized the homage scene in the finale, made Sachs give up his laurel crown and had Beckmesser return to take part in the joyful conclusion. In a final stroke of originality, a beaming, avuncular Wolfgang Wagner himself came on stage and joined Sachs's and Beckmesser's hands in a demonstrative reconciliation.

The first year's performance was generally judged disappointing. Wolfgang and the conductor, thirty-four-year-old Mark Elder, did not see eye to eye on the musical interpretation; Wolfgang had his way but critics were not impressed with the result, and Elder was not asked back. Three of the principals—Siegfried Jerusalem (Walther), Bernd Weikl (Sachs), Mari Anne Häggander (Eva)—were considered less than ideal. The outstanding soloist was Hermann Prey, whose Beckmesser stole the show.

Not until 1985 did Wolfgang attempt *Tannhäuser*, which he staged in early New Bayreuth style. Concentric circles as the design feature, the use of light to emphasize mood and action and starkly simple sets were all revived. The second act featured little more than a backdrop of rounded arches, apparently modelled on the canopus at Tivoli. The stage pictures were dignified, classical even, but by now they were an anachronism and blatantly conflicted with what outside producers were at this time putting on the Festspielhaus stage. Once again critics saw the weak point of the production in the directing, which was disparaged as lifeless and empty, or in the words of one observer a case of 'dumping the principals down on the stage and leaving them there until it was time to move them off again'. While Richard Versalle (Tannhäuser) and Cheryl Studer (Elisabeth) had mixed reviews, the conducting of Giuseppe Sinopoli in his Bayreuth première was considered masterful. The music did not save the production from the audiences, however, which booed the first season's performances with great zest.

With even greater gusto did they jeer Wolfgang's 1989 *Parsifal*. This production prompted much headshaking; with no evident concept of staging or interpretation, it appeared that Wolfgang had run out of ideas. The meadow scene of the first act was a bare floor with four enormous crystalline stalactites which moved and turned to become the interior of the temple of the grail but which several reviews suggested might more appropriately have accommodated the priests of *Aida*. In the second year of the production, Wolfgang introduced a startling innovation at the end when the grail was uncovered by Kundry, as the brotherhood's token woman, apparently Wolfgang's concession to feminism. Although the acting was criticized for lifelessness, the singing by Hans Sotin (Gurnemanz) and especially by Franz Mazura (Klingsor) and Waltraud Meier (Kundry) was very well received. Not so William Pell's Parsifal, which took some hard critical knocks. Putting its finger on a wider problem, the *Frankfurter Allgemeine* commented, 'Wolfgang Wagner's loyalty to immature singers is humane but not conducive to artistic quality.' James Levine's conducting was the slowest reading since that of Knappertsbusch; some found it dignified and impressive, others limp and boring. 'One felt oneself back in Cosima's era', sighed a critic.

Wolfgang Wagner entered upon his final years as Festival leader as he had begun in 1951. In the common view he was a canny and highly competent administrator, an efficient and generally well-liked manager, a disappointing producer, a poor stage designer and an inadequate director. He had kept the Festival moving with infallible efficiency despite increasing competition from other festivals, the scarcity of good Wagnerian singers and omnipresent financial constraints.

The Wagner dynasty itself remained as divided and unhappy and jealous and quarrelsome as ever. Time and death—Winifred's in 1980 and Friedelind's in 1991—did nothing to lessen the animosities or to clarify the epic question of Wolfgang's eventual successor as head of the Festival. Over this issue the battleline was starkly drawn, with Wolfgang and Gudrun, who had long since become the Festival's eminence grise, pitted against the composer's various great-grandchildren. And as much as ever Wagnerian life imitated Wagnerian art. Wolfgang continued to regard the next generation as so many scheming Ortruds and Telramunds, seeking by calumny and scandal to seize what was not theirs and for which they had no qualification. And they more than ever viewed Wolfgang as a stuporous Fafner clinging to his loot—with Gudrun as Alberich hoping to be the ultimate beneficiary—while they, the Siegfrieds and Brünnhildes meant by destiny to liberate the treasure, impatiently awaited the moment of show-down.

9

'Do you know what you saw?'
(*Parsifal*)

'Zwei Seelen wohnen, ach! in meiner Brust,' Wolfgang might have said with Goethe's Faust. Two souls lived, alas, in his breast as well: a conservative, uninspired one that was manifest in his own increasingly old-fashioned productions and an experimental, daring one that was evident in ever more avant-garde productions which he commissioned from outside producers. Beginning in 1969 Wolfgang in effect turned over the Bayreuth stage to others to put on their own shows. The crisis confronting the Festival after Wieland's death had forced him to face the fact that he could not manage on his own. With artists abandoning the Festival and Wieland's productions coming out of the repertory, he had little choice but to look elsewhere for fresh ideas and new techniques.

The basis of this radically new approach was one that had animated the two brothers in refounding the Festival in 1951: to demolish Bayreuth as a temple where the faithful worshipped and to replace it with a *Werkstatt*, a workshop, where Wagner's operas would be subject to continuing reevaluation and experimentation. Wieland had always regarded his new productions as works in progress, to be corrected and improved with each new season. This is why Bayreuth had earned its postwar reputation as living opera theatre and why audiences found going there an adventure every year. There was also a less platonic reason for the change. Continuous rejuvenation and provocative performances were necessary to compensate somewhat for the self-imposed limitation of a restricted and unchanging repertory.

And so, after nearly a century of attempts, the aim of achieving perfect, model performances—Richard Wagner's original intention in establishing the Festival—had been recognized as an impossible ideal. The workshop concept now became the hallmark of post-New Bayreuth. Keeping Wagner's works alive, Wolfgang insisted again and again, meant constantly reinterpreting them to make them relevant to contemporary audiences. 'The continuous, active contact with what is

273

topical, with our present day, that is what we encapsulate in the idea of *Werkstatt* Bayreuth' is the sort of comment he made over and over.[1] By the same token the Festival was no longer to be the end point but the launching platform of a career for singers, conductors and producers. Performances were to be as meticulously prepared as in the past, but the overriding objective was to carry on experimental opera theatre. The risks involved and the demands on Wolfgang's own restraint were bound to be considerable.

There had already been one outside producer. Back in 1951, when Wolfgang was preoccupied with administration and Wieland was struggling with his *Ring* and *Parsifal*, it had been necessary to call in Rudolf Hartmann, head of the Munich Opera and a friend of Wieland's from his Munich days, to produce *Meistersinger*. Hartmann and his stage designer Hans Reissinger put on a good old-fashioned version of the work which was splendidly conducted by Herbert von Karajan and marvellously sung by Otto Edelmann (Sachs), Elisabeth Schwarzkopf (Eva), Hans Hopf (Walther) and Erich Kunz (Beckmesser). Hartmann's interpretation, no doubt reflecting the still difficult times, played down the humour and emphasized the serious, human side of the work. As such it carried a poignant meaning to the audience, some of whose members responded with tears during the holy German art monologue and with rapturous cheers at the end. The work itself and the conservatism of the production were intended by Wieland as a deliberate artistic and political pacifier to the old guard, which had otherwise witnessed its traditional Wagner being blown to pieces that season.

How different it was in 1969. In that year Wolfgang turned to August Everding, a Munich theatre director, and Josef Svoboda, a Prague architect and stage designer, in the hope of getting a *Fliegender Holländer* with a bit of *Gewitter und Sturm*. While not overcoming all the problems of a work inherently difficult to stage, they provided a production that was ingenious and intriguing. Everding consciously stepped away from the New Bayreuth approach and presented the opera as an allegorical, romantic ballad. Svoboda's settings established an appropriate mood of romanticism, mystery and even menace.

Svoboda followed an essentially architectural approach. He extracted from the opera a few critical themes which he simplified and made the nucleus of the production. Ignoring the romantic naturalism of the composer's stage directions and combining elements of modern realism and abstraction, he made the stern of Daland's boat and the bow of the Dutchman's ship the central visual focus. These dominated the stage and remained fixed through all three acts, so that the opera could proceed without a change of scenery or a pause or a curtain. Daland's fishing boat occupied the foreground of the stage and was the principal acting area. The Dutchman's ship seemingly swept in from the obscure distance, its huge black, threatening prow dramatically towering over Daland's boat. From there, forty feet above the stage floor and in a glittering,

August Everding's 1969 *Fliegende Holländer* was not a mythic-psychological ballad but realistic music theatre, an interpretation reflected in Josef Svoboda's stark stage props and dramatic lighting effects.

sinister light, the Dutchman delivered his great monologue. It was a thrilling scene.

In the second act the Dutchman's ship was made to vanish through the legerdemain of lighting technology, while the deck of Daland's boat was transformed by the highlighting of props—a door, a portrait and fishing nets—into the interior of Daland's house. The nets were intended to hint at both Senta's imprisonment and the world of fantasy in which she lived. The unreality of her world was also suggested by the Dutchman's portrait which came to life and moved inside its frame and then disappeared when he arrived in person. In the final act, lighting brought into focus a broad flight of stairs—in effect the village street and site of the townsfolk's revelry. The finale was conventional, Senta ending it all by jumping into the sea.

Everding's directing and Svoboda's staging as well as the lighting and costumes had a good press, though some critics were left uneasy by the combination of abstraction and realism, and behind that of Everding's conventionality and Svoboda's originality. The singing—by Leonie Rysanek (Senta), Donald McIntyre (Dutchman), Martti Talvela

(Daland), Jean Cox (Erik), Unni Rugtvedt (Mary) and the season's discovery, René Kollo (Steersman) — by and large received rave reviews. Such was not the case with Silvio Varviso's conducting.

Worthy as it was, the Everding-Svoboda production failed to restore the Festival's old excitement. At some point Wolfgang hit upon the idea that the best way to liven things up was to have provocative and heterodox interpretations. He therefore calculated that it would be necessary to bring to Bayreuth directors who were out of the main stream of Wagnerian opera, indeed who had little or no knowledge of Wagner or even of opera. And so for a new production of *Tannhäuser* he asked the famous Milan dramaturge Giorgio Strehler and, when he declined, Götz Friedrich, stage director of the East Berlin Comic Opera. Although Wolfgang had often engaged East German soloists—they were cheaper than singers from the West—his inviting an East German producer was a bold step at the time and risked offending at the very least the Bavarian government and the equally conservative Friends of Bayreuth, both of which were vital financial contributors. It was also a great artistic gamble. Friedrich had never before produced Wagner; Wolfgang had never attended a Friedrich production. More than that, there was a fundamental difference between the avant-garde of Bayreuth and the avant-garde of East Germany.

Friedrich was an alumnus of the kindergarten of Walter Felsenstein, the East Berlin Comic Opera's famous practitioner of realistic music theatre. East German producers followed a distinctive approach, no doubt strongly influenced by the political situation in which they worked. They tended to unmask situations and people. They treated the historic context of a work along with the circumstances of the composer's own life as no less important than its theatrical and musical form. Traits of this school were dynamic presentation, dramatic clarity, precise pictorial representation, a stark profiling of the characters and exact directions to singers. The productions tended to be hard, cold and spare. Directing was so central that the approach was known as *Regietheater*. These were the techniques that guided Friedrich, his designer Jürgen Rose and the choreographer John Neumeier.

Not since Wieland's day had such original thought gone into a Bayreuth production. But while Wieland's starting-point was to think through a work as though it had never before been staged, Friedrich's was more drastic still: 'We who do opera, who do music theatre, must ask ourselves anew in each individual case why this work should be performed, for what purpose and for whom it is to be performed.'[2] His answer in this case was that *Tannhäuser* held a timely message for society. The clue to the work was to be found in the background against which it was written—in Wagner's struggle against an oppressive social order, a remnant of the very social hierarchy which confronted the protagonist in the opera. The drama gained real bite when it was seen not in the traditional way as the story of a man torn between erotic and spiritual love—between Venus and Elisabeth and between Venusberg and Wartburg—but as the chronicle of an artist in his relation to society, everywhere and at any time. In Friedrich's view, Tannhäuser's dilemma was how to maintain his creativity and his integrity when this required on the one hand preserving his freedom from social norms and on the other forging those links with society which an artist needs to communicate his message. The opera therefore told the old but never-old story of the artist who is treated as an outcast because he does not conform to the prevailing social mores. As such it was autobiographical, Friedrich pointed out in an essay in the Festival programme, not just of Wagner the artist but of Wagner the political rebel of 1849. It was also, as he did not point out, partly biographical of Friedrich himself, the artist in a Communist state.

As produced in 1972, *Tannhäuser* was a parable of 'the journey of an artist through inner and outer worlds, in search of himself', in Friedrich's words.[3] The journey led him from an 'artificial paradise', symbolized by the Venusberg, to a world of ideological coercion and social oppression, epitomized by the Wartburg and Rome. Self-realization was as impossible in the one as it was in the other. Yet 'the historical and at the same time the contemporary greatness of Tannhäuser grows out of his struggle to understand that the artist can only realize himself by communicating with society'. Rebellion is 'creatively revolutionary', Friedrich maintained, when it culminates in 'an awareness of religion and commitment, even though it may be a new commitment or a religion as yet unknown'.

In this version, earthly and heavenly love were regarded not as antitheses but as different sides of the same coin—Venus and Elisabeth were for the first time sung by the same soloist—and Elisabeth died not a saint but an old, broken and lonely creature. Yet Friedrich did not replace the orthodox uncritical view of the Wartburg with a new uncritical view of Tannhäuser. At the end the hero died not a redeemed sinner but a man whose tragedy lay in his failing to find commitment. As the place of religion was redimensioned, so the concept of redemption was reinterpreted. The ultimate message Friedrich hoped would come through to a late twentieth-century audience was that a credo of social tolerance should replace faith in miracles.

The stark novelty of the interpretation was visually evident as soon as the curtain opened, and the curtain opened with the first notes of the overture which, defying precedent, was itself staged. Tannhäuser was seen fleeing from the 'real world' of the Wartburg to the fantasy world of the Venusberg. There, in Friedrich's frothy prose, the 'images of a youthfully naive love and the vision of the possibility offered by the love between man and woman become increasingly frenzied and turn suddenly into destructive orgasm'. The Bacchanal was presented not as reality but as fantasy, as a sexual and sado-masochistic nightmare among the dead and depraved, thus demonstrating that sensual excess inevitably leads to barbarism, cruelty and death. Appropriately enough, the settings throughout the act were bare, mysterious, threatening and ugly.

The hall of song of the second act was a bleak and forbidding rostrum formed by fourteen sharply rising steps. This symbolized a domineering and hierarchical society, which demanded effort to achieve acceptance and which threatened precipitous descent if rejected. It was a clear metaphor of the lot of the artist in the Third Reich, encouraged when he supported the regime, driven into exile or the concentration camp when he did not. Although the third act was portrayed as a world of unremitting desolation, it concluded with what Friedrich intended as an appeal for understanding of those who forsook comfort and conformity in the search not for faith but for truth. Here was an opera by Wagner the revolutionary rather than by Wagner the Christian redemptionist.

The fresh breezes that Wolfgang hoped would waft over the Green Hill now reached hurricane force. Not since the notorious Paris performance of *Tannhäuser* in 1861 had a Wagnerian work set off such a furore. Then it was a small group of troublemakers; now it was just about everyone. Music critics complained less about the interpretation,

The hall of song as a symbol of disguised tyranny and obligatory social ritual in Götz Friedrich's 1972 *Tannhäuser*. Having challenged the one and violated the other, Tannhäuser has been expelled by a show of raw power (drawn swords) leaving Elisabeth uncertainly poised between two worlds. In this 1977 photograph are Hermin Esser (Tannhäuser), Gwyneth Jones (Elisabeth), Bernd Weikl (Wolfram) and Hans Sotin (Landgrave).

even when they grasped it, than about the idiosyncratic directing, bizarre choreography, barren sets and above all the provocative costumes. The dress of the Landgrave's retinue looked suspiciously like storm-trooper uniforms and that of the pilgrims returning from Rome conspicuously like an oppressed proletariat coming back from the factory. More than anything else the costumes gave rise to the impression that this *Tannhäuser* was about class war, totalitarian police and salvation for the artist in a socialist state. Any chance that critics and audiences might have been somewhat placated by the excellent singing of Gwyneth Jones (Elisabeth and Venus), Bernd Weikl (Wolfram) and Hans Sotin (Landgrave) was destroyed by Hugh Beresford, whom many considered to be the worst Tannhäuser since Pilinszky in 1930–31.

No one was more caustic about the production than the conductor himself, Erich Leinsdorf, who refused to return the following year—a severe loss since he was one of the few remaining great Wagnerian conductors. Even the emotions recollected in the tranquillity of his memoirs were sour. Leinsdorf accused Friedrich of having compromised his artistic integrity for the sake of politics. In his preparations the producer 'must have reread the whole opus of Marx, Engels, Trotsky, Liebknecht, and the lot. What he did not read up on was Wagner.'[4] Friedrich had excised Tannhäuser's redemption in fear 'for his own safety on returning to East Berlin if he staged anything as Christian as all that'. Leinsdorf also charged the producer with artistic incompetence. Placing the second act singers on a podium resulted in the voices vanishing into the flies rather than flowing into the auditorium. The pilgrims' crucifix was so heavy that the choral members carrying it sang flat in three out of four passages. And the scene in which Elisabeth crawled off stage and Tannhäuser on made Leinsdorf wonder whether he was unaware of some 'special predilection Wagner had for reptiles'. But the original sinner was Wolfgang Wagner, to whom Leinsdorf imputed 'calculating dishonesty' for inviting Friedrich solely *pour épater les bourgeois*.

A shocked bourgeoisie was certainly the result. Seldom if ever in theatrical history could there have been such a stunning example of life imitating art, such a perfect transposition into an auditorium of what had just been performed on stage. In an afternoon Friedrich had become Tannhäuser, while the German Establishment of 1972 had become the Thuringian Establishment of the thirteenth century. Friedrich was denounced as a dangerous red who was a threat to the Federal Republic and who should be sent back to East Germany. Some accused him of turning the opera into a Communist attack on Nazism, others of using it to celebrate the inevitable triumph of the poor over the rich. A *New York Times* reporter heard members of the audience shout 'revenge' at the producer and saw an elderly woman 'swinging her evening bag over her head as if she was going to throw it' at him. The paradox of course was that Friedrich, the putative Communist propagandist, had spent his career contending with the ideological oppression of the East German Communist regime.

Anti-clerical, anti-religious, anti-establishmentarian—Friedrich's was the most blatantly ideological production ever to have gone on the Bayreuth stage, and it marked an important moment in the Festival's history. Wolfgang, who stood by his producer, was himself considered guilty by association. He received bomb threats and piles of poison pen letters addressed to him as 'the red director of the Festival' and labelling him a 'gentleman Communist' and a 'propagandist of Soviet ideas'. Especially and almost unanimously outraged was the Friends of Bayreuth Society. So Wolfgang had his wish. Nothing could better have proved that Wagner's works still spoke to the contemporary world. And nothing could better have demonstrated that mixing politics and culture still produced dynamite in Germany. Only there could an opera performance have set off such an explosion. All was soon forgiven, however. The next year audiences cheered the production to the rafters.

Friedrich's rough, tough and disturbing work was followed in 1974 by a svelte, tasteful and reassuring *Tristan* created by the Everding-Svoboda team. It was pure *son et lumière*. The stage was stripped almost clean; lighting—used with scrims, wires, cords and the like—appeared transformed into substance. In the second and third acts images of foliage were projected onto countless cords, which acquired an almost glass-like translucence. Colour and light seemed liquid. The scenes gained at once surface and depth, palpability and mystery. The effects ravished the eye with visual magic. Changes of colour and modes of lighting set the atmosphere of each scene and mirrored the mood of the music and action.

The first act was set on the bow of what looked like a sleek modern cruise liner. The scene was dominated by the conventional sail, which Svoboda had added at the last minute when other ideas proved unsatisfactory. In keeping with Everding's interpretation, each act was punctuated by a shift from the real world to the private world of the two lovers. After Tristan and Isolde drank the love potion, for example, there was a sudden blackout after which the two were bathed in a pool of deep blue light while behind them the sail glistened in moonlight. The second act was a shimmering scene of indistinct shapes and voluptuous colours, modulating from rich green to autumnal rust and, during the love scene, an inky blue. In the final act streamlined walls framed the scene, against a background of an enormous, glittering abstract tree.

Everding had hewn out a path different both from Wieland's scenic minimalism and Friedrich's harsh abstraction. His productions were eye-teasing and human; his characters were real people with whom the audience could identify themselves. He introduced any number of small touches—such as Tristan's enraptured look as he caught sight of Isolde a moment before he died—that many critics found deeply affecting. The strong directing and the visual beauty were excelled in the initial

Act II of Everding's 1974 *Tristan*: Svoboda's string cord technique created an impression of plastic, three-dimensional coloured light. Lighting was modulated to reflect the mood of the music and the characters' psychological state.

year by Carlos Kleiber's conducting—widely judged the great success of the season—and by the outstanding voices of Catarina Ligendza (Isolde), Helge Brilioth (Tristan), Donald McIntyre (Kurwenal), Yvonne Minton (Brangäne) and Kurt Moll (Marke).

In planning for the centenary *Ring*, Wolfgang Wagner first turned to Ingmar Bergman and then to Peter Brook and, when they declined, asked Peter Stein, the iconoclastic Berlin theatre director, who agreed on condition that Franz Josef Strauss, the conservative Bavarian politician, would be prohibited from attending the performances. Wolfgang, who had in the meantime signed up Pierre Boulez, then accepted the conductor's recommendation of Patrice Chéreau, a young theatrical producer with little operatic experience and whose only brush with Wagner was to have slept through a performance of *Die Walküre* in Paris in 1972. Even that degree of contact was greater than his set designer, Richard Peduzzi, or costume designer, Jacques Schmidt, could claim. The 1976 *Ring* was bound to be a gala event; with an all-French team in charge it was certain to be a controversial one as well. In fact it turned out to be the most sensational production since 1876.

281

Chéreau, without preconceived notions but teeming with ideas, made up in imagination what he lacked in depth. A director through and through, he saw the *Ring* first and foremost as a vehicle for exciting acting, and this approach prescribed not only the sets but, even more, the stage direction, which became the most important element of the new production. Here was *Regietheater* as never before done at Bayreuth. The drama itself he regarded, with no originality, as an allegory about power, the way it is used and how it destroys. What was novel were the staging, costumes and directing through which he presented the characters not as gods but as ordinary people who lived not in a mythical universe but in the everyday world we know. Chéreau's was therefore not a timeless *Ring* but one with specific historic references, the late nineteenth century being the temporal centre. Nor, most heretically of all perhaps, did he treat it as a single drama but as four separately interpreted and staged parts. And while Chéreau denied that he had followed any single controlling idea, the one unifying element was an underlying social critique, though more Shavian than Marxist— *Rheingold* signifying the pre-industrial world; *Walküre*, early capitalism, with Hunding as the first entrepreneur; *Siegfried*, the age of nineteenth-century industrialism; *Götterdämmerung*, the inter-war period of proto-fascist capitalism.

But it was not his interpretation as much as his visual images that— to put it mildly—arrested attention. With great wit and even greater bluntness he raised the curtain on a huge hydro-electric dam, a producer of metaphorical power which it stored in the form of gold in its base. The treasure was guarded by three voluptuous tarts—sex being an even stronger lure than money—who first tempted and then rejected the grubby worker Alberich. In the following scene the Wotan family, housed in a renaissance-style palazzo and handsomely arrayed in late nineteenth-century dress, were preparing to move, when the most gigantic giants ever to appear at Bayreuth arrived to foreclose the mortgage. Part of the eventual pay-off, the ring, was gratuitously hacked out of Alberich's hand by Wotan, thus demonstrating the sadistic brutality of capitalist dealings. In due course Wotan and his family trooped off to Valhalla, which combined the features of a Tuscan hill town and Wall Street.

Walküre opened not in Hunding's hut but in the spacious courtyard of his classical-style palazzo. The mighty ash tree was in place, though dead and decayed, with the sword waiting to be extracted. The ensuing love scene was played with a passion that almost qualified for an X-rating. The second act began not on Wagner's 'wild rocky mountain top' but in the vast drawing room of Valhalla, whose meagre furnishings comprised a huge dressing mirror, a pendulum suspended from an invisible ceiling and a straight-back chair. Fricka appeared in a white décolleté gown and Wotan, though never without his Bronze Age spear, in a stately morning coat. Confiding his troubles to Brünnhilde,

Rheingold, Scene 1 (1976): the most provocative setting in Bayreuth's history. 'At the beginning of *Rheingold* there is this thing on stage which could be a dam, but it could also be a lot of other things' (Patrice Chéreau).

Wotan sang to her via his reflection in the mirror; but after being persuaded by Fricka to let Siegmund die, he was unable to bear the sight of himself and, in an impressive gesture, covered the mirror with his dressing gown. The third act opened to a nightmare setting in the Valkyries' cemetery, veiled at times behind puffs of smoke, to which the Wish-Maidens transported dead heroes in carts drawn by live horses. In the final scene, the walls of the burial ground parted to reveal what Chéreau intended as a glacier but which reminded observers of sites as various as an Aztec pyramid and the Matterhorn. There it was that Brünnhilde was put to sleep.

The visual assault continued unabated in *Siegfried*, which showed Mime not only with a gigantic space age forge but also with a battered suitcase for a quick get-away from his rowdy ward. In the second act Fafner turned out to be a huge toy dragon on wheels, which was hauled around by stage-hands. At the moment of his death, he turned back into his original giant form and then expired. Siegfried did his dreaming not in a shimmering forest but in a defoliated copse; the wood bird which led him away was in a cage. In *Götterdämmerung*, action began on

283

Brünnhilde's promontory and moved to the great hall of the Gibichungs, which was a loggia constructed of classical columns and furnished with a single modern chair serving as Gunther's throne. Gunther himself appeared in a twentieth-century dinner jacket and Gutrune in a coeval frock from the Rhineland's best couturier. A sleazy, ill-shaven Hagen wore a crumpled dacron suit while Siegfried, who arrived in a shabby gamekeeper outfit and medieval breastplate, changed into black tie for his wedding. Both the second act and the final scene of the opera took place along a boundless stretch of water, facing which were the deserted and burnt-out tenements of the New York City dockland. Suggesting an ecological sub-theme, the third act opened back at the old hydro-electric dam, which was now rusted and without water, the Rhine having meanwhile dried up. At the very end an enormous crowd of people—of all ages and social groups but mostly young and working class—put the seal on the drama by turning and facing the audience with an expression of dazed hopelessness.

Such were some of the stage pictures and it was largely these that brought down the house. The initial scene, with the hydro-electric plant and the street girls, caused a shock from which no one quite recovered. The moment the curtain opened, a mood of indignation surged through the auditorium. As the *Observer*'s music critic commented:

> I had not previously experienced in the theatre protest as furious as that which greeted *Das Rheingold*. But it paled before what was to come. By the time we had reached *Siegfried* with its mechanized anvil, a lawyer from New York had let it be known that he had whistles for anyone who cared to blow them, and in *Götterdämmerung*, Gunther and later Siegfried himself in dinner-jackets, Hagen's men carrying submachine guns, these contributed to a pandemonium that twice nearly brought the performance to a halt. When the producer, Patrice Chéreau, and his designers, Richard Peduzzi and Jacques Schmidt, bravely presented themselves on the stage alongside the conductor, Pierre Boulez, they were greeted by a sustained howl of rage. It was not a pretty sound.[5]

The sound was only part of what was the greatest uproar in Bayreuth's history, the audience divided into one mob roaring in favour and one screaming against. On opening night there were bloody brawls, Wolfgang Wagner's new wife had her dress ripped and another woman had her earring torn off—and the earlobe with it. There were death threats and bomb threats; friendships and marriages were said to have been broken. On many evenings that summer the shouting and catcalls followed Boulez and Chéreau into restaurants after the performance. Some of the big contributors, such as Siemens, were said to have threatened to withhold future support; the Friends of Bayreuth offered to bankroll an entirely new production if Chéreau's were scrapped. Wagner fundamentalists formed yet another group, the Aktionskreis für das Werk Richard Wagners, to fight the latest apostasy. And there was an open insurrection by the orchestra.

Why such a violent reaction? To some extent it was the old *Bayreuther Geist* again. Despite its idiosyncrasies, the production was essentially no more 'revolutionary' than the centenary versions put on in Kiel, Kassel, London, Milan, Geneva and, most provocatively, in Leipzig. But what could pass without offence in the outposts of Wagnerian civilization, was still a sacrilege at the shrine itself. Wieland had committed sacrileges as well, but he was at least a Wagner and a German and he had not perpetrated them on the most sacred of occasions. 'Have you seen what *he* has done to *our* Wagner!' was 'the one and only lamentation' which the reporter of *Nouvelles Littéraires* heard on the streets of Bayreuth that summer.[6] Profanation was thus in one way or another the issue. To the political conservatives the production was insufferable because Chéreau had not simply knocked the Germanic gods off their pedestals—Wieland had done that decades earlier—but he had mocked them and their world. To the musical conservatives it was intolerable because it was not serious opera but burlesque, vaudeville, cabaret, science fiction, satire, grand guignol. There was one voice that spoke forthrightly for both groups. Winifred Wagner was quoted as saying that if she ever met Chéreau, she would murder him. To see the *Ring* well done, she maintained, it was now necessary to go to Salzburg—a remarkable concession in light of the long competition between the two festivals. However, when she met Chéreau a year or so later, she admitted to him that it was better to be enraged than to be bored. That was increasingly the view of audiences as well, and at the final performance in 1980, the ninety-minute ovation was almost as impressive as the original ruckus.

The critics reacted in much the same way. All of them found striking moments—'some of the most moving and impressive touches I have ever seen in opera' was typical—though each had his own favourites. There was wide acclaim for the flair and expertise of the directing and the soloists' acting. 'The fury would have been less intense if Mr Chéreau had simply bungled his job; the real aggravation is that his production makes so many illuminating, often unkindly truthful, points about *The Ring*,' stated *The Times*.[7] While many French critics were mortified that it was a French producer who created such a scandal, *Le Monde* forthrightly defended Chéreau. His production proved 'that it is possible through hard work to find something new to harvest in this sterile terrain'.[8]

But there was more censure than praise. The *New York Times* characteristically dismissed Chéreau as 'a director going amok' and his production as having 'very little to do with the *Ring* cycle'. Serious critics stressed several points. The production lacked the intellectual and visual coherence, the timelessness and universality of Wieland's *Ring*. Instead it was a confused collage of myth, psychology, social comment and environmentalism. The presentation was an incomprehensible blend of the mythical, medieval, mid-nineteenth-century and contemporary, with an incompatible collection of stage pictures. The sets and acting often blatantly contradicted the score. And the underlying interpretation was based on merely one of the composer's themes—social revolution—and therefore drastically diminished a noble epic.

The allegation of its being a Marxist *Ring* was a red herring. In fact, in its hostility to science, industry and urbanization, the treatment marked an unintended throw-back to German conservatism and fascism. It was anti-modernist more than anti-capitalist, reactionary more than revolutionary. What was subversive about the production was its handling of the drama. Up to then even the most iconoclastic treatments acknowledged the essence of Wagner's stage directions and the overall balance of staging, acting and music. That link was now broken. After Chéreau nothing, to coin a phrase, could be the same.

No less of a storm raged over the conducting, which Boulez frankly intended to be as heterodox as the staging. Some no doubt disliked his interpretation because of the production, but even some who liked what they saw were shocked by what they heard. A good many critics agreed with a majority of the orchestra members that Boulez had not mastered the score. They complained that he attenuated the score's grandeur and produced a reading that was, despite some gorgeous moments, bloodless. 'Like Chéreau on the stage,' wrote the *Observer*, 'he presents a partial and small-scale view of the work as a whole.' At the same time Boulez was praised for achieving exceptionally 'fine-grained and translucent textures' as well as 'a lyrical tenderness that is new in his conducting'. Such was also the view of *Le Monde*, which credited him with having 'achieved a perfection of detail, a transparency, a finesse and an exceptional equilibrium'[9]—the traits for which Boulez was celebrated.

In a way the conductor's main problem was Chéreau. Ironically, in a penetrating article in the Festival programme that season, Boulez had emphasized the supremacy of the score: 'Wagner the musician possesses a force of conviction that manifestly exceeds that of Wagner the dramatist.' Yet by universal consent, it was the dramatic spectacle that was supreme and the music was reduced to a subordinate level—not least of all because of the conductor's idiosyncratic interpretation.

In a *Ring* that was not especially well sung, the vocal inadequacies were to some extent overlooked because of the outstanding acting. Peter Hofmann's Siegmund was the undoubted vocal highlight of the season. Karl Ridderbusch poured his personal loathing of the production—including his own costumes—into the roles of Hunding and Hagen and performed them outstandingly well. Gwyneth Jones (Brünnhilde), Donald McIntyre (Wotan), Hannelore Bode (Sieglinde), Yvonne Minton (Waltraute), Zoltan Kelemen (Alberich), Eva Randova (Fricka), René Kollo (Young Siegfried) and Jess Thomas (Siegfried) received mixed notices.

Twelve changes of scene in the twinkling of an eye, breathtaking choral ensembles, exciting drama, lighting as though by Caravaggio—Harry Kupfer's 1978 *Holländer* was both a technical and an interpretative triumph.

For a new production of *Fliegender Holländer* at the 1978 Festival Wolfgang added to his stable of producers the head of the Dresden Opera, Harry Kupfer, another Felsenstein protégé. With his stage designer, Peter Sykora, Kupfer presented the opera in the post-New Bayreuth style of dream-like—or nightmare—realism. Or surrealism, in this case. His interpretation easily maintained Bayreuth's exceptionally high standard for this work.

With singular imagination the opera was presented as taking place purely in Senta's fantasy. Dominating the performance, the maid was on stage from beginning to end. The curtain rose on the overture to find her standing on a platform above the stage almost as though in a trance. At the crescendo of the storm motif the Dutchman's picture fell from the wall; she retrieved and held it to her bosom while standing throughout the act, a silent witness to all that followed. The Dutchman's ship appeared within two enormous cupped hands which opened to reveal the blood-red vessel and the Dutchman in gold chains. The chains loosened and he was propelled onto the land. What originally seemed

287

like a prison ship or slave galley was transformed in the second act into a flower-laden love boat, while Senta and the Dutchman sang their great duet. The final act, with brilliantly choreographed group scenes, concluded with Senta's defenestration and the crowd's disapproving stare at her dead body.

Some understood the treatment as a psychodrama about a schizophrenic; others construed it in a more Ibsenesque vein, as a woman's rebellion against the constrictive norms of bourgeois society with death as the only mode of resistance possible. All agreed it was a tragedy without redemption, without transfiguration, without pity. Perhaps the highest accolade came from those who credited Kupfer with having ingeniously turned this early work into one of the most relevant and powerful of Wagner's operas.

Although in the première year there was both unstinting critical praise and equally vehement disapproval, in time there was general agreement that the production was one of the great postwar successes. Technical wizardry made it possible to perform the opera as a series of rapidly changing tableaux, the fleeting impressions of Senta's fantasy world. The decors adroitly blended stark realism with subjective supernaturalism. Yet full success in the first year rested on the dramatic tour de force of the young Danish soprano Lisbeth Balslev as Senta. Without her, the *Neue Zeitschrift für Musik* commented, the production would have been 'unthinkable'.[10] Simon Estes (Dutchman), Matti Salminen (Daland), Robert Schunk (Erik) and the remainder of the cast were all highly praised. Appropriately the harsh Dresden score was played, conducted by Dennis Russell Davies in the spirit of the production. The audience cheered with enthusiasm.

Seven years after having provoked a scandal over *Tannhäuser*, Götz Friedrich returned to Bayreuth. In the meantime he had produced *Tristan* in Scheveningen, the *Ring* in London, *Parsifal* in Stuttgart and *Meistersinger* in Stockholm. Now he was to do *Lohengrin*. With its miraculous legend, romantic fairy-tale aspects and its nationalistic references, the opera was a challenge for leftist producers. Friedrich cut through the problems by perceiving a fundamental parallel between *Lohengrin* and *Tannhäuser* in the persons of Tannhäuser and Elsa. Both were social rejects and both were searching for self-realization and truth; the former followed a course that led to rebellion and death, the latter retreated into a state of inner emigration that ended in self-destruction. Unlike other producers, Friedrich regarded *Lohengrin* as Wagner's saddest work, and the production reflected the bleakness.

Visually the production marked an important alteration of style. On the one hand Friedrich adopted much of the abstraction, the stylization and the symbolism of Wieland's 1958 version, similarly giving a central role to the chorus and designing the sets appropriately. On the other hand he rejected the colour and sumptuousness of the earlier production, without fully retaining the post-modernist realism that he had imbibed from Felsenstein. To design the settings Friedrich recruited the German kinetic artist Günther Uecker with whom he had successfully collaborated on *Tristan* in Stuttgart.

Lohengrin's traditional sapphire and silver was replaced by black and steel, and throughout the performance the stage floor itself was covered with a sheet of lead, meant to symbolize the patriarchal–militant social order which underlay the action. As in his *Tannhäuser* production, Friedrich opened the curtain on the prelude, revealing Elsa as though immersed in a nightmare. The first act began not in a pastoral setting along the banks of the Scheldt but in a science-fiction chamber, which one observer described as 'the largest yet most claustrophobic indoor structure which Bayreuth has known'.[11] It was a cold and even ominous scene in which rising stands for the Brabantine and Saxon knights were ranged on either side of the stage, against a black wall decorated with steel studs. Lohengrin arrived in a blinding light on a revolving disc— 'like a glittering batman from outer space', as one sour critic put it[12]— manifesting his deviancy from the strict and orderly world of Brabant. The bridal scene took place in a sombre chamber, described by Uecker as a 'cathedral of love', decorated only with steel rods and a huge feathery bed on which the lovers declaimed their feelings.[13] Visually it recalled Wieland's abstraction and symbolism.

Act I of Friedrich's 1979 *Lohengrin*. Conceived as 'stage sculptures' and designed with choral acoustics in mind, Uecker's sets linked visual realism with conceptual myth.

The production had a good reception. Friedrich was credited with having successfully merged legend, romantic fairy tale and historical epic into a smooth whole, while reassessing the very notion of miracle. But though his stagecraft was widely praised, Uecker's decors did not go over well. The mildest criticism was that the studs, rods and light amounted to an art exhibit rather than an integrated element of the production. According to other comments, they were 'hideously inapt', 'simply defied belief', constituted 'an evening replete with visual out-rage' and desecrated the second act with 'the façade of a '50s office block in New Brutalist style'. Audiences, however, liked the production or at least were not offended. Whether the traditionalists had largely died out by now, were numb or simply found this interpretation undisturbing, there were no jeers to sully the enthusiastic applause.

Critics generally liked the singing in the première year. Most praised Peter Hofmann (Lohengrin), Ruth Hesse (Ortrud), Leif Roar (Telramund), Hans Sotin (Heinrich) and Bernd Weikl (Herald), though faulting Karan Armstrong (Elsa), a young American in her Bayreuth debut, for a persistent wobble. Edo de Waart's conducting did not earn him an invitation to return, and he was replaced by Woldemar Nelsson, who romped briskly but effectively through the score.

For a new production of *Tristan*, Wolfgang Wagner first asked Patrice Chéreau, who declined. Daniel Barenboim, who had meanwhile been engaged to conduct, insisted on having Jean-Pierre Ponnelle who had just produced and designed a bizarre *Ring* in Stuttgart. Ponnelle's only preconceived notion was that Isolde should not be present on stage at the end but exist only as a figment of Tristan's fevered brain. Otherwise he developed his staging and directing as he went along. Although it teetered on the verge of disaster up to the moment it went on stage in 1981, the production offered Bayreuth a fairy-tale version of the work such as had never before been seen there. Tristan and Isolde were transformed into Pelléas and Mélisande. Melancholy was present but little tragedy; heart-melting beauty but little heart-breaking sadness.

The visual enchantment was marvelled over for years. The second act was especially memorable: a gigantic tree glittered with tiny lights—or were they moonbeams or perhaps fireflies?—under which the lovers rippled their fingers in a limpid pool of water. Some found it all too saccharine; one hard-hearted critic claimed the couple resembled Hänsel and Gretel rather than an Irish princess and a Breton knight. The last act was performed, as intended, as though it were Tristan's agonized hallu-cination. Hence, Tristan was given an additional twenty-five minutes to live, dying at the end in the arms of Kurwenal and the Shepherd. After the première year, no one else appeared on stage; Marke and Melot were visible merely as shadows while Isolde lacked even that degree of palpability—singing her Liebestod from the orchestra pit.

Critics rather liked the soloists. The principles were René Kollo

Jean-Pierre Ponnelle's 1981 *Tristan*, Act II: With changes of lighting, the scene appeared at first sumptuous and enticing, later desolate and threatening.

(Tristan), an American debutante Johanna Meier (Isolde), Hermann Becht (Kurwenal), Matti Salminen (Marke) and Hanna Schwarz (Brangäne). There was no consensus about the conducting. Like the watches in Pope's essay, music critics never agree even though each is always firm in believing his own. During the seventies and eighties in Bayreuth, however, watches seemed to be set on entirely different time zones. Conductors were regularly judged by critics to be some of the best and by others some of the worst ever to lift a baton in the Festspielhaus. And so it was with Daniel Barenboim. There were those who dismissed him out of hand as a symphonic conductor with no feeling for opera. And there was, among others, *Oper und Konzert* which went so far as to write, 'At last Bayreuth has found a great Wagnerian conductor.'

The 1982 centenary production of *Parsifal* was placed in the hands of Götz Friedrich who, with the designer Andreas Reinhardt, contrived to invent some of the most unusual settings seen at Bayreuth. Taking as the starting-point Gurnemanz's words to Parsifal, 'You see, my son, here time is one with space', Reinhardt designed sets that were at once poetic and realistic and where time and space seemingly joined, or perhaps dissolved. For the first time in history the Festspielhaus stage was rid of even the slightest hint of Joukowsky's Byzantine-style temple. 'Within

291

The grail's temple in Act I of Friedrich's 1982 *Parsifal*. The space, hermetically closed to the outside world and evocative of a catacomb or mausoleum, symbolized the isolation and introversion of the brotherhood of the grail.

this space,' Reinhardt said, 'I wanted to destroy the conventional visual images and inspire the public to search for new visual possibilities.'[14]

That he certainly did, by creating an acting space that seemed to defy both normal perceptions and the laws of physics. The setting looked as though he had taken the Palazzo della Civiltà Italiana near Rome and turned it inside out and laid it on its side. This produced a succession of chambers inside a tower, with the audience at the foot, facing the top. The effect left an impression that 'behind' was 'above' and 'depth' was 'height'. The walls of these chambers were formed of arched cells, appearing at times to be catacombs or tombs or at one point a space capsule that transported Gurnemanz and Parsifal to the temple. Klingsor's castle was a hi-tech lab. The Flowermaidens, a headache for every producer during the previous ninety-nine years, were convincingly erotic—too much so for at least one critic, who found the scene closer to a brothel than a magic garden. Although that interlude was shrouded in darkness, the lighting and colour of the production were otherwise sumptuous. Idiosyncratic as it was, the staging aroused remarkably little criticism.

Friedrich's was a secularized *Parsifal*, a social commentary without religious connotations. An élitist, closed society had lost its compassion and humanity, bringing the brotherhood close to ruin. At the end, which was also a beginning, the closed society opened itself, the knights laid down their swords and helmets, and women entered the world of the grail. Although the utopia of a peaceful society was not ensured, it was at least held to be within reach. The underlying notion was the world's need of compassion as 'human social concern'. A weakness, even for those who liked the production, was the difficulty of finding a nexus between the way Friedrich staged the work and the meaning he wished to impart to the opera.

One person at least liked neither the staging nor the interpretation. James Levine deemed the production intolerable. Whether for that reason or not, he gave the score a sacerdotal reading that ran directly counter to Friedrich's intent. *Oper und Konzert* commented that Levine's conducting brought out the beauties of the score but lacked dramatic zest; he turned *Parsifal* into what it is not—'a religious service with beautiful music'. When Levine refused to conduct the production after the 1988 season, Wolfgang Wagner kept his conductor, retired the production and replaced it with his own version.

The first season enjoyed an above average performance. Peter Hofmann was considered an ideal Parsifal in voice and appearance; Leonie Rysanek made a fine comeback as Kundry; Simon Estes was an impressive Amfortas; Hans Sotin's Gurnemanz, Franz Mazura's Klingsor and Matti Salminen's Titurel were all praised.

Since 1951 Bayreuth had witnessed productions that were conventional and scandalous, beautiful and ugly, dull and thrilling, and that were cheered and jeered. With the *Ring* in 1983 it had one of its most magnificent flops. The production had been commissioned by Wolfgang Wagner for the last of the centenaries, that commemorating the composer's death.

In planning this *Ring*, Wolfgang decided to begin by selecting a conductor, and sounded out Georg Solti, whom he had unsuccessfully tried twice in the past to bring to Bayreuth. Solti agreed on the understanding that the production was to be an old-fashioned, romantic treatment of the work, without psychological interpretation, political analysis or stylistic abstraction. To produce and direct the work, Solti recruited Peter Hall, who was completely in accord with Solti's approach. As Hall saw it, Wieland and Wolfgang had done symbolic *Rings* to highlight the psychological element in the operas; Chéreau's political interpretation had been a reaction against that; his was to be a reaction against Chéreau's. He intended not only to follow the composer's stage instructions down to the last frog, ram, horse, bear and bird but also to accentuate the neglected sensual and sexual element. 'I wanted to see a

Ring based on nature, about the weather, about rain, and clouds, water and mountain tops, and fire,' he said.[15] In turning to William Dudley to do the designs, he made clear that he wanted real water, real fire, real trees, a horse that looked like a horse, and a carriage drawn by real rams.

This great leap back—not just over Wieland's and Wolfgang's versions but even over Preetorius's—was contrary to every artistic trend in Bayreuth for at least half a century. No doubt for that very reason such a production had for years been a dream, not just of old Wagnerians but even of some new Wagnerians who longed—if just once—to experience a really old-fashioned, naturalistic *Ring*, albeit without the swaying backcloths and mellow glow of flickering gas lamps but still breathing the atmosphere of 1876.

So the time for this sort of approach may have come. But Hall ominously linked to it a robust English anti-intellectualism. In taking on the project, he had characterized the *Ring* the '*biggest* great work of art ever created'.[16] But on encountering the 'craggy naïveté' of Wagner's text, as he put it, he said he came to see the *Ring* as 'a child's fairy story elevated into an adult myth'.[17] While it is true that Wieland Wagner in his last days had spoken lightly of producing a *Ring* in the style of Walt Disney, he would not have shared Hall's stated aim of producing a *Ring* simple enough for 'a twelve-year-old to understand what is happening'.[18]

On such shaky premises, this highly accomplished team went forward in the autumn of 1980 to construct their production. They began at the beginning. Impressed by the impact of Chéreau's opening scene, Hall and Dudley decided that the first stage image to hit the audience would set the tone for the entire work. They decided to create a splash by having naked Rhinemaidens sing and swim in a huge tank of real water, with their images projected into the auditorium through mirrors. Easily conceived, in practice it was impossible to dispose of fifty tons of water in the interlude of two minutes and forty-five seconds before the next scene. It therefore proved necessary to design and construct a costly and highly complex platform to cover the tub. The platform, it then occurred to Hall, would make an excellent foundation for the entire production. Accommodating the tub and platform, however, required strengthening the stage to support the additional 65 tons of weight, installing a vast heater for the water, putting in a new system of pipes to fill and empty the tank and constructing a hydraulic system for the platform under the stage. Only two scenes into a work of thirty-six individual scenes, the producer and designer were already ensnared in technical gadgetry and engineering problems—not to mention spiralling costs.

As work progressed, things went steadily awry. Sets and costumes were hopelessly late; special effects were dreamed up, created and tossed aside; the budget was overspent; resignation threat followed resignation threat. The British team could not speak German; the Germans did not

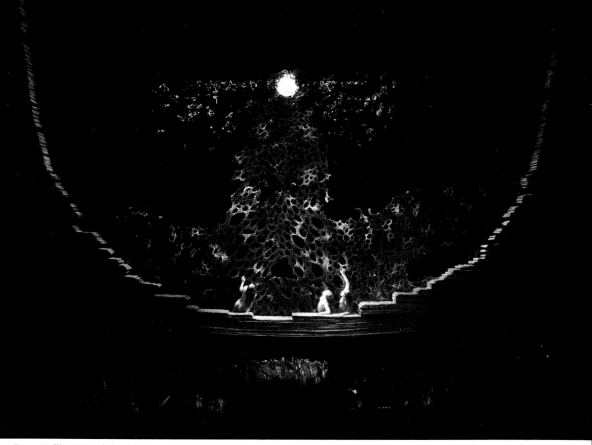

Peter Hall's 1983 *Rheingold*, Scene 1 (1983): 'The things that trigger me in the *Ring* are the first scene of *Rheingold*, where you've got to put your cards on the table, as Chéreau did' (William Dudley).

know English. The stage crew thought Hall and Dudley rigid, demanding and ungrateful; they thought the staff unwilling, inefficient and hostile. And the producer never sought the counsel of Wolfgang Wagner, with his incomparable experience as a stage manager. The grand result was that a few hours before the première of *Götterdämmerung*, following three years of labour, the final scene was still being worked on. Even in Bayreuth's well-planned universe, productions develop as they go along and sometimes hang on the brink of calamity before pulling themselves together at the last moment. This one fell into an abyss.

The production might have been more appropriate for the centenary, since some considered it a failure on a level with that of 1876. It left Friedelind Wagner enraged. After talking incoherently to an interviewer about British bombing raids during the war, she declared, 'This is the worst amateur show I have ever seen in a theatre. Peter Hall has no idea of the *Ring*, nor of directing. . . . This is the downfall of Bayreuth.'[19] Echoing her apocalyptic fears, the redoubtable critic Claus-Henning Bachmann captioned his review 'Bayreuth-Dämmerung' and picked the production apart, atom by atom. Now it was the turn of British critics to be mortified. 'Circus-style giants with plastic hands and faces, a hobbyhorse Grane, two stuffed rams for Fricka, and *Hänsel and Gretel*, even Walt Disney-like settings, just do not work,' wrote the editor of *Opera*. It was this failure of effects—as in 1876—that was one of the weaknesses. The *Sunday Times* thought the hall of the Gibichungs looked like an old-fashioned railway station. 'The wild mountain top resembles Greenland rather than a romantic primitive landscape'; 'the magic fire glowed like a great, red neon ring as though some huge outdoor advertising sign', stated the Hamburg *Abendblatt*. The production was also faulted for stylistic incoherence. A 'jarring juxtaposition of styles drawn from a century of Wagnerian history', the *New York Times* commented. The *New Yorker* found it 'a puzzling mixture of literalness ... and bleak, ineffective abstraction'.

Most critics professed amazement that such flabby directing and acting could have come from a director of Hall's experience. And they were troubled by the lack of any conceptual coherence. Hall in turn was genuinely taken aback by the notion that he should have had some animating interpretation. Almost as though a *Ring* in Bayreuth were a Christmas pantomime in London, he lamely explained at a press conference after the première, '. . . I believe in naïveté in the theatre. I would like this production, visually and in its actions, to make sense to a child.'[20]

The production was not without eminent defenders. These stressed that Hall and Dudley had provided any number of beautiful scenic pictures. 'A poetic, smooth, illusionistic staging,' wrote Joachim Kaiser. *Die Zeit* praised the production as 'well thought through; it has stature; it is lively; [there are] moving scenes of overwhelming beauty'. In the view of *The Times*, for three-quarters of the length it was 'visually stunning'. More ambiguously, Walter Bronnenmeyer said it was as impressive as a Snow White film.

There were those who loved its traditional naturalism. The arch-conservative *Aktionskreis für das Werk Richard Wagners* formally thanked Hall and Solti for the production, and the group's publication, *Richard Wagner Blätter*, mounted a spirited apologia, portraying the attacks on Hall as part of a conspiracy. Music critics, it maintained, followed a party line just as much as they had in the Third Reich. Unless a production purveyed a Marxist-socialist or a left-liberal point of view, they condemned it out of hand. Consequently few reviews of this *Ring* were fair; many were vicious and *ad hominem*. The level could be gauged, according to the journal, by the *Frankfurter Allgemeine*'s having mocked Hall for his lower middle-class background, as the son of a railway station-master and grandson of a house painter and a rat exterminator.

The performances of the première year were poorly sung, with German critics writing of a *Sängerdämmerung*. Again, the team had courted trouble at the outset. They excluded anyone who had sung in

Chéreau's *Ring* and then made matters worse by taking hair-raising gambles on unknown soloists for principal roles. Few of these worked out. Reiner Goldberg had to be excused as Siegfried at the last moment and was replaced by Manfred Jung. Jung may not have been a great heroic tenor musically but he was doubtless a great heroic tenor morally in tackling the role, and it was thanks to him that the performances could take place. Hildegard Behrens just as courageously sang her first Brünnhilde; she was judged both credible and creditable — as close as Bayreuth came to a vocal discovery that summer. Siegmund Nimsgern also made a promising start with Wotan but fell out as a result of illness. Among the other roles, Jeannine Altmeyer (Sieglinde), Hermann Becht (Alberich), Matthias Hölle (Hunding), Aage Haugland (Hagen) and Peter Haage (Mime) had good reviews. Siegfried Jerusalem (Siegmund) had a mixed reception.

Expectations for Solti's conducting had been high. He was the last great Central European romanticist, a musical perfectionist and a remorseless coach and rehearser. But he had the usual first-year difficulties dealing with the covered pit. Since what came out of it during rehearsals was predictably not his kind of big sound, he experimented with the pit cover to get the colour and sharper climaxes he liked. Eventually he was satisfied that he had achieved the desired balance. But it was a harrowing ordeal. 'At the end of each performance I had the feeling I couldn't go on any more,' he later said. 'It was not just the exhaustion, it was the heat. People have no idea what the suffering is in that pit.'[21] The critical reaction ran the gamut, only more so. *Opernwelt* went so far as to claim that his conducting qualified him to be the successor to Furtwängler; Bachmann found it the most conspicuous weakness of a conspicuously weak production.

What was more unforgivable than the failed production was the subsequent attitude of the triumvirate who had created it. Well-established *Werkstatt* principles dictated that the producer, conductor and designer should regard the first year as merely a start and return in subsequent years to root out weaknesses and develop the production further. In this case, however, all three members of the team simply washed their hands of it. A rightly aggrieved Wolfgang Wagner commented to the *Financial Times*, 'Peter Hall and Georg Solti left us with a ruin. Neither had the courage to stand by their work and bring it to completion.' Despite concern that not enough tickets would be sold in future seasons, Wolfgang kept the work in the repertory. Peter Schneider took over from Solti and Michael McCaffery, one of Hall's assistants, did his best to tidy up the sets and strengthen the acting, until eventually the production became, if not a success, at least no longer a painful embarrassment.

In 1987 Wolfgang turned to a film director, Werner Herzog, to see what he could do with *Lohengrin*. The result had its peculiarities but,

Lohengrin as fabled medieval romance in Herzog's 1987 production. Gierke's stage images, as here in Act I with its cold winter light, barren branches and snow-covered river bank, were poetic, painterly visions after the style of Caspar David Friedrich.

thanks to the staging designs of Henning von Gierke, was outstandingly beautiful. The mood of this production was one of disillusion, not miracle; the kingdom of Brabant was one of frigidness and desolation, a world of ice, snow, black sky, moon and stars. The opera opened on the frozen-over Scheldt and in a further meteorological reference, Lohengrin arrived in a laser-beam swirl of ice. The second act took place in the ruins of the minster, and the bridal scene of the final act took place outdoors against a background of ice-covered mountains. In an even more novel gesture, Elsa did not die at the end of the opera but joined hands with Ortrud—as snow began to fall.

The cast included Nadine Secunde, in her Bayreuth debut, as Elsa and Paul Frey as Lohengrin; Gabriele Schnaut sang Ortrud, Ekkehard Wlaschiha, Telramund and Manfred Schenk, the King.

For opera audiences—as for laboratory mice in psychological experiments—the greater the expectation, the greater the potential for disappointment. One of the most eagerly awaited productions in years was Harry Kupfer's *Ring* in 1988. Kupfer's prior Bayreuth success, his iconoclastic productions elsewhere in Germany and the Vienna Opera's rejection of his proposed *Ring* as too avant-garde led to hopes of a thought-provoking masterpiece, possibly even the *Ring* of the century. When unveiled, the production found none to love and very few to praise. And the little praise it received was counterbalanced by the coruscating sarcasm and withering criticism of some whose hopes had been highest.

Even before *Rheingold*'s opening chords, the curtain parted on a grim and mysterious scene. There on a seemingly endless grey road lay a corpse, and there in motionless silence looking on were clutches of men and women in trench-coats, their hats shoved down and collars pulled up. Here, evidently, was the conclusion of some earlier and sinister drama. Yet it was apparently also the introduction to another drama— Wagner's. For when this got under way, there was the same pitiless highway. On the highway were, again, some very dubious-looking characters. These, however, were vaguely familiar; yes, they were the Valhalla gang, and behind the mafioso sunglasses was their *capo*, Wotan. On learning about the gold treasure stolen by Alberich from an aqueous green laser-lit river bottom, Wotan descended to a hi-tech factory, manned by Nibelung robots in white overalls, to retrieve it. The dirty deed done and the loot handed over to the giants—even larger and more cataleptic than their Chéreau and Hall forebears—Wotan and his family ascended in a rainbow-coloured lift to their glass skyscraper Valhalla, strewing self-congratulatory confetti on the way aloft.

Despite the programmatic descriptiveness of the music itself, the prelude to *Walküre* was staged, showing Siegmund staggering along life's endless highway, observed through a heavy fog by Wotan. Hunding's hut was a sleek metallic construction, furnished with an ultra-modish dining table and matching aluminium tree stump. In a scene where irony bordered on burlesque, the third act opened with the Valkyries swarming around tumbrels filled with dead heroes and bounding up and down what appeared to be a fire ladder. Otherwise the final act, as well as the whole of the second act, took place on the unadorned road of destiny, concluding with Brünnhilde's being put to sleep in a laser-beam box of fire.

The visual highlights of *Siegfried* were more striking still. Mime's forge was a discarded industrial boiler—or was it a beached U-boat?— while the second act décor might have been a post-modern, nightmare version of a Piranesi prison. The Wood Bird came not out of the forest but out of Wotan's pocket and was fixed on the end of his spear where it danced a jig. Fafner, a beast with metallic tentacles, reverted to his original giant form at the moment of Siegfried's lethal stab. The third act took place back on the grey road of history, again in a heavy fog.

A television motif characterized the beginning and conclusion of *Götterdämmerung*. In the prelude the Norns strung the rope of destiny along TV antennae; at the conclusion small groups of glitterati stood in small groups watching the downfall of the world on TV sets—we the blasé observing our own end, cocktail glasses in hand. Between these

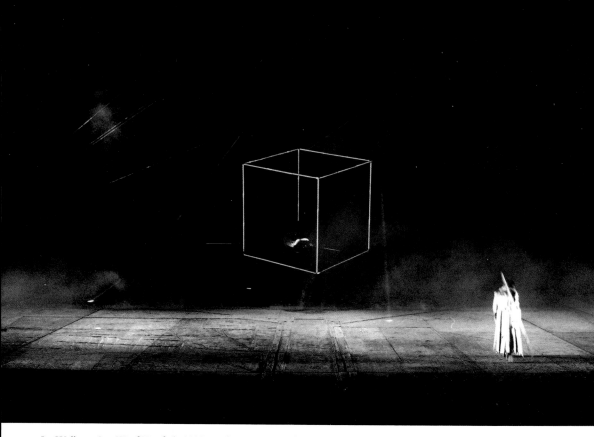

In *Walküre*, Act III of Kupfer's 1988 production, Loge does his tricks with laser beams, encasing Brünnhilde in a fiery cube as Wotan looks on from the pitiless highway of destiny.

two scenes Brünnhilde and Siegfried were at home in a bunker, the Gibichungs at home around a space-age quadripod and the Rhinemaidens at home in a rusting pump station. As the final curtain closed, a little boy and girl stole off, signifying that tomorrow was another day.

In essence this *Ring* was a parable of how the power-hungry cheat, lie, bully, terrorize and kill to get what they want, destroying the innocent along the way and themselves in the end. Though anything but a novel interpretation—Wieland Wagner's second *Ring* was just as explicitly grim—this was a *Ring* suffused more than any previous one with a sense of moral and physical panic. The Chernobyl disaster, which had occurred while Kupfer was working out his interpretation, seemed so manifest that the production was labelled by some as the 'Chernobyl *Ring*'. For this reason, perhaps, it was visually the ugliest production ever seen in Bayreuth. In Kupfer's view, opera must be provocative, must force people, as he said, 'to face up to the problems of the day'. Ubiquitous contemporary reference was therefore essential. Wagner's Forest Murmurs, for instance, were heard against a background of physical horror—presumably epitomizing the distance between pristine nature in its original state and the world environment in its current state. Hence this was the most despairing of *Rings*. At the end the children may have escaped, but they were sure to find themselves back on the same infinite highway of destiny, the entire cycle of expectation and disappointment to be repeated—including the dread possibility, one writer feared, of another Kupfer *Ring*.

But this *Ring* was not just tragedy, it was also farce. *Siegfried* was done as slapstick comedy, to the point where a critic said he half expected Fafner to get his come-uppance not by a sword through the gizzard but by an old-fashioned cream pie in the face. It was at the same time an unmasking exercise. The prime movers—Wotan, Alberich and Hagen—were not mere villains but low-class thugs. Siegfried was also redimensioned, into a jolly, innocent, fun-loving lout. Mime became a homunculus reincarnation of a climbing, dangling, lurching Harold Lloyd. The costumes alone were a giveaway. Wotan strode about like a real cool dude, in a long sleek coat with fur collar, broad-brimmed hat, jeans, low-cut black T-shirt and cowboy boots. Siegfried was clad in a blue jump-suit until changing for his wedding into what the *Süddeutsche Zeitung* described as 'a mixture of Elvis Presley outfit and Liberace frippery'. He was, the writer quipped, 'ready for Las Vegas'.[22]

A large part of the problem was Chéreau. As Hall had reacted *against*, so Kupfer had reacted *to* him, the former producing an unconvincing contrast, the latter an inferior pastiche. Like its 1976 ancestor, this *Ring* had an unfavourable reception in its first year, but this time the mood did not soften greatly in subsequent years. On certain points there was a solid consensus. Chief of these was that Kupfer's liberties with the drama falsified it. Not only did Wotan appear where he had no right to be—such as at Siegfried's funeral—but was seen to be manipulating events in violation of Wagner's plot. By turning the Wood Bird into Wotan's instrument, for example, the central idea of Siegfried as 'freer than the god himself' was destroyed. The production was also judged by critics to have left too many enigmas. 'Up to the last many of us believed that at some point the Kupfer concept would reveal itself. But *Götterdämmerung* brought no solution to the puzzle,' reported the Munich *Abendzeitung* in a typical view.

The settings themselves, by Hans Schavernoch, had few admirers. The stated aim of establishing a link between the stage and the contemporary world was achieved by paradox and irony, but the effect was often unconvincing. What was one to make of the quadripod? And were not the Norns' antennae embarrassingly obvious? The laser lighting, by Manfred Voss, was held by some to be enthralling, by others worthy of a small-town disco.

The strength of the production was Kupfer's directing, in particular the psychological interpretation of the characters and their relationships. 'Rarely has the relationship between Wotan and Fricka (a real marriage, not just a henpecked husband) or the sexuality of Siegmund and Sieglinde or the physical closeness of Wotan and Brünnhilde been so powerfully conveyed,' stated the *New York Times*.[23] Yet even here Kupfer's work was considered flawed. No one had a good word to say for the way singers—when not lying flat on their backs—were kept in perpetual motion. And what motion! Crawling, kneeling, rolling, running, climbing; manic activity that was compulsive and distracting and that often made it difficult for soloists to sing and downright dangerous to act. 'Who is crazier,' asked *Oper und Konzert*, 'those on the stage, or we who do not drive such unmusical nonsense off the stage by a storm of laughter?'[24]

Musically at least it was assessed to be a good *Ring* and one that improved with age. The mainstays of the production were Graham Clark's Loge and Mime, John Tomlinson's Wotan, Nadine Secunde's Sieglinde, Linda Finnie's Fricka, Günter von Kannen's Alberich, Matthias Hölle's Hunding, Philip Kang's Hagen and Waltraud Meier's Waltraute. Substitutions after the first year—Anne Evans for Deborah Polaski as Brünnhilde in *Siegfried* and *Götterdämmerung*, Poul Elming for Peter Hofmann as Siegmund and Siegfried Jerusalem for Rainer Goldberg as Siegfried—strengthened the performances. About Barenboim's conducting, critics could not make up their collective minds. 'A triumph,' said *Figaro*; 'I have rarely heard better playing at Bayreuth,' commented the *Observer*. Perhaps a greater number were unimpressed, though everyone agreed the conducting gained in conviction with every passing season.

Revolutions devour their children, as the saying goes, and the revolution launched by Wieland in 1951 was consumed after his death by changes no less drastic. In his effort to keep Bayreuth at the centre of the Wagnerian world, Wolfgang had turned to producers who might provide renditions of the operas that would show them to be relevant to the contemporary world and make them provocative, novel and exciting. It was in the belief that this was more likely to come from the unorthodox that he often selected those with little or no experience of Wagner or even of opera. Once under way, the innovatory process became self-reinforcing and ever more daring. What had been done by Wieland on a high intellectual plane was now accomplished by deliberate provocation and scandal; the scalpel was replaced by the meat cleaver.

The resulting productions have been characterized by a radical re-interpretation of the dramas. Many of the ideas, it is true, were variants on Wieland's concepts or were inspired by what he had begun. But the new versions were in their way as novel as his had been. Occasionally the operas were mined for ideas of contemporary relevance. Man's violation of nature, as in the Chéreau and Kupfer *Rings*, was such a preoccupation that Wagner almost emerged as the spiritual founder of the Greens. Some original themes were altered. The composer's notion of the redeeming love of a self-sacrificing, heroic woman was deemphasized or banished entirely; women acquired more independent roles, becoming in the process more human and often more tragic. Elsa and Kundry no longer died at the end; Elsa and Ortrud were reconciled; women were admitted to the temple of the grail; the Rhinemaidens were prostitutes. There were fewer heroes and fewer villains. Wotan in particular was increasingly shorn of his stature and even his dignity, Siegfried seemed less an adventurous superman than a gormless adventurer and even dear old Sachs was no longer simply a tender-hearted matchmaker but also a bit of a cheat, though at least he was endowed with the grace to make up with a now-forgiving Beckmesser. The secularization begun by Wieland was taken further; miracle, religion and superstition were discredited. The dramas were often more tragic, less hopeful. Although they dealt provocatively with social conditions and were critical of bourgeois society, these versions were not explicitly political, much less Marxist, however much they may have been misunderstood by some music critics. Certain operas were placed on a new plane by treating the action as taking place solely in the imagination of one of the protagonists—Tannhäuser, Elsa, Senta, Tristan.

Scenographically the productions were equally innovative. The abstraction and symbolism of the fifties and sixties were replaced by realism, but realism of a brutal post-modern, almost surrealistic sort. Even overtly conservative approaches, such as those by Everding and Svoboda, were inventive in their use of sets, light and colour, facilitated by Bayreuth's wondrous lighting technology. Some productions were designed to suggest a dream—or nightmare—world. Beauty was often shunned and settings were deliberately ugly, expressing a world with little hope and less mercy. One of the most original staging features was the layering of time periods and styles, most strikingly in the Chéreau and Kupfer *Rings*. This syncretic approach was based on the notion that, while the work was overtly about Nordic myth, it was rooted in the period when written—that is, the mythic aspect was a metaphor for the problems of the nineteenth century and by extension those of the present. Wotan could therefore wear a frock coat or jeans and yet carry a Bronze Age spear as a symbol of power.

Dramaturgy enjoyed unprecedented importance. The director was dominant, even in cases where Wolfgang Wagner initially gave authority to the conductor. In the work of some producers, in particular the Felsenstein alumni, directing had clear priority over the staging and the music. Some works were transformed into psychodramas, with an attempt to penetrate the mind of the main character and stage the opera through that state of mind. In a few cases, most notably Chéreau's *Ring*, the dramas were presented as exciting theatre, great dramatic adventure, a vehicle for all sorts of novel ideas and treatments. Notions picked up from other art forms, such as film, were introduced, expanding the parameters of orthodox operatic art. In all, there was a clear

shift of emphasis from music to drama, from the aural to the visual—
perhaps fortunately in view of the often unreliable singing in this
period.

Beautiful, exciting, shocking and even scandalous, these productions
made Bayreuth one of the liveliest places on the cultural map. But under
the pressure of competing with others—or even sometimes with their
own earlier work—producers were driven to ever further extremes of
originality and provocation so that by the last decade of the century it
was difficult to think that any possibility remained of unsettling a Festival
audience short of actual murder, rape or cannibalism on the
Festspielhaus stage.

Yet for all the excitement, the question arises—as it has at every
juncture in Bayreuth's history back to Cosima's era—whether what is
being presented on the stage is faithful to Wagner's intent, whether it
elucidates or obstructs the meaning of the music dramas, whether a
production brings the work nearer intellectually and emotionally, forcing audiences, as Wagner hoped, to see themselves and their own world
in it. Many of the post-New Bayreuth novelties—or infidelities—
neither originated at nor were unique to Bayreuth. But performed on
the Green Hill they gained a special validation.

An artist is never fully aware of the depths of his own creations, as
Wagner himself acknowledged on more than one occasion. Since
Wagner's works seek to encompass the entire spiritual cosmos, to
explore the inner meaning of human life, they offer the possibility of
unending adventure. Contrary to the belief of Cosima, Daniela Thode,
Hans Pfitzner, Adolf Zinsstag, the *Aktionskreis für das Werk Richard
Wagners* and all the other Wagnerian dogmatists over the decades, there
is neither a final objective meaning to any of the operas nor a platonic
ideal of a production which, once found, remains forever valid. Time
marches on and perceptions of the world are overturned. Even the
dullest-witted member of a contemporary audience cannot regard the
works in the same way as did someone who attended fifty or a hundred
years ago. A great opera is like a precious gem, to be turned over and
over and looked at from different angles. And the strength of Wagner is,
in Harry Kupfer's words, that his 'range of ideas is so vast, so inexhaustible in fact, that even when dealing with the same work a second or
third time, one always finds new facets. . . . It is as though the work itself
changes and suddenly reveals things that one simply did not notice
before.'[25]

Finding new meanings through reassessing the dramas has been the
essence of Bayreuth's work since 1951. Whatever their weaknesses,
these new interpretations have brought out fresh aesthetic dimensions
and explored the psychological, political and social themes buried in the
operas. They have saved the works from becoming museum pieces or
simple entertainments. But if the Solti-Hall *Ring* ultimately failed because it had nothing new to say and was not even good entertainment,

certain other productions ran into trouble because they were so novel, subtle and complex, so far over the heads of even a Bayreuth audience, that some producers—Friedrich, Kupfer, Chéreau—were prompted to write substantial explanatory tomes which viewers had to study if they wished to understand what they had seen.

These productions also raised what has become the most insistent question of contemporary Bayreuth: were these Wagner's works that were being put on stage? As greater and greater liberties were taken, some productions seemed—like many novels turned into Hollywood films—little more than 'an adaptation of a story' by Richard Wagner. The justification for such licence was essentially summed up in a comment of Kupfer's that he was faithful because he fulfilled the intentions not the letter. The argument—used by every producer since the days of Cosima and Appia—begged the question, though, since it is precisely Wagner's intentions that have been at dispute since his death. It might have been more persuasive simply to maintain that his fidelity was to Wagner the master provocateur, the man who was always out of step with the times, the composer who took pleasure in challenging society's complacency.

Patently some features of these productions were not Wagner. Staging the preludes and indeed adding an entirely new scene in Kupfer's *Ring* were most obviously pure invention. Whatever these adjuncts contributed dramatically, many believed that they compromised the composer's intention of creating a mood for the action that follows. But such revisions were merely one aspect of the deeper change wrought by director's theatre: shifting the fulcrum of performances from the aural to the visual to the point where the critical balance of the acting, staging, text and music was upset. The intense concentration on staging so subverted the notion of sets as a silent, facilitating background for the music-dramas that it was at times impossible to 'hear' the music for the 'sound' of the physical presentation. In addition the staging itself was on occasion blatantly dissociated from the score. Even admirers of Chéreau and Kupfer were troubled by having to hear, for instance, the luxuriant Forest Murmurs against a visual accompaniment of squalid desolation. Nothing exposed the sacrifice of the aural more clearly than requiring soloists to sing while lying prone or clambering up and down a steel scaffold.

Post-New Bayreuth also tampered with the substance of the dramas. Some characters—Friedrich's Elisabeth, Kupfer's Senta, Ponnelle's Tristan—were transformed in a way that left open whether they were still Wagner's creations. Plots as well were not only adulterated but at times ignored and even invented. Did not Ponnelle's handling of the third act of *Tristan* destroy the contrast between the world of day and the world of night, make nonsense of King Marke's final words and deprive the finale of its poignancy, indeed its meaning? Were not such gestures as Wolfgang Wagner's bringing Sachs and Beckmesser together—

touching as it was and reflective of the laudable postwar German desire for reparation and reconciliation—contrary both to the composer's intention and to psychological plausibility? Many felt that nothing was gained and that such interpretations smacked of gimmickry. So the dark suspicion grew that a guiding principle of some producers was simply: when in want of ideas, shock.

No doubt it *is* preferable to be outraged by novelty rather than bored by convention, as Winifred Wagner admitted, provided that new meaning is uncovered and an audience is stimulated to ponder it. And those who want their Wagner as fairy-tale opera in the style of Cosima's romantic naturalism can always find it in New York. But the issue for Bayreuth—and for contemporary operatic production—is establishing where interpretation leaves off and violation starts, where inspiration stops and self-indulgent exhibitionism takes over, where independent critical judgement ends and trendy uncritical conformity in fear of being considered an old fogy begins. After all, the composer's motivation in establishing his own opera theatre was to prevent the disfiguration of his works.

As it enters its second century, Bayreuth is a simulacrum of the German nation much as it has always been. Through sacrifice, hard work, patience and eminent good sense, the Federal Republic rose from ashes and ignominy to become the world's best-governed country, with a benign social system and an economy the envy of the world. It gradually came to terms with its past and learned the crucial difference between national pride and nationalism. Similarly, the Festival emerged from moral, political and financial bankruptcy and through great effort and imagination achieved a position of unchallenged eminence. It too eventually freed itself from its fascist past and became a model of good management and inventive activity.

Bayreuth has always had its ups and downs. There have been periods when its performances were qualitatively no better than or even as good as those in other opera houses. Yet Bayreuth remains what it has always been and what has never been duplicated elsewhere: a genuine festival which enjoys the exceptional devotion of artists and audiences, a great historic tradition, incomparable conditions of performance, a devotion to the same seven works and, above all, the Festspielhaus itself. All this ensures that it will remain a special place. Whether it will remain the supreme interpreter of Wagner and the world's most exciting opera theatre will obviously depend on the quality of its productions and performances. The Festival remains outstanding in areas where the management has control—the chorus, orchestra and productions. Its weakness lies in areas it cannot control—the quality of singers and conductors.

But even at its worst—which is rarely bad—one can only concur with Shaw, who observed in *The Perfect Wagnerite* that the performances 'are often far from delectable. The singing is sometimes tolerable, sometimes abominable.' But, as he insisted, 'Those who go to Bayreuth never repent it.'

Notes

Introduction

1 Letter of 17 April to August Röckel in Carl Friedrich Glasenapp, ed., *Bayreuther Briefe von Richard Wagner (1871–1883)* (1907), 83–4.
2 *Sunday Times*, 3 August 1930.
3 Nicola Buda and Manfred Bockelmann, *Unsterblicher Wagner—lebendiges Bayreuth* (1983), 119.
4 *Opera*, 1986, 67.
5 *Welt am Sonntag*, 23 May 1976.
6 Joseph Wechsberg, 'A Reporter at Large' in *The New Yorker*, 18 August 1956.
7 Hermann Schreiber and Guido Mangold, *Werkstatt Bayreuth* (1986), 214.
8 Buda and Bockelmann, 106.
9 Wechsberg, *New Yorker*, 18 August 1956.
10 Schreiber and Mangold, 223.
11 Buda and Bockelmann, 246.
12 Karl Böhm, *Ich erinnere mich ganz genau: Autobiographie* (1974), 126.
13 *Sunday Times*, 3 August 1930.
14 *Gondroms Festspielmagazin 1987*.
15 Stephen Fay and Roger Wood, *The Ring: Anatomy of an Opera* (1984), 106.
16 *Neue Freie Presse* (Vienna), 14 August 1876.
17 Egon Voss, *Die Dirigenten der Bayreuther Festspiele* (1976), 69.
18 Dietrich Mack, *Der Bayreuther Inszenierungsstil* (1976), 65 and Voss, 69.
19 Voss, 69.
20 Willi Schuh, ed., *Richard Strauss: Betrachtungen und Erinnerungen* (1957), 92.
21 Voss, 66.
22 Fay and Wood, 105.
23 Schreiber and Mangold, 100.
24 Antoine Goléa, *Entretiens avec Wieland Wagner* (1967), 17.
25 Fay and Wood, 105–6.
26 Wechsberg, *New Yorker*, 18 August 1956.
27 Schreiber and Mangold, 214.
28 Stefan Jaeger, ed., *Götz Friedrich: Wagner-Regie* (1983), 39.
29 *The Perfect Wagnerite*, Preface to 1922 edition.
30 Schuh, *Betrachtungen*, 92.
31 Herbert Barth, ed., *Bayreuther Dramaturgie: Der Ring des Nibelungen* (1980), 173.
32 *Richard Wagner in Bayreuth* (1873), 4.
33 31 July.
34 'At the Shrine of St Wagner' in Robert Hartford, *Bayreuth: The Early Years* (1980), 154.
35 Igor Stravinsky, *An Autobiography* (1936), 59.
36 Hartford, 222.
37 Karen Monson, *Alban Berg* (1979), 79.
38 Albert Lavignac, *The Music Dramas of Richard Wagner and His Festival Theatre in Bayreuth* (1898), 52.

Chapter 1

1 *Richard Wagner in Bayreuth* (1873), 7.

2 Carl Friedrich Glasenapp, *Das Leben Richard Wagners*, 6 vols (1894–1911), vol. 3, 424.

3 *Richard Wagner in Bayreuth*, 6–7.

4 Richard Wagner, *Gesammelte Schriften und Dichtungen*, 10 vols (1887–8), vol. 3, 8ff.

5 Ibid., 42ff.

6 Richard Wagner, *Mein Leben* (1914), part III, 14.

7 20 September in *Richard Wagners Briefe an Theodor Uhlig, Wilhelm Fischer, Ferdinand Heine* (1888), 58.

8 12 November, ibid., 118.

9 30 January in *Briefwechsel zwischen Wagner und Liszt*, 2 vols (1887), vol. 1, 162.

10 *Mein Leben*, part III, 135.

11 Letter of 4 May 1864 to Eliza Wille in Hanjo Kesting, ed., *Richard Wagner Briefe* (1983).

12 Letter of 26 November 1864 from Ludwig to Wagner in Heinrich Habel, *Festspielhaus und Haus Wahnfried* (1985), 25.

13 Letter of 5 January 1865 in Otto Strobel, ed., *König Ludwig II. und Richard Wagner: Briefwechsel*, 5 vols (1936–9), vol. 1, 45.

14 Letter of 1 May 1865, ibid., 90.

15 Letter of 16 September 1865, ibid., 182.

16 Letter of 4 February 1867, ibid., vol. 5, 60.

17 Letter of 20 November 1869 in Strobel, vol. 2, 292.

18 Letter of 1 March 1871 in Strobel, vol. 2, 320.

19 Karl Heckel, ed., *Briefe Richard Wagner an Emil Heckel: zur Entstehungsgeschichte in Bayreuth* (1899), 39.

20 Habel, 335.

21 Letter to Feustel of 12 April 1872 in Carl Friedrich Glasenapp, *Bayreuther Briefe von Richard Wagner (1871–1883)* (1907), 78.

22 Glasenapp, *Das Leben Richard Wagners*, vol. 5, 29.

23 Habel, 336.

24 26 March 1872.

25 27 March 1872.

26 5 July 1873.

27 14 September 1873.

28 24 September 1873.

29 Letter of 13 June 1873 to Anton Pusinelli in Glasenapp, *Das Leben Richard Wagners*, vol. 5, 91.

30 Martin Gregor-Dellin and Dietrich Mack, eds, *Cosima Wagner: Die Tagebücher*, 2 vols (1976–7), 4 December 1873.

31 Heckel, 74.

32 Strobel, vol. 3, 29.

33 Friedrich Nietzsche, *Der Fall Wagner* (1888), section 5.

34 Letter of 1 October 1874 in Strobel, vol. 3, 41–2.

35 Ernest Newman, *The Life of Richard Wagner*, 4 vols (1933–47), vol. 4, 469.

Chapter 2

1 Ernest Newman, *The Life of Richard Wagner*, 4 vols (1933–47), vol. 4, 436.

2 Gustav Adolph Kietz, *Richard Wagner in den Jahren 1842–1849 und 1873–1875: Erinnerungen* (1905), 202.

3 Carl Friedrich Glasenapp, *Das Leben Richard Wagners*, 6 vols (1894–1911), vol. 5, 199.

4 Richard Fricke, *Bayreuth vor dreissig Jahren: Erinnerungen an Wahnfried und aus dem Festspielhause* (1906), 9 May.

5 Ibid., 22 July.

6 Ibid., 9 August.

7 Newman, vol. 4, 471.

8 Heinrich Porges, 'Die Bühnenproben zu den Festspielen des Jahres 1876' in *Bayreuther Blätter*, September 1881, 262–3.

9 Angelo Neumann, *Personal Recollections of Wagner* (1908), 9.

10 Lilli Lehmann, *Mein Weg* (1913), 287.

11 Porges, *Bayreuther Blätter*, June 1880, 150.

12 Fricke, 22 June.

13 Fricke, 8 June.

14 Newman, vol. 4, 456.

15 19 August 1876 in Saul Padover, ed., *The Letters of Karl Marx*, 310.

16 Modest Tchaikowsky, *The Life and Letters of Peter Ilich Tchaikowsky*

(1906), 182.

17 Letter of end August/early September in Padover, 312.

18 *The Times*, 10 June 1876.

19 Letter of 12 July 1876 in Otto Strobel, ed., *König Ludwig II. und Richard Wagner: Briefwechsel*, 5 vols (1936–9), vol. 3, 81.

20 Letter of 7 August 1876, ibid., 82.

21 Letter of 12 August 1876, ibid., 83.

22 Glasenapp, vol. 5, 286.

23 Ibid., 287.

24 15 August 1876.

25 Glasenapp, vol. 5, 294–5.

26 Letter of 12 August 1876 in Strobel, vol. 3, 83.

27 18 August 1876.

28 Letter of 11 September 1876 in Strobel, vol. 3, 90.

29 Martin Gregor-Dellin and Dietrich Mack, eds, *Cosima Wagner: Die Tagebücher*, 2 vols (1976–7), 9 September 1876.

30 Ibid., 5 November 1876.

31 Ibid., 21 October 1876.

32 Ibid., 24 July 1878.

33 Ibid., 29 September 1878.

34 14 August 1876.

35 *Neue Freie Press* (Vienna), 13 August 1876.

36 Alexandra Orlova, *Tchaikowsky: A Self-Portrait* (1990), 57.

37 *Bergensposten*, quoted in Robert Hartford, *Bayreuth: The Early Years* (1980), 63.

38 *Kölnische Zeitung*, 18–23 August 1876.

39 19 August 1876.

40 *Neue Freie Press*, 18 August 1876.

41 Orlova, 56.

42 *New-York Times*, 3 September 1876.

43 Reported ibid., 4 September 1876.

44 *Interludes* (1922), 65.

45 *The Times*, 19 August 1876.

46 Ibid., 29 August 1876.

47 Gisela Zeh, *Der Bayreuther Bühnenkostum* (1973), 28.

48 Letter of 25 January 1854 in La Mara, ed., *Briefe an August Röckel von Richard Wagner* (1894), 42.

49 Newman, vol. 4, 411.

50 'Nüchterne Briefe' in *Schlesische Presse* (Breslau), August 1876.

51 *Menschliches, Allzumenschliches* (1878), section 2.

52 Newman, vol. 4, 544.

53 Gregor-Dellin and Mack, *Cosima Wagner*, 23 September 1878.

54 Letter of 31 March 1880 in Strobel, vol. 3, 172.

55 Gregor-Dellin and Mack, *Cosima Wagner*, 20 August 1880.

56 Letter of 28 September 1880 in Strobel, vol. 3, 182.

57 Letter of 24 October 1880, ibid., 185.

58 24 July 1882.

59 Glasenapp, vol. 6, 502.

60 Newman, vol. 4, 609.

61 Letter of 8 September 1882 in Strobel, vol. 3, 248.

62 30 August 1882.

63 *Jenseits von Gut und Böse* (1886), section 256.

64 Vol. 78, 353.

65 Felix Weingartner, *Buffets and Rewards* (1937), 78.

66 'Das Bühnenweihfestspiel in Bayreuth 1882', *Bayreuther Blätter* 1882, vol. 5, 322.

67 Quoted in Newman, vol. 4, 671.

Chapter 3

1 Julie Kniese, ed., *Julius Kniese, Der Kampf zweier Welten um das Bayreuther Erbe* (1931), 128.

2 *Sunday Times*, 27 February 1938.

3 'Zettel zu *Parsifal* Proben 1884' in Dietrich Mack, ed., *Cosima Wagner, Das zweite Leben, Briefe und Aufzeichnungen 1883–1930* (1980), 37–40.

4 5 August 1884.

5 Letter of 8 September 1886 in Mack, *Cosima Wagner*, 68.

6 Letter of 6 April 1888 to Felix Mottl, ibid., 148.

7 Letter of 8 April 1888 to Felix Mottl, ibid., 149.

8 Felix Weingartner, *Buffets and Rewards* (1937), 146.

9 Ibid., 149.

10 Anton Seidl, 'Über das Dirigieren' in *Bayreuther Blätter*, 1900, 294.

11 Letter of 19 April 1888 to Ernst van Dyck in Mack, *Cosima Wagner*, 150.

12 Lilli Lehmann, *Mein Weg* (1913), 197.

13 Anna Bahr-Mildenburg and Hermann Bahr, *Bayreuth* (1912), 16.

14 Walter Bronnenmeyer, *Vom Tempel zur Werkstatt: Geschichte der Bayreuther Festspiele* (1970), 45.

15 11 November 1888.

16 Albert von Puttkamer, *50 Jahre Bayreuth* (1927), 121.

17 *Nord und Süd* (Breslau), April–May 1889.

18 Richard Du Moulin Eckart, *Cosima Wagner: Ein Lebens- und Charakterbild*, 2 vols (1929, 1931), vol. 2, 477.

19 11 November 1888.

20 *Kölnische Zeitung*, 22 July 1889.

21 *The Hawk*, 13 August 1889.

22 *The World*, 1 August 1894.

23 *The English Illustrated Magazine*, October 1889.

24 *The Star*, 19 July 1896.

25 *The English Illustrated Magazine*, October 1889.

26 Letter of 11 April 1903 to Hermann Count Kaiserling in Mack, *Cosima Wagner*, 630.

27 Letter of 13 May 1896 in Paul Pretzsch, ed., *Cosima Wagner und Houston Stewart Chamberlain im Briefwechsel 1888–1908* (1934), 464.

28 Letter of 11 September 1891 to George Davidsohn in Mack, *Cosima Wagner*, 256.

29 'Die ersten zwanzig Jahre der Bayreuther Bühnenfestspiele' in *Bayreuther Blätter*, 1896, 45.

30 *Erinnerungen* (1923), 135.

31 *Bayreuther Blätter*, 1896, 46.

32 29 July 1891.

33 24 July 1891.

34 Letter of 12 December 1886 in Mack, *Cosima Wagner*, 79.

35 *Bayreuther Blätter*, 1936, 112.

36 *The World*, 8 August 1894.

37 28 July 1894.

38 *Mein Weg*, 207.

39 Moulin Eckart, vol. 2, 443.

40 Franz Trenner, ed., *Cosima Wagner-Richard Strauss: Ein Briefwechsel* (1978), 108.

41 Peter Pachl, *Siegfried Wagner: Genie im Schatten* (1988), 153.

42 Letter of 22 January 1894 in Voss, 22.

43 Letter of 9 November 1905 in Voss, 39.

44 Letter of 18 January 1894 in Mack, *Cosima Wagner*, 367.

45 10 August 1896 in Dietrich Mack, *Der Bayreuther Inszenierungsstil* (1976), 9.

46 *Mein Weg*, 199.

47 23 and 25 July 1896.

48 Puttkamer, 153.

49 7 August 1930.

50 Letter of 24 March 1889 to Carl Friedrich Glasenapp in Mack, *Cosima Wagner*, 176.

51 Letter of 9 May 1901 in *Bayreuther Blätter*, 1901, 221–6.

52 Moulin Eckart, vol. 2, 812.

Chapter 4

1 George R. Marek, *Cosima Wagner* (1981), 259.

2 *Hamburger Nachrichten* in Peter Pachl, *Siegfried Wagner: Genie im Schatten* (1988), 205.

3 Anna Bahr-Mildenburg and Hermann Bahr, *Bayreuth* (1912), 32 ff.

4 Albert von Puttkamer, *50 Jahre Bayreuth* (1927), 138, 140.

5 Susanna Großmann-Vendrey, *Bayreuth in der deutschen Presse*, 4 vols (1977–83), vol. 3, 2, 57.

6 Puttkamer, 168.

7 Pachl, 265.

8 *An Deutschlands Jugend* (1918), 83.

9 Bahr-Mildenburg and Bahr, 51.

10 'Nach 1913' in *Bayreuther Blätter*, vol. 37 (1914), 4.

11 5 August 1908.

12 *Deutsche Tageszeitung*, 15 August 1909.

13 24 July 1908.

14 *Berliner Tageblatt*, 28 July 1909.

15 *Vossische Zeitung*, 31 August 1912.

16 *Neue Freie Presse* (Vienna), 15 August 1912.

17 Vol. 79, (1912), 425.

18 *Hamburger Nachrichten*, 24 July.

19 Großmann-Vendrey, vol. 3, 2, 59.

20 *Hamburger Fremdenblatt*, 25 July 1911.

21 *Grenzboten*, vol. 70 (1911).

22 *Erinnerungen* (1923), 144–5.

23 Martin Gregor-Dellin and Dietrich Mack, eds, *Cosima Wagner: Die Tagebücher*, 2 vols (1976–7), vol. 1, 8.

24 Erich Ebermayer, *Magisches Bayreuth:*

Legende und Wirklichkeit (1952), 151.

25 *Hitler* (1973), 181.

26 Ebermayer, 174.

27 August Kubizek, *Adolf Hitler: mein Jugendfreund* (1953), 142.

28 Eberhard Jäckel, ed., *Adolf Hitler: Sämtliche Aufzeichnungen 1905–1924* (1980), 53.

29 Ibid., 1034.

30 *Oberfränkische Zeitung*, 14 November 1923 in Hartmut Zelinsky, *Richard Wagner: Ein deutsches Thema* (1983), 169.

31 Werner Jochmann, ed., *Adolf Hitler: Monologe im Führer-Hauptquartier 1941–1944* (1980), 224.

32 Letter of 5 May 1924, Jäckel, 1232.

33 Letter to Alexander Spring in 1923 in Michael Karbaum, *Studien zur Geschichte der Bayreuther Festspiele* (1976), 2/65.

34 Jochmann, 307–8.

35 8 May in Elke Fröhlich, ed., *Die Tagebücher von Joseph Goebbels: Sämtliche Fragmente*, 4 vols (1987), vol. 1, 178–9.

36 *Bayreuther Tageblatt*, 5 September 1924, Pachl, 342–4.

37 Letters to Fritz Busch and wife in Egon Voss, *Die Dirigenten der Bayreuther Festspiele* (1976), 45–6.

38 Voss, 43.

39 Peter Pachl, ed., *Kurt Söhnlein: Erinnerungen an Siegfried Wagner und Bayreuth* (1980), 31.

40 21 April 1927 in Dietrich Mack, *Der Bayreuther Inszenicrungsstil* (1976), 98.

41 Letter of 11 May 1930, ibid., 99.

42 *Sunday Times*, 10 August 1930.

43 *Berliner Tageblatt*, 24 July 1930.

44 Letter of 1921 to August Püringer, Zelinsky, 165.

45 *Sunday Times*, 2 August 1930.

46 Jochmann, ed., 308.

47 2 August 1930.

48 Letter of 1 January 1915 in Ernst zu Hohenlohe, ed., *Briefwechsel zwischen Cosima Wagner und Fürst Ernst zu Hohenlohe-Langenburg* (1937), 339.

49 Carl Gustav Jung, *Collected Works* (1970—), vol. 10, 214.

50 30 September 1928.

51 2 August 1930.

52 *Neue Musikzeitung*, vol. 49 (1928),

611.

53 *Gesammelte Schriften*, 3 vols (1925–9), vol. 3, 315.

54 7 July 1927.

55 Bronnenmeyer, *Vom Tempel zur Werkstatt: Geschichte der Bayreuther Festspiele* (1970), 62.

56 *Neue Musikzeitung*, vol. 49 (1928), 597.

57 *Erinnerungen*, 143.

Chapter 5

1   Letter of 4 August 1933 in Michael Karbaum, *Studien zur Geschichte der Bayreuther Festspiele* (1976), 2/85.

2   *Sunday Times*, 10 August 1930.

3   Berndt Wessling, *Furtwängler* (1985), 223.

4   *Allgemeine Musikzeitung*, 24 July 1931.

5   *Vossische Zeitung*, 19 June 1931.

6   Letter of 22 March 1932 in Harvey Sachs, ed., *Arturo Toscanini dal 1915 al 1946: l'arte all'ombra della politica* (1987).

7   *Inside the Third Reich* (1971), 60.

8   *Zeitschrift für Musik*, July 1933.

9   *Musikblätter des Anbruch* (Vienna), vol. 15, 1933, 10.

10 Summer Issue, 1933, 117.

11 Erich Ebermayer, *Magisches Bayreuth: Legende und Wirklichkeit* (1952), 197.

12 Karbaum, 2/77.

13 Ibid., 2/112–13.

14 Norman Cameron and R.H. Stevens, eds, *Hitler's Table Talk 1941–1944* (1973), 215.

15 Werner Jochmann, ed., *Adolf Hitler: Monologe im Führer-Hauptquartier 1941–1944* (1980), 225.

16 *Inside the Third Reich*, 149–50.

17 Jochmann, 225.

18 Friedelind Wagner and Page Cooper, *Heritage of Fire: The Story of Richard Wagner's Granddaughter* (1945), 88–9.

19 Letter of 29 April in Harvey Sachs, *Toscanini* (1978), 224.

20 Letter of 28 May, ibid., 225.

21 *Sunday Times*, 6 August 1933.

22 *Frankfurter Zeitung*, 7 August 1933.

23 Otto Strobel, ed., *Neue Wagner-*

Forschungen (1943), 21.

24 Frida Leider, *Playing my Part* (1966), 161.

25 15 August 1933.

26 Entry of 23 October 1937 in Elke Fröhlich, ed., *Die Tagebücher von Joseph Goebbels: Sämtliche Fragmente*, 4 vols (1987), 311.

27 Entry of 3 November 1937, ibid., 323.

28 Fred Prieberg, *Kraftprobe: Wilhelm Furtwängler im Dritten Reich* (1986), 289.

29 7 August 1936.

30 'Under the Swastika' in *Modern Music*, November–December 1933.

31 *Sunday Times*, 6 August 1933.

32 *Berliner Tageblatt*, 24–27 July 1933.

33 Dietrich Mack, *Der Bayreuther Inszenierungsstil* (1976), 56.

34 Karbaum, 2/94–5.

35 Albert Speer, *Spandau: The Secret Diaries* (1976), 103.

36 Karbaum, 2/112.

37 *Heritage of Fire*, 143.

38 Johannes Jacobi in *Münchner Neueste Nachrichten*, 27 July 1938.

39 7 August 1936.

40 Letter of 7 September 1945 to Walter von Molo in *Letters of Thomas Mann 1889–1955*, 2 vols (1970), 481.

Chapter 6

1 *Frankfurter Zeitung*, 18 July 1940.

2 *Fränkische Presse*, 20 May 1947.

3 Letter of 5 April 1947 in Michael Karbaum, *Studien zur Geschichte der Bayreuther Festspiele* (1976), 2/125.

4 Letter of 3 July 1947 quoted in American Military Government postal intercept, National Archives, Washington.

5 Wolfgang Seifert, 'Die Stunde Null von Neubayreuth' in *Neue Zeitschrift für Musik*, vol. 132 (1971), 11.

6 *Gondroms Festspielmagazin 1991*, 4.

7 *Siegfried* programme 1991, 15.

8 Geoffrey Skelton, *Wieland Wagner: The Positive Sceptic* (1971), 85.

9 Walter Panofsky, *Wieland Wagner* (1964), 14.

Chapter 7

1 *Ich erinnere mich ganz genau: Autobiographie* (1974), 200.

2 'Denkmalschutz für Wagner' in Oswald Georg Bauer, ed., *Wieland Wagner: Sein Denken: Aufsätze, Reden, Interviews, Briefe* (1991), 41.

3 *Opera*, 1952, 517.

4 Ibid., 1958, 630.

5 *Richard Wagner's Music Dramas* (1979), 158.

6 Andrew Porter in *Financial Times*, 25 January 1978.

7 *Opera*, 1963, 76.

8 Ibid., 1954, 535.

9 *Nachklang: Ansichten und Erinnerungen* (1987), 176.

10 'Überlieferung und Neugestaltung' in *Festspielbuch*, 1951.

11 *Wieland Wagner: The Positive Sceptic* (1971), 141.

12 'Überlieferung und Neugestaltung'.

13 *Oper und Drama* in *Gesammelte Schriften*, vol. 3, 64.

14 Nicola Buda and Manfred Bockelmann, *Unsterblicher Wagner—lebendiges Bayreuth* (1983), 41.

15 Walter Panofsky, *Wieland Wagner* (1964), 18–19.

16 Skelton, *Wieland Wagner*, 177.

17 *The Listener*, 7 February 1963.

18 *Wieland Wagner*, 186.

19 Joseph Wechsberg, 'A Reporter at Large' in *The New Yorker*, 18 August 1956.

20 *Neue Westfälische* (Bielefeld), 22 July 1967.

21 'Weltdiskussion um Bayreuth', in Gisela Zeh, *Das Bayreuther Bühnenkostum* (1973), 83.

22 Antoine Goléa, *Entretiens avec Wieland Wagner* (1967), 50.

23 Wechsberg, *New Yorker*.

24 Buda and Bockelmann, 41.

25 *Rheingold* programme, 1966.

26 Skelton, *Wieland Wagner*, 177–8.

27 4 May 1951 in Bauer, *Wieland Wagner*, 141.

28 Goléa, 32.

29 *Wieland Wagner*, 178.

30 Skelton, *Wieland Wagner*, 180.

31 Goléa, 119.

32 *Tristan* programme, 1968.

33 *Tannhäuser* programme, 1955.

34   *Opernwelt*, September 1964.
35   *Opera*, 1959, 585.
36   *Meistersinger* programme, 1958.
37   *Christ und Welt*, 24 June 1966.
38   Bauer, *Wieland Wagner*, 141.
39   Egon Voss, *Die Dirigenten der Bayreuther Festspiele* (1976), 60.
40   Wechsberg, *New Yorker*.
41   Buda and Bockelmann, 136.

Chapter 8

1   *Playboy*, July 1976.
2   *Der Spiegel*, 1 March 1976.
3   *Welt am Sonntag*, 23 May 1976.
4   *Der Spiegel*, 1 March 1976.
5   27 August 1955.
6   Joachim Kaiser, *Leben mit Wagner* (1990), 235.
7   13 August 1969.
8   *Münchner Merkur*, 20 July 1970.
9   *Süddeutsche Zeitung*, 13 August 1976.
10   1 March 1976.
11   *Süddeutsche Zeitung*, 19 October 1966.
12   *Der Spiegel*, 1 March 1976.
13   *Bayreuth: Rückblick und Vorschau*, 1977.

(1983), 305.
2   Stefan Jaeger, ed., *Götz Friedrich: Wagner-Regie* (1983), 8.
3   *Tannhäuser* programme, 1972.
4   Erich Leinsdorf, *Cadenza: A Musical Career* (1976), 22ff.
5   15 August 1976.
6   5 August 1976.
7   4 August 1976.
8   23 July 1976.
9   1 August 1976.
10   September/October 1978, 411.
11   *Opera*, 1979, 20.
12   *Neue Zeitschrift für Musik*, 1979, 605.
13   Jaeger, 165.
14   Ibid., 212.
15   Stephen Fay and Roger Wood, *The Ring: Anatomy of an Opera* (1984), 37.
16   Ibid., 4.
17   Ibid., 37.
18   Ibid., 37.
19   *Abendzeitung* (Munich), May 1984.
20   Fay and Wood, 203.
21   Ibid., 210.
22   3 August 1991.
23   30 July 1988.
24   August 1988.
25   Dieter Kranz, *Der Regisseur Harry Kupfer* (1988), 104.

Chapter 9

1   Herbert Barth, *Der Festspielhügel: Richard Wagners Werk und Wirkung*

Bibliography

Bayreuth is discussed to a greater or lesser extent in virtually every book about Richard Wagner and is at the least mentioned in a good many studies of opera and German history since 1876; it is also the subject of a vast periodical literature. This list is limited to those books that were consulted during the writing of this work.

Introduction

General surveys and histories

Anon.: *Bayreuth 1876–1976* (1976)

Anon.: *Festspielnachrichten: Beiträge 1957–82: Wagners Werk und Wirkung* (1983)

Herbert Barth: *Der Festspielhügel: Richard Wagners Werk in Bayreuth* (1989)

Herbert Barth, ed.: *Bayreuther Dramaturgie: Der Ring des Nibelungen* (1980)

Herbert Barth: *Richard Wagner und Bayreuth in Karikatur und Anekdote* (1970)

Herbert Barth, Dietrich Mack and Egon Voss: *Wagner: A Documentary Study* (1975)

Hans-Joachim Bauer: *Richard Wagner Lexikon* (1988)

Oswald Georg Bauer: *Richard Wagner: Die Bühnenwerke von der Uraufführung bis heute* (1982)

Carl-Friedrich Baumann: *Bühnentechnik im Festspielhaus Bayreuth* (1980)

Walter Bronnenmeyer: *Vom Tempel zur Werkstatt: Geschichte der Bayreuther Festspiele* (1970)

————: *Richard Wagner: Bürger in Bayreuth* (1983)

Peter Burbidge and Richard Sutton, eds: *The Wagner Companion* (1979)

Erich Ebermayer: *Magisches Bayreuth: Legende und Wirklichkeit* (1952)

Eric Eugène: *Les idées politiques de Richard Wagner et leur influence sur l'idéologie allemande (1870–1945)* (1978)

Germanisches Nationalmuseum Nürnberg: *Die Meistersinger und Richard Wagner: Die Rezeptionsgeschichte einer Oper von 1868 bis heute* (1981)

Volker Gondrom, ed.: *Bayreuth-Brevier: Ein Führer für den Festspielgast* (1970)

Susanna Großmann-Vendrey: *Bayreuth in der deutschen Presse* (4 vols, 1977–83)

Robert Hartford: *Bayreuth: The Early Years* (1980)

Michael Karbaum: *Studien zur Geschichte der Bayreuther Festspiele* (1976)

Hanjo Kesting, ed.: *Richard Wagner Briefe* (1983)

David Large and William Weber, eds: *Wagnerism in European Culture and Politics* (1984)

Albert Lavignac: *The Music Dramas of Richard Wagner and His Festival Theatre in Bayreuth* (1898)

Dietrich Mack: *Der Bayreuther Inszenierungsstil* (1976)

Hans Mayer: *Richard Wagner in Bayreuth 1876–1976* (1976)

Barry Millington and Stewart Spencer, eds: *Wagner in Performance* (1992)

Barry Millington, ed.: *The Wagner Compendium: A Guide to Wagner's Life and Music* (1992)

Jean Mistler: *Richard Wagner et Bayreuth* (1980)

Edwin Müller and Gottfried Ginter: *Richard Wagner als Welterneuerungslehrer: Der Ideengehalt der Bayreuther Weihespiele nach des Meisters eigenen Worten* (1955)

Ulrich Müller and Peter Wapnewski: *Richard-Wagner-Handbuch* (1986)

Geoffrey Skelton: *Wagner at Bayreuth: Experiment and Tradition* (1976)

Siegmund Skraup et al.: *Der Fall Bayreuth* (1962)

André Tabeuf: *Bayreuth & Wagner: Cent ans d'images* (1981)

Egon Voss: *Die Dirigenten der Bayreuther Festspiele* (1976)

Wolf Siegfried Wagner: *Die Geschichte unsere Familie in Bildern: Bayreuth 1876–1976* (1976)

Gisela Zeh: *Das Bayreuther Bühnenkostum* (1973)

Hartmut Zelinsky: *Richard Wagner: Ein deutsches Thema* (1983)

Festival operations

Nicola Buda and Manfred Bockelmann: *Unsterblicher Wagner—lebendiges Bayreuth* (1983)

Stephen Fay and Roger Wood: *The Ring: Anatomy of an Opera* (1984)

Hermann Schreiber and Guido Mangold: *Werkstatt Bayreuth* (1986)

Alfred Soos: *Das Bayreuther Festspielorchester: Geschichte und Gegenwart* (1988)

Structure and acoustics

George C. Izenour: *Theater Design* (1977)
Richard Leacroft: *Theatre and Playhouse: An Illustrated Survey of Theatre Building from Ancient Greece to the Present Day* (1984)
Jürgen Meyer: *Acoustics and the Performance of Music* (1978)
Edwin O. Sachs: *Modern Opera Houses and Theatres*, vol. 1 (1897)
Alexander Wood: *Physics of Music* (1975)

Chapter 1

Anon.: *Briefwechsel zwischen Wagner und Liszt*, 2 vols (1887)
Anon.: *Richard Wagners Briefe an Theodor Uhlig, Wilhelm Fischer, Ferdinand Heine.* (1888)
Joachim Bergfeld: *Von Tribschen nach Bayreuth: Richard Wagner zur Verwirklichung seiner Festspielidee* (1958)
Wilfrid Blunt: *The Dream King: Ludwig II of Bavaria* (1970)
Houston Stewart Chamberlain: *Richard Wagner* (1896)
Carl Friedrich Glasenapp: *Das Leben Richard Wagners*, 6 vols. (1894–1911)
———, ed.: *Bayreuther Briefe von Richard Wagner (1871–1883)* (1907)
Martin Gregor-Dellin and Dietrich Mack, eds: *Cosima Wagner: Die Tagebücher*, 2 vols, (1976–7)
Heinrich Habel: *Festspielhaus und Haus Wahnfried* (1985)
Karl Heckel: *Die Bühnenfestspiele: Bayreuth: Authentischer Beitrag zur Geschichte ihrer Entstehung und Entwicklung* (1891)
Karl Heckel, ed.: *Briefe Richard Wagner an Emil Heckel: zur Entstehungsgeschichte in Bayreuth* (1899)
Grete Holle: *Wachsen und Werden der Bayreuther Idee nach Wagners Schriften und Briefen* (1941)
Hermann Kaiser: *Der Bühnenmeister Carl Brandt und Richard Wagner: Kunst der Szene in Darmstadt und Bayreuth* (1968)
Gustav Adolph Kietz: *Richard Wagner in den Jahren 1842–1849 und 1873–1875: Erinnerungen* (1905)
La Mara, ed.: *Briefe an August Röckel von Richard Wagner* (1894)
Lore Lucas: *Die Festspiel-Idee Richard Wagners* (1972)
Ernest Newman: *The Life of Richard Wagner*, 4 vols (1933–47)
Detta and Michael Petzet: *Die Richard Wagner-Bühne König Ludwigs II.: München Bayreuth* (1970)
Sophie Rützow: *Richard Wagner und Bayreuth: Ausschnitte und Erinnerungen* (1943)
Geoffrey Skelton: *Richard and Cosima Wagner* (1982)

Otto Strobel, ed.: *König Ludwig II. und Richard Wagner: Briefwechsel*, 5 vols (1936–9)

Richard Wagner: *Gesammelte Schriften und Dichtungen*, 10 vols. (1871–83)

————: *Mein Leben* (1914)

Chapter 2

Joseph Bennett: *Letters from Bayreuth* (1877)

Oskar Berggruen: *Das Bühnenfestspiel in Bayreuth im Hinblick auf die bildende Kunst* (1877)

Peter Cook: *A Memoir of Bayreuth 1876* (1979)

Henry Coutagne: *Richard Wagner et le théatre de Bayreuth* (1893)

Carl Dahlhaus: *Richard Wagner's Music Dramas* (1979)

Manfred Eger: *Wagner und die Juden: Fakten und Hintergrund* (1985)

Gustav Engel: *Das Bühnenfestspiel in Bayreuth: Kritische Studie* (1876)

Walter Engelsmann: *Erlösung dem Erlöser: Richard Wagners religiöse Weltgestalt* (1936)

Richard Fricke: *Bayreuth vor dreissig Jahren: Erinnerungen an Wahnfried und aus dem Festspielhause* (1906)

Julius Hey: *Richard Wagner als Vortragsmeister* (1911)

John Jackson: *The Wagner of Bayreuth* (1891)

Max Kalbeck: *Das Bühnenfestspiel zu Bayreuth: Eine kritische Studie* (1877)

Julius Erich Kloss: *Twenty Years of 'Bayreuth' 1876–1896* (1896)

Erich Kloss: *Richard Wagner und seine Künstler: zweiter Band der 'Bayreuther Briefe' (1872–1883)* (1908)

Lilli Lehmann: *Mein Weg* (1913)

Paul Lindau: *Nüchterne Briefe aus Bayreuth* (1876)

————: *Bayreuther Briefe vom reinen Thoren: Parsifal von Richard Wagner* (1883)

Angelo Neumann: *Personal Recollections of Wagner* (1908)

Friedrich Nietzsche: *Richard Wagner in Bayreuth* (1873)

————: *Der Fall Wagner* (1888)

————: *Menschliches, Allzumenschliches* (1878)

————: *Jenseits von Gut und Böse* (1886)

Alexandra Orlova: *Tchaikovsky: A Self-Portrait* (1990)

Martin Plüddemann: *Die Bühnenfestspiele in Bayreuth: ihre Gegner und ihre Zukunft* (1877)

Richard Pohl: *Bayreuther Erinnerungen* (1878)

Heinrich Porges: *Bühnenproben zu der Bayreuther Festspielen des Jahres 1876* (1886)

Hans Michael Schetterer: *Richard Wagner's Bühnenfestspiel: Nachklänge an die Aufführungen des Jahres 1876* (1876)

Martina Srocke: *Richard Wagner als Regisseur* (1988)

Charles Villiers Stanford: *Interludes* (1922)

Modest Tchaikowsky: *The Life and Letters of Peter Ilich Tchaikowsky* (1906)

Felix Weingartner: *Bayreuth 1876–1896* (1904)

Chapter 3

Marie L. Bablet-Hahn, ed.: *Adolphe Appia: Oeuvres Complètes*, 4 vols. (1983–)

Anna Bahr-Mildenburg and Hermann Bahr: *Bayreuth* (1912)

Geoffrey Field: *Evangelist of Race: The Germanic Vision of Houston Stewart Chamberlain* (1981)

Ernst zu Hohenlohe, ed.: *Briefwechsel zwischen Cosima Wagner und Fürst Ernst zu Hohenlohe-Langenburg* (1937)

Julie Kniese, ed. *Julius Kniese, Der Kampf zweier Welten um das Bayreuther Erbe* (1931)

Dietrich Mack, ed.: *Cosima Wagner, Das zweite Leben. Briefe und Aufzeichnungen 1883–1930* (1980)

George R. Marek: *Cosima Wagner* (1981)

Karen Monson: *Alban Berg* (1979)

Richard Du Moulin Eckart: *Cosima Wagner: Ein Lebens- und Charakterbild*, 2 vols (1929 and 1931)

Paul Pretzsch, ed.: *Cosima Wagner und Houston Stewart Chamberlain im Briefwechsel 1888–1908* (1934)

Albert von Puttkamer: *50 Jahre Bayreuth* (1927)

Winfried Schüler: *Der Bayreuther Kreis von seiner Entstehung bis zum Ausgang der wilhelminischen Ära: Wagnerkult und Kultusreform im Geiste völkischer Weltanschauung* (1971)

Willi Schuh: *Richard Strauss: Jugend und frühe Meisterjahre* (1976)

———, ed.: *Richard Strauss: Betrachtungen und Erinnerungen* (1957)

George Bernard Shaw: *The Perfect Wagnerite: A Commentary on the Ring of the Nibelungs* (1898)

Igor Stravinsky: *An Autobiography* (1936)

Franz Trenner, ed.: *Cosima Wagner—Richard Strauss: Ein Briefwechsel* (1978)

Siegfried Wagner: *Erinnerungen* (1923)

Felix Weingartner: *Buffets and Rewards* (1937)

Kurt Wilhelm: *Richard Strauss persönlich* (1984)

Chapter 4

Fritz Busch: *Pages from a Musician's Life* (1953)

Norman Cameron and R.H. Stevens, eds: *Hitler's Table Talk 1941–1944* (1973)

Bernhard Dopheide: *Fritz Busch* (1970)

Shirlee Emmons: *Tristianissimo* (1990)

Joachim C. Fest: *Hitler* (1973)

Elke Fröhlich, ed.: *Die Tagebücher von Joseph Goebbels: Sämtliche Fragmente* (4 vols, 1987)

Eberhard Jäckel, ed.: *Adolf Hitler: Sämtliche Aufzeichnungen (1905–1924)* (1980)

Werner Jochmann, ed.: *Adolf Hitler: Monologe im Führer-Hauptquartier 1941–1944* (1980)

Carl Gustav Jung: *Collected Works* (1970—)

Zdenko von Kraft: *Der Sohn—Siegfried Wagners Leben und Umwelt* (1969)

August Kubizek, *Adolf Hitler: mein Jugendfreund* (1953)

Kurt G.W. Ludecke: *I Knew Hitler* (1939)

Peter Pachl: *Siegfried Wagner: Genie im Schatten* (1988)

Hans Pfitzner: *Gesammelte Schriften*, 3 vols (1925–9)

Walther Rathenau: *An Deutschlands Jugend* (1918)

Lord Redesdale: *Bayreuth in 1912* (1912)

Kurt Söhnlein: *Erinnerungen an Siegfried Wagner und Bayreuth* (1980)

Chapter 5

Hildegard Brenner: *Die Kunstpolitik des Nationalsozialismus* (1963)

Paul Bülow: *Adolf Hitler und der Bayreuther Kulturkreis* (1933)

————: *Bayreuth: Die Stadt der Wagner-Festspiele 1876–1936* (1936)

Berta Geissmar: *The Baton and the Jackboot* (1944)

Fritz Hallwich, ed.: *Im Umkreis der Kunst: Eine Festschrift für Emil Preetorius* (1955)

Walter Heist: *Emil Preetorius: Grafiker, Bühnenbildner, Sammler* (1976)

Martin Hürlimann, ed.: *Wilhelm Furtwängler im Urteil seiner Zeit* (1955)

Meta Kropf: *Bayreuther Festspielsommer von damals (1936–1944)* (1977)

Frida Leider: *Playing my Part* (1966)

Erika Mann, ed.: *Thomas Mann: Wagner und unsere Zeit* (1983)

Karl Hermann Müller: *Wachet auf! Mahnruf aus dem Zuschauerraum* (1935)

Emil Preetorius: *Das szenische Werk* (1944)

————: *Richard Wagner: Bild und Vision* (1942)

————: *Zum Problem der Wagner-Szene: Bühnenbilder und Figurinen zum Ring für Bayreuth 1934* (1935)

Fred Prieberg: *Musik im NS-Staat* (1982)

————: *Kraftprobe: Wilhelm Furtwängler im Dritten Reich* (1986)

Harvey Sachs: *Toscanini* (1978)

———— ed.: *Arturo Toscanini dal 1915 al 1946: l'arte all'ombra della politica* (1987)

————: *Reflections on Toscanini* (1991)

Albert Speer: *Inside the Third Reich* (1971)

————: *Spandau: The Secret Diaries* (1976)

Otto Strobel, ed.: *Neue Wagner-Forschungen* (1943)

Bruno Walter: *Theme and Variations* (1947)

Friedelind Wagner and Page Cooper: *Heritage of Fire: The Story of Richard Wagner's Granddaughter* (1945)

Berndt Wessling, ed.: *Bayreuth im Dritten Reich: Eine Dokumentation* (1983)

————: *Toscanini in Bayreuth* (1976)

————: *Furtwängler* (1985)

Joseph Wulf: *Musik im Dritten Reich: Eine Dokumentation* (1963)

Chapter 6

Bernd Mayer: *Bayreuth: Die letzten 50 Jahre* (1988)

Werner Meyer: *Götterdämmerung: April 1945 in Bayreuth* (1975)

Wolfgang Seifert: 'Die Stunde Null von Neubayreuth' in *Neue Zeitschrift für Musik*, vol. 132, 2–12 and 69–77 (1971)

Richard Wilhelm Stock: *Richard Wagner und seine Meistersinger: Eine Erinnerungsgabe zu den Bayreuther Kriegsfestspielen 1943* (1943)

————: *Richard Wagner und die Stadt der Meistersinger* (1938)

Chapter 7

Oswald Georg Bauer, ed.: *Wieland Wagner: Sein Denken: Aufsätze, Reden, Interviews, Briefe* (1991)

Karl Böhm: *Ich erinnere mich ganz genau: Autobiographie* (1974)

Dietrich Fischer-Dieskau: *Nachklang: Ansichten und Erinnerungen* (1987)

Hermann Glaser: *Kulturgeschichte der Bundesrepublik Deutschland* (1985–)

Antoine Goléa: *Entretiens avec Wieland Wagner* (1967)

Victor Gollancz: *The Ring at Bayreuth: And Some Thoughts on Operatic Production* (1966)

Friedrich Herzfeld: *Das neue Bayreuth* (1960)
Claude Lust: *Wieland Wagner* (1969)
Kurt Overhoff: *Manipulationen* (undated typescript)
Walter Panofsky: *Wieland Wagner* (1964)
Karl Heinz Ruppel: *Wieland Wagner inszeniert Richard Wagner* (1960)
Walter Erich Schäfer: *Wieland Wagner: Persönlichkeit und Leistung* (1970)
Viola Schmid: *Studien zu Wieland Wagners Inszenierungskonzeption und zu seiner Regiepraxis* (1973)
Geoffrey Skelton: *Wieland Wagner: The Positive Sceptic* (1971)
Penelope Turing: *New Bayreuth* (1971)
Wieland Wagner, ed.: *Richard Wagner und das neue Bayreuth* (1962)

Chapter 8

Herbert Barth, ed.: *Wolfgang Wagner: Zum 50. Geburtstag* (1969)
Oswald Georg Bauer: *Wolfgang Wagner: Arbeitsprinzipien eines Regisseurs* (1979)
Joachim Kaiser: *Leben mit Wagner* (1990)
Hans Jürgen Syberberg: *Syberbergs Filmbuch* (1976)

Chapter 9

Joachim Bergfeld: *Ich wollte Wagner vom Podest holen: Anmerkungen zur Bayreuther Ringinszenierung durch Patrice Chéreau im Jubiläumsjahr der Festspiele 1976* (1974)
Élisabeth Bouillon: *Le Ring à Bayreuth: La Tétralogie du Centenaire* (1980)
Pierre Boulez, Patrice Chéreau et al.: *Histoire d'un Ring* (1980)
Jarka Burian: *Svoboda: Wagner: Joseph Svoboda's Scenography for Richard Wagner's Operas* (1983)
Stefan Jaeger, ed.: *Götz Friedrich: Wagner-Regie* (1983)
Dieter Kranz: *Der Regisseur Harry Kupfer* (1988)
Erich Leinsdorf: *Cadenza: A Musical Career* (1976)
Michael Lewin, ed.: *Der Ring: Bayreuth 1988–1992* (1991)
Jean-Jacques Nattiez: *Tétralogies Wagner, Boulez, Chéreau: Essai sur l'infidélité* (1983)

Index